VILLAINS

VILLAINS

The Inside Story of Aston Villa's Hooligan Gangs

Danny Brown & Paul Brittle

with Pete The Greek, Clarkey
& Andy Browne

MILO BOOKS LTD

First published in November 2006 by Milo Books

This paperback edition published in February 2008

ISBN 978 1 903854 67 9

Typeset by e-type

Printed in Great Britain by
Cox & Wyman Ltd, Reading, Berkshire

MILO BOOKS LTD
The Old Weighbridge
Station Road
Wrea Green
Lancs PR4 2PH
United Kingdom
www.milobooks.com

Authors' Note

We would like to straighten out our fundamental position at the start of this book, which is that we are no longer football hooligans. We don't believe in or condone any form of football violence on or off the pitch today. This is just a public documentation of our past.

Tribute by Joe Egan

There are some things in life you cannot buy. Mike Tyson's old trainer the legendary Cus d'Amato once told me you will be judged by your actions, not your words. Danny Brown is a guy who put his life on the line for me, not for money or favour but out of loyalty and friendship. Best of luck Danny.

Your friend Joe Egan
Author of Big Joe Egan: The Toughest White Man on the Planet

Before reading any further, please spare a few thoughts for the following who are no longer with us. These lads were worth more to Aston Villa than any player ever could be and each and every one played their part in our social history. They may be gone but certainly never forgotten.

Ray Barnes
Steve Barnes
Paul Beard (Beebo)
Pete Bishop
Geoff Broomhall (Boots)
Eddie Corkhill
Malcolm Costello (Coke)
Patrick Edwards
Gary Exton
Gez Flynn
Des Gallagher
David Garner
Steve Groves
Gary Harwood
Chris Hassan
Paul Heath (Paulie)
Andy Kitson
Gary Lyttle

Kevin Maloney (2-stone)
Gary Morgan
Dave Moore
Kevin Murphy
Robert Neale (Nelly)
Steve Norton
Neil O'Mara
Steve Powell
Adam Powers
David Rammel
Dave Ravenhall
Micky Rivers
Barry Sheery
Michael 'Spoon' Somers
Dougie Thompson
Andy Timms
Bunny Weir
Paul Yates (F-Man)

CONTENTS

THE SPEECH

OKAY, LISTEN UP lads. Can I have your attention? *Stop talking and fucking listen!* We are here tonight to do a job. The bullying and the harassment of innocent Villa lads around the town, the bullshit they have been spouting for years about what they are going to do to Villa when they come up, it ends tonight.

Words are cheap, it's time for action to put all the myths to bed because if we don't these fuckers will be unbearable and everything they have been spouting will be seen as true. You all have faced these cunts down the years and you know it's just a numbers game with them. Well take a look around you and see, we have the numbers and we have the quality. Nobody is going through this firm tonight.

Now those who ain't sure about it, fuck off now, because it will get heavy and you will have to fight. We cannot afford passengers tonight. We are going on their manor, we are taking it to them. It will be seen as a piss-take, so just leave if you are having second thoughts, because if you are not committed and if you do run when it comes on top, then you are going to get battered by us anyway.

We cannot afford any mistakes, we can't afford spectators, this is what we want, it's our chance to put the record straight, and when Andy and Dennis give the word we move as one. No silly singing, no half-heartedness, we keep it tight, no stragglers, no hanging back, no backward steps, not one fuckin' inch.

We walk to their place as a Villa firm and when they come, we stand and go into them. This is the old boys, the C Crew and the Steamers reunion, our finest, no messers, you are all top lads, front liners each and every one and that's why you're all here.

So this is it, let's finish it tonight once and for all, let's do it for the Villa!

Yam Yam
Club Sensations, Moseley Road
7pm, 16 September 2002

INTRODUCTION

ASTON VILLA FC is one of the biggest and best-supported football clubs in Britain, the giant from England's second city with a long and distinguished history in the game, culminating in an unforgettable European Cup victory in 1982. The story of their terrace army, however, has never been told – until now. Like all major clubs, Villa have had their hooligans and hardmen, who have been involved in some of the fiercest terrace battles of the past four decades. *Villains* traces their gangs from the 1960s up to the present day. Through first-person testimony, it reveals for the first time the antics of the Steamers who, led by a band of colourful and fearless characters, put Villa on the hooligan map. Eventually they were superseded by the C Crew, a multi-racial gang who came together during Birmingham's Two-Tone period and the parallel casual era.

This was the heyday of hooliganism, and the Villa Park faithful clashed with the toughest and most violent gangs around. At the helm were legendary figures such as Pete the Greek, who famously headbutted a police horse, and 'Black' Danny Brown, who was jailed in 1981 for one of the most infamous football-related attacks. This book charts the lives of in particular, five match-day boys who became leading members of the Steamers and C Crew firms and whose love of Aston Villa eventually led to very severe consequences for them all. Many others have also contributed, and the story is brought up to date with tales of the more recent Villa Youth.

A word on the title. Villa fans are often known as 'Villans' (without the 'i'). Well, all of the lads in this book are true fans, but in recognition of the fact that many of our activities have been frowned on by the authorities, not to mention the law, we have chosen to alter it slightly to *Villains*. You get the message.

A number of people had been asking various respected Villa lads for a few years about doing a book, and finally at a social function at the HQ of Villa's older lads, in a well-known establishment in the Moseley area of Birmingham, it was agreed that they would get together and write about their past exploits. The book has two authors but is a collaboration of five well-known faces who have not only drawn on their own experiences but also enlisted the support and help of other Villa front line lads to ensure a true portrayal of events. The dream and vision of those five people at the initial meeting on 23 March 2006 to bring this book to fruition is dedicated to all Villa fans, past and present, who have stood on those battle lines. This is your story, your rollercoaster ride of emotion following our beloved club Aston Villa. Enjoy.

BLACK DANNY

I was born and originally brought up in Gloucester, not exactly a hot bed of football but due to my Mom and Dad splitting up I first moved to Birmingham at the age of 9 with my Mom and 3 brothers and 2 sisters. I was the favourite with my Dad and he was settled in Cardiff and asked me to move there with him, so for a year I sampled the delights of Welsh hospitality living in Ninian Park Road which is of course around the corner from Cardiff City Football Club. It was never going to work out long term as I missed the rest of the family and it was difficult as Dad was out working as a painter and decorator. I was always left to my own devices and I found out a lot about Cardiff City Football Club due to the fact our next door neighbour was a bloody fanatic. He and his mates would take me up to the valleys to watch Cardiff City train. But my dad never allowed me to go to a single match, saying it was a hellhole, and despite my neighbour trying to turn me into a plastic Taffy, there was only ever going to be one club for me. Despite many lows and not too many highs, I look upon myself to be very fortunate that that club turned out to be Aston Villa.

We moved around a lot in my early years and I suppose the first real home we settled in was in Handsworth, ironically living in Villa Road. At the bottom of the road was the Baptist church where my club, Aston Villa, was formed in 1874. You could say it was fate but I was not aware of its significance until the years went by, my thirst for knowledge of the Villa took a hold of me and I became well aware of where I lived and the part it played in the glorious history of Aston Villa Football Club.

In those school days I would get myself into scrapes as the local kids would rag me about my West Country accent, as we all know how cruel kids can be and like it or not if you are different you become an easy target and they always seem to pick on you. Being the new kid on the block, complete with a funny accent, made me that easy target, and at first it seemed like I had a fucking bull's eye on the back of my school pants. All the other kids were settled in school by the time I arrived on the scene and had already established their mates, and while I have always been one to make friends over a period of time, it takes me a while to suss them out before I can trust someone. That's just the way I am and always have been but at the time it did not help my rise in the popularity stakes.

I did eventually make friends with people but started out by gaining some respect for sticking up for myself and getting a reputation as a lad who could have a fight. I was winning more than I was losing and I certainly seemed better at that than what I was doing in the classroom! Reputations are built on 50 per cent fact and 50 per cent stories and sure enough the storytellers embellished the facts, something that would follow me throughout my life. Sometimes it helped but sometimes it gave me major problems, particularly in those early school days.

Like all kids having older brothers, I wanted to hang out with them because what they were doing was far more interesting than anything me and my mates from the neighbourhood got up to. Without realising it I was a right pain in the arse to them. My brothers, whatever they say, are not football fanatics, in fact one of them is a Man United fan so that tells its own story! My major beef with them is that if your team loses it affects your weekend, it puts you in a bad mood, you hardly want to go out or pick a paper up the next day, at least that's how it is with me, yet to them it was always the same:

'It's only a game, Danny!'

That was bullshit because Villa was my life, in fact it was my whole life for a long time. Men always remember their first girlfriend but the Villa meant more to me than some slag who teased you with a bit of a grope up top for weeks while you wasted your pocket money on her in the hope of that little bit more a little bit lower down. Even today when I don't go as much to the game as I used to, I feel the same way. It's simple: you never forget your first love do you?

My first love was forged in the old Third Division in 1972, a year when we won that league and where it was commonplace for 30,000-odd fans to turn up at every home game, massive crowds that swelled to 40,000-plus for the bigger games. My earliest recollection was when we played the Brazilian team Santos at home, a night game where the great Pele came to Villa Park and drew a gate of 54,000. Some may find it hard to believe but I am a bit of an anorak for history on the Villa and it was a pity that it wasn't a subject at school because I would have been top of the class in that!

The first match was on a Saturday, and oddly I am not sure of the opposition that day but my brother and cousin were going to the game. All week I had nagged them to take me along, but to them I was a nuisance, almost an embarrassment. Although I was only two years younger, when you are twelve two years is a big gap and it was not cool to have your little brother holding onto your shirt tails. But when they made their way out the house I followed them, walking four steps behind. Every now and again they would look back and shout, 'Fuck off you little twat, do one.' I ignored it and carried on.

I walked up through the streets and watched kids in the road kicking balls about and a few people in claret and blue scarves. Typically of me I was just quietly taking it all in, not thinking about what to expect, as to me it was just a Saturday out of the house doing something different. That was about to change. As we neared the ground – we were now on Trinity Road – I looked and stared almost in disbelief at the size of the crowd. There were thousands and I mean thousands of people around me. I had never seen so many people in my life and they were going all in one direction, to Villa Park.

Apart from the crowd, the thing I noticed most was the Trinity Road stand and its steps up to the upper tier. It was an old-fash-ioned, traditional stand, very grand in its day, and a place that a lot of people associated with Aston Villa in those days. What a view it gave, as you could look back and see Aston Park, which is also full of history and tradition.

The stands were for the rich and privileged and for the dads and their lads. We were years away from having a hope in hell of getting in there, in fact funds were non-existent and we had no hope of even getting into the Holte End. I watched people queuing up to get into the L section, a huge expanse of terrace that housed thousands. The other side of that end was K section and an area we used many years later during a period I call the C Crew years – which will be explained later.

Hundreds who could not go into the ground gathered at the top of the park, as from there you could see a corner of the pitch and try to catch snippets of the play when the ball came towards the Holte End. I can still remember the noise of the crowd, the 'oohs' and 'aahs' as shots and headers nearly went in and the clapping if some-thing had happened on the pitch worth applauding.

With about 20 minutes to go, the gates would be opened to let out those who wanted to leave early and miss the rush. That was our opportunity to get in free and watch the rest of the game and that's what we and thousands of kids all over the country did every week.

It was a crazy sight as a lone steward would try to stop literally hundreds of youths pushing and scampering past the people who were on their way out.

I was past him with ease and soon on the terrace, thinking how huge the Holte End was. It seemed to go back forever and full of people, many standing at the side of these red metal barriers with scarves dangling down reading their match-day programmes. I didn't say a lot, I just watched what others were doing and took it all in: the singing, the pushing, the swaying as the ball came up our end. More than anything, I was transfixed by those eleven players in claret and blue. I was hooked. I didn't really see the other team; that day I inherited invisible claret and blue glasses and I wear them to this day!

From that day there was no going back. I no longer needed my brothers to take me to the game; from then on I went to Villa Park on my own. I couldn't sleep on a Friday night with excitement, knowing that next day I was going to watch the Villa, it's a feeling that is hard to describe if you are not a football fan and that feeling never leaves you totally. My Saturdays started early and it wasn't uncommon for me to be sitting in Aston Park at eight or nine in the morning, waiting for the gates to open, fully seven hours before kick-off at three o'clock (the norm before TV ruined the kick-off times). I became the master of finding all the nooks and crannies to sneak in free of charge; there was always a way of sneaking in and I did it. I just hope Doug Ellis doesn't blame me if it affected the transfer funds at the time. I felt that I couldn't miss anything. I also loved to watch the crowds and the people. It became such a big part of my life that I didn't want to hang around the house when I could be at the ground.

I was blissfully unaware of the problems with trouble in those early days. It was just about the football, nothing else, and I certainly don't remember other teams' supporters in the Holte End. That would change. My earliest recollection of seeing trouble was probably a League Cup quarter-final with Millwall. I was 15 at the time and we were now living in Erdington, so my route to the ground was different, as I had to go down Witton Lane and through Stockland Green to get home.

I remember this huge mob of Villa running Millwall and the Villa lads, decked in the traditional Doc Marten boots, clambering over each other to get at the Londoners. What I didn't know at the time was that a year earlier, Villa supporters apparently took a hell of a bashing in London, resulting in some refusing to leave the safety of the train station. So for this Villa mob it was payback time, something that I appreciated over the coming years after I had taken a few kickings of my own. It give me a buzz watching my own team's mob running another mob. You tend to think that you are almost untouchable. It was only when I started to travel away that I realised everything I had seen that night was common all over the country and Villa were not always going to come off best.

I had started to go away and like most I went to other Midlands grounds first. In those early years Villa travelled in their thousands. Probably because the team were on the rise after coming so close to going out of business in 1968, there was a euphoria about the place. All this time I was learning my trade and was starting to become as interested in what was happening off the field as on it. I knew for instance that in the Holte End different mobs were occupying different sections: you had the Kingstanding mob on the right side and Quinton/Erdington lads on the left.

I was picking up information all the time and was hearing a lot about the main man at the Villa, a guy who was truly a terrace legend. He was known as Pete the Greek. I was thrilled when it turned out he was someone my older brother, Popeye, used to know very well as he was a warrior who was known and respected at the Villa by all. Then there was a mob called the Steamers, who at the time were the main mob, earning their reputation in brawls that made national papers. Their row with Manchester United supporters at a service station resulted in all football coaches being banned from motorway stop-offs without prior appointment.

I just wanted to be near to it all. I was naïve about how it all worked but found that the farther up North you went the more hassle you could get, and if you were black you didn't even need to advertise you were a Villa fan; sometimes the colour of your skin in certain places was like wearing a Villa shirt. I was proud of my club and naturally assumed that if you went to the football you wore your colours, and I would go away with my two scarves tied around my wrists. When I started to go to games outside of the Midlands, it did not take me long to realise that it was not always a good idea to advertise that you were not a local. Being black was enough to spark it off, wearing colours at times was fuelling the fire.

One incident that sticks out was Middlesbrough away. It was different from my jaunts by train around the Midlands, as I went by coach, not a coach full of lads but one of the supporters' coaches run by the Villa Travellers Club. I should have got off when I noticed the number of people on there with packed lunches and dozens of badges to show they were 100 per cent anoraks. But I stayed on and it was a long journey to a horrible town which, like most northern towns, seemed to be cold, wet and windy. The first thing that hit me when we landed in enemy territory was, *where are all the usual thousands of Villa fans getting off the trains singing, chanting?* They just weren't around.

Ayresome Park was not the most inviting of places either. I suppose we were spoilt, as Villa Park has always been a top ground and I think we regarded everywhere else as a shithole. Well this was not just a shithole, it was a very unfriendly shithole. We got off the coaches and the few coppers that were around just pointed us in the direction of the ground and off I went, head down, with the small following of Villa and their incredible collection of badges. It was a relief to get in the ground, as the whole place was shifty, even the police horses seemed to look at you funny and it was one of the few grounds where you would not dream of trying to bunk in the home end. It was a case of have your money ready and get in the place before you took a dig.

Once inside, the nightmare truly began. We were put in a corner which was uncovered and open to the elements and before long I was freezing. With the small following we had we couldn't even create body warmth because there weren't enough of us. As I stood there shivering, I noticed a mob of Boro who seemed intent solely on staring at the Villa fans as opposed to what was happening on the field – and it seemed I was the main attraction. At 6ft 4½in I am hardly likely to blend in, and being black made me a magnet for the opposition support, something I had to live with for many years. The abuse started with the name calling, 'black bastard', 'nigger', all the usual stuff that was prevalent at that time in football. Then they started with the threats, the cut-throat gestures, the pointing to the exits and the shouts of what they were going to do.

I tried to ignore it and not look back or catch anyone's eye, but it was relentless. Then a programme seller walked over and said, 'You're going to get killed outside, they hate blacks up here. You won't go home alive.'

I got the attention of the few Old Bill at the bottom of the terrace and pointed over to the demented morons, saying, 'Them guys are threatening me. You see him in the donkey jacket?' To my dismay, the copper shrugged his shoulders and said something like, 'Well you shouldn't have fucking come here then, should you.' I had never experienced so much fear or loneliness, the feeling was a horrible feeling, though it was something I would experience at many times in the future.

Somehow I did manage to get home alive that day, but to suffer 90 minutes of torment and realise that these were not the same Villa supporters I had witnessed turn over Millwall was a wake-up call that we weren't invincible and that I was certainly not safe, given both the colour of my skin and my desire to wear my club's colours. I had to learn quick. I thought that by no longer wearing colours to away games I wouldn't get noticed.

The season after I had taken a particularly bad kicking at Liverpool [see Chapter 9], and shortly after I went to Chelsea and convinced myself I would be safe by going in the Shed. To blend in, I thought I would buy something in blue and white and in a state of panic I went to a rosette seller and bought the biggest Chelsea rosette you have ever seen. Of course, I needed a lot more than that to blend in, as they were one of the most racist clubs in the country and I would have stuck out less had I painted myself white and attended a National Front meeting. A few other Villa lads from Erdington spotted me and I winked at them but even though they had no Chelsea colours on, they blended in a lot better than I did – which may have been because I was the only bloke in the Shed with a rosette on that was ten years out of date!

I quickly learnt from my mistakes and although I took a few beatings away from home I also enjoyed watching Villa mobs get the better of away fans on my walks back through Witton Lane. I started to understand what it was all about and to know where the action was and that Witton Station was the place to get amongst it at home if you had any old scores to settle. Believe me I soon had a few, even though I had only been going for a couple of years.

On the pitch, Villa were flying. They won the League Cup in 1977, beating Everton after three games that I was fortunate to witness – I owe the Norton brothers (Eddie and the late well respected Steve) a debt of gratitude as I had missed my coach and they stopped to let me on. Ron Saunders had created an exciting team and it was a great time to be a Villa fan. I had also watched a Villa mob in action at Leicester City, where they cleared their end, and it seemed to me that we suddenly had thousands of 'lads'. I felt safer in the knowledge that we had a big following and were often able to do as we pleased with the numbers we had (though that myth would be blown out of the water at West Ham in 1980).

I was still more of an observer than a participant in hooliganism but my turning point was in 1978, when we played Everton at home. I hated the Merseyside crowds with a vengeance, as on my visits there I'd had hot tea thrown in my face, been spat on, racially abused and taken a beating off a mob of Liverpool thugs. Everton to me were fair game and I wanted pay back. This game would later be referred to in the old *Villa Times* magazine, in which the club made an announcement about certain sections of Villa fans who were standing in the North Stand intent on causing trouble and the headline bluntly read, 'We don't want you at Villa Park.'

It wasn't long after a new stand had been built, the North Stand, which replaced the old Witton End, a large uncovered terrace which held 14,000 and was bigger than our closest neighbours' main end, the Tilton Road. The Witton Lane had for a number of seasons seen Villa lads going in and starting to fight with the away fans, as there was no segregation, but with this new stand they split the bottom terraced area into two, with the Villa to the left and the away lot to the right. There were seats above but that area has always been regarded as a family stand and it is vary rare for any trouble to break out in there.

It was one of those games when I couldn't wait for the final whistle. I was eager, thirsty to get involved and I had made my mind up that I was going to get hold of an Everton fan and make him pay for the shit that I had suffered in his backyard that season. When the game ended, the Everton fans were allowed to come out at the same time as Villa, which was even better, as plenty of our lads had already left and were lying in wait. There was pure hatred in the air, as it wasn't just black blokes who suffered at the hands of the Scousers. We had all heard numerous stories of lads getting picked off in Stanley Park and people getting slashed, mugged and relieved of shoes and sheepskin coats. That was the way it was there for many years and people were sick of it.

The walk from the away section to Witton Station isn't long, and unlike at some grounds where you have many opportunities to ambush away fans returning to the train station, at Villa you had to strike fast. These were the days before CCTV and if the away mob went the wrong way you were able to get at them. We had some of our best rucks in the streets surrounding Witton Station. As the Everton lot came out I felt a dryness in my mouth and my heart was beating faster; it was always like that for me before a row. Other lads would show no emotion but were equally if not more aggressive, but I always felt pre-fight row nerves. I could almost feel the veins in my neck bulging as I waited.

Sure enough, as they came they went directly opposite into Station Road and we were into them, I say 'we' as I wasn't paying much attention to anyone else, I just went in not looking back for others to follow. I always had the feeling when I was running with the C Crew that we were all together but this was pre-C Crew days and I cannot say I was totally aware who was with me, but I simply didn't care. I had gone past that and felt safe in the knowledge that this was my turf and I was going to make someone feel how I felt on those bad away days.

I found my victim but he caught my eye and panicked. Villa were running the Everton lads in different directions and he tried a different route and went towards one of the houses. He started banging on this house door, shouting to be let in, and as I got near an Asian guy opened the door and the Scouser burst in, assuming I wouldn't follow or hoping he could hide inside. He was wrong on both counts. I followed him into the back room. The Asian family, sitting down for their evening meal, watched in astonishment as the Scouser tried to get out the back door with some skinny black loon in hot pursuit. There was no way out and I got him and dragged him outside.

I was lost in a trance. All that pent-up aggression was fuelled from when I had been on the receiving end and I was in a total frenzy. I was pulling at him trying to get him to look at me and I think if I had had a knife that day I would have used it. It was the first time I had felt like that but I have lost count of the times since when I have felt the same way. The Joe Bloggs in the street couldn't understand how a football game could get to me but if you have had a row at football most of you will know that buzz and I had a glazed look like some guys on drugs. This was my heroin and it became my addiction. The unfair thing is that they send football hooligans to prison eventually, not to some cushy rehab clinic where they try to cure you.

By now I had totally lost it and was jumping on him, kicking him about the body like a rag doll and every impact was getting harder. I was giving no thought to it other than I wanted to hurt him. He was curled up with his hands over his face trying to protect his body so I tore at the scarf tied around his neck and was trying to yank him up by it so I could inflict the blows onto his face. I decided to take his scarf as a trophy and looked back sneering at him like the warrior I felt I was. The devil on my shoulder popped up and said, 'Well done Danny.'

I got home and can't deny that part of me felt ashamed that I had let the club down and that I wasn't being a true fan. That was typical of me: I was always having the angel/devil debate with myself, but the devil was winning a lot more and if the angel popped up I shut my eyes and it soon fucked off. I had started my career as a football hooligan (Black Danny was born) and it was something I would become notorious for around the country. But unlike some of the so-called firms who had one leader, one main face or one mouth-piece, Villa had plenty of men like me. I was just one of many who fought for the club over the years, men who I respect and men who respect me, and I am fortunate enough to have those men with me now as we put the record straight about Aston Villa's hooligan mobs over the years.

For me, Paul Brittle was, pound for pound, our main lad in what became the C Crew. The kid was on another level, brave, fearless, nuts and above everything loyal to the Villa and his mates. This kid was going on the Steamers' coaches at eleven years of age when other kids were going with their dads in the seats, so at an early age he was getting a taste of it. People who have fought with him and against him will know what I mean about him and it was a privilege to have him by my side.

BRITTLE

I lived in the Lea Bank area of Birmingham with my parents and three sisters before we moved to Northfield. Mom and Dad split up, with Dad moving to Penrith in Cumbria when I was four. I had a very happy child-hood and suppose you could say I was popular at school, as I was the joker in the pack. I have always valued my friends. I am fiercely loyal to them, sometimes to the point of blind loyalty. It has been my downfall on occasions. But I am fortunate to have made more friends than I have lost. Some I would give my life for and I don't say that lightly, as those who really know me will testify.

School though was a problem because I was a rebel. I just wanted to have a laugh and fool around and the teachers could see I was a disruptive influence. Throughout my life, accepting authority has always been difficult, so I rebelled against it. It resulted in me fighting with teachers and even the headmaster. I think my dear old Mom was tired of trying to cover up for her lad and after me being expelled three times she realised they knew there wasn't much chance of changing me.

I think the violence stemmed from mixing with older kids who were street brawlers and the whole life of watching the rows in the streets. I was transfixed but whereas some it frightened, with me it was a drug. I couldn't walk away from it; I had to go over and watch. As I got older I seemed to be fighting almost daily. I could never turn the other cheek.

The one thing I never was, was a bully. I once got called that in prison when the Governor found us all pissed-up on homemade potato beer and for whatever reason thought I had made the others drink it. In fact I was just trying to make life easier for my mates who were inside. So when he said it, I replied, 'I have been called a few things in my life, some of them right, but never a bully.' I then hit the fucker, but he was a cheeky cunt and deserved it. The next thing I remember is waking up in the hospital wing of Lincoln Prison and it didn't exactly help my early release date but as usual the consequences were the last thing on my mind.

I started going to football around 1970 and it wasn't Villa, it was the Albion, a game they won 6–1. Then I went to a few games at Blues but my first impressions were, what a shithole. At this point I didn't have a club as such, it was just something to do. Then a lad called Keith Taylor, who was five years older than me, took me to my first game at Villa, in 1970 against Bristol Rovers in the old Third Division. I can't remember the game, the score or even much about the players but I can remember the ruck.

The Holte End of course I do remember, and the ground itself was far superior to the Hawthorns or the Sty. But what sticks out is the old Trinity Road terraced area and the Bristol Rovers lads that were in there. I noticed that there were thirty Villa lads and suddenly they were over this small fence separating the Holte End from the Trinity Road and straight into 'em, fighting before the Old Bill moved in to calm things down. I thought, *this is fucking great*. I was eight at the time and at the end of the game went round to the Trinity Road from the Holte, where a copper said, 'Son, you don't want to go round there, there's going to be trouble.' I was thinking, *I know that's why I want to go there*. I lost Keith - I had gone off on my own and forgotten he was with me. I just wanted to see the fighting.

From that day, Aston Villa was the club for me – and the result off the pitch was more important than on it. Yes it was great and still is if we win, but to win the row and get the result off the pitch was the main thing. My mom had the search party out for me as Keith came back into the street without the young mate he was supposed to be looking after. She probably worried that, me being just a dot, I couldn't look after myself.

I started going down the Villa regular and my whole week became about the weekend. I couldn't wait for Saturday and the two-week break for a home game soon proved too much. I needed to go to away games and began to beg/steal/borrow to see the Villa, or really the football row.

The year we won the Third Division championship, Blues also got promoted from the Second Division to the First, and Birmingham City Council decided to hold a joint civic reception on the same day, one in the morning and one in the afternoon. Villa had theirs in the morning, then a huge mob decided to walk to St Andrews to smash the place up – at least, that was the general feeling. This mob could have been 1,000-strong, it seemed to go on forever. As we got to Digbeth it started to get out of hand, with people attacking cars in the streets and general Seventies-style mayhem, almost as if we had just got off a football special.

The crowd were chanting, 'We want a leader.' Then this guy, small but built like a solid brick shithouse, jumps on the bonnet of a car screaming, 'I am your fucking leader!' I had just met Pete the Greek.

I got to know Pete later really well. Here was a true legend. The bloke goes down in folklore and there are that many stories about him he could do three books on his own.

I was at the Hawthorns with Villa one season, I think it was 1973. We had lost and Pete wasn't happy. He was headbutting a lamppost continually in front of the Albion fans, shouting, 'Come on Albion, you want some?' There were no takers. It was complete lunacy but in the back of my mind I admired him, wanted to be him and loved the fact they wouldn't take him on. People will not believe what he was capable of. Simply he was the original Man Without Fear. He wasn't part of any mob, he was just Pete the Greek and our main man, a one-man effing army.

I was also taken in hand at an early age by some of the older lads doing the business for the Villa. They would go on and be major players in the Steamers gang. One lad who looked after me and showed me the ropes was Dewar, a top lad and fuck me could he row. I looked at the likes of him, Melvyn and obviously the Greek and just wanted to be like them, sounds corny but it's true. These were the major influences on my life and now I wanted to be a part of it.

My first action was an important League Cup game away to Crewe in 1974. Thousands of Villa had travelled and seemed intent on wrecking the train station. It was the first time I had seen Alsatian dogs used to control the fans. A Villa lad in the crowd threw something, I'm not sure if it was on the pitch or at the home fans, but the police came in to arrest him and I saw my chance. As a copper bent down I kicked him in the head. I ain't saying it was hard but he flipped and tried to chase me. I was in between the legs and away. I can't describe the feeling, it was a real buzz and started me on the road to football violence.

I have seen some terrible things when I was in prison and lived by the rule, don't let no one fuck with you. Don't show weakness, it clouds your thinking in certain situations. For example, in the Eighties we had been rowing with Leicester at their place for most of the day and were really giving them the runabout. I wanted to find them for another row; maybe it was the suicide button in me. I walked into a pub and it was all their main lads. I couldn't exactly walk back out as I was now amongst them, I had to just give it everything I had. There was no choice but to run in and hope I got in the first few digs, then they might think I was a nutter and back off. But this wasn't a Pete the Greek at Albion, they wanted me, and I got bashed with ashtrays, pool cues, bottles, fists and boots until I was almost unconscious.

I had blood streaming out the back of me eyes, I was aching, bruised, I had probably taken the worst beating I have ever taken and I was being passed around for each one to have their piece of me. After what seemed like an age I saw glass coming towards my face and shouted, 'Go on you cunts, kill me.' But they didn't. I thought, *mugs, you should have killed me*. That's how the violence got me. I was on self-destruct. I couldn't back down and nearly paid with my life.

The first C Crew lad I ever met was Jimmy Ryan. We were both aged about ten or eleven and were hunting for scarves at the station when we got talking and teamed up. We stayed in contact and often trekked across Brum to call for each other. All of a sudden Jimmy disappeared and I'd forgotten all about him until one day he appeared at my front door. I'd guess we were around twelve at the time. Jimmy explained that he'd been sent to Approved School and was on his toes because he hated it there. I was only too pleased to offer him accommodation and for the next two months he lived in the shed at the bottom of my garden with myself and my sisters taking it in turns to take tea, toast and whatever else we could out to Jim. We went to the games at weekends.

My mother never realised she had a lodger in the shed but one night when Jim was feeling low he phoned his own mum and agreed to meet her for a chat about things. I told Jim it was the wrong thing to do but he insisted on going and when he met his mum she had brought the police and his social worker with her. I told him to make a run for it but he saw it through and went back.

Jimmy remains a good mate to this day, and little did I know as they took Jimmy back with them that my friendships with people down the Villa would grow like the roots of a tree. By the time I was nineteen, I knew hundreds of lads and was helping to organise a lot of the things happening off the pitch at the time. Brittle was my name but certainly not by nature and meeting up with the rest of the lads from the C Crew brought the happiest times of my life.

You come across certain people in life you say you can trust with your life. Andy Browne is one of those people. He is quiet, unassuming and keeps in the background, weighing up situations. His biggest passion is his training. If you ever wanted a bloke by your side then Andy is the bloke you would choose.

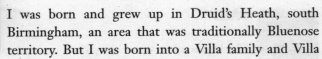

ANDY BROWNE

I was born and grew up in Druid's Heath, south Birmingham, an area that was traditionally Bluenose territory. But I was born into a Villa family and Villa has always been my team. One of my earliest memories is when my brother got me an LP record of the commentary of the 1971 League Cup final between Villa and Spurs. At the time Villa were in the Third Division but you could hear that their support was exceptional and when Spurs ended up as winners and went up to collect the cup, the background noise was of the Villa fans singing, 'Aston Villa, Aston Villa, we'll support you evermore.' I loved that part of the record and would play it over and over.

At school I became close friends with a lad called Tommy, who is a good friend to this day. Tommy was very similar to me as he too had been born into a family of Villa fans. Another good schoolfriend at the time was Jamie, the only Blues friend I have ever had, also a very good friend to this day. Jamie was a game kid, very likeable and comfortable with our firm. The first game I went to was a home game against Fulham. My older brother Johnny Browne took me to the game. I was very young and can't remember too much about it. The one thing that sticks in my mind is that it was a night game and

I was fascinated by the floodlights , one corner was the A the other a V. Soon I was going more regularly and it wasn't long before me and Tom were going together on our own.

My first ever hero was a player called Willie Anderson, a winger who used to score lots of goals for us. I was devastated when I found out that Villa had sold him to Cardiff. Overnight, Cardiff became my second team and this liking of them stayed with me for several years. When I first began to meet the lads, when I was 16 or 17, I used to talk about Cardiff so much that it became my nickname. Nobody called me Andy, they all called me 'Cardiff'.

I have met my closest friends through the Villa: Paul (Brittle) and Sean, who are golden lads, like brothers to me really, and not forgetting Jimmy Coley, Pete Moore and Dave Fin.

DANNY

Clarkey is a few years older than me and somebody we all looked up to. Although he was a Steamer and not C Crew, a lot of us see him as one of us because he has been in enough fights with us. I never thought he got the true recognition outside of the Villa ranks he deserved, not that he would crave it. Speaking to a lot of the other lads, the thing that sums him up is that everyone agrees it is reassuring to see him on your side. He is as famous for his frontline appearances as he is for his 'Do you believe in the Villa' party piece.

CLARKEY

I was first approached about getting involved in a book about eight years ago but I wasn't that interested, mainly because I was wary that it would be just another book of biased exaggeration and the right people wouldn't get involved because of their new found careers/lives. Having said that,

I do need some persuasion and it's taken me eight years to get this far. I might as well apologise to everyone now who I have promised to meet or to ring and then not done so. It's nothing personal lads, I just get waylaid or suffer lapses with my addiction problem – women. Hopefully when it mattered, I never let anyone down. Certainly nobody has ever let me down and I'm proud to have so many Villa lads as my pals.

Okay, that's all the *Trisha* stuff out the way; let's get on with it. I met with the other four lads and we all agreed that if we do a book then it will have to be the full story, the defeats as well as the wins, but above all else it must be about the crack. For me it was as much about the laugh with your mates as it was about the buzz of being in the middle of a row. Don't get me wrong, whenever it 'went' my focus was on what was in front of me, not who was next to me. I suppose you could call it a tribal thing but I can honestly say that I never went out of my way to hurt anyone – except when we played the Blues.

I am first and foremost a Ladywood lad, Birmingham born and bred. I have lived there for the majority of my life apart from a two-year stint in Germany after I came out of prison. I was born 48 years ago and have one brother and two sisters. My dad was very strict with me as a kid and I would feel the force of his belt on numerous occasions. It was only when I was about 15 that I began to get on with him and I understand now that it was his way of instilling discipline into me. I went to school at Harbourne High and by the third year there I had earned my spurs and was cock of the school. Once you are up there, you have to accept that there is always somebody who wants to have a go at you and I think this is true in many aspects of life.

The first game I ever went to was in 1968, West Bromwich Albion against Everton just before the same two teams played each other in the FA cup final. I went with a mate from school. A couple of years after that, I went to my first Villa game with another mate from school, Belch. I became a Villa fan and me and Belch began going on a regular basis. By 1974, we had left school and had money to travel to away games.

A turning point for me came in December of that year when we played at Colchester in the League Cup. I was an apprentice at the same place as Belch and to get the day off work we told our foreman that we were in a sponsored swim. Well, with what happened I was certainly in at the deep end. We won the game and at the end there was a pitch invasion from the Villa fans. I thought to myself, *fuck it, I'll have a piece of this*, and ran onto the pitch as well. I had only got a couple of yards past the touchline when I bumped into a copper, spinning him round. I was weaving my way through trying to avoid the Old Bill getting hold of me when I suddenly felt the thud of a truncheon into my stomach and I doubled over.

'Get off the pitch you black bastard,' was all I heard in the half-cockney, half-bumpkin accent they speak in down there. I looked up to see the copper I had bumped into standing over me. As I tried to get my breath back, I saw a right hand fly in and knock the copper to the floor.

'You don't do that to a Villa fan, you cunt.'

The owner of the right hand helped me up and we ran back into the terrace. I had just met Hicky, another lad who remains a good friend to this day. Unfortunately it wasn't enough; the Old Bill made sure I was going nowhere. I got my first nicking and was kept overnight. The coach I had come on drove round to different police stations looking for me but had to give up in the end. I was kept overnight and in the morning was given a caution. Because of my age they also gave me my train fare back to Birmingham. Belch went into work next morning and explained I had caught a cold at the swimming gala. The things you do for the Villa, eh!

The following Saturday we were away to Bristol City and again me and Belch decided to go, only this time we caught the football special down there. And who was sitting opposite us on the way down? Only Hicky from the previous Wednesday at Colchester. We got on really well and Hicky introduced me to all of his mates, who were sound and they told us to pop into the Imperial Hotel before the next home game as that was where they drank. I had just met the Steamers and it wouldn't be an exaggeration to say that my life changed from that moment onwards – and changed for the better. Here were a bunch of lads that would fight and die for me and I would do the same for them. Little did I know at the time that we would certainly do our share of fighting over the next 20 years.

After our victory at Colchester in December, we went on to win a two-legged semi-final over Chester City to reach Wembley. It was also to be my first taste of football violence but strangely enough it wasn't with Norwich, who were our opponents that day, but with Millwall. I wasn't aware at the time but Millwall were old acquaintances of ours and there was big history between the two teams from the previous few years. Not only that but whenever Villa made an appearance in the capital it usually followed that Millwall would appear at some stage during the day, and this day turned out to be no different.

We were drinking in the Greyhound when word began to spread that a mob of Millwall were not far up the road. The pub half emptied and around 200 Villa charged up the road, away from Wembley. What started as a slow jog turned into full pelt as the Millwall mob came into sight. I would say there was a maximum of 70 Millwall but they stood their ground and it was toe-to-toe for a short while, with the usual few on the floor. It didn't last long and we soon got the upper hand. Millwall were forced to have it on their toes. I am not going to try to pretend it was a major result because it wasn't, not with those odds, but it was the first time I'd been involved in hand-to-hand combat and I had loved it. To put the icing on the cake, I saw my team win the cup at Wembley that day as well.

I honestly believe that this book could have been based on any five from a number of between 50 to 75. There are a lot of people who are main faces who have been involved in this shit for a long while. I've met a lot of characters along the way and some very dangerous people in their own right. For my part, I did it off and on for thirty years but my time is now definitely over. I wouldn't have missed it for the world. I love the Villa, love the lads and love the crack. I have had the privilege to stand on the front line of both the Steamers and the C Crew and I have a lot of good memories.

An Audience with Pete The Greek

DANNY   **PETE**

There couldn't be a terrace book on Aston Villa without mentioning Pete the Greek. He was simply a legend, possibly the best-known face of any terrace legend at Villa, in any era. You can talk to any old Villa lad from the Seventies or the Eighties and they will have a story on Pete. I have seen him in battles, gone side by side with him, but never got to know the man personally or asked him if some of the stories about him were true. I wanted to know his opinions on the Seventies firms and relive his battles with him.

Pete, when did you first go down the Villa and why?

I was 18. I hated football. I lived in a hostel with another 20 lads and some suggested going to the Albion and some to the Blues, but one lad called Tony said, 'Come to the Villa.' He explained that there was always fighting with the away fans. That sounded all right to me and in 1971 I went to my first game, but no, I can't remember who against other than Vic Crowe was the boss.

Where did the name Pete the Greek come from?

Well when I started going down the Villa and I didn't know anybody, I was always fighting and people kept saying, 'That Greek bloke's fighting over there again.' The name stuck but the truth is I am not Greek, I am half Arab, half English.

When did you first get nicked and have you done time for the Villa?

I had only been going to the game for six months and got nicked fighting at Forest outside the Trent End. I actually got sent down for that and another three times, including Forest again, and believe it or not in the same spot outside the Trent. Then Albion for fighting in the Brummie Road, and Derby. Other than that I have done a total of ten stints in the nick, mostly for violence.

I have to ask you Pete, did you really headbutt a police horse?

Yes I did, when we played Man United at home in 1975. I did some crazy things, I know, like headbutting lampposts or walls. It worked me up, got me in the mood. I got nicked for it and when the judge sentenced me they sent me to a psychiatrist for six months.

Pete, sorry mate, that is fucking funny, can we stop the interview for a minute while I compose myself. What did the horse do by the way?

It wobbled.

I was always the football fan first and the rowing came later. Was it the same for you?

No, I loved the fighting. I would get blokes talking to me about Villa needing a new full-back or a midfielder. I used to just agree but couldn't give a shit really. *Let's go and find a row, you boring cunts.* I know it sounds funny but it took me eight years to work out the offside rule. The bastards changed it just as I had worked it out, then I just gave up trying to work it out after that.

My brother Popeye used to tell me stories about you, he said you would do press-ups and pull-ups on lampposts in the street?

Yes, I was a fitness fanatic and would walk up to a lamppost and pull myself up 20 or 30 times, then walk up to the next one and do the same. I would do press-ups on the train as I was going to the game. I prided myself on keeping fit and I was also boxing at the British Leyland club and was a useful light-middleweight. When you have got yourself a name, and I was proud of my name, I wanted to make sure I didn't let myself down.

You had a habit of going into firms on your own, would you class yourself as a loner or part of a firm?

I was originally on my own and yes I just used to steam in and didn't think about the numbers. Sometimes it worked, sometimes it didn't. I later ran with the Quinton mob because at the time my area, Ladywood, didn't have a mob. The Quinton mob were very good lads and even when I went in the nick Millwall lads who I met inside would talk about them. Blues also had good lads from Quinton.

Okay, but what about the legendary one-man assault on Bolton at their place?

Oh yes. I was bored, the lads were in the pub and I wanted a row, so when I saw them come round the corner I just ran into them and they ran off. They realised later it was just me but I didn't care when they came back, it was part of the fun.

Were you there for the Millwall game in '73?

Yes I was and was one of the group of Steamers who went in their end. We might have only lasted 20 minutes but no one was doing that at Cold Blow Lane then. I saw Millwall's Harry the Hatchet put an axe in Dave Gillette's head I think it was. It was the worst terrace fight I have ever been in and we had it toe-to-toe but 20 minutes is a long time in a fight. We did eventually get bashed. Groombridge did a lot of damage that day and went head-to-head with Tiny on their own end. We didn't win but that's the way it goes sometimes and we certainly weren't the train lot, who got smashed. Millwall lads I spoke to said even West Ham hadn't done that in those days. Groombridge should get a special mention; on the railway station he went straight into their firm on his own but he then had to do a retreat up the railway track.

Was it true there was a lot of history then with Millwall and Villa?

Yes, there was. We were a big club and a scalp to them and after the incident up there we made sure we repaid them big time at Villa Park, and whenever we were in London we ended up in a row with them. They even sprayed on a wall close to the ground, 'Villa turn back.' So you knew they would turn out for us. But London grounds you were never sure who would turn up to fight. We played Orient away and ended up having it with West Ham there.

What about the Shrewsbury incident?

Oh that was funny, you're talking at their ground. I pulled the fence separating Villa from their main lot and ran into them. There was only ten of us and they ran. A bit disappointing really.

You became famous for your headbutts. What about the Carlisle incident when the lads were locked out and you butted the gate and it opened?

I'm surprised you remember that. I was drunk and the Villa lads couldn't get in, so it had to be done.

The Seventies were a great era for football violence and it's what got me into it watching you lot. What's your memories?

It was good fun. I was young and on adrenalin and every away game we would try and take the home ends, it was where the fun was. In the Third Division we were the big club, with 30,000 gates, so when we went to places the whole town would turn out. I had some great rucks at the oddest of places. I got bored with the Holte so went in the Witton End to mingle in with the away fans and have it with them. It was more fun. I thought the Villa lads in the Seventies were as good as any, can't ever remember us getting battered at Villa Park.

Bradford away was a good row, they just seemed to swap ends at half-time and 250 of them thought they would come into the Villa section and the Old Bill let them. We didn't, and ended up getting the better of them but it was toe-to-toe stuff, the proper fighting.

Would you class yourself as a Steamer?

Yes I do and proud of it, there were some very good lads in that firm and hard bastards who wouldn't run, and that's all you can ask.

Who was the main man in that group?

It's hard to say, they were all good, but if it was one it would be Dewar – but I've got to say it's close. Those lads made me feel a king for a day in 1975. I had just come out of prison on the Thursday for another stint on behalf of AVFC and we were at Wembley for the League Cup final versus Norwich and I think it was Godds paid for my ticket and the lads my beer. They held me up on their shoulders, a great day and I never got the chance to thank them but if they are reading this then they will know how chuffed I was.

Have you ever run or bottled a straightener?

I have never run but I sometimes think I should be dead by now with the rows I have been in and the bashings I have taken. I was never the hardest. I had a good nut and wasn't afraid and I was mad but there were others just the same like Groombridge. He was a good friend and good to have on your side but he once wanted to do something even I backed out of. Andy Gray, the Holte End hero, had left Villa to go to Wolves and not long after, we played them. He wanted us to get on the pitch and batter him to fuck. Anyone who knows Groombridge knows he meant it but I thought I would end up doing six years for it, so bottled the straightener. Ha ha. Groombridge was nuts and as good as anybody to have in the row.

Pete, I grew up on stories of you like most Villa lads of my era did. My oldest brother used to call you a warrior and remembers you getting into fights with the mods and rockers, seaside stuff. Is that correct?

I was a skinhead back then and had a claret and blue Lambretta with 60 mirrors and parked it for every game at the Witton Arms. Along with about 30 other Villa lads we used to go and drive to the seaside towns and get into some good scrapes.

What's your view on our rivals, Blues?

I rated the old lot, got some good lads, and other than the Windsor incident when we bashed 'em I always felt neither of us got major results against each other. To me it was fifty-fifty. I did get nearly half-killed twice in Boogies going back 15 years ago, when I went in their pub on my own and they recognised me and jumped on me. I was about to be thrown through the window when a lad called Dove stopped them.

You don't seem bitter about it?

Why? It happens and was a long time ago. I don't like Blues but I respect their older lot.

What about the other Midlands firms?

The Wolves Subway Army were very good but Albion were piss-poor. I got to know Mutley at the detention centre and he was old school and he was their main lad in my opinion. They just couldn't hold it when we played them, they were wank. That's why I went in the Brummie Road, as it wasn't a problem, but got nicked in the process. I was surprised when I heard about the Uplands [see Chapter 13] but apparently they have got a good set of lads these days and don't run away like they did in the old days.

Coventry, we always used to go in their main bit. Thirty of us tried to take their whole end one day but again they were nothing special. I remember being in the Mercat pub at one game and two Cov blokes I was drinking with tried to take the piss out the Villa, no respect, so had to bang 'em out. Can't have the Villa being slagged. The only other firm I rated from the Midlands was Forest, who were very game. I had some great battles with them, even met and became mates with them. I became mates with the late Paul Scarrott as we were in the nick together.

Are there any firms that you rate from the Seventies?

Millwall was an evil place to go to and I got my biggest hiding there. Nobody could take liberties there but at least we had a go in their end. After that it's West Ham, another top firm in their day. I also rated Everton, had a lot of good rows with them as well. What amazes me was the likes of Spurs, we ran them all over the place in Wembley in 1971 and there was no more than 100 of us and yet now they are supposed to be a top firm. Portsmouth was another tough place to go, along with Cardiff; I've got the scars to show you from both of those places.

Pete, what's the score with your relationship with the Old Bill?

Coppers! They don't like me, even now I get grief off them. One day in the Holte six of them were kicking me down the stairs and I actually bounced down each step. I have given a few a hard time though over the years but fuck 'em.

Are there any teams that surprised you?

Oxford, 1973. I expected it to be place full of silly students and we went in their end, as we would do everywhere back then. Fair play, they got a crew of lads who steamed the Villa at the back of us. Some right wankers though at the back, them Villa kids should have stood and fought. By them running they caused a crush that could have got somebody killed. I tried to stop crushing the little girl underneath me but I thought we were going to be goners, all of us. It was a Hillsborough situation.

What's your views on the C Crew?

They are good lads, like yourself, Brittle, Andy, Pattison, etc. You didn't run and you did more than your bit for the Villa. Enjoyed some good battles with you Danny and do you think the Queen might recognise us in next year's honours list, maybe an OBE for services on behalf of hooligans?

Any regrets Pete?

Well the Villa and the fighting cost me my marriage but she gave me the ultimatum either give up the Villa and the fighting or I walk out. So I said, 'Bye, close the door on the way out.' I was just fanatical about it, I couldn't give it up. She was a good woman though. I have met some great people and made great mates and enjoyed it while it lasted.

Pete finally it's got to be asked. You know your pal Groombridge, he is not here to answer in person and I'm not sure if it's true or is an old fisherman's tale, but it has to be asked. About his time working in the morgue, did he really cut off a dead woman's head and put it in a bag?

(Pause as Pete chuckles.) Yes. He was 18. He bet a mate that he would do it and bought a pen-knife for one-and-six, went into the morgue and cut the head off. He brought it into the pub wrapped up in a bag. The bloke thought it was a dummy head as all the blood was drained from it. He was feeling it and got a bit of a shock when he found it was real.

Fucking hell Pete, that is scary.

Mmm. He won the bet, a fiver! He was a bit mad Groombridge, got done for it, but we all did mad things back then.

Think we will wrap it up at that, give my best to him. Like yourself he was a Villa legend even if he did try and stab me once, ha ha!

1 AS I WALKED UP TO THE STEPS OF THE HOLTE END

CLARKEY

In 1968, Villa were on the brink of bankruptcy when local businessman Pat Seward managed to persuade the travel king and inventor of the bicycle kick, Doug Ellis, to come in and buy into the club and launched a share scheme where a band of loyal Villa supporters helped stop our great club folding. Maybe it was general apathy or the fact the board in charge couldn't run a piss-up in a brewery but it was only eleven years after we had won the FA Cup and we were on the road to nowhere as a club.

One of our older lads, Klepto, from the Sutton area of Birmingham, recalls those days in the Sixties off the pitch:

There was no real organisation in those days, you would just get pockets of a dozen or so Villa lads. Probably the very first mob as such in the late Sixties was a mob of greasers from the Glebe area of Birmingham who had a bit of a run-in with Millwall on the steps of the Holte End. I can also recall another mob that was formed around the same time was the 'Dougal', which a few of the older lads like Boots (RIP) ran with, although nobody knows where this name stems from.

There was a large group of lads who used Peppers, the function room at the Queens Head in Erdington, and eventually Villa lads started to drink in Brum town centre. The first city centre Villa pub was the White Swan on Edmund Street. It wasn't long before the first ever 'unofficial' coach firm started up, using Stockland Coaches.

Prior to our relegation to the Third Division, two incidents stick out in my mind. One was Queens Park Rangers, who not as famous as their Glasgow namesake but were another Rangers who came into the Holte End in big numbers and stayed for the duration of the game in the late Sixties. The other was Millwall in there around 1967.

Villa also went on a bit of a cup run: we took First Division Southampton to a replay at Villa Park and beat them before we drew Spurs away in the fifth round of the FA Cup. We took thousands, and what with it being the FA Cup and the club on a bit of a false dawn, largely down to the influence of Tommy Docherty's charismatic personality, there were so many Villa there that day we ended up in Spurs Shelf End and took their end.

We managed to just beat relegation in 1969 but worse was to come as a fan. April 1970, and the unthinkable happened. Aston Villa were relegated to the Third Division for the first time in their proud and illustrious history. This just two years after the club nearly folded, only to be saved from the brink of bankruptcy by deadly Doug and a loyal band of supporters who pledged money into a share scheme. It was akin to Manchester United being relegated to the Second Division in 1974 and for a club the size of ours it was a huge embarrassment that we were now to be playing the likes of Rochdale and Bury. Our local derby would be Walsall. Our neighbours rejoiced and we became the butt of many jokes, causing passions and tensions to run high. When Birmingham supporters carried a coffin into the workplace at British Leyland to celebrate our relegation, a mini-riot broke out on the production lines.

Yet many Villa supporters now look back at this era with fond memories and see it as a turning point in our history when fans and players became almost as one, everyone rallying round for the cause. It seemed to galvanise our support. Our last home game in the Second Division drew a crowd of 32,000. We all felt that we were still a big football club, indeed a sleeping giant; the trouble was, we were in a bastard coma.

Nobody in the lower divisions had seen a club as big as Aston Villa before and we were a major attraction. We were averaging crowds of 30,000-plus and other clubs were recording their highest home attendances whenever we were in town.

These were the days of the away football specials when thousands would travel and for Villa supporters it was all new and exciting, as Villa would take over whole towns, never mind football grounds.

Those days of decline also brought some of the best days you could imagine. Some instant memories: football specials, butchers' coats, Doc Martens, monkey boots, brogues, turned-up Levis, two-tone Sta Press, sheepskins, leather coats, crombies, Ben Sherman, Jaytex, terracing, the taking of ends, silk scarves, the sound of hundreds of pairs of boots running down the road or the terracing, the sound of a boot going in on the opposition, no mobiles, no real organisation and very little police intelligence.

The main mobs were from Quinton, who called themselves the Quinton Stars, Erdington and Kingstanding and the main faces of that era were the likes of Amy and Terry Smith, Jim Hegarty, Venny McKay, Dave Gillette and the infamous Pete the Greek. They were the people we young kids looked up to. The objective and the fun for them was getting in and taking the home ends and then staying put. The Villa skins were doing this on a regular basis at the likes of Reading, Chesterfield, Preston, Swindon, Shrewsbury, Wrexham, Notts County, Chester, Port Vale, Fulham and Rochdale. I have detailed some of my own accounts from the memory bank and the likes of Raggy, Pete and Hicky have given me some of their stories.

RAGGY CHESTERFIELD

It was the first game of the season, and with the novelty factor thousands of Villa fans travelled to Chesterfield to see our first game in the Third Division. We went by the old football special and we really were the big club in the division; nobody of our size or stature had been in that division before. We arrived at the station and the Old Bill kept us in while people gawped, stared at us and what seemed like the whole town wanted to see what was going on. We were like a circus attraction. This happened on a regular basis, people had never experienced this size of travelling support before in their towns and cities.

We took over the place and the Villa fans took both of the ends, forcing the Chesterfield in there onto the pitch. Our manager, Vic Crowe, came onto the pitch appealing for calm with the Villa support, as the lads were creating mayhem all over the ground. We were enjoying ourselves and it was a great feeling to go to these places and take over. I don't think Chesterfield town, never mind the football club, had seen anything like it, but a plus for them was that it drew a record gate of 16,000, almost double their average gate.

This was the start of things and set a trend for our two seasons in the Third Division. This happened on a regular basis as the travelling support gave these little clubs much-needed gate revenue but also big headaches in how to control us. Of course there were occasions when the whole town did turn out and they wouldn't just roll over and let Villa mobs do as they pleased. The word had got round the rest of the Third Division about the numbers we were taking and the likes of Bradford and Barnsley were different propositions, both rough Yorkshire towns who didn't take kindly to people taking liberties there.

BRADFORD CITY, 1972

We had been there the season earlier and had taken good numbers and met with little resistance but the next season was very different, as people were starting to wise up to Villa. We were in an era of seemingly endless strikes and this time there was a rail strike, resulting in a reduced travelling support from Villa. What greeted us at the game was bizarre. At half time the Bradford fans simply switched ends. They came out of the one end as a mob and casually walked round the side of the pitch and into the end we were occupying and the police just watched. That was the signal for everybody to get stuck in but they had good numbers and were attacking us from everywhere. The Villa lads had to stand firm or it would have been even worse. A lot of our lads travelling home in coaches and cars had wounds from an epic battle.

BARNSLEY

We didn't have any fear of, or probably respect for, most of the clubs we were visiting, it was just the norm for us to go in their ends. The first season we went to Barnsley we all went into the home end and the Old Bill put a thin blue line between us and the Barnsley lot. The Tykes didn't take kindly to Villa on their territory and throughout the game there was fighting as they attempted to get us out and reclaim home soil.

On the way back to the station there was a battle royal going on, as they were looking to salvage pride and give the mobs from Villa Park something to take home. The running scraps culminated in a real large battle with them at the marketplace. I wouldn't say it was a victory for either firm but it was on top and worse was to come.

Our next visit there was a night game and we went again by football special, only this time it was a 13-carriage train and we only managed to fill the first two carriages.

As we approached Barnsley station the train stopped at a level crossing and we found the wheeltappers and shunters welcoming committee waiting for us. We felt like scabs going through the Yorkshire picket lines. There were hundreds of them. They weren't happy with us for our previous exploits there and were determined there would be no repeat. We managed to get to the ground safely and paid into the side end. The Barnsley mob were not aware we were in there until the game had started. The walk back to the station after the game was as bad as it got and we had to run the gauntlet. They definitely were no mugs.

Apparently we were the only firm at the time that had managed to stay in the Barnsley home end for the whole game but over the two games we had to fight to earn that accolade.

PETE OLD PRESTON AND THE QUINTON MOB

The Quinton mob were one of the original Villa mobs. They did themselves credit at Cardiff, and with the old enemy West Bromwich Albion against their Smethwick mob, and at various other locations during Villa's trek through the lower divisions. Preston was one I remember vividly.

Getting off the first of two football specials at Preston, we felt a million dollars. We had some good lads and had to march through the town centre to get to the ground, Deepdale. As we marched along the pavement of the High Street singing 'Power to the Villa', we felt we could take on the world. As we approached the ground, a mob of Preston were waiting and we ran straight into them, some Villa going one way after some Preston and some going another way. We were with the mob nearest the ground and after gaining the upper hand were put on the back foot by the arrival of more Preston. We gave them a few kicks and tried to push on towards the ground but were beaten back by sheer numbers. Some vicious kickings were given to a few Villa who got caught.

Our lot had to retreat back down the road when we saw a huge mob coming up towards us. To our relief it was the second football special arriving, led by a short skinhead lad wearing a sheepskin. Behind him was the rest of the Quinton mob. A roar went up and we turned and joined the Quinton mob running at the Preston. After a few quick kicks and punches the Preston turned and ran. The last we saw of them before the game was as they disappeared over the horizon of the park next to the ground.

To add insult to injury we then went straight into the Preston end, ran the few Preston in there and by the start of the match had completely taken the home end.

A Villa fan climbed up a flagpole in the ground and nicked the Preston flag, much to our amusement.

After the match my lot were not troubled until close to the station, when we had a run-in with a nasty lot of Preston who were obviously out for revenge after what had been done to them. Thankfully a load of Villa came down from the station and assisted us in rounding off a very good day.

One of the lads, Gary, was with Pete the Greek at Preston that day. He recalls:

We had gone on the earlier special and when we got there we just came straight out of the station. A small group of us went the wrong way, ending up in a cul-de-sac with a large mob of Preston at the other end. The Greek didn't bother waiting for reinforcements and started to break up somebody's fence and hand out the bits of wood to us. Now we thought it was on top but he turned it round single-handed and went charging into the Preston mob, who by now were not so keen.

Just as he was going into action, the other football special pulled in with all the lads on and they got it from both directions. The Greek was never one to wait; I remember the sight of him at Blackpool railway station, wearing a yellow motorcycle helmet, running head first straight off the train and fighting with the Old Bill. A good bloke to have on your side with the numbers against you but not one for organisation really. He went, you either followed or you didn't. He was his own army.

PETE OLD SWANSEA CITY

As a 16-year-old, this was one of my first real offs following years of being on the fringes of trouble and developing the buzz for football violence. We travelled by football special and made our way to a pub near the ground. About 20 Villa were in the pub and were making themselves heard. Standing outside the pub gave us a good view of a large mob of Swansea lads coming round the corner towards us.

We ran into the Swansea, punching and kicking, as more Villa backed us up from out the pub. I took a heavy smack to the ear and was booted before getting in my first punch on the nose of a Swansea lad who doubled up and got a boot in his face. We heard more Swansea coming down the road and Villa made a withdrawal up the road towards the ground, leaving two Swansea on the ground but having to help one of our lot to get away.

We went in the ground on the halfway line, not realising that was their main end, to be met by Villa lads who had obviously already taken a kicking. One had all the bone on his elbow exposed from being kicked down the terracing whilst others had facial injuries. As more Villa turned up, the regular Villa fans went behind the goal, with the lads going on the halfway line to confront the Swansea. Swansea were eventually kicked out of the halfway line and Villa tried to get in their end. Throughout the match there were little offs as both sets of lads tried to get at each other.

After the match, we got separated from the main Villa mob when we chased after a small mob of Swansea. Big mistake! On the roads back to the station, Swansea were walking single file down both sides of the road, checking everyone to see if they were Villa. There were about eight of us and the way we were dressed left no doubt as to who and what we were. We ran. Our bottle went and there was no way we were taking on 100-plus Swansea. We took a few kicks and punches and headed round some back street, which somehow led us back to near the station.

Other Villa were in a similar situation and we grouped together to face up to the Swansea waiting just by the station, plus the mob somewhere behind us. Some Villa were also coming back out of the station and good numbers were now gathering. A roar went up as Swansea charged and Villa went into them, boots flying. The sound of hundreds of boots running is something you can never forget, and then that special sound as boot meets body. The off lasted a good few minutes before police turned up with dogs and split the two sets of lads up.

Swansea earned a lot of respect that day and maybe a few lessons were learned, as we certainly thought they would be a pushover, having never encountered them before. The same applied to a lot of the 'smaller' clubs we met that season – but when the Villa were in town every nutter from miles around seemed to turn up to meet us.

ROTHERHAM UNITED

Villa went into the Rotherham home end, which ended up being split 50-50 between Villa and Rotherham, with a thin police line down the middle. There was constant fighting throughout the match with a steady stream of stretchers taking away the injured. A lot of those were for leg injuries from kicks to the shins. After the match it was very confused with fighting everywhere. Another place where Villa didn't get it all their own way, but a great day out.

PETE OLD CARDIFF CITY

My memory is surprisingly vague about this one, I think in those days it wasn't anything special, just another away day watching the Villa, whereas nowadays it would be talked about before and after the event for weeks. We were with Aidan and his lot and some dope had been smoked en route. As we approached the ground in a mob of 20 or 30, a much larger mob of Cardiff appeared. They all seemed much bigger and older than us, with many wearing metal-toe-capped boots.

We were forced down a side street by the ground, which turned out to be a dead end with a brick wall at the end. We were trapped with nowhere to go – all we could do was stand and get mullered or make a run through the Cardiff mob. We all agreed that we would run at, and hopefully through, the Cardiff. Heads down and arms like windmills, we ran through the Cardiff, punching and kicking whoever we could and receiving much worse back. Two Villa got caught and were given a bad kicking but credit to the Cardiff they didn't follow through and left the Villa to drag themselves away to safety. I don't remember the match and don't remember getting back to the station.

We will never see those days again. I'm just proud to have been involved with some great people in some great times that will never be forgotten.

RAGGY

In the Sixties, Villa had actually taken Cardiff's home end but when we travelled there in 1972 it was a very different prospect. It seemed they had dragged them in from the hills and valleys and had the numbers to deal with us. Villa were in and out of their end all the way up to the start of the game. Just before kick-off the Villa lads, who were mainly those from the train, were pushed round onto the side terrace. It was to and fro with both sets charging each other throughout the first half.

At half-time the sheer numbers of Cardiff got the better of Villa and we ended up on the pitch across to the other side, where the coach firm was standing. It was a long walk back to the station and the Villa needed to stick together or it would have been too on top.

 HICKY (of the Steamers) SEALAND AIR RESCUE

We had instances like at Mansfield Town, where the likes of Notts Forest joined up to have a pop at the Villa and some of ours came off worst, but it was all part and parcel of it in the seventies. In truth it was never as sinister as the Eighties, where violence went to another level.

The very first firm name for a Villa crew that I remember other than the local area names was taken from a coach hire company used for away games called Sealand Air, organised by Rosco. They used to travel the length and breadth of the country and on one occasion en route to Middlesbrough the coach broke down just outside

Mansfield. The Sealand Air mob decided to take in the Mansfield v. Swansea game and give some payback to the locals who had given them a rough ride the season before. In bizarre circumstances, this mob of 50 lads ended up running the Mansfield out of their home end and taking up residence there, much to the bewilderment of the players on the pitch, who stopped playing to watch the local police escorting Villa out of the end 15 minutes into the game.

Everywhere the Villa went we took large numbers, many of whom were well up for trouble, although that's not to say that we didn't come unstuck at some grounds because we certainly did. In those days it was accepted that if you travelled away with the Villa you would find trouble and you stood a good chance of getting some sort of injury. Once you got the buzz there was little you could do about it, you just got on with it. One thing that always amazed me was that the main Villa lads were not just 'hooligans' purely out for trouble, they were also Villa fans and Villa was in their blood. It was more a case of fighting for the honour of Aston Villa. I remember talking to one of the main lads on a football special and he could name just about every Villa player going back to the war. That knocks on the head all the talk about 'they are not supporters, they are just thugs'.

CLARKEY

On the football front the first season saw us taking the Third by storm, backed by fanatical support home and away. Along the way we went on a League Cup run that saw us play Manchester United, who boasted the likes of Best, Law and Charlton, in a two-legged semi-final. Over 12,000 Villa supporters made the trip to Old Trafford and that night saw fighting before and after the game. We felt we were back in the big time and for the home leg a Third Division club drew 62,500 – and we beat them 2-1, with Pat McMahon scoring a diving header just two days before Christmas Day to give all Villa supporters the best present you could ever wish for.

Who could stop us? We were on a roll but ultimately that cup run was our downfall for promotion, as we had a horrendous two months in February and March in which we won only one game, although we did have a League Cup final to look forward to against Spurs. Those who were there or saw the highlights on *Star Soccer* on the Sunday know we completely outplayed them for 75 minutes but Martin Chivers scored two decisive goals in another heartbreaker. As Alan Mullery lifted the cup, all you could hear was, 'Aston Villa, we'll support you ever more.' He ended up sticking two fingers up at the Villa supporters – I never liked the cunt after that!

The next season we again played before massive crowds, including 46,000 for a local derby against Walsall. The 48,110 for our promotion rivals Bournemouth was a higher attendance than either Everton or Manchester United attracted for their home games that day. It was also the first ever Third Division game to be shown on *Match Of The Day* and later a documentary was shown on BBC that explored the fanatical support of Aston Villa. That gives you an idea of the crowds Villa were attracting and the size of the club. Remember there were hardly any away fans travelling to Villa Park back then.

When we went to Notts County, we took a staggering 20,000 fans, swelling their crowd to 34,000. It was like being part of a revolution and we even signed a Liverpool player who was prepared to drop two divisions, Ian Ross. When he was debating signing for Villa, the great Bill Shankly said, 'Ian, in ten years' time there will be a Super League and Aston Villa will be in it.' It signalled our intent that we were on the way back.

We started to get our act together on the pitch after a stuttering start, with 'Andy, Andy Lochead in the air' scoring 25 goals and Bruce Rioch smashing goals of the month every week. Our final home game drew 45,000 against Chesterfield; effing Chesterfield, I ask you! When people talk about loyalty and support then let's get it right, we were up amongst the best. That season even saw a great Villa youth side playing before crowds of 20,000. We had a crop of youngsters who would win honours for the club in later years and the likes of Gidman and 'Walks on Water' Brian Little saw us win the FA Youth Cup 4-2 at Anfield, with Villa supporters occupying the Kop for the night. It was refreshing to beat Birmingham over two legs in the game dubbed 'the battle of the super boys', Little winning hands down against Trevor Francis.

In the following season, 1972/3, back in Division Two and long before the three-up, three-down system, we finished third but way behind the two that went up, Burnley and QPR. The best away following that season seen at Villa Park was probably Leeds in the cup. Leeds United were the best side in England at the time and we held them to a 1-1 draw at Villa Park, where Rioch scored a gem and again 46,000 turned out. Tommy Docherty used to say that if Villa shirts were hanging on a washing line 20,000 would turn out just to watch them dry and Don Revie after that game said the support from the Holte End was magnificent, better than Liverpool's Kop. I wouldn't argue. Was there a better sight than a packed Holte End in the Seventies, with a capacity of 28,000? I don't think there was. The noise and the passion almost sucked the ball in at times, it was worth a goal start to the team.

The 1973/74 season saw us finish a very disappointing fourteenth but again we had a great FA Cup run in which we beat Arsenal after a replay, drawing a crowd of 48,000 at Villa Park. A certain Ulsterman, Sammy Morgan, terrorised Bob Wilson over the two games. Arsenal came in the Holte that night at the bottom but were very quickly despatched.

The Millwall game that season gets covered in detail later [see Chapter 4] but the other one that sticks out was Cardiff City, who made a very poor attempt to get near the Holte End. They got sussed on Witton Lane and an attack led by the Greek saw their mob of 100 Taffs caught front, back and side by Villa lads. The only option they had was to jump the turnstiles on Witton Lane and that's what they tried to do but with that many they were never all going to get over and in the squash a lot took heavy beatings before the Old Bill on horseback saved them.

Vic Crowe was sacked as manager in 1974 and Brian Clough was touted as his replacement. Cloughie had already been praising Villa as a sleeping giant with massive support but surprisingly we went for a guy not even in the reckoning, Ron Saunders. Doug Ellis got that right because he proved to be our most successful manager and despite him later leaving us to ply his trade with the unwashed up the road he gave us seven unforgettable years.

That season we started off slowly but stayed in contention just behind the leaders, Man United and Sunderland. We didn't really take off until after Xmas and then we really kicked in, along with a glorious cup run that saw us beat Norwich 1-0 at Wembley. We won 14 of our final 16 games, gaining promotion at Sheffield Wednesday, where never mind take the ground, we took the fucking city. Villa had 15,000 at that game. We took their large, uncovered Kop and made it the Holte End for the night. Their hooligan book *Flying With The Owls*, or should it be *Lying With The Owls*, mentions us in the Kop but says we didn't hold it and after the game we wouldn't come out. No, we held it all game, and yes we wouldn't come out – we were too busy celebrating on their pitch as we had won promotion back to the First Division. Villa were back in the big time and for the first time in our history had European football to look forward to.

The final home game against Sunderland drew over 57,000. I doubt we will ever see a gate like that again at Villa Park, with thousands locked out. My abiding memory of that game is thousands of Mackems dressed in red Doc Marten high-leg boots. There wasn't any trouble at the game, it was a total party atmosphere and at the end the pitch was engulfed in thousands of fans celebrating a fantastic season of a League Cup and promotion double.

While all that was going on things were getting organised off the pitch as well.

2 THE STEAMERS

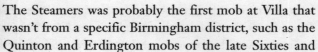

CLARKEY

The Steamers was probably the first mob at Villa that wasn't from a specific Birmingham district, such as the Quinton and Erdington mobs of the late Sixties and early Seventies. It was a collection of different pockets of lads that drank in the town, originally at the Imperial Hotel, then later on they made the Hole In The Wall pub in Dale End their office. As one of the lads looking on, they had a fearsome reputation and every terrace youth wanted to be a Steamer and their match day antics have gone down in Villa terrace folklore. They were one of the main reasons why I got involved in football violence. To get an invite onto a Steamers coach was almost like getting an invite from the Queen, as it wasn't something they handed out lightly, and you had to be able to stand and fight your corner, not 'shape'. Some of them didn't take too kindly to the young pups but others did, and like apprentices we learnt our trade from them.

The Steamers had a close bond and they probably had as many laughs as they had fights. They were a close-knit firm who drank, stood and fought together most days of the week. Some great stories of these lads have passed down into football folklore, like Groombridge's attempts to take the Luton end in the Seventies, when he had a cunning plan he shared with the other Steamers. He told them he would pretend to faint, get taken out by the St John

Ambulance, and once he was near to the Luton end would jump off the stretcher and dive into the Luton fans. He told the other Steamers that would be the cue then for them to run across the pitch and attack the end. Sure enough, after pretending to faint he was taken out, and as he was going round the pitch he jumped off the stretcher and dived into their lads. But the other lads were laughing that much they couldn't join him, so he proceeded to try to take the Luton end on his own. Unfortunately he got battered and nicked.

Groombridge was a total nutter. Sean from New York reminded me of one night when he took us on one of his suicide missions in town to a Blues pub where he gets into the pub and stands in the middle of them pointing at each one in turn asking them if they want a straightener, with no takers. He then turns to me, forgetting that I was Villa and also with him, and says, 'What about you?' I replied, 'I came in with you, John.' That was Groombridge all over, once the red mist came down he was gone.

These were the stories we grew up on, these were the people that were the stuff of terrace legend and you would sit and listen to these incredible tales with mouths open, waiting to hear how they had conquered opposing firms. I suppose the stories got exaggerated as they went round, but as I got to know people like Groombridge well I think some of them were played down; the bloke was a lunatic, but thankfully a Villa lunatic.

I don't know what the kids expected to see – blokes ten feet tall – heavyweight boxing champions, Magnificent Seven types – but such was the mystique about these guys that I was almost thinking people would queue up to get their autographs. There were so many stories about Pete the Greek, for instance, that he was like William Wallace of *Braveheart* fame, who people thought was seven feet tall and had the strength of ten men. Well, Pete wasn't seven feet tall but he had the physique of a pocket battleship. He was one on his own. His idea of a good Saturday night was taking his missus out to well-known Blues drinking haunts so he could have his Saturday night row, and he had a few of those all right.

At away games, people would say, 'The Steamers are here,' and it meant the other Villa supporters felt safe, but more than anything proud, that they were representing the Villa. They were our SAS of the terraces. For games against Blues, the Hole in the Wall pub would fill, then the Red Lion nearby, and thousands – and that's no exaggeration – would congregate around Dale End, waiting for the Steamers to leave the pub to walk to the ground so that they could follow. The Steamers made you feel part of an army.

Everyone of that age group claims to be a Steamer but the truth is that the original Steamers were no more than 50 lads, and there is a hat that is still in circulation today with the original names on it. Without being disrespectful to anyone, the names of those legends were the likes of Foxy, Melv, Mouse, Groombridge, Big Sean, Big Pete, KC, Rosco, Steve, Coogie, Hicky, Godds, Dewar, Roff, Deano and Martin, D.Dub, Ginger, Raggy and many more. Those that I have been able to track down and who were willing to speak recall some of the battles and funny incidents of that golden era.

FOXY

I thought the name actually came from a song of the time, 'Dreamer, you're nothing but a dreamer' by Supertramp, but consensus is that it was from a beer called Newquay Steam Ale that some of the lads were drinking every night whilst they were holidaying in Newquay. At the time the likes of Terry Smith were always referring to steaming into people when talking about a row and it was just a name that got bandied about a lot. The song, though, was forever on the jukebox in the old Imperial Hotel and we would all break out into 'Steamer, you're nothing but a Steamer'.

We had some great cracks and there were some great characters. One of our lot allegedly is the only guy with an FA Cup winner's medal; well, he didn't win it but screwed an ex-Leeds player's house and nicked his medal. I am not going to make us superheroes but it was a good firm and it was a family, a Villa family, that we had created. Big Pete had started off the balloon craze where we had gone to the likes of Stoke, Derby and Southampton and there were thousands of balloons and it became the norm for the travelling hordes to take them, letting them out as the teams appeared on the pitch. You also had the sights of Villa fans upside down, legs dangling out in the shape of a 'V', and there were then tens of copycat legs and V's on the Holte End, spawned by the Steamers. It was the kind of atmosphere that was created. We liked a drink or two or three and I think Ansells and M and B breweries must have taken a fortune off us.

Some say it started that night game at Man City when we stood our ground but we were wearing tee-shirts with 'Steamers' a season before that. Hicky reckons it was Antwerp away that it started but we will cover all of these and more in this chapter. All I know is I wouldn't have missed it for the world.

FOXY MAN UNITED SERVICE STATION ROW

Villa were playing Chester City away in the semi-final, first leg of the League Cup in 1975, and Man United were playing at home against Norwich City in the other semi-final. We had actually played each other four years earlier at the same stage of the competition when we were in the old Third Division and they were on the decline then but still had the likes of Best, Law and Charlton playing for them. The first game was at Old Trafford and Villa had taken 11,000 supporters up to the game. There was fighting on and off all day and in the return leg it was much the same. There was always a bit of niggle between Villa and United in them days but this night in 1975 deserves a special mention. It was the year before the Steamers were officially formed but it was basically the same lads who were scrapping for a few seasons earlier.

The usual policy for night games was to set off after an afternoon pub session, which meant leaving at 2.30pm due to last orders. This time we had an extra pint at last orders and left by coach at 3pm. We were barely out of Birmingham when people already wanted a 'piss break' and ten miles up the motorway, after persuading the coach driver, we stopped at Hilton Park services in Cannock. We arrived and then it was the usual rush of 50 blokes trying to get to the toilets.

As we were running to the loos we could hear chants of 'United, United' echoing throughout the building. Before we knew it, we were under siege from a bombardment of plates, saucers, cups, trays, in fact anything that wasn't held down was coming in our direction. We started to return everything that had been thrown at us and it developed into the biggest food fight you could witness – and we were not in the mood to lose. They may have started it but despite their numbers – there were two coaches of them to our one – we were certainly going to finish it.

We started to get the upper hand and the United lads were now trying to get out anyway they could, as our lot were going forward not backwards. In the middle of all of this Melv is boxing away in a corner with one of their lot. It was a hilarious sight as things were flying past their heads and now and again Melv would duck a flying cup or plate but continue boxing this lad. The restaurant itself was like something you see in a tsunami disaster area, there wasn't anything that hadn't been trashed. The walls were covered in blood.

We hadn't finished with United, they brought it on and they were going to pay for it. They were running out the exits and jumping out of the broken windows, panicking, but we were not letting it finish there. They were demolished and looked a sorry sight, covered in half-eaten food and bits of crockery, with blood all over them. They were in total disarray and were climbing over the motorway and running down the hard shoulder to escape us.

It didn't take long for the Old Bill to arrive and we didn't have time to get back on the coach. Three of our lads managed to avoid getting nicked by hiding underneath the coach but 49 of us weren't so lucky and we all got nicked and missed the game. The row made headlines in both regional and national newspapers and the incident resulted in all football coaches being banned from motorway service stations without prior approval.

We ended up in court and couldn't believe it when we all got there to find that the United lot were appearing on the same day. We found out they were diehard United fans from Corby. Our case was adjourned for dinner and as usual we went for a pint but the pub was three deep and a few of us went to the next pub. This one was full of the whole United lot from the services. Whilst they looked a lot smarter and hadn't got half their dinners down them this time, they weren't happy. A few words were exchanged and it could have got moody but nothing happened. We had had our result and fun at the service station against superior numbers and went straight through them, they were the supposed top hooligan firm of that era but they came a second best to the Steamers that day.

D. DUB ANTWERP 1975

The Saturday before our first European game we played Arsenal at home. After the game, we were all in the Golden Eagle on Hill Street in Birmingham city centre. There were around 25 of us when suddenly 15-20 of Blues' lads came in. They began to ask, 'Who's George?' None of us knew who George was, but in true Spartacus style, one after another the Steamers replied, 'I'm George.' It soon kicked off and by the end every Bluenose was either lying on the floor or had run off. A well-known face of theirs called Punch-Drunk Albert tried to get back up, so I bashed him with a stool and knocked him back out. As we were leaving I threatened the barman with what would happen to him if he rang the police. It was a good start and set us up nicely for our first excursion into Europe.

ROSCO

On September 17 that year Villa played their first ever game in European football, away to Royal Antwerp in Belgium. Like many football fans, the first time I ever left these shores was to follow my football team and along with nine others I went to Antwerp for a week. I had no passport at the time but back then you were able to get hold of a permit that allowed you into certain countries. What I didn't realise was that this permit was only for one day and mine was dated for the day of the game. The Belgians were very good and allowed me into the country on condition that I would admit to having sneaked in if I was caught. With this in mind, I made sure none of our party stepped out of line up until the day of the game.

We spent the whole of the Monday on the piss and had begun to do exactly the same on the Tuesday when we discovered where the team was staying and headed there straight away, arriving just as they'd finished a light training session. Everybody was very friendly but a special mention must go to Steve Hunt, Ray Graydon and the late Terry Weir, the official photographer; a photograph of us actually appeared in a match programme shortly afterwards.

The day of the game was spent meeting up with the other Villa supporters around the town and by the ground and a good time was had by all. I think the less said about the game the better, as we were well beaten, so afterwards a serious drink was needed. As the night wore on, we were told of a bar where the players were drinking, so we headed there and bumped into about six of them, including Steve Hunt, Sammy Morgan, Jim Cumbes, Leighton Phillips, John Gidman and Frank Pimblett. All were top drawer except for Pimblett, who was a bit offish. Steve Hunt wouldn't let us buy a round; Leighton Philips got behind the bar and started dishing out the drinks and Jim Cumbes told us to make sure we 'gave it to the Blues' when we played them. Sammy Morgan was fantastic and was absolutely fine when one of the lads accidentally knocked his glasses off and then stepped on them. We carried on drinking through the night and finally retired at around five in the morning, with the result of the game now the last thing on our minds.

FOXY MAN CITY, 1976

At the time I was working on a site with 'the Loon' and as this game was on a Wednesday night we both took the day off, meeting in the Hole in the Wall at opening time. As usual, the coach left at 3pm and when we landed in Manchester I was stinking drunk. That didn't stop me and Melv getting a few more beers in before kick-off and maybe the drink took hold but we went and purchased tickets in the seats opposite the Kippax.

We had a bird's eye view of the Villa and Man City mobs in the Kippax going hammer and tongs at it and we both said at the same time, 'Let's get over there.' That was easier said than done from our position but a few minutes later we had managed to get to our lads and were in the thick of it. The fighting was raging and nobody seemed to be taking a back step, it wasn't running battles it was people standing there getting stuck in to each other. The fighting turned onto the Old Bill and you now had both Villa and Man City fighting them as it became a three-way scrap.

Eventually the Old Bill got a hold on things and the match passed off without any further interruption. After the game, we managed to persuade the coach driver to stop while we went for a drink and we found another pub not far from the ground in Moss Side. It wasn't long before we'd attracted the attention of Man City lads and soon we were out of the pub and fighting them on the road. At one stage, we chased a group of black lads away from the pub but they kept on coming back, each time with bigger numbers. One time when we charged them I went one step too far and kept going after them whilst everyone else had stopped. I found myself on my own. I got surrounded and the last thing I remember was someone swinging an iron bar at me.

I was woken up by a copper and I realised I'd been knocked out. Another copper brought a bloke over to me and asked, 'Was this the one who did it?' I threw a punch at the bloke and copped him bang under the chin. Needless to say the OB weren't impressed and took me back to where the coach was parked. Unfortunately the coach had left and I was shocked when the OB said they'd catch it up. I found out later that they had been with the coach and knew it wasn't far away.

When they caught up with the coach and got me on, the lads could hardly recognise me. I looked like the Elephant Man, had lost my two front teeth and my nose was broken. Someone got me onto the back seat and they cleaned my face up with a can of Breaker, although some of the lads were cheesed off that good beer was wasted on me and was one less for us to drink.

We got back to Brum in the early hours and Melv and me went over to the tea wagon, where we bumped into another pal of ours, Gaz O, who had got his jaw broken from the fighting outside the pub. It was that kind of night.

CLARKEY

We had done very well inside the ground, holding our own, and before the game had chased a gang of what seemed to be mainly mixed-race lads off without much of a problem. But outside we met with another firm; these were black lads who were carrying plastic carrier bags. I was wondering what they had them for until they started taking chains out. I then realised they hadn't brought their packed lunches with them.

We had no choice but to get into them, but with the lads we had you knew from past fights everybody would back everybody else up. The row kept going on for ages. You would put one lot away and another lot would appear. We at one point seemed to be surrounded, as they were attacking us from the front and the back. I was absolutely knackered, there just didn't seem to be any let up in it, and I knew that if I dropped my guard I would get hurt.

There was a brief stand-off before I was right back into the thick of it again and it just seemed like one after another. We finally got the better of them and then the Old Bill came. I was glad to get on the coach but looked at the lads and some had taken a proper kicking – but stood up to it. It was the day in most people's eyes that the Steamers became official and still goes down as one of the best rows of all time considering the numbers we had. After that day, the name was known around the Villa terraces and whilst it could be argued it was going before, this was the game that put us on the map as a firm.

At around the same time, however, came a very eventful day at Villa Park that we can't brush under the carpet and pretend never happened. It doesn't make good reading for Villa lads. This was a so-called friendly between us and one of the biggest teams in Scotland, and most who remember that day will admit it was certainly not friendly but a day that goes down in terrace folklore. George, an old Witton Warriors veteran, takes up the story.

GEORGE OUR DARKEST HOUR: GLASGOW RANGERS, 1976

I had got to my local, the Crossways, which was on the edge of Kingstanding and right in the Perry Common area of Birmingham, early, around 10.30am. It was the norm for me to stop off there, have one, then go on into town to meet the rest of the lads. I knew something was wrong when I got in there and there were eight Jocks up the bar. They bought me a drink – now that's the only thing I was going to get off them all day. They had told me that Glasgow Rangers had laid on cheap travel for all their fans as a thank you; they also said that most had travelled down the previous day and there was about 15,000 making the trip down.

I finished my pint, got on the bus and went into town as normal and as soon as I came into town I could see all these young kids carrying the old bumper eight-packs of beer and walking round the streets. When I got off the bus I think I could be forgiven for thinking I was on Glasgow High Street, there were hundreds of Jocks walking around the town centre and it looked as if they were doing as they pleased. At an old clothes shop of the time, Nelson House, the Jocks were walking in and taking whole racks of clothes out. These were the days of the star jumpers and multi-buttoned trousers and it seemed every Jock had helped himself to a set of these.

I got to the Pen in the Wig pub just round the corner from the Hole in the Wall and found some of the Villa lads but there was no more than ten, so we decided to get to the ground. The stories were already coming in of the Jocks playing up in Aston the previous night, pissing in people's letterboxes and ransacking the Asian corner shops. We got to Sixways Aston and met up with some of the lads from Kingstanding. We now had about 25, a mixture of Steamers and KS, but what we were about to see was the most gut-wrenching sight for any Villa lad. As we walked up Witton Lane it was like being at Ibrox: there were thousands everywhere, but worse, we looked into the Holte End from the road and the top of the terracing was a mass of blue and white and Union Jacks.

The Jocks had been playing up so much in Aston, and none of them had digs, that the police decided to open the ground in the middle of the night and put them in there, more for public safety than anything. Prior to that, they had already been climbing the walls to get in. There was no cover on the Witton Lane stand then so it was obvious that they were going to go under a roof. We moved onto Aston Park and just stood watching it. I was angry, frustrated, humiliated if you like. We were proud of the Holte End, it was our holy ground and nobody had taken the Holte. I had been on many away grounds in the old Third and Second divisions where we had taken whole ends and met with little resistance. Maybe we didn't have it all our own way but nine times out of ten we did. Taking the likes of Sheffield Wednesday's kop was seen as no big thing, and those that had come in the Holte, like Bristol Rovers and Arsenal in a cup game, were dealt with and didn't get anywhere near taking it. Blues had come in 1971 and got smashed and one year Albion's two main men, Mutley and Bowie, had come in on a reconnaissance mission and were found out and smashed. Other than that it was rare and certainly not with the numbers we were looking at for away firms to come in.

All the other lads were feeling the same and we had amassed

about 50 of us by now, including Fast and Big Jim Hegarty. We thought we had to do something, just what I don't know, so we decided to go in the Holte End via the entrance from the Trinity Road. We got to the bottom and then some twat pulled out a tricolour from his jacket. It was the proverbial red rag to a bull, only this was a fucking army of raging bulls and all hell broke loose.

We did hold our own until the Old Bill came over and put us in the corner of the Holte. I looked around. We hadn't got the full firm by any means but we had a good set of lads, the likes of Hogg, who used to run the coaches after Rosco, the Guss brothers, and I kept thinking that if we had the full firm we just might have a chance of regaining the Holte.

As soon as the second goal in the second half went in, a Villa lad from the Witton End jumped on the pitch with his tricolour and that was it. Down to sheer numbers, they forced us on the pitch from our own end. The players made a dash for the tunnel and it was literally every man or woman for themselves. It badly hurt our pride but in an official crowd of 17,000 only 5,000 were Villa and less than two per cent wanted to have a go back. The odds weren't exactly on our side and this lot were not only pissed but they had no fear, it was like the Vikings on the rampage.

Now I went to the England-Scotland game in 1977 and this was exactly the same, the cunts were everywhere and anywhere. But outside the ground we decided to make a stand, a last stand if you like. We were raging mad; you have to understand what it felt like. We grouped on Witton Lane and met the marauding Jocks head-on. Other Villa were on their toes and buses were being diverted, it was sheer chaos. The lads held firm and we managed to fight and push them back past the Holte End entrance. Gus got nicked and you even had the Jocks who had been pissing through people's letter boxes taking refuge in those very same houses now as we were seething and looking for some payback.

The police on horses and more dogs than you see in Battersea Dogs' Home regained control and got between our little mob and them. The police weren't interested in nicking Brummies and when they found Gus was a Brummie they let him out the panda car. What they didn't know was that Gus was carrying and when he got let out he went straight in and stabbed two Jocks.

We made it home and the whole radio and television coverage was about the match being abandoned. It seemed that every part of Birmingham had a story about Jocks in their area smashing up boozers and generally terrorising Joe Public. I was restless and thought I had to get into town to see what was happening. When I got up there, at about 8.30pm, it was like a ghost town, deserted other than pissed-up Jocks milling about. The Old Bill had closed the pubs. I wandered around and went by the main police station, Steeplehouse nick, and there were tens of coaches. They had just rounded them all up. There were also Rangers lads who had spent out and wanted the Old Bill to pay their train fares home.

After wandering around for an hour, I went onto Broad Street, which was very different back then to today's 'golden mile'. It was home of the Rum Runner, which became famous through Duran Duran but was a popular drinking haunt with Villa lads. It was a relief to find this open, possibly the only place open in Birmingham town centre. In there were other Villa lads – Clarkey, Groombridge, etc. – and we had a good 20 and all of us were pissed off, angry, frustrated. I didn't feel afraid that afternoon like I did at Millwall, I was just very very angry and that was the general feeling amongst all of us.

We then heard Scottish accents, there must have been 30-odd of them and there was no two ways about it, they were copping it, so we told the doorman that we couldn't let it go as they had taken major liberties in the city, never mind Villa Park, and we needed payback. It went off, and with the doorman and even the DJ joining us we locked the doors and gave them a beating they wouldn't forget and something to take back to Glasgow. It must have been 15 minutes of brawling but our anger was boiling.

The shout went up, 'Old bill!' and we dispersed at 1.30 am to find all the taxis and late night buses had been taken off, so I had to walk back to Erdington. The lesson of that day was that we had not taken the game seriously and whereas we were used to turning places over in the old Third on a regular basis, we had allowed it to happen to us here. We made sure it never happened again and gave a few more clubs the same treatment, with Leicester City one that sticks out in my mind a year later, when we totally trashed the whole city.

CLARKEY

The one most important thing that should be said about the Steamers is that with them it was the day out and the crack first, the fighting was always second on the agenda, and most of the lads I have spoken to have stressed to me that the crack side of things needs to be put over. I have chosen a couple of away games from the mid Seventies that I think typify what travelling to watch games was and to a certain extent probably still is for football lads:

DEANO LEEDS AWAY, 20 DECEMBER 1975

I have been going to watch Villa games since 1969 and when I reached the age of 16 I was allowed to go to games with a group of lads who called themselves 'the Dougal'. I have no idea what this name meant or where it came from but they were a great bunch of lads. Boots, Shof and JB were the first lads I knew, with Boots being a bit of a hero of mine back then.

As the years passed, the Steamers arrived and great times were had by all. It wasn't all about fighting rivals; it was also about having a laugh, especially at away games. This is why I have chosen to write about my twentieth birthday, the day we played Leeds away. The lads involved were myself, my brother Roff, JB, Melv and Foxy.

The week before, we were in the Hole in the Wall and Foxy overheard myself and Roff planning with JB a trip to Leeds the following week. Not only did Foxy tell us that him and Melv would come, he also volunteered to drive us up there in his new Mark 3 Cortina. On the morning of the game we set off with two bottles of vodka, a couple of cartons of orange juice and a portable cassette player that Melv had brought with him. With Foxy and Melv on board it was jokes all the way up there.

When we hit Leeds, Foxy pulled up alongside a bloke who was walking along on the pavement. Melv wound down the window and asked him if he knew where a pub was called the Ring of Feathers.

'Can't say I know that one mate,' came the reply but Melv assured him it was around there somewhere.

'No, don't know it mate,' said the bloke, so we drove off, stopping about ten yards further up.

Melv then yelled back to the bloke, 'We know where it is now, mate.'

The chap hurriedly caught us up and asked us where it was, as he was interested to know himself.

'It's round the duck's arse,' Melv told him.

It may sound corny now but at the time the car erupted with laughter and the bloke looked absolutely stunned.

We did the same thing a second time, only this time we were on a hill and some bloke had his head inside the window whilst talking to us. Foxy let his foot off the brake and the bloke walked backwards while talking at the same time as the car rolled down the hill. Eventually he asked Foxy to put the brake on. One by one we lost it but gathered our composure to deliver the punch line simultaneously.

'It's round the duck's arse!'

We eventually stopped off at a pub and we got talking to some local Leeds lads who told us we were too far away from the ground to walk but we could follow their car to the ground. After the game we agreed to go back with the lads to the same pub and were following behind them when JB suddenly popped up with 'round the duck's arse' for no apparent reason. We all began laughing again and Foxy was laughing so much he banged into the car in front with the Leeds lads in it. Their car had a deep dent in it but ours was fine and the lads told Foxy not to worry and that we would sort it out when we got to the pub.

We started driving again and Foxy suddenly shouted, 'Sweeney!' turned sharply off the road and put his foot down. Luckily we lost the Leeds lads and also found the motorway. After about an hour we pulled off into some little village and stopped at a pub. There was a hatch in the hallway and we ordered our drinks there before entering a small bar. JB went in first and was sent flying, as the room was in darkness. Melv followed and did exactly the same before I found the switch and turned the lights on and there underneath Melv and JB was a naked young couple in a rather compromising position. We all casually walked in and sat down and Foxy told them not to stop on account of us but they both left in a hurry.

After a few pints we decided to head back to Brum to try to catch last orders. Just after we hit the motorway, Melv shouted, 'Someone's nicked my tape player,' and JB noticed the last bit of the vodka was also gone. A couple of minutes later Foxy suddenly said, 'This isn't my car, it's done too many miles,' and did a U-turn on the M1. We got back to the pub to find a bewildered man trying to get into Foxy's car. Our car pulled up, we all got out, Foxy said to the bloke, 'Sorry mate, wrong car,' and we all got into the right car and drove off. The look on this bloke's face was a picture. My only disappointment was that Melv had got his cassette player back and we were subjected to the BeeGees yet again.

It became obvious we weren't going to make last orders in Brum, so we stopped about 25 miles away for the last hour. While we were in this last pub, I noticed JB had a Villa badge covering up a hole in his polo neck jumper, and began to pull at the hole. At this point the others joined in and before JB knew much about it, all he was left with was the collar.

When we got back to Brum, myself and JB decided to go to a club in town called Rebeccas, so they dropped us there. The sight of JB with his bomber jacket zipped up to the top with just a frayed collar on underneath will stay with me forever. Luckily we knew a girl who worked at the club and she lent him a blouse for the night.

When they arrived at Roff's mother-in-law's house, Roff invited Foxy and Melv in for a drink. Roff's mother-in-law is Italian and I think I should stop here but next time you see one of them, ask them what happened. I have to say I have been to some great games and I've had some great birthdays but that day will never be beaten. I was at a fundraiser for one of our lads recently and Foxy asked me if I remembered the day we went to Leeds. How could I ever forget? That is why, out of all the great times I've had in over 30 years of going with the Steamers, that was my favourite trip.

ROSCO   NEWCASTLE AWAY, SEPTEMBER 1975

While I suppose many people will be talking about the punch-ups that occurred up and down the country, I would like to talk about some of the good times I've had and the great friendships I have formed. All of my immediate family are Blues fans, but when I was very young I was taken to a Villa game by an uncle and from that day Villa has been my team. I am eternally grateful to my uncle as it has enabled me to meet so many wonderful, wonderful people who have become lifelong friends. I want to focus on a crazy weekend back in September 1975 and a trip to Newcastle.

The story actually starts on the Friday night, as we were travelling up overnight to meet up with a mate who lived in a pub up there. The only driver among us was Foxy, so it was him who hired a minibus to take twelve of us up there. We left the Windsor at around midnight and as we drove out of the car park Foxy seemed to bounce off everything within ten yards of the van, finishing off by hitting both gates on the way out. A few of us began to wonder if this was actually such a good idea as Foxy had probably drunk more than any of us but most fell asleep and before we knew it, we were waking up just outside Newcastle at the pub our mate worked in.

We all started drinking again at around eight in the morning and after the game we headed straight back to our mate's pub, where we stayed until closing time. We were all serious drinkers on that minibus but at around ten o'clock, one of the lads who I will call 'Vern', couldn't drink any more, so he went upstairs to sleep for a couple of hours. We were on the verge of stopping the night when three of the lads said they had to be back to play football the next morning, so after saying our goodbyes we set off at around midnight. We had been travelling for about half an hour when somebody asked Vern a question but he didn't respond and we all realised at once that we'd left him asleep in the pub.

By this time half the lads were asleep but those who were awake spotted a Chinese takeaway that was still open and a few of us went in to order some food. As we were waiting quietly for our food to come, Melv appeared in the shop stark bollock naked, saying, 'How about this for a load of bollocks you Chinese bastards.' We almost doubled up in laughter as three of them chased Melv out of the shop and down the road with meat cleavers in their hands. We picked Melv up further down the road and then went back to the pub for Vern.

At around four in the morning, Foxy decided he couldn't go any further, so he pulled over in the middle of nowhere and went to sleep. Most fell asleep but two of the lads went for a stroll and some fresh air. Only half an hour or so had passed when Foxy jumped up feeling right as rain and set off again, leaving the other two walking around in the country. This time we had driven for about 45 minutes before realising we were two light and again we turned round and went looking for them, eventually finding them about an hour later.

We finally got back to Brum at around nine in the morning, dropping everyone off, including the three who were going straight back out to play football. Me and Foxy arrived back at Yenton Van Hire about half ten and they missed all the gashes and bumps we had done over the journey and gave us our money back no problem. We both then headed towards the Windsor for the rest of the day.

FOXY BARCELONA, 1978

We had all decided to go to Lloret de Mar for the week when we played Barcelona in the UEFA Cup. When our planeload arrived at the hotel, we found out that Big H and his crew, who had already been there for two days, had had some problems the night before in a club called Coco's which was attached to the hotel. The first thing we did was to rename the club the 'Trevor Francis Disco'. After we had all got ourselves sorted, we met up in the hotel bar and had a few drinks there before heading on to the Trevor Francis Disco.

As soon as we entered the club, it was obvious that there was an atmosphere in there and it didn't take us long to suss out who the main mouthpiece was. Me and Melv had an argument between ourselves to see who was going to chin the mouthpiece and in the end we tossed a coin and Melv won. He went outside with him and I held everyone inside but I struggled to hold them back as both English and Spanish were pushing to get outside, so I gave up trying and let them all out just as Melv was finishing off the Spaniard. When everyone got outside it developed into a free-for-all, with tables and chairs going in all directions, and it didn't take long to take the Spaniards out.

The following morning, we woke up to find all the hotel reception staff were carrying guns and during breakfast the Spanish police arrived. There were 60 of us staying in the hotel and by the time breakfast had finished all but eight had been nicked. I was lucky as I had a room to myself and was not about at breakfast, so I organised a whipround to see if we could sort out some bail money for the lads. Obviously on reflection there was never going to be a chance of eight lads raising bail money for 52.

After I had collected all the money I could, I made my way to the police station to try to get the lads bailed. As I arrived, I could hear Villa songs booming up from the cells. At this point I really did the lads a big favour by going up to the OB on the desk and saying, 'Moneyo, releaso the lads.' Needless to say my charm got me nowhere and the Old Bill kept the money. Fortunately they released everyone a couple of days later and everyone got to see the game, where it was something else to witness 90,000 passionate supporters in a stadium that was breathtaking. It was the game the old Cornetto song 'One Aston Villa' came from and was copied by every other football club in England.

ROFF STEAMERS (ENDALE) FC

The season 1980/81 was not only memorable for Aston Villa winning the First Division title but was also the time when some of the Steamers decided to form a Sunday afternoon football team in the old Selly Oak League Division Three, long before the professional game was played on the Sabbath. At the time, the Hole in the Wall was our second home and ruled the town. This was well known by the football fan fraternity. When we applied to the league, because of this reputation we decided to call ourselves Endale F.C. a.k.a. Dale End, after the road the pub was in.

The first few games were cricket scores against, but word got around to the lads and a handful of us who played regularly on Sunday mornings helped out. We stopped the rot and started to win games, moving up the league. The team was Hicky, Perks, JB, Roff, Pinky, D.Dub, McGon, Mart, Les, Foxy and R Leader, C.S.Den, K.C. (manager) and Big P (assistant). Team selection was usually whoever turned up unscathed and not in nick after the Villa and Saturday night drinking session.

One of the lads, CS, played semi pro and started helping us out. He would usually score two or three goals a game but had to play under another name and attribute the goals to Foxy due to his contract. He was so successful (40 goals) that the league secretary asked if 'Foxy' would consider playing for the district team. Obviously Foxy declined, he wasn't a bad player but not that good.

Word soon got around in the league that Endale F.C. was the Steamers from 'the Hole' and teams started to fear playing us. We never bullied teams but took no prisoners. I remember playing a team called Rubery and one of the main Bluenose boys, JJ, from the Quinton mob played for them. It was a hard-fought but fair game and both teams had mutual respect for each other at the end of play. We won 3-2.

The League Secretary started attending some of our games; I would like to think it was because of our attractive football but suspect it was because of the occasional flare-up. Unfortunately CS had to stop playing when this occurred but we still reached the semi-final of the Premier Cup. We played a team called IMI, who had not lost a game for three years. We came comfortably out on top 3-1 and made the final.

This was played at the Civil Service ground in Elmdon on a Thursday night. Our opponents were a team of black guys called Cal Thorpe F.C. from Balsall Heath. They regularly won the league and cups most years. On this night their second team were also playing in a final. The Civil Service ground in those days had two pitches, one lower level and one upper. We played on the low level pitch and were holding our own. CS couldn't play but we were playing some decent stuff. It was quite close but once they scored halfway through the second half things started to get nasty.

D.Dub took a player down and was warned by the ref; another tackle and he was sent off. The opposition started to retaliate and it soon developed into a melee. Their second team and supporters saw the commotion and started running over the hill. It was like something out of *Zulu Dawn*. We almost burst into 'Men of Harlech', something the C Crew have been known to do, for obvious reasons. We gathered in the centre of the pitch and stood firm. A few punches were thrown, followed by a stand-off. We were outnumbered three to one but held our own.

The referee called for both captains to calm things down. However this was difficult because he had sent one of ours off. With ten men and the game turning into a kicking match, we eventually lost our heads and the game 4-0. Afterwards a few words were said but I think both teams had a mutual respect for each other. They were a good, well organised team; we were a bunch of Villa mates.

In the clubhouse afterwards, the other team playing were also Villa. We both went on to celebrate reaching the finals, dancing on the tables and looking forward to going to Highbury in two days' time, where Aston Villa would go on to lift the First Division Championship and be crowned champions – but that's another story.

The following season, we were promoted from Division Three to the Premier Division. A great comradeship continued from following AVFC to playing local football and still does to this day.

Footnote: In the 1870s, a footballer called Archie Hunter came down from Scotland to Birmingham looking to play for a team called Calthorpe. He ended up at Aston Villa, where he was a prolific goalscorer but had to play under the name A.N. Other that season because he was not a registered player. Spooky.

ENDALE FC
Manager: K.C.
Assistant: Big P
Team: Hicky, Perks, J.B., Roff, Pinky, D.Dub, McGon, Mart, R.Leader, Foxy, C.S., Les, Den
Squad lads: Eddie, Mad Martin, Dean M

BRITTLE STEAMING FROM THE BOARDROOM

Mack the Sock, as he is affectionately known, got his name for owning just about every market stall in the Midlands that sells socks. He made his dough and a lot of it, about £1.5 million. Now it was never enough to buy his beloved Villa (although the way we were going he should have held on a few years), but being the businessman he was he saw an opportunity in Northampton Town FC and the fact that there was a potential redevelopment of the ground with the council. So he bought the club, and if there has ever been a more unlikely chairman, one who could call on the likes of me and Pattison and the Steamers as his boardroom guests, then I would like to meet him.

There are a lot of stories about Mack, some of which we could never get printed, but one of the more printable where we all won't get done for libel is the one where he gave the then manager of Northampton, Theo Foley, a Rolex watch for his achievements. On receiving the watch, Theo got very emotional and thanked Mack, who proceeded to tell him, 'Don't worry Theo, it ain't real, it's fake. I got it in Thailand.' Mack was and still is a character. He once tried to sell me Northampton Town's car park for 40 grand. Quite what he thought I was going to do with a car park I don't know. On another occasion, me and Gary Patt, with a few other Villa lads were on a train going down to watch Northampton and we got into a conversation with some of their lads, who were complaining and moaning about their chairman. The abuse got too much, and I think it was Gary who turned round and said, 'It's your unlucky day lads, Mack is a very good friend of ours,' and we kicked seven kinds of shit out of them. I don't think it altered their view of Mack, and when there was a growing the-board-must-go campaign the most bizarre sight was some of the Steamers, as his newly appointed set of directors, in the boardroom to face the now not-so-angry mob.

Mack is one of life's gents. He may talk cobblers at times but I never expected him to buy a football club nicknamed Cobblers.

BIG H BIG H IS A STEAMER

(Big H was asked if he was prepared to be one of the lads fronting the book, but typically of him he was modest and said there are enough out there who deserve to be fronting it rather than me, but said he would be honoured to contribute. H was a big part of the Steamers, maybe not right at the start but certainly afterwards.)

I started supporting Villa at an early age and began to go to watch games in the early Seventies as a schoolkid. Because I was so big for my age, I was always getting asked to go with kids from my local areas of Weoley Castle and Bartley Green who were three, four and five years older than I was. I started to go to away games on coaches run from Weoley Castle. They were eventually stopped because of all the trouble we were causing.

At around the same time, me and a mate I will call 'China' used to go over to Frankley services on the M5, which weren't too far away from where we lived, every Saturday night to see if we could bump into any fans travelling home from various places. We used to collect scarves as trophies off our victims and China got hold of a Man United scarf that he particularly liked and even went as far as to sew a Villa badge onto it. A few weeks later we were at Bristol and the OB came in to investigate an incident that had been caused by someone in a red and white scarf. The scarf was passed down a line of us and guess who was at the end of the line? Yeah, me. Bang, I was nicked straight away. Maybe they thought I was older, I will never know, but I was actually 14 at the time and as a juvenile this meant that an adult had to come and collect me. So it was that my mother's plans for Saturday evening went out of the window as she jumped onto the next train to Bristol.

I had been nicked with another lad who was 18 and as such didn't need an adult with him to get his bail. I think the OB were crafty at this point as they released us both at the same time and basically both into my mother's hands. Both of us had tickets for the football special, which had long gone, so my mother ended up paying for tickets home for us both on top of the fare she'd paid for herself. We were back down in court on the Monday and I ended up getting something silly like a £10 fine whereas the whole episode had ended up costing my poor mum over £40.

I didn't give Bristol much thought afterwards and was soon carrying on as normal, although things didn't always go according to plan. A visit to Anfield one year definitely fell into that category. I got sussed as soon as I entered the ground, they were all pointing me out saying things like, 'It's the big darkie from last year.' I was not bothered, as I was with a load of mates and the game passed without further incident. Outside, on the other hand, was a completely different ball game. I had a sixth sense that we were being followed, so I dropped my programme and as I crouched down to pick it up, my worst fears were confirmed as about 20 of them were about to pounce. At six foot seven I stood out like a sore thumb and it suddenly sunk in why nobody wanted to walk with me.

The first Scouser aimed a kick at me and I blocked it while at the same time I swung for him and took him out. It looked quite good as it goes, even if I say so myself, and I felt cocky, my only trouble being the 19 other Scousers who wanted to have a pop at 'the darkie'. I have never had a martial arts lesson in my life but for some unknown reason I took up a kung fu pose. The cries of 'get the darkie' immediately changed to 'get the grasshopper' as I lashed out, trying to keep them at bay. They kept edging closer and closer in and began to go round the back of me as well. One of them pushed the bloke in front of him towards me but I managed to put him down with a right-hander. Unfortunately this was the trigger and I made the split-second decision to go on my toes. I headed towards the coaches at what seemed like 100 miles an hour with these 20-odd Scousers hot in pursuit and now reverting to their original mode of 'get the darkie, get the darkie'.

Can you imagine my relief to reach the first coach and leap on? Well multiply that by ten – and then imagine how I felt when I realised I'd jumped on a coach full of Liverpool fans! By this time my pursuers were outside the coach as I was told to get off at once. I jumped off windmilling, managed to break through the gauntlet and the chase began again. I jumped onto another coach but again to my horror it was a Liverpool coach, only this time everybody on board had seen what was going on and not only did they let me stay on board, they drove me round to where the Villa coaches were parked. With that kind gesture my opinion of Scousers changed; well, for all of five minutes it did.

As the next couple of seasons came and went, our little group from Weoley Castle began using the Hole in the wall pub in town, which was also where the Steamers were drinking at the time.

Whilst we all got on with them, our little group still tended to do our own thing, although we were by now travelling to away games on the Steamers' coaches. I think the turning point was when we went to Barcelona in the UEFA Cup. Almost everyone from the Hole in the Wall put down deposits for a week in Lloret. We played the first leg at Villa Park and with five minutes left the holiday was about to be cancelled as we were 2-0 down and most of us were saying that we wouldn't go to Spain and would save ourselves paying the balance of around £50 for the holiday. Bear in mind that I was an 18-year-old earning around £20 a week at the time. All that changed as Villa scored two goals in the last five minutes to leave the first leg all square and it was Spain here we come.

Foxy tells the Barcelona story further up the chapter but for me this was when I really became close with the Steamers. Foxy actually saved my life that week as I had collapsed and swallowed my tongue due to the amount of alcohol I'd drunk. When we got back we were all a lot tighter and things moved on from there. Everyone always says to me, 'Of course you're a Steamer, H,' but in all honesty I don't feel I am because I wasn't there at the start of it all. What I do feel is very, very privileged and very fortunate to have met and to have been associated with so many good people at the Villa.

By the late Seventies I had taken up boxing and had joined Birmingham City Boxing Club, something I still get ribbed about to this day. The funny thing is that half the boxers at the club were Villa lads. One night we fought against Aston Villa Boxing Club, who Danny [Brown] boxed for, at Joe Gallagher's testimonial dinner; Joe was a Birmingham City player at the time. I was supposed to fight Danny's brother that night but they wouldn't let us fight because I was 17 stone and Danny's brother was only just over twelve. It was because of these situations that the super-heavy-weight division in amateur boxing was introduced. Out of my first 16 contests I only actually fought on five or six occasions because my opponents were too small. One night we had a contest in Cornwall, I travelled all the way down there on the coach and when we arrived at the venue, which was a golf club out in the sticks, I discovered that I wasn't able to fight because the distance between the stage and the ceiling was less than my height, and that was without allowing for my afro.

I began to get quite a good reputation in the ring and all my pals from the Hole in the Wall began to come to watch me fight. Every year Birmingham City used to fight an amateur boxing club from Ireland; one year we would go to them, the following year they would come to us. This particular year we were entertaining them at the Deritend Ex-Servicemen's Club, which is now known as the Porsche Club, in Small Heath. There were spaces for 200 people to watch. I personally sold 120 tickets and there was probably more like 300 people there on the night.

Being a heavyweight, my fight was the last one, so throughout the night I'd been out talking to all the lads. I'd even had a couple of pints of Guinness. I caught a glimpse of the guy I was going to fight, Wally Burke his name was. I will never forget it. Wally was skipping and shadow boxing in the mirror in the toilet as I went in for a piss.

'All right mate,' I said.

'Yeah, great,' he replied.

The contest was level at four-all with only my fight left and my trainer was saying things like, 'Don't pay any fucking notice of your mates, just get in there and box.' But as he was talking, all I could hear was a barrage of Villa chants coming from the main hall.

'Yeah, allright then, fine, whatever,' I replied.

As I walked into the hall, a wall of noise – 'BOOM BOOM, BIG H, BOOM BOOM, BIG H' – greeted me. All the Villa songs began to come out, it was absolutely fucking brilliant. It was like I was on another planet, I felt like I was lifted into the ring by the crescendo. I could hardly hear the bell as the noise was that loud when we started. I began to wave at the lads and wink at them whenever I could while at the same time boxing. 'Big H is a Steamer, Big H is a Steamer,' they kept chanting.

With about 30 seconds to go in the first round, Wally came in and caught me right on the button of the chin and I just sat on my arse on the floor. The whole place went into a deadly silence; I could almost sense the disappointment in the crowd. I got up and the referee checked I was okay as I began to ask myself why I did all that. I messed about for the remaining few seconds of the round until the bell went. As soon as I got back to my seat, my trainer double-slapped me across the face, left then right.

'Don't you ever fucking do that again. Listen to what I tell you, forget your fucking mates, are they in here with you?'

His words really hit home when he said that. After that I went back out and I couldn't hear a thing. Bang, bang, jab, jab, a couple of right crosses, dropped him twice, broke his nose and he had nine stitches above one of his eyes. The referee stopped it in the second round.

I began to struggle to find opponents because of my size but it had its advantages as well, like the time I was invited to spar with a guy from London who was tearing up trees at the time called Frank Bruno. He was due to fight a giant similar to my size in the name of Jumbo Cummings. Unfortunately I broke my thumb about a week before the session and had to pull out. Maybe if I had sparred with Bruno he wouldn't have got put down because in the fight he was put down and came back to win. Harry Carpenter asked him the immortal question that night, 'What did you think about that punch Frank?' Bruno replied, 'What punch, Harry?' I don't know if he gave his trademark pantomime laugh but it started the banter between them two.

After that my enthusiasm began to die down a little bit because I would be training all week on my own, which I found soul-destroying, only to find that again and again I would have no opponent when contests arrived. I continued to watch the Villa of course and continued to enjoy the crack and the pisstakes with blokes like Andy, Brittle and Clarkey. Like any other Villa fan I could tell you a story or two about Pete the Greek but my favourite memory is of the time we were at Old Trafford in 1974 and arrived at the ground off a special train. As we got to the ground without a police escort, they seemed to come at us from all directions; it was like a deluge as they attacked us from all sides. As I looked behind me into the melee, I spotted Pete bobbing up and down, throwing a few punches and then disappearing amongst all the bodies before reappearing to throw some more punches. It was a sight I will never forget and to me sums Pete up, a true warrior and a man who will not give an inch.

I think when I look back that I was lucky not to be killed or to be in prison for some of the things I got up to, and while I always knew it was wrong, it didn't stop me. I have met so many friends over the years that have become part of my life and I can't imagine my life without these people.

DEWAR

I didn't want to get involved in the book because I think, *why should we talk about it and brag?* It's not my style and I don't want to big up myself or the lads. There are so many untold stories though about the crack we used to have, the funnier things. People like Stritch could tell so many funny stories from the old days of the Imperial Hotel and the Hole in the Wall but maybe that don't sell books. I would just like to say that a hero of mine as a kid was Mouse, now he was a legend and a leading player in the early days of Villa hooliganism. I have a lot of time for Brittle and remember him as a young lad coming on the coaches. He was that small we used to put him on the luggage rack. We took him under our wing and don't think you will find anyone who doesn't like or rate him.

3 MILLWALL WHEN IT WAS MILLWALL

BRITTLE

Would any book on football violence be complete without a mention of Millwall or West Ham? Encounters with both firms were turning points for Villa's boys. If West Ham was a turning point for the C Crew, then without doubt Millwall had the same effect on the Steamers. We were involved in some epic battles with them in the Seventies. Because of the size of Villa and the fact that Millwall were forever playing their football in the Second Division, we were seen as a scalp and someone they could have it with on a consistent basis, home and away. I have sat down with the likes of D.Dub, Raggy, Rosco, Hicky and H to get their stories of 'Millwall when it was Millwall'.

D.DUB MILLWALL AWAY, 1973

Some of the older lads like Rosco had been before and were there in the late Sixties, when they were going for the record run of home games undefeated and the Villa ended up winning 1-0 when they were one game off the record. Not a wise thing to do at the Old Den. They invaded the pitch to take it out on the ref, who had awarded us a penalty. The thing is, with Millwall back then it was almost the norm. They hated anything and everything that wasn't off their manor and gave you a welcome you were never going to forget. Rosco is old school and if you need to talk to anybody about Villa home and way in the past 40 years, he is your man, so we were not under any illusions; it was never going to be a picnic. The names Millwall, the Den and Cold Blow Lane put the fear of the devil into people and there is no doubt that some who normally travelled to away games were known to pull a sickie for this fixture.

So to 1973, our first game of the season and it was away at Millwall. Half of us went on the special train from New Street and another 100 went on two coaches from town. A special train holds 800, and for the first away day of the season we would normally have taken double that, but this time there was no more than 400 on board. We made good time down to London and arrived at New Cross Gate station at around half past one.

The first 50-100 out of the station were immediately attacked and run back inside. One of the lads, Andy Tibbs (RIP), was hit over the head with an axe and was hospitalised for the rest of the day. You have to remember there was little organisation back then and the train was certainly not full of 'lads' in this first lot, it was a mixture of ordinary fans and some lads, yet the Millwall fans waiting for us to arrive were anything but ordinary, they were like a pack of wild animals and we were their prey.

By the time we had got our lot off the train, most of the lads among us had got themselves together and we charged back out and ran 50-odd Millwall back to The Station, a pub up the road. I think we were lured there by those 50, because as we reached the pub, loads of Millwall came out of a side road, armed to the hilt with batons, poles, bars, knives and just about anything else you could think of that you wouldn't want a Millwall fan holding. At the same time, more Millwall came out of the pub with bottles and glasses. We had been well and truly ambushed. Millwall were geared up for it and we ran back into the station again, along with the few West

Midlands railway police who had come down with us on the train and had followed us out.

We took a fair few casualties and by the time the London Old Bill arrived to calm things down, the 400 had halved to about 200. Some went off on their own and some even decided they were not going out of the station again. To be fair it was mostly scarfers who melted and the 200 that stayed together was mostly lads. The Old Bill then escorted us to the ground. I was 17 and one thing that really struck me (not the only thing that day, as it goes) was that while our lot all seemed to be aged between 15 and 20, most of the Millwall lot looked like they were around the 25 mark or more, and that is a big difference at that age.

We all got in the ground together and it was fairly empty at the time. It seemed that one side was seated and three sides were standing and that you were able to walk all the way around the three sides. Almost straight away we attracted the attention of a Millwall mob, as most of the ogres from the Station ambush had followed our escort to the ground. As the Millwall approached us – unbeknown to me – our mob, which numbered about 80 at this stage, backed away. A mate of mine, TC, shouted, 'D, we're running!' but just my luck, I didn't hear him and kicked out at the bloke who came nearest to me. The bloke looked at me as if I was not a full shilling, as if to say 'What are you on?' and it was then that I realised there was nobody left with me and I was surrounded, with nowhere to escape.

I noticed a gap in the fence to my right and made a beeline for it as the howling mob came at me. As I went through the gap, the mob were spitting, shouting, kicking and punching me. The gap in the fence had enabled me to get onto the pitch and I walked towards the centre circle, not really knowing what to do next, almost in a daze. Fortunately nobody came on after me, which was a miracle in itself, as this lot seemed to have the run of the place. As I looked back into the terraces, I saw baying mobs in all three sides, so I headed towards the seating area. As I approached, I began to hear applause and I realised there were Villa fans in there and they were clapping me.

I climbed into the seats, relieved that my ordeal was over, only to be nicked straight away. I wondered what the charge was going to be: saving my own life in a public place, perhaps, or maybe breathing on the Cold Blow Lane terrace? I was taken to a police caravan within the ground where they seemed convinced that I had a knife and searched me vigorously. I was released after they had searched me and headed to the opposite end of the ground, hoping it would not be as bad.

The first thing I saw as I got onto the terrace was a Villa fan being held with a knife against his throat. My luck hadn't changed. It was a horrible atmosphere and you could just feel the hatred they had for us. They wouldn't rest till they got you, if it took all game and all night they weren't letting any of us out of South London without some sort of beating.

The two coaches had also made good time down to London but the passengers were told by their drivers as they reached the outskirts of the capital that they were only going as far as Marble Arch and everyone would have to make their own way to Millwall from there. Raggy was among those on the coaches and recalls getting off the tube train at New Cross Gate. He was greeted by 20-odd Villa fans from the special train who had decided they were not going to leave the station again. 'Don't go out there, it's madness,' one of them said to Raggy, but having got this far he had no intention of spending Saturday afternoon inside New Cross Gate station. The 100-handed coach firm walked straight to the ground with no sign of any Millwall. Luckily for them all the Millwall were by now inside the ground making sure the Villa train mob had a warm welcome.

Raggy recalls the graffiti on the wall across from the station: 'It said, "If you come you will get done, Villa," then 200 yards further up was, "If you have got this far, you have done well." Now imagine what was going through our minds. They had actually gone to the trouble of spraying our name on the wall. We should have felt honoured but were thinking, *oh fuck*.

'It was very intimidating and a great tactic. You almost felt like

Neil Armstrong going where no one else had been before, but on the other hand, did you really want to? We got to the ground easily enough but as soon as we paid into the terracing it was immediately on top for us, as Millwall were everywhere. Some paid for a transfer from the terracing to the seats and others just jumped over the fence. One Villa lad got stabbed up the arse trying to scale it but I don't think anyone stayed in the standing area.'

Rosco was having his own issues on the terraces: 'I was in the ground with one pal standing next to a copper. I was hoping I hadn't got sussed when a Millwall lad on the other side of the copper says, "I am going to slash your facking face to bits, you cunt," showing me his wooden ruler with three razor blades screwed to it. Another guy who was top of the class in woodwork; Millwall seemed to have a lot of lads who were very good in that department. The copper chucked the bloke out and I watched as he merely came in the next entrance. Now I don't mind a ruck but I draw the line at that.'

Meanwhile, I had found another group of Villa fans to stand with after being released from the police caravan. As we gathered to re-group, Millwall came down the stairs to us and we were attacked from either side. At this stage, it is fair to say that almost everyone was completely demoralised and we all dispersed without much resistance. Most people paid into the seats but I couldn't afford to, so I stayed on the terraces on my own.

With 20 minutes to go, I decided to get out of the ground along with the other Villa in dribs and drabs, but of course Millwall spotted what was going on. Outside the ground, the police surrounded the Villa and almost immediately the Millwall surrounded the police. I saw a copper take a knife off a Millwall fan, clip him round the ear and say, 'I have told you before about carrying knives.' I couldn't believe it, after they had been so obsessed with nicking me when they thought I had a knife.

We got back to the station without anything happening and the loudest cheer of the day went up as twelve or so Millwall lads on the opposite platform got run by Godds and a few others. One of them even ran down the tracks but after what we had been through that day we were in no mood to give people squeezes. Another Millwall lad came down onto our platform and got dragged onto our train when it arrived. He got a bit of a going over and was thrown off somewhere by Watford up the line when the train came to a stop, a little bit of payback for what they put me through.

The thing was about Millwall, they had a reputation and they lived up to it. It was never a place for the faint-hearted but even then it exceeded expectations. Unless you went you could never really explain what it was like going there. It was as bad as people say, and worse.

HICKY

The Villa that did make it had to endure the gauntlet of walking to the ground. The locals were out on their balconies throwing stuff at us and pointing out anybody they thought was Villa to the troops on the ground below. We managed to get to the ground and for some reason about 20 of us got onto their home end. We didn't last long, 20 minutes maximum, and if it wasn't for Dave Gillette fending them off with a carving knife we would never have survived, but Dave waving the knife like a demented loon gave us just enough time to scale the fences into the seats for some safety. Not everyone escaped; one of the lads got slashed across the arse as he scaled the fence.

When you see 70-year-old grandads threatening you and screaming, 'You northern bastards,' it was a bit different to the Chesterfields and Fulhams. They were really showing us some good old South London hospitality from the whole community. Halfway through the game one of them even decided to throw a rock at our keeper.

Would you believe it, the Villa only go and score. Everyone was thinking, what's it going to be like if we beat them? Fortunately we drew but outside was as bad as, if not worse than, if we'd won. A Villa fan on New Cross Road had a paving slab put across his bonce and any Birmingham-marked car had a waiting committee. They were sitting on the bonnets and once you got near your car you got another beating and your car damaged in the process. I really thought that someone was going to get killed that day and I would never experience that feeling anywhere else on my travels in 35 years.

I have to admit I smile when I hear people say they took a firm to Millwall or 'We put on a show there' and all that claptrap. This was the Seventies, when there wasn't the policing, there wasn't the segregation and there were no hangers-on in Millwall's firm. This was Millwall when it was Millwall! For me and others it was the start of some really good battles with them, some we lost and some we won, but we'll never forget that day.

D.DUB MILLWALL AT HOME, 1974

After what had happened on the first day of the season, there was obviously a top turnout by Villa for the return game at Villa Park. It was a disappointment, as no Millwall mob turned up. This was not a surprise; for some reason back then it happened a lot. Throughout our two years in Division Three, whilst you would have every local man and his dog turning out when Villa came to town it was very rare for teams to bring anything to Villa Park. Division Two had followed a similar vein and despite major scenes at places like Notts Forest and Cardiff, neither side brought big numbers to Villa. Now Millwall had followed suit.

The following season, however, it was a different story. When they came up this time they came with a mob, all in white butchers' aprons. They were typical grizzly Millwall types and not only that; they came into the Holte End. There was a mass brawl on the terraces, with Villa fans wielding bicycle chains at them. It ended with Millwall being fucked onto the pitch but not before one of their main faces, 'Tiny', had been stabbed by a well-known Erdington lad. Millwall were taken round to the Witton End but there was more fighting outside and a certain amount of revenge was extracted for the previous season's horror show.

A few weeks later we were away at Fulham and most of our lot travelled down on the football special train. We were escorted from the tube station to the open end at Craven Cottage. This was very rare for London Old Bill in those days, as they never seemed bothered about things like that. When we got into the ground, there was a possible explanation as to why the Old Bill were so interested in us: the home end was full of Millwall not Fulham.

The game passed of peacefully enough and at the end the Old Bill kept us in the ground. It turned out that they wanted to get Millwall away first and as we began our escort back to the tube station, we caught glimpses of Millwall's escort some 500 yards ahead. We could see them all the way back to the station. As we came within sight of the tube station we were held up and watched as Millwall all went onto the platform, which was above us as we stood on the road. Within a minute or so a train sped up, stopped and the Millwall mob all got on. Within the blink of an eye they were gone. We were then allowed onto the platform to wait for our train back to Euston. The train duly arrived and we all boarded and headed to Euston. We went a couple of stops or so down the line and my mind began to drift away from football and onto what I was going to do when we got back to town. My thoughts were brought to an abrupt halt as the train pulled into Earls Court.

The whole platform was taken up by Millwall's mob. All hell broke loose. Some Villa got off the train, some Millwall jumped on, some Villa barmies standing by the doors were trying to get out of the way and some Villa lads were pushing in the other direction to try to reach the melee. Suddenly the train doors closed again and three of us were left on the platform. All the Villa were banging on the doors and windows and pressing the emergency buttons as we began to start praying for a miracle. All of a sudden a big Millwall bloke stepped forward and said, 'Leave these three alone, they've got bottle,' and with that they all left the platform and reappeared on the other side. We were obviously relieved but fair play to that bloke. Whoever he was, they certainly listened to what he said.

CLARKEY MILLWALL AWAY, 1975

We played them right at the top of our form, beating them 3-1. Villa were in the seats and as you would expect Millwall came in at the end of the game and into the seats looking for the 'Brummie cants'. Some of the lads got trapped and had to jump onto the pitch, making their exit via the players' tunnel with Millwall in hot pursuit. The only upside was that they got into the players' changing rooms and ate the sandwiches laid on for the Millwall team.

BIG H

About six of us were going on the train. After the previous year's problems, British Rail were not putting on a special and most Villa fans were going down on coaches. When we arrived at New Street, we were pleased to find out that we could buy tickets at 'special train' prices and so we all headed off to London. We met up with a couple of other Villa fans on the train and our numbers swelled to a mighty 17!

We caught the tube from Euston and the nearer we got to Millwall the more and more home fans got on, until the train was packed with people wearing blue and white. One bloke we had met on the way down was pissed and started singing a Villa song. I swear to God that is the closest I have ever been to knocking a fellow Villa fan out.

We got off the train and stuck together, walking through what I could only describe as a maze of all these little roads, then over and under bridges, and the only reason we knew how to get there was because we were following all the crowd. I began to start seeing the graffiti that other people had told me about, things like 'Turn Back Now'. We finally reached the ground, and bearing in mind I'm only 15 at the time I don't mind admitting this was the most scared I've ever been at a football match. As we walked up the steps to the terrace, they were all wearing donkey jackets with plastic across the back and they all seemed to have no necks and were all grown men. It was like I was surrounded by 100 Lenny McLeans.

I was almost at the top of the steps and could see into the ground when I felt someone grab my jacket from behind. *Oh no*, I thought, *here we go.* But to my relief it was just someone who had tripped on the steps and had grabbed hold of me to stop his fall. I assured him it was definitely not a problem. We walked around to the other end of the ground, hoping in vain to find a mob of Villa, and then realised that all the coaches had paid into the seats. This is God's honest truth now, I saw two blokes standing not far from me openly displaying machetes. I thought to myself, *what the fuck am I doing here?* and that feeling didn't change when one of them grunted to me, 'One Brammie barstard cams near me and I'll cat his fackin' balls orf.' I suddenly learnt how to speak cockney and replied, 'Yeah, right.'

Villa won the game 3-1 and as soon as we scored the last goal, a lot of the home fans started making their way into the seats where the Villa fans were. We could see the Villa fans scattering from where we were standing and decided it was time to make a move, hoping everyone would think we were cockneys going round to join in. It worked and we headed straight back to the station.

On the way back, we bumped into a cockney Villa fan who had got run before the game and had been stabbed in the arse as he tried to climb a fence to get away. He had missed the match because he'd been in hospital having his arse stitched up but he took us under his wing and told us that if anyone said anything, he would do the talking. Thankfully we didn't need him to do it and got home in one piece but without doubt that was the scariest experience I have had at a football match.

CLARKEY MILLWALL AT HOME, LEAGUE CUP, 1976

Now we were a First Division side and enjoying a good run in the League Cup, while Millwall were in the Second Division. The draw was made for the quarter-final and it came out Villa versus Millwall. We just knew it would be a top turnout. This was a year before the famous *Panorama* documentary about Harry the Dog and the Treatment and one-man assaults on terraces. I think that programme did more to encourage football violence than anything else; it was the most talked about programme on the terraces for years. So here we are facing them in their heyday, and having met them a few times and with the rows we had with them, they were no secret to us. Certainly for most of my age group none of us had come up against anything like them before or since.

They treated it like a cup final and brought thousands and from very early doors were camped outside the old Witton Arms. They were a very impressive mob and everyone looked like the proverbial bulldog chewing a wasp. I wasn't in the Witton End but have heard the story of the Greek in there and his antics, but after the game was a sight to behold. It seemed every Villa lad, young and old, was on hand. I'm not sure if there was a recruitment campaign going on or if it was due to the fact that our local media had printed a story called 'Terror at the Den' about the train ambush a few years earlier, but the firm of lads was quantity and a fair amount of quality.

The Millwall coaches were parked on a large wasteland area called the Serpentine and when the game finished they made their way there only to find a huge mob of Villa lying in wait. The younger element bombarded them with bricks, stones and empty, discarded bottles found on the wasteland. Some of the Millwall lads were making a stand and were coming forward, not going backward, but that's when the older lads took over.

The Steamers and those of similar age were into the Millwall lads and it was now them on the back foot. The Millwall firm were being attacked from all sides, no stand-offs, no jumping about waving arms, no worrying about getting life for dropping litter at a football ground, this was fist and boot, go down, get up, wipe the blood away and go again. Millwall lads were even under coaches trying to escape the onslaught and were being dragged out and beaten. This time it was us making sure everyone got a beating.

The youngsters made sure the coaches and trains had a reminder of Birmingham hospitality and the Steamers made sure that Millwall went back with stories to tell their own grandchildren, like we had a few years earlier. It was a great result for Villa against a top outfit and was the last of our battles of the Seventies with probably our best opponent of that era. That was when Millwall was Millwall, and their proper lot will remember Villa for some good battles.

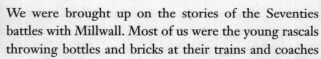

DANNY MILLWALL, 1980

We were brought up on the stories of the Seventies battles with Millwall. Most of us were the young rascals throwing bottles and bricks at their trains and coaches in 1976. The *Panorama* documentary about their firm was legendary and this game was a chance to meet the first TV hooligan celebrities, people like Tiny, Ginger Bob and Harry the Dog, only we didn't want their autographs, we wanted their scalps. We wanted to row with their top boys, just like the Steamers had years before. It's always nice to have Millwall on your CV and now it was our turn.

The firm was predominantly C-Crew lads from Erdington, Kingstanding and some of the Aston Tramps (see Chapter 5) that night. We were always looking to test ourselves and I suppose we were like anorak hooligans in a sense. Whatever game was on at Villa Park we wanted to be there and fight the travelling firm. So here we were at an FA Youth Cup semi-final against Millwall, hoping they are going to bring a firm, and they didn't disappoint, bringing a coach of their lads to the game.

Because it wasn't a first-team game, like most reserve or youth games they only opened one stand, in this case the Trinity Road stand. They housed Millwall in the upper section right-hand corner and Villa in the lower section. The game was a real niggle match and Villa had a couple of bruisers in their side who could mix it on the pitch – Noel Blake and Robert Hopkins – both of whom later left Villa to go across the road, but the only football medals they were to ever win in their career was the FA Youth Cup playing in claret and blue. I wonder if they have the photos still on their sideboards, especially Hopkins; he was Youth captain but like Blake, who could never cut it at the Villa, they just weren't good enough. Blake left Villa under a cloud, something he was forever reminded about by Villa supporters when we played them. Hopkins was friendly with some of the Blues' match-day lads even when he was playing the odd game for Villa. Maybe it was Brittle dropping the nut on him one day on New Street ramp that made him so bitter, or the fact he scored an own goal in a cup tie against non-league Altrincham to send his beloved Blues out of the FA Cup.

The Villa youngsters were well up for it and gave no quarter. The referee seemed to struggle to maintain control on the pitch and we are told afterwards that when the game had ended, Villa and Millwall had their own row outside the changing rooms, with Blake leading the Villa players into the confrontation. Throughout the game, Millwall's firm went through their friendly repertoire of songs – 'We Are Evil', 'No-one Likes Us' – the songs that went along with their terrace notoriety. Their lads were made up of some older, typical docker types and some young bucks like ourselves. It was going to be a good test for us.

Most of our crew that night were from the local surrounding areas. We decided we would have it with them on Aston Park and were pointing to them to say, 'Out there later after the game.' We left early. It may have been a big game to the likes of Blake and Hopkins but it was a fuck-all game to us and we needed to make sure we were prepared. There are always some games you are going to need to be well prepared and to me this was one of them, we weren't often going to get the chance to pit ourselves against Millwall because they had never been in the top flight up until then, so things had to be right. We needed to give a good account of ourselves.

Outside the ground, work was being carried out on a community playground in the park so there was a ready-made array of weapons available in the form of bricks and concrete slabs. We collected the bricks and rubble and put them behind the trees that sprawled across Aston Park and waited for Millwall to come out. We had taken the best vantage point and as soon as they came out and onto the park there was no pulling back. We bombarded them with missiles and they really didn't have a chance. I heard a few years later that one of theirs got put down by a concrete slab hurled by a big skinny black lad. Well that was partly true; it was a house brick to be honest.

We had about 25 of us, no more, but if you have an arsenal of weapons it can make up the numbers. We are going to have it as a result, anyway.

4 WE ARE THE WITTON WARRIORS

MOSES

The Witton End, pre-1977/78, was a large, uncovered end that could probably house 14,000. It was considered the away end but in truth unless it was Blues or Man United you would often get home supporters mingling in with the away fans. The older lads like Pete the Greek started to use this more than the Holte as there was more fun to be had and you were starting to get a lot of Erdington and Kingstanding, Castle Vale lads would be in there too, mostly from areas like Short Heath, The Ridgeway, Finchley Road, The Crossways, Stockland Green, The Norton, Pype Hayes, they were the ones who would try to seek out the opposition's lads without getting noticed too early, by their foes or the Old Bill.

The Holte End had previously become split into two sections. You would get right-side and left-side chants and, commonplace at the time, you would get half chanting 'Rangers' and the other half 'Celtic' if the sheer boredom of game warranted. There was even a full-scale row one night between the two top halves of the Holte, with one poor bastard getting volleyed in the face for being a right-sider – and this was the Villa v. Liverpool night game in 1976 when we won 5-1!

One memorable night in the Witton End in 1977, Millwall were the visitors in a League Cup game. They brought a proper firm up. Villa had been turned over at Cold Blow Lane in '73 (see Chapter 3), so many of the lads were itching for payback. I am a few years older than the likes of Black Danny and Brittle so was probably at it a few years earlier. I ran with the crew from Perry Barr, a good set of lads, the likes of Jonah, the Pettit Brothers, Muzza and Cliff, we had a good 20, most of us coming from the Perry Common school. The Witton End became our manor. This night the fighting had already started before the game out by the Aston Hotel and what used to be called the Witton Arms, Witton Island as we know it, so I knew it was going to be a busy night. They brought a top firm with them, with the full set of old grizzlies that Millwall were famous for at the time, but it was a quarter-final so they were always going to travel in numbers.

You hear lots of stories about terrace scraps and legends but what I am about to tell you is gospel: it was the first time I have ever seen a shooter brought to a game. God's honest truth, one of the Millwall lads brought a shooter wrapped up in newspaper with elastic bands round it. Talk about coming prepared. Millwall were in the Witton in numbers, but so were some Villa. Millwall obviously had the numerical advantage but we had a right game fucker called Pete the Greek. The cockneys knew who the Greek was without actually knowing him by face. One big black lad stepped up and growled, 'I want your top man, Pete the Greek.' It was Tiny, a South-east London terrace legend, and one game cunt himself. Pete stepped out, probably fucking smiling if I remember right, and they both walked up towards the old refreshment bar, which was at the back of where the Corner Flag restaurant is now. They walked up the steps of the old terracing right to the top, where the old 'piss corner' was on the left, tucked out of sight of any Old Bill. Hundreds then gathered in a circle around them, with probably hundreds more watching from the old grass bank at the back, because if you were on the slope at the back of the terraces you could look to the left and see the spot.

These guys were warriors, gladiators, call it what you like but they were having it toe-to-toe and completely knocking the bollocks out of each other, with no quarter given. Nobody else got involved, everyone was glued to this row, it was like an old school playground ruck with blood, everyone wants to see for themselves who is cock of the school and here we all were, watching these two top geezers fighting to see who was the cock of their clubs, cage fighting without the cage and something that would have a lasting impression on me and the lads. It was about bottle, about pride for your team and what it meant. This was it.

I would love to say Pete won but he didn't. Neither did Tiny. It ended due to the sheer numbers watching. With more and more now looking at the fight rather than at the pitch, it alerted the police, whose presence called it a night for these two. I wish I had a camera that night because the two shook each other's hands and casually walked up the red steps and back to where the rest of their respective boys had gone. Any youngsters reading this probably will think it's rubbish but back in the late Sixties and early Seventies it was a regular occurrence for Pete the Greek to have a straightener.

After the game, Millwall did take some casualties on the Serpentine and Aston Park, across the road from the church. It was one of the biggest Villa mobs I have ever seen. Some Millwall ran at the park, but the others just stood and took what I can only describe as a serious beating. They were well and truly done that night, although again they were as game as fuck. It was sheer numbers and revenge for 1973 that fuelled this bitter hammering. Fair play to the Millwall lads that stood and took it.

When they rebuilt the old Witton end in 1977 and renamed it the North Stand, I think it put a lot of the older lads off. They thought it wouldn't be the same so they stopped going in. This led to a younger crew taking over, predominantly the lads I went with plus another good set of lads from the Rose and Crown in Erdington, like Kev C, Rob, Fordy, Pete, Sparra, Stropper and Doc. At the time I always thought the Perry Common lads were top notch, they were the ones I went to the match with. I didn't go on the C Crew coaches other than for the Leeds game. We went by cars or minibuses and so we did encounter different things to the other lads, and so I saw things differently I suppose. Our firm was good with a strong bond, everyone could have it and because we were close nobody would shit out on you and leave you roasting. I felt comfortable with them all, they were like family. I still see some of them now. It's a pity I have lost touch with others because they were good lads. We had a 17-year-old, Jimmy Coley [see Chapter 10], who ran with us for a while and who went on to become a player in another league really, and you could tell then that it was always going to happen.

I ended up C Crew like the rest of my own firm, and while most of the C Crew would occupy the lower Holte End, with spotters strategically placed along the bottom and by the entrances to repel invaders, I always thought we needed a firm next to the away fans. You've got to make it difficult for them on your manor and most grounds then in the old First were doing the same thing, having a firm next to the aways. A lot of ours used to sing the old 'We are the Witton Warriors' stuff but though it sounds odd, when people have you on this icon pedestal I can't be seen to be doing all that. It wouldn't have been the done thing. I had to be above that.

The Witton Warriors were not a firm as such, we were a branch of the C Crew but we did a lot of damage for the cause and I like to think we made it difficult for away fans. Sometimes being black came in handy and I exploited it to the full and got away with things my white mates couldn't; for instance in them days I would always carry two scribers on me, the ones you used in metalwork. I hid them in my hair plaits or dreads and I could easily whip them out. I got the idea from the number of times I came into contact with blades, down to them Scouse bastards.

One memorable row with Liverpool was before the New Street slashings [see Chapter 9]. I was no different to most black lads who travelled with the Villa to the new 'City of Culture' – we all had a rough time there and can even remember the fuckers singing 'We only want the black fellas' in the old Anfield Road end. Seven of us jumped over into them, fronting them with, 'Here's your black fellas,' and due to this I was up for it whenever they were in my city. I used to get amongst the away fans by standing in their section, then as we were all walking out I would just smash one of the fuckers. This was the signal for my crew to steam in; it always caused disruption and confusion among them and gave you that split-second advantage. We would pile in, do the damage and get the fuck out before anyone got lifted by the Old Bill.

One time I was right amongst the Scousers and all the Villa were on the opposite side of the road down Witton Lane. Bottles and bricks were flying over the road and the Old Bill were smashing everyone with their truncheons, kids from both sides, trying to keep us apart. I knew I needed to act quick to cause that few seconds of disruption but some Villa lads had acknowledged me and I was sussed, not difficult looking back now as I was the only black face amongst them. So like a gunslinger goes for his guns, I went for mine, only these were two metal scribers and my holster was my dreads. I whipped them out and slashed the bloke nearest to me; it was either him or me as I saw it. That was the spark for what was to come. I knew we had them, I saw the terror on their faces. They were pushing and shoving each other as not one of them wanted to be at the front. The Old Bill would batter one mob of Villa back but another crew of Brummies would slip in and dish out the digs before getting the truncheon treatment.

I can recall the Pettit brothers at another game, they were great lads, as game as fuck. It was against Man United. There was now a fence in the Witton end dividing the away crew and our lot. In pure frustration and not being able to wait until the walk outside, the two brothers jumped the fence into them and both got nicked. Another memorable battle was when Man City came; it was the opening of the North Stand. City had a proper good firm back then, they could have it home or away. It didn't go all our way that night and if I am honest it was well on top, with a few Villa taking injuries.

The game prior to that, they had erected a fence to split the Holte End. They planned to split it into two and put away fans in one side of it, the cheeky cunts. They had got fed up with the antics of our lot in the Witton end and so thought the best plan of action was to split the biggest end in the country! You have to wonder sometimes if these people understand the mentality of football supporters and what their main end means to them; the Holte was sacred ground and that's coming from someone who hardly ever went in there! It was the largest terraced goal end in Europe at its peak, housing 28,000, more supporters than some entire grounds. It was strange going to Liverpool to see the famous Kop of which everyone has heard, then realising how small it was in comparison to our own main end. The Holte end was that big that we all felt it impossible for anyone to take, and no one but Glasgow Rangers has ever done it in my time. The reason they took it is that most of them had scaled the walls before the gates had opened, the Old Bill then kept letting them in and fucked all the Villa off, but that is spoken about more elsewhere so I'll leave it at that.

The night of the Man City game, people were more intent on removing the fence from the Holte, all armed with screwdrivers and hammers as if they were doing a job at work. Chants went up of 'The fence must go' and go it did! They managed to remove it but meanwhile our lot had our own battle going on with Man City's firm. They were in our end, the Witton, but they weren't so easy to remove.

Some of the happiest days of my life were back then, doing battles with loads of good crews. All the London clubs brought good firms, QPR brought a great firm a year earlier for the semi-final of the League Cup and we had a proper tear-up with them that night in the Witton end, outside the away exits and then again on Witton station.

I am not going to pretend I was a Villa fanatic because I wasn't. I was a Leeds fan to start with who got sick of the racist stuff at Elland Road. I suppose that, along with peer pressure from my mates who were Villa mad, changed me. I had seven great seasons down the Villa, rucking almost every game; in fact it is hard to think of a game when it didn't go off in one form or another. It was a phase in my life I don't regret but it's a long time ago now for me. I knew when it was time to get out, unfortunately for some of our firm that wasn't the case and they have paid the price.

BRITTLE

Saturday, 21 August 1976, Division One, Aston Villa 4, West Ham United 0. This is the one that some who were keen-eyed youngsters at the time point to as the catalyst for the formation of a firm that would spend many years on the terraces of the Witton End. A good firm from the Crossways pub, lads all early to mid-twenties, walk up Witton Lane from Witton Island, stop at the visitors' entrance and casually pay in. There are about 25 of them, led by Terry Smith and Jim Hegarty, Stan, Injun Joe and other faces. Another 20 or so young Brummies who are hanging around the area to see the famous West Ham firm realise what is happening and follow them in.

They all walk along the wide gangway that separates the front section of the Witton end from the back. The end is not yet full, so it is easy for the West Ham firm stood on the open back terrace to see who is in front of them. They quickly realise these lads are not cockneys. A few Londoners move forward and start taunting the Brummies, who carry on towards the other side. Nothing happens for a while. The cockneys are waiting for the right moment, the Villa lads are assessing if this is a suicide mission. A few police stationed in the Witton end realise what is happening but there is not enough of them to prevent the obvious.

At once, West Ham make their move down the terraces to their right. At the same time, Villa move up on to the upper terrace. In a flash, it is off. Villa did not get the upper hand, most of the lads present who spoke about it recognise this, the advantage of numbers in West Ham's favour made it impossible. But what was witnessed was a brutal show of defence by a number of boys that would go down in local terrace folklore.

The main Birmingham face was a certain Terry Smith, a fearless leader of his boys and a terrace warrior of the highest calibre, and this row elevated him to main face status. There were injuries suffered on both sides; it would only be fair to say Villa took more than their London rivals. But the sight of the shirtless Terry Smith, going hammer and tongs with some top Londoners, made sure that the rest of the Villa boys stood and battled it out. This was a proper row: blood spilling on both sides, bystanders moving out the way quickly for safety but with eyes fixed firmly on the battle as they flee, feet and fists flailing each other, some go down, get up and back at it, some go down, get up and fuck off into the safety of the crowd, for them enough is enough. The Holte End in full voice, 'Hello, hello, Witton aggro, Witton aggro,' as the fight rages. Slowly the numbers doing battle dwindle to a few, this is last-men-standing stuff, but the last men standing are all good enough and kicking the living shit out of each other. This fight dies when the last men are fucked and not before, it doesn't die because there is victory but because there is nothing left, it is brutal.

West Ham's boys retreat to the central section of the upper Witton End and Villa down to the section by the players' tunnel, still trading insults. Time lets both sets of lads catch their breath and lick whatever wounds they have. Both firms, now regrouped, want more, for them it is game on, but police reinforcements are now there to intervene. They gather Villa's firm and surround them, pushing them back towards the players' tunnel, penning them in. West Ham lads are pushed back up the terrace in the same manner, the main characters now laughing with each other, praising each other's efforts, the youngsters buzzing at the sight of their own going toe-to-toe with a top firm and giving nothing away, trading blow for blow, not winning but not running. This has been a top battle and they know it.

Villa's firm are rounded up and escorted around the pitch to the Holte End. The lads know that this had looked good, and from a hooligan's point of view that is a victory. They duly accept the praise that is given to them from their counterparts who have witnessed the row from the Holte. For these lads this is it, it is everything, fuck the game, let's relive what's just happened on the terraces. This is the kind of terrace battle that stays in the memory of a hooligan for life, and to youngsters that may not yet be 100 per cent sure, it is a row that makes your mind up for you. It decides for you what you are going to be doing every Saturday afternoon from now on.

DANNY THE ASTON TRAMPS

Not the most stylish of names and not one the lads themselves came up with, but that's the name they were given and they did a different job to other Villa firms. The two founder members of the Aston Tramps were brothers Thomas and Danny Griffin. They both had this belief that they were urban guerrillas. I've seen this duo view a minibus full of away fans from 300 yards out, zoom in on it, trash it and turn it on its side, pull out the occupants then beat the fucking daylights out of them, all in 90 seconds flat. That's how deadly this pair was.

Most of their firm came from the Aston, Witton and Newtown areas, the roads surrounding the football ground, the maisonettes off Lichfield Road and ones facing the Adventurers pub. Their job was to get the away fans that travelled in cars or minibuses. They picked people off and let's not glorify it; they trashed the motors *and* robbed people of their belongings, money and clothes. They were especially good of a night game, where you had lads balaclava'd up long before the hoodies. They got the ones the C Crew and Witton Warriors missed on coaches or trains. The lads who would mind the cars around Villa Park were part of the crew too. The only other place like it for surrounding roads back then was Maine Road. Those that thought they would have a pleasant walk through Aston Park to get to their vehicles were in for a big shock as Thomas, Danny and Co. would be waiting for them behind trees or even on the bonnets of their cars as they got back. Some of these lads became members of the C Crew.

The Aston Tramps were ideal on semi-final days (semis are often played at Villa Park as a neutral ground) and in 1980, when West Ham played Everton, they joined with the C Crew to pick off mobs of both clubs. A West Ham firm were caught on Aston Park as a bit of payback for the Upton Park clash and that same day I was getting stuck into Everton fans in one of the side roads while the lad we called 'Custard Creams' was having his dinner with his family. I was right outside his front room with a metal pole beating some Everton lads with it and Custard Creams was pretending not to notice while his family were muttering their disgust.

The likes of Victor from Newtown was an original member, as were Robin and the late Chrissie, all very good lads who went on to become faces at the Villa. The mob itself was just very good at what it did.

5 CONGRATULATIONS, YOU HAVE JUST MET THE ICF

DANNY

The Seventies had come and gone and we were getting ourselves together on and off the pitch. Off it, we had started to take good numbers away and were a match for most at home, while on it we really did look like we had a side who could challenge for major honours. On 8 March 1980, both of those statements were put to bed and it was a case of back to the drawing board!

By then we had reached the quarter-finals of the FA Cup and like supporters at most clubs we had a belief that this could be our year. In the previous round we were drawn to play at Blackburn and I had gone by train to a game which saw Villa take a huge following, as cup fever was beginning to take hold of us all. In those days we were always reminded of 1957, the last year we had won the FA Cup; at Villa it is similar to England and everyone harping on about 1966. At least the World Cup is only every four years; we have 1957 thrown at us every fucking year, and it still hasn't changed. At Blackburn, Villa fans took over the pubs and generally had the run of the place. The home fans were run ragged. It was a no contest, like going to Coventry for us only further to travel.

I think we all expected to do the same at West Ham, as we had been allocated the South Bank terrace and 8,000 Villa were making the trip. Now maybe we dismissed West Ham lightly or we didn't read the papers but it was nothing like Blackburn. Some lads had travelled there a few seasons earlier and experienced problems but it wasn't as if we had taken any numbers or a firm then. We had also had a run-in with an unknown young firm making their way in the world of football violence at Villa Park two seasons earlier, who we coped with easily enough. They actually came in the Holte End but whereas West Ham in their published account will have you believe they took the Holte, the truth is they didn't get far before they were forced onto the pitch and up to the Witton End, to a so called 'heroes' welcome'.

They call it their first major foray into football violence. They also call it the birth of the Inter-City Firm. Either way, little did we know that we would meet them two seasons later and this would be a more serious, experienced, clued-up firm who were far better than the youngsters who had been brave or daft enough to come on the Holte End, even though they were neither big or hard enough to see it through.

After we had beaten Blackburn Rovers in a replay, the draw against West Ham was a decent one for us, given that they were a Second Division side who at the time weren't even doing well in their division. So on and off the pitch we fancied our chances. I don't think anybody was thinking that it would be on top with the numbers we would take, in fact we didn't expect any firm to come through us with those numbers. We made a major error on that one.

Most Villa fans out of the 8,000 that travelled to Upton Park that day will have a story about their experience. Here are a few. They make, for Villa lads anyway, unpleasant reading. Moses was a well known face at the time and he remembers the day well.

MOSES

Five carloads of us had gone from Kingstanding, the usual suspects plus Fat Bazz. It was a good firm. I considered us the baddest, maddest fuckers around; I mean, no-one fucked around with these boys, did they? No one would run, would they? Everyone was a stand-on geezer, weren't they?

We didn't even make it to London before we ran into our first row. The lads decided they needed to fill up before London as we had forgotten to take a full load – only this wasn't petrol, it was cans of beer. We ended up stopping off for a beer or two in Northampton just as the pubs opened at 11am. Now with these lads we didn't exactly welcome newcomers into the crowd, we were a bit isolated and didn't take kindly to anybody butting their noses in on our business. Well, the locals decide to get interested in our drinking, something was said and before you know it the touch paper was lit and we were in the middle of a pub brawl. We lost five lads in the process who got nicked. That now leaves four cars on the way to West Ham.

We got to the ground. I ain't much of a drinker, I'd had a few, and I looked round and could see a good crew where we were standing. Yes, it was going off but we weren't in the thick of it where we were standing and I wasn't aware of how bad it was going off. The game was a tight affair and a typical cup tie. They got a disputed penalty over a nothing cross that Ken McNaught handled and Ray Stewart banged in the penalty. It was a fucking sickener and I just wanted to get out of the ground and get away.

'I'm off,' I said to the others. 'Meet you at the car,' they said. I just couldn't watch them cunts celebrate.

As I get out the exit, they slammed the door shut. Three of us had made it outside but we saw they had lads milling about, so I knew it was on top. We tried to get back in but it was too late, they weren't opening the doors and we were on our own. We start to walk towards Upton Park station and I was thinking if I could blend in with my green khaki combats, as they were all in green flying jackets, their match-day gear.

I then get spotted: some blond-headed cunt giving it, 'Got the time, mate?' That old chestnut. We now have 25 on our tails and there is no other option but to leg it. One goes one way and me and Jonah another, although I am hobbling which slows me down, but there is a reason which will soon be made clear. We get to an Asian shop and Jonah gets there first. He gets in and slams the door.

'Jonah, let me in. Jonah, let me in. For fuck's sake Jonah, let me in!'

He froze in panic and didn't know what to do, but he didn't open the door. I was on my own. I am fucked but I have one last option – my dog collar. I have moved on from my days with the metal scribers in the dreadlocks [see Chapter 4] and now have a dog collar attached to a chain with a metal ball bearing welded on by my brother. I hide it in my shoe but the ball bearing gives me a problem when I walk. The things you do for football violence, eh?

I pick up a bottle from the floor, smash it against the wall, take out the dog chain and swing it round like a mad cunt. As far as I can see I am fighting for my life. I catch the first fucker with it and whoosh, his face splits and the show of blood gives me the seconds I need to run. I get up the street and two black guys offer to help me but at a price.

'Man, give us what you have in your pockets and we will protect you from the guys after you.'

I am a kid, I ain't got tuppence in my pocket, so I take my choice and it's the chain. One cops it straight in his face and I make a right mess of him, so much so that he is screaming in pain. The other one knows he will get it next so leaves me alone. The mob is still after me and now I am panicking. I don't know the area or where I am but somehow I get myself into the neighbourhood and some back street houses. I am hiding in a back garden, hoping they have gone. I go and knock on a back door at random and a bloke opens it.

'Fuck off, we don't want no blacks here.'

I hadn't the time to tell him I wasn't actually selling anything or was a Jehovah Witness; I was just trying to save my black ass. I ran into the next garden and hid behind the bins. I was holding a bin as a shield, shaking and terrified, there was nowhere to run. Then I broke to the back door, knocked it and thank God it was a black face. He invited me in when I told him my story and soon I am being given fish soup with his family watching *The Fosters* on the television. I was safe, even if the soup was shite.

I waited till the coast was clear, shook my saviour's hand and made my way back to the car. All the lads were there but everyone had the same story to tell, one of terror, and all were carrying injuries or scars or bloodstains on their clothes. I saw Jonah, a lad I had known since I was five. I wanted to bang him out for leaving me but we were old mates so I left it. But I was severely pissed off with him, the result, the shit I had been through and the soup!

We decided we needed a drink. We weren't that far from the ground but we pulled into a pub; it was full of 'Appy Ammers'. *Well sorry; you are going to get it for what every one of us has just been through.* We trashed the pub and whilst we didn't bring weapons inside we used everything in there: ashtrays, bar stools, tables, the lot. We left the pub unusable and every one in there injured; I know that cos Big Jim made sure no one was left out.

It had been going off for a good ten minutes when I went outside to just get away from it, thinking the Old Bill had to be on their way. Twenty of us were causing serious havoc, this was a pub riot, not a brawl. West Ham lads were coming out trying to get away. The rumour later was that I threw a West Ham lad through a window. I am not sure; I just threw him against the window and it bust.

Now Big Jim is a terrace legend, a six foot, four inch, proud Irishman who never backs down and for me is up there with the Greek. He has lost it and is punching every fucker in there, making sure no one leaves unless they are going out on a stretcher. Those who know him will know what I mean. We were screaming at him, 'Jim, leave it will you, that's enough, the Old Bill will be here,' but he ain't listening to me or anybody. We had to drag him out and he was even fighting us, he completely lost it and wanted to kill somebody. Eventually we managed to get him into the car.

His mood lightened up on the way back, probably by about Coventry. We had also stolen the tills and the whisky and other bottles from the pub. We were lucky we never got nicked but we knew nobody could have gotten our car registrations. The pub was totalled. It was some small payback for what we had endured during the day.

DANNY

We had gone by coach from the middle of Brum town centre, the first coach run by Andy and Brittle at that time. We had a bit of a sing-song and the mood was good. It was the quarter-final of the FA Cup, our Holy Grail, and all the talk was of what we did at Blackburn, where we'd had the run of the place. In our naivety we thought that at West Ham and little old East London we would be doing the same. We parked in some dodgy back street and as we walked to the ground with a police escort we knew we certainly weren't going off to find a nice pre-match boozer for a drink.

I sussed something out and said to the lads, 'They are amongst us.'

'What do you mean, they are amongst us?'

Whack! A couple of ours got chinned. That was what I meant! This was totally different to previous games, they were just steaming in to us, the Old Bill were as relevant as the lampposts or the cars we were passing, they didn't give a flying fuck. They also seemed older, in their mid-twenties, while we were 18 or 19. No one was going to take liberties on their manor that day.

We got into the ground and I looked at the thousands we had brought, thinking, *you may have had a result outside, West Ham, but with the firm and numbers we have it's going to be a lot different.* Well, that's what I thought at the time. We were standing halfway up and in the middle, and from nowhere, like Ninja Turtles, a guy would spring up next to you, hit you and disappear. I couldn't work out what was going on, only the fact people were getting hit and we couldn't find out who was doing what. Twenty-seven years later, I found out that the rumour that West Ham terrace legend Bill Gardner was a steward that day, looking after crowd control, was true. Bill had a key to the dividing gate and kept letting the ICF through to us. I suppose it was akin to putting the Krays in charge of a bank. He later admitted it was one of his best days at Upton Park in the Eighties. Yes, I bet it was.

At half-time, with the game evenly poised at nil-nil and in my opinion set for a replay, I noticed three black lads dressed in green flying jackets. I knew they weren't Villa and instinctively said, 'Get 'em

Villa, West Ham are in here.' Whack, I felt my nose explode as I took a hit, possibly from a knuckleduster. A gap opened up in the terracing as it does when it kicks off and fighting broke out around me. I was holding my nose when the police came in and nicked me. *Nice, any chance of nicking the Cockneys who were throwing the punches in a Villa end?* I was dragged around the pitch still holding my nose, taken past the famous chicken run, led down the tunnel and into the first aid room.

The copper decided he wasn't going to nick me and said, 'You can go back on the terracing.' What was I going to be nicked for, spilling blood on the terraces? I came up the tunnel just as the players reappeared and remember seeing Trevor Brooking, the gentleman sportsman of West Ham. He was not a bit like the bastards we had come across. The copper took me back past the chicken run and I felt like the bloke standing too close to the train as they tried to suck me in with the usual, 'Kill the bastard, throw him in here.' I was shitting it.

It certainly changed my mood. I was silent for most of the game. Their nutters were still coming in, throwing punches and disappearing and the stewards and police took not a blind bit of notice. I was just glad to get the draw and get out of there. As the game finished and we were out of the cup, I saw poor old Boris, one of the lads. Another season up in smoke. The chant of 'On the pitch!' went up from the disgruntled Villa following and I was straight over that fence but when I looked back only three had made it over. I tried to get back to the Villa end but got another good clumping.

I finally managed to get back into our end and now just wanted to get away. We made our way out and, Jesus, four of us – me, Lloyd, Buster and Reggie – got steamed by proper geezers, docker types. We disintegrated and ran in every direction.

I got back to the coach and everybody there had a tale of woe. No one had escaped an injury of some sort. To put this into perspective, if you read the Steamers' accounts of Millwall [see Chapter 3] this was on a par with it for us. The upstarts had found their own 'Millwall', if you like.

Then West Ham appeared by the coach and I thought, well they have done me twice, maybe it's third time lucky. We all went into them and this time we did a lot better and got our only result of the day. The ones that stood got filled in and the rest were on their toes but I wasn't finished. The guy I had my eyes on was obviously a local and went into his house, using the key to get in. He was about to close the door when I kicked it open and proper did him. It made me feel a bit better.

The odd thing was that back on that coach there was a sense of pride amongst the lads. It was probably our first major ruck against top-notch opponents. Yes we may have come off worse but we didn't bottle it and we felt like we had been in a proper row.

I got back to Brum and went straight round to my missus' house – and who is sitting there nice and cosy but one of our crew who had cried off and missed the game, a lad called Wolfie. Now I don't know what he thought he was playing at or if he thought I was some kind of mug, but like those West Ham geezers who were coming in to our end and then disappearing, he went. Only this geezer never showed his face in Brum again.

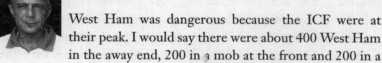

BRITTLE

West Ham was dangerous because the ICF were at their peak. I would say there were about 400 West Ham in the away end, 200 in a mob at the front and 200 in a mob on the side. The ones at the front got a bit of a hiding and at one stage their bottle went completely but the ones at the side were a different kettle of fish, these were obviously their top lads and they were all blokes, no kids amongst them, which was unusual back then. We kept going in at them but we just could not move them, it was their manor and they knew their strengths. Because they had their backs to the wall, it meant we could only go in at them from one direction, which worked for them.

No way could you move them, man. They were a firm and a half. There was even a big gap at one stage all around them and I clocked one bloke who was old enough to be my father with a green flying jacket on and I told my mate standing next to me that I wanted to do him. Bear in mind that I was only nineteen or twenty at the time, I went under a barrier and ran up and banged him one. Everyone followed me in again but we still could not move them and I have to give them untold respect as they stayed there all game.

Outside I thought 'yeah we are going to have a right row with you cunts' because I knew there was more Villa about than just the ones rowing with the West Ham on the side. I will be honest, I was very disappointed because when we got outside there was hardly any Villa about and the ICF were everywhere. I was with a couple of lads but that was it – West Ham were still up for it but there weren't any Villa. We got back to where all the coaches were parked and it had been well on top for a lot of people outside. West Ham had been an organised firm; we had been a disorganised group of individuals. I made up my mind at that moment that if I was going to have anything to do with it, I was never going to let Villa be so disorganised again. We had been up against the best in the country in my opinion and maybe we could learn from them.

Villa finally got themselves firmed up by the coaches and took a walk back down the side street. This time we did give it to some West Ham who had got a little bit too cocky but it was nothing compared to what had gone on throughout the whole day. In the ground we hadn't done too bad; outside I was very disappointed and the little result we had at the end didn't mean much compared to what had gone on before.

DEL BRITISH LEYLAND CARS

I had gone with lads from the Hunter's Moon pub in Castle Bromwich, the first pub you hit as you come off Junction 5 of the M6 northbound and a pub that was as infamous for weekend brawls as it was for grab-a-granny nights. Some of us had learned more about fighting there than on the terraces. It was just one of those pubs.

There were five of us in total, including Pridd and Mickey, who were proper pissheads who always wanted to get to away games for pub opening time. We'd had rows before, as they had a habit of parking their car smack in the middle of the away fans and normally right behind their main end, it was a standing joke when you went away with them but they didn't give a fuck. We got to West Ham and sure enough were there for opening time. They managed to find a pub full of West Ham. While the other three were wary of being the only five in a pub that was gradually filling up with cockneys, Pridd and Mickey had put their money on the pool table and were playing pool against all comers. Like the Jasper Carrott sketch 'No cowin' Bovril' they now were shouting the rounds at the bar in the broadest Brummie accent. I was watching to see if there was a reaction but in fairness there wasn't.

With me being the only black face in there and East London having the reputation as racist, I was thinking all the time, *watch your back*. Pridd and Mickey were good lads and could have it, and I didn't mind having a row myself, but five would never be enough. Fortunately the West Ham left us alone, but one of our lads, Budgie, was getting nervous and didn't stay. He said, 'Look, I am going to the ground, see you in there.' None of us thought anything of it, the lad wasn't a rower, just a good Villa lad.

It was pretty crazy in the ground and you had to have your wits about you, but walking back to the car, which seemed to be parked the other side of the fucking world, was like a scene out of *The Warriors*. We finally managed to get there and it was a relief, but the problem was there were only four of us. We sat and waited for Budgie, and with everything that had gone on in the ground we were worried that he had been hurt or even hospitalised.

We sat there for what seemed ages and then we could see them, a firm of West Ham. There must have been 100 of them and it was obvious they were looking for Brummies, or Northerners as they think of us. They looked at us and from a walk they broke into a run. Now Mickey has been known to stop the car and get the wheel-brace out at other places, but this was West Ham and there were 100 lads, not 20, so fuck it, *start the car, let's get out of here!*

British Leyland and Longbridge in Birmingham were not renowned for making reliable cars and we were in one of the worst, an Allegro. It lived up to its reputation. The car wouldn't start and we were soon trapped inside it in the middle of a frenzied attack. The windows were going in, the panels were being booted and they were rocking the thing side to side, while Mickey was furiously turning the key and it just wouldn't click.

'For fuck's sake Mickey, start it!'

Just as they were banging on the roof, the engine fired up and we managed to get away from them, even though they still gave chase. Those few minutes seemed like a lifetime and I was as scared as I have ever been in my life. We got to the top of the road and pulled the car over by a copper. We were lost and seriously worried that we were going to go the same way as the Allegro. We asked the copper for help but he replied, 'I'm from the other side of the river.' That was it, so we were on our own. After frantically driving around, we went to the nearest hospital, worried that our mate Budgie was in there, but he wasn't, and we eventually had to head home. All the talk was of how we hoped he was okay but Mickey kept moaning and muttering about his car and the damage to it. He was a big Paddy and he wasn't in a good mood.

We pulled into the Hunter's car park and Wib, another lad, said, 'I bet Budgie is up the bar.' We got out and looked at the damage to the car. Nobody said anything to Mickey but it was ready for the scrapheap.

We walked in and Budgie was at the bar.

'Where you been?' said Mickey.

'I hitched a lift on a coach. I wasn't walking back to the car, it was mayhem.'

Mickey didn't reply, he just went over and hit him. He also got rid of the Allegro and bought Ford cars thereafter.

6 THE C CREW ARE COMING TO TOWN

BRITTLE

You have to go back before that first game on 16 August 1980, Leeds away, and understand how the firm first got together. My early recollections are from the Steamers days when I first met a skinny black kid who became good mates with me and was later to become known as Black Danny. Because I was always going round with lads five or six years older than me, I got to know a lot of the Steamers from an early age, and by the time I was 14 I would be travelling regularly to away games on the Steamers' coach.

One particular game, we were away at Everton and I was with a pal of mine from round by me when I clocked Danny on the coach. He stood out because he was my age but we never spoke. When we got there, all the Steamers went into a pub for a drink, it may have been the Blue House. In those days, you weren't even allowed in pubs at 14 or 15 so we went on a walkabout. We couldn't exactly sit outside with a bottle of pop and a packet of crisps, could we?

We bumped into a few more young lads off different coaches and ended up about 30-handed, aged between say 14 and 17. We soon bumped into a firm of Everton heading towards us and I straight away thought we were in trouble, as none of the Steamers were about to look after us; we were going to have to look after ourselves.

I told everyone not to run and I threw a few punches at a geezer who came at me. All of a sudden I saw a long arm come past me and BANG, the bloke hit the deck. Danny had him. That was the first time I ever met Black Danny. With this, the Everton all had it away on their toes and I can't describe the feeling as we were running after them. My confidence was sky high.

This was probably the turning point for me, because I realised that, yes, we could do it. Before, I was always in the background, wanting to be a geezer. That day I was at the front, I never ran and I did my bit, and although I was probably the smallest kid there, I was giving the orders out and people followed me. It's all right giving the orders but if nobody listens to you, you're in trouble, aren't you? When we got back to the pub, the Steamers couldn't believe what we'd done.

ANDY

You have to go back to 1978, really, to understand where it started. While the Steamers were still the main firm at Villa, and very much in their prime, the more me and Tom went to games and got ourselves involved in bits and bobs, the more lads we got to know and before we knew it, we had a right little firm of young upstarts who were meeting up regularly. One of our most popular meeting places was the Aston Hotel on Witton Island, an ideal place to spot away fans getting off the trains. Our numbers began to grow as more and more lads got to know each other and there always seemed to be someone who knew some-body else – I suppose we were what you would call a 'Youth firm' these days.

At one home game against Liverpool, I was nicked and ended up getting six months' detention in Whatton Detention Centre. When I landed there I had no idea a lot of the others were already in there, so you can imagine my surprise when we first got there to hear shouts of 'Come on you Lions' and 'Cardiff's here', meaning my nickname, Cardiff. My arrival swelled the Villa ranks in the nick and we completely took over the place. My pal Tommy was already in there as well as people like Brittle, Joycey and Heaffy. I also met a lad with 'Leicester City' tattooed across his chest. I don't have any tattoos but I really liked this bloke's and always planned to have 'Aston Villa' across my chest but never got round to it. The bloke said to me as we passed, 'I suppose you're Villa as well aren't you,' and then began to tell me of the rows that took place the previous season when we went to Leicester and cleared their end, and that Villa had a proper firm.

We were running the place and you couldn't go anywhere in the whole nick without hearing the word Villa mentioned. One day when I was working, the screw in charge of me was reading the paper. 'Anything about the Villa in there?' I asked him politely. I was shocked by this answer. He threw the paper to the floor and shouted, 'Villa? Fucking Villa? I'm sick to death of hearing about Villa. From the minute I get here till the minute I leave, all I fucking hear about is Villa.' I've always thought how lucky that screw was – after all, how many of us can say we go to work and hear about the Villa all day long? It was the same when we went to the church there on Sundays. Every Sunday they would sing a gospel type of hymn that went, 'Jesus loves the children, oh yeah.' All you would hear in the church as the hymn was sung was, 'Jesus loves the Villa, oh yeah.' It was so funny to hear that blasting out every week, although the screws weren't laughing.

It was also in Whatton that I became close to Brittle. We knew of each other before Whatton and I can remember being on the same coach as him to Middlesbrough once, when it was bang on top, but it was our time in Whatton that laid the foundations for our friendship and was the first time I really got to know him. I would say that we hit it off straight away in there and became inseparable. To this day Brittle is my closest friend and we are very strong together if and when we need to be. I think that was the first season where the magistrates and judges had been ordered to dish out prison sentences for football lads, with the idea being that it would give people a short, sharp, shock. As far as I was concerned, it helped us come together as a group and talk about how to organise ourselves when we got out and it also pushed Brittle and me towards each other.

I was released on the Friday in time for a home game against Liverpool, of all teams, on the Saturday. I got nicked right outside the away end before the game – the 'short, sharp shock' didn't seem to have worked.

During our time away together, me, Brittle, Tommy, Joycey and Heaffy, among others, talked about how it would be great to get an organised, proper firm, a new firm that could go to away grounds, get noticed and make our mark. We all shared that same passion, now we had the same ambition, and that's how it started, long before a name was ever thought about.

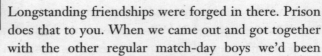

BRITTLE

Longstanding friendships were forged in there. Prison does that to you. When we came out and got together with the other regular match-day boys we'd been running with before the nick, a new firm was formed. After the West Ham game, certain people realised that they would have to take things a little more seriously if we were to be a credible outfit. So some of the lads took up boxing, like Buster and Lloyd. Danny was already boxing anyway for the Villa at the old Holte Hotel but also some of the lads got very serious into weightlifting, the likes of Jimmy Coley were already bang into it anyway. I had tried the boxing bit but ended up just wanting to bite the other bloke's head off. Fuck them Queensberry Rules.

The little pockets of mates and groups of lads from across all the areas of Brum started to mix together. Introductions were made, somebody was always a mate of somebody else and before long we had a good firm of lads. It sounds corny but it's true, we were like one big family back then. People were watching each other's backs.

We would get on the coach and everyone would be sitting in the same place with the same mates, for example Joycey always sat with Heaffy. We were creatures of habit and it created a bond.

Some would play cards, some would just want to talk, others were silent, waiting for the off. It was fun, it was exciting and we were the new kids on the block. The Steamers were a good outfit but never had the numbers we could pull. It was a snowball effect: from running one coach we could count on the regular four coaches and at our peak took seven coaches. Where we had been the ones going on their coaches, it started to be the other way round and they came on ours. Not everyone was particularly happy about us but as time went on we earned our stripes.

We had run coaches before, like West Ham away in 1980, but our first real one as a firm, when we had decided from the outset to go to every game that season, was Leeds away. Myself and Andy were the organisers. The name C Crew came from one of our top front line soldiers, Boris. As with the Steamers, there were many rumours about its origins. Some thought the name came from our jaunts to the seaside, but the founder member is adamant it was based on where we stood in the corner of the Holte End. This was our position to defend and any opposing fans that tried to come in the Holte were dealt with.

A few seasons earlier, we'd had London teams try to get in via the bottom of the Holte, with some success, so we were spread in both the upper and lower right-hand sides as you looked at the pitch before we eventually all were based in the bottom right-hand corner. The name C Crew was abbreviated from Corner Crew and it started to spread. One guy got a bit confused and in his eagerness for instant recognition had a tattoo with the words 'Sea Crew' proudly emblazoned on his arm, not the brightest thing to do but the thought was there. One C Crew lad off the Bromford called Smiffy had a banner at an away game in the Andy Gray era with 'Andy Grey is bionic', so spelling wasn't our game.

In those days our social calendar was all about the C Crew lads. We would drink together during the week, some of the lads shared digs together and Friday nights we would all meet up at the Hole in the Wall with our birds. Our women put up with a lot when you think about it, as because of our reputation and notoriety we always ended up rowing with Blues lads who wanted to make a name for themselves. Isn't it funny how they always seem to have a pop when you are out with your missus. There are loads of tales about this. I was forever brawling on the late bus and my missus would wade in with her stiletto heels, while Danny was jumped on the ramp by 20 Blues when he was with his missus.

You could say it went with the territory, and yes, we got ourselves into scrapes throughout the week, it wasn't just match day for us, we were at it 24/7, but that was the life we were living. We had a strong front line and I mean proper, a good 40 who were all willing to put themselves on the line. It would be difficult to pick anybody out as they were all very, very good and very important to what we were trying to achieve. The C Crew consisted of white lads with the wedge haircuts, girls both Asian and white, black lads, mixed race, lads from Quinton, Erdington, Kingstanding, Lea Hall, Chelmesley Wood, Kings Heath, Coleshill, Bromford, Maypole, West Heath, Shirley, as well as the usual Villa strongholds. For some games we could turn out 400 but the hardcore was a good 200 and when some lads couldn't make the game others were able to lead the crew. This was not about a few individuals; it was organised, it was quantity and above anything it was quality.

DANNY THE C CREW MEET THE NATIONAL FRONT

It was a Sunday in 1979 and we were really starting to get together and earn our spurs. I look back now and think how naïve we were at times, but we had no fear and we wanted action. Millwall were playing at Walsall and our plan was to meet in the city centre and get the train to Walsall to find Millwall for a tear-up. There must have been about 25 of us, with all the usual frontline faces (Heaffy, Joycey, Reggie, Lloyd, Buster) ready for a row. Millwall of course had that notoriety factor and it was still only a couple of years after the *Panorama* documentary, so fuck the Sunday roast, let's get over to have it with the Treatment or Halfway Line lot, or those loons dressed as mummies.

As we walked down Corporation Street in the town, going past the Odeon cinema, one of the lads said, 'He's in there, Maquade.' Maquade was one of Blues' main lads, a skinhead who was a National Front sympathiser and had a firm of lads with him who hated blacks and Irish. I thought, *yes, I am having him*, and walked towards where they told me he was, which was a pub blown up by the IRA five years earlier now called Bar St Martin. Outside the pub were a few skinheads in their regimental Doc Martens, braces and Fred Perry tee-shirts.

I went in and scanned the boozer, and fucking hell, there was a face I knew instantly from the various television programmes about him and especially the coverage he had received on *World In Action*. It was Martin Webster, the leader of the National Front. I was almost elated that we had bumped into a real prize, a guy who to most young West Indians was our Adolf Hitler. Without going over the top, imagine being a young Jew in wartime Poland and Hitler is on your doorstep. What an opportunity to get to him.

I turned to the lads and said, 'Give me a minute, don't do anything till I give the orders.' I then went for a piss in the pub loo. It was full of skinheads but I wasn't interested in them, I wanted Webster, he was my target. I had forgotten about Millwall and most of the lads had too, there would be other opportunities to have it with another football firm but to have it with the NF was too big an opportunity to miss.

Before I was active on the rowing scene, I had been as an observer a number of times at National Front marches in Birmingham, which seemed to be a regular occurrence, mainly due to the publicity they could get on the back of the 1974 pub bombings. At these marches I witnessed some real battles, which seemed to attract people from all walks of life: left-wing students, blacks, Irish, whites, and football hooligans who just wanted the ruck and who were on both sides of the march, and of course baton-happy Old Bill.

One of these marches was on a winter Saturday afternoon in Digbeth city centre. The Villa home game and the Blues away game were both called off due to waterlogged pitches. The national press landed. They were hooked up at every viewpoint, taking shots. I still remember it as if it was yesterday. The proudest moment of that day for me was seeing my old history teacher, Mr Edwards, fronting the National Front while seated on the shoulders of this big Rastafarian guy, giving the V-sign. That shot made the front cover of every newspaper in the country the next day, with the words 'racist scum get out of Brum'. That day was surreal. Villa Steamers were getting stuck into Blues skinheads who were in the middle of the National Front march, with one of them pleading innocence as Foxy from the Steamers was bashing several kinds of shit out of him. In those days Blues were very much National Front sympathisers.

Getting back to the pub, I came out of the loo to hear, 'Danny, Danny, they're leaving.' Webster and the NF lot were now on the move, going in the direction we had originally come from. We shadowed them, picked up the pace and broke into a trot, then started the chant, 'We hate National Front, we hate National Front.' They turned and faced us, a mob of 40 skinheads looking like a Sham 69 reunion, with their Doc boots, braces and bleached jeans. This was no time for any stand-off, we went straight into them, white, black and Irish lads uniting under one flag, the C Crew flag. Fists and boots flew in and we were soon getting the better of them, and even though a lot of their lads were older they didn't seem up for a row.

We forced them back and then ran them the length of New Street to the alleyway by the Britannia Hotel, but we couldn't get to Martin Webster. The evil bastard was not front line helping his troops, he was getting out of the way and didn't want his hands dirty. Just as we got close, a car pulled up in a screech of tyres and four big old lumps jumped out, armed with hammers. Our adrenalin carried us through and they couldn't force us back but they did a professional job of getting their leader away from a very hostile situation.

We had done very well. It was the start of a personal crusade for me and the C Crew lads, that whenever we knew there was a NF march then we would be there. We were not allowing that filth in our city. He may have lived to fight or hide another day but the message was out and I hope Webster carried a few scars from that day. For all the hired muscle he had, they were no match for a set of lads fighting a cause. After that day, I became a marked man by the National Front. They would drive round Erdington, firmed up, looking for me. They even printed calling cards with the words 'Black Nigger Danny Wanted Dead or Alive'. Birmingham City also picked up on that technique of intimidation, printing their own cards calling for my head.

The Handsworth Riots

The History Book Version: The two Handsworth riots occurred in the inner-city Handsworth district of Birmingham during the summers of 1981 and 1985. They were allegedy caused by heavy-handed policing and drug-related problems, fueled by a nationwide wave of uprisings in the wake of the April 1981 Brixton riot. Other reports claimed that the local African-Caribbean community felt aggrieved at the increase in Asian-owned businesses that were prospering in the area. Violent racism existed in the city from both cultures. It has been argued that the riots really arose from poor social conditions, racial discrimination, poverty, unemployment, and dilapidated housing.

The first riot took place on 10 July 1981. The second, larger riot took occurred between 9-11 September 1985 and was reportedly sparked by the arrest of a man near the Acapulco Cafe, Lozells and a police raid on the Villa Cross public house in the same area. Hundreds of people attacked police and property, looting and smashing, even setting off fire bombs. Two people were left dead, two were unaccounted for, 35 were injured, over 1500 police officers were drafted into the area, around 45 shops were looted and burned, and the cost of the damage ran into many hundreds of thousands of pounds. The second riot was seen as the spark for similar riots across the country, notably on the Broadwater Farm Estate in London.

That's the official history book version, but it doesn't tell the whole truth. First of all, the 1981 riot was in my opinion more intense and bigger. The part the C Crew played in it, on that hot summer weekend in 1981, will always be remembered by those who were there, but you're not going to read about it in any history book, that's for sure. The Tories were part of the problem, not least their leader Margaret Thatcher. She once made a quote saying any woman who understands the problems of running a home will be nearer to understanding the problems of running a country – ha, ha, ha! She had also made her views on race known with her speech, 'Don't play the race card with us.'

Just like the C Crew, the Cool Cats, Man City's top firm, were multi-racial and were about to do their own thing in Moss Side. As the C Crew marched up Lozells Road towards Soho Road, black and white youths were together. Most of the shop windows were boarded up. Some of the lads thought I was mad taking the firm into Handsworth, but I knew different. This was my old manor, I learned my trade on these very streets and I knew we would be all right.

By the time we got to Villa Cross, we had well-known black heads from my school days marching with us, even law-abiding citizens joined the pack. I felt like a drum major going to war with his merry men. We went past my old house on Villa Road and I looked over at number 46 and started thinking about Enoch Powell's famous 'Rivers of Blood' speech delivered in Birmingham some years before. The little devil popped up on my shoulder and said, *keep it up son, don't fuck up now!* We are now at the top of Villa Rd looking on towards Soho Road and we couldn't believe what meets our eyes …Brittle is standing there by Monte's nightclub with a firm of C Crew lads! He and the rest of the lads were well up for it.

We stood around waiting for the orders, waiting for it to go off.

I showed the lads all the Handsworth firms from the area, my older brother's Popeye Crew, the famous Finch Road Crew, even the Aston and Newtown boys had turned out, all the firms from North Birmingham regions were presents with their braves. My brother, Popeye, was doing bird at the time – that was nothing new with him, as he seemed to spend a lot of time in the nick. Years later, he would be involved in Britain's biggest ever prison riot when the inmates took control of HMP Strangeways in Manchester. Some of his firm, the older lot, called me over.

'Young Popeye, who the fuck are these white guys with you?'

I told them they were my firm, the C Crew special forces, the boys from Villa Park.

'I've fought with these guys all over England,' I said. 'They have the courage of Indian warriors.'

They smiled and said, 'You're as mad as your brother.'

Standing and waiting was like being in hell's kitchen. This was going to be some uprising. Black and white British youths were going to do what Northern Irish youth in Belfast and Derry had been doing for years. As the sun went down that night, we were ready for the confrontation, and for the next forty-eight hours, the C Crew and the Handsworth firms fought a running battle with the West Midlands Police, while Handsworth burnt to the ground. We didn't care about the free market, what the fuck was that? What Mrs Thatcher didn't understand was that rioting was the voice of the working class, black and white. Youth in other parts of the country rioted too. Toxteth in Liverpool burnt down. Jimmy Gittins, a Man City match-day boy, got nicked for his part in the Moss Side riots after leading the Cool Cats into battle and was sentenced to four years in prison. 'Young black hooligan gets four years,' I hear you law-abiding citizens cry. Well for the record, little Jimmy Gittins is not black, but he was a football hooligan – and was proud of it too. I later became good friends with Jimmy at HMP Swinfen Hall when I was serving three years.

I also took part in the 1985 riots. The C Crew were no longer so active. Lloyd had received a long prison sentence, Brittle was in and out of prison like an yo-yo, something that would never change for the kid over the years, while Ravenhall was doing his own thing with the Villa Youth. Things had changed in Handsworth. Most of the young lads would now hang out at the Acapulco Cafe or the Villa Cross pub. A crew from Erdington Slade Road called Spears had moved to Handswoth at the time and were at war with the local lads. Coming from Erdington and growing up in Handsworth, I felt I had loyalties to both sides, so I decided from the start of the riots that I was going to be a lone sniper, doing my own thing.

One night the Birmingham City Zulus landed with a big crew, thinking they could jump me, as I was own my own. This was typical of them. When my brother's crew saw what was going on, the Zulus were warned that this was North Birmingham and I was classed as a blood brother on this turf. No one was going to bully me on this manor. Mr X was packing a firearm and the ball was in their court. Deep down, I'm glad they never made a move, as they would have gone back to the south side in body bags, trust me.

7 CHAMPIONS OF ENGLAND, PART ONE

DANNY

VILLA under Ron Saunders won promotion in his first year in charge and then he assembled another team that we thought could go on and seriously challenge for major honours. Things were looking up. We won the League Cup in 1975 and then built possibly the most exciting side of my lifetime, with the likes of Gidman, Gray, Little and Deehan. We won the League Cup again after three epic games against Everton in 1977 and that season also finished fourth in the league and got to the quarter-finals of the FA Cup. All this trainspotter or anorak stuff is important as most people have the likes of myself and many of the lads down as outright hooligans; well yes, we liked a fight but that does not mean that we were not mad about the Villa either. If it meant no row and us winning, most were happy; a row and a win and it was happy days all round.

The following season we made it to the quarter finals of the UEFA Cup, losing to a Johan Cruyff-inspired Barcelona, then in 1980 we once again got to the quarter-finals of the FA Cup, losing to West Ham, while finishing a creditable seventh in the league. Under Saunders we had faith, he was a messiah, our Bill Shankly and out of the same mould. Very dry and deadpan was Ron and under his stewardship we never finished out of the top eight once we returned to our rightful place in the top tier of English football.

In 1979 he lost patience with Gidman and Gray and sold them, even though Gray was the darling of the Holte End. Despite cracks beginning to appear we trusted him and he started to rebuild another side around a solid spine in Jimmy Rimmer and Ken McNaught, and somehow he converted Alan Evans and Kenny Swain from strikers to defenders. Along with the industry and dependability of Mortimer and Bremner, he had the skill and tricks of Gordon Cowans, Gary Shaw and Tony Morley and it was plain to see that he was only missing one final piece of the jigsaw, a centre forward who could score goals, lead the line and put himself about a bit – which made the sale of Gray somewhat mystifying. Ron had tried the likes of Donovan and Geddis and it hadn't worked so he went out and bought Peter Withe, even though he had played for our bitter rivals previously. We pinned our faith in Saunders, never wavered in our belief that he would make us champions again and in the 1980/81 season he delivered the championship dream, within seven years of taking over a Second Division side.

It was not just on the pitch where we were getting our act together. Off it we were learning fast. With improved performances came bigger support and with that, as is the case with most clubs, that support becomes more troublesome. Again this is important, as I know many people will say that we only had a decent firm when we were successful. That is nonsense. For years we had a hardcore following who gave in the main as good as it got. The so-called glory years carried it on to a new level and made us a formidable outfit. During this time, Brittle had progressed through the ranks and had started to get us organised and was, as he is now, one of the main respected faces on the scene.

BRITTLE

The West Ham cup game had taught us a lot of lessons about the importance of being organised. By the time the 1980/81 season came around, we were well up for it and as organised as we could have been. The first game of the season was Leeds away and that was as good a test as you could get. Andy and I had struck a deal with National Travel at Digbeth coach station where we could order coaches to suit the number of people that turned up. That day in August saw 100 turn up, so we ordered two coaches. I have to be honest and say that when I saw the 100, I didn't feel over-confident. I didn't see many of the Steamers on the coaches and it looked a very young firm. A lot of the lads had got the wedge haircuts that were popular with the Scousers and dressed like Scousers. They might have looked good in Liverpool but they stood out there at the Mayfair nightclub, where we waited for the coaches, and looked far from a frightening group of fighters who were on their way to take on one of the most respected mobs in the country.

One of the lads, Moses, was for some reason a Leeds fan and had been with their away firm at the Midlands grounds. He was telling us all about the Leeds bird called Ellen who used to get stuck in and was a rower, even glassing one unlucky bloke who thought she should be at home knitting instead of trying to take off his face. Our lads were a bit jumpy about that but as the crew developed we had our own birds on the firm who were better looking and came in very handy, like Donna and Pauline. Pauline in the home game that season ended up chinning the Leeds bird Ellen, so having women in the firm does help because blokes are wary of hitting a bird. They also managed to sneak tools into games for the lads even if the General was always saying, 'You can't bring birds away.' He saw it as a weakness taking them and didn't want them around us, but many of us agreed that apart from sexual and kitchen duties they did have their uses!

I knew almost everyone on the two coaches and while I knew we had some very good lads with us, I worried about our age. The majority were young and Leeds had been right up there as a very game firm for many years. When we got there and began to walk to the ground without an escort, all sorts of things were going through my mind. Here were me and Andy trying to get it together and it could all go pear-shaped at the first game. As we got near the ground, the chants of 'Leeds, Leeds, Leeds' started and we began to get bombarded with bottles and glasses, which were coming down on us from a balcony above a pub. Leeds were on both sides of the road and coming straight at us.

I must admit to being a bit surprised when our lads went straight into them. Not one backward step was taken and our only problem was ducking and dodging the glasses and bottles being lobbed from the balcony. There was hands-on fighting and everyone stuck together. Leeds kept backing off and in the end the bombardment stopped because we were right in amongst them and they were hitting their own. Leeds had scattered by the time the police arrived on the scene and it was only when the OB had us in an escort that they came back. At one stage, as were walking alongside a row of buses, Leeds came in between the buses for another go but it was never going to develop further due to the police presence.

The game passed off peacefully enough and we were escorted back to the coaches and out of Leeds without any more incidents. On the way home, the coaches stopped off at a pub called the Derbyshire Yeoman in Derby, and as soon as we arrived some Villa fans came over to us and told us they were on a minibus and were having grief from a coachload of Grimsby on their way back from somewhere like Shrewsbury The cavalry charged and the Grimsby retreated without a murmur. It was a superb ending to a first outing.

Unfortunately the OB arrived at this point and took the coaches off to the local station. It turned out that there was a couple of Steamers on the coaches after all, and after what had happened to them at Hilton Park back in 1975 they decided it was best to do one there and then. As it went it was the wrong call because nobody got charged, we were all released and back in the Hole in the Wall long before those who'd left the coaches at Derby.

After the success of the Leeds trip, things began to snowball. By now Moses' firm were using the coaches as well as a few other separate groups, and after trips to Man City and Leeds again in the League Cup, anyone who was anyone was using the coaches. The firm went from strength to strength.

On September 6, we were due to play at Ipswich. Andy and I

decided to take one coach on to Great Yarmouth after the game, with a second going straight back to Birmingham. Ipswich were not really taken seriously as a team with a firm, and it was one of those days where you went for the crack and the football, with little expectation of a row.

The football wasn't up to much and we lost 1-0. Ten minutes from the end, about 20 of the lads decided to go out and try and get into the Ipswich section for a play-up. Before they made it amongst the Tractor Boys, they were spotted and 30 Ipswich came out, including a group of black lads. Now two months earlier, Heaffy and Ozzie had been in Brum town centre, by the landmark Rackhams on Corporation Street, when they had bumped into Cud and his Blues firm, which was the norm for a Saturday night . The pair nodded to each other and re-enacted their own Butch Cassidy and the Sundance Kid scene, clasping hands and charging the Blues, taking a few slaps as they went headfirst into them. Just as it was looking as if the numbers would get the better of them, the cavalry arrived in the shape of the C Crew. Although Ozzie was going head to head with Cud, the Noses were now on the back foot and ran into Oasis Market, with Cud taking refuge among the leather jackets. No worries, it happens to the best of them.

This time, Heaffy and Ozzie weren't so lucky. As Heaffy raised his fist to smack one of the black lads, BANG BANG BANG, he was cracked three times. It turned out these lads were martial arts experts and knew what they were doing. Heaffy was knocked clean out, and this time Ozzie was clean out alongside him, horizontal in fact, with no cavalry to repel the enemy. However, Jimmy Coley wasn't budging and stood over Ozzie to fight off all these martial arts lads. Seeing that the numbers were certainly not in his favour, Jimmy saw out of the corner of his eye an old bloke with a walking stick, and quickly took it off him, using it to protect his pal and fight off the Ipswich lads. He was too busy to notice that the old bloke was also on the floor now, having fallen over. Jimmy dragged Ozzie of out the way and Moses pulled Heaffy out, saving them from a proper hiding. As they said afterwards, you don't leave your mates, do you?

The lads made a hasty retreat back to the coaches and met the rest of us, who were amazed that they had come unstuck at a place like Ipswich. That firm had had it with Cockneys, Scousers, Blues, Leeds and Man United and nobody had got the better of us. Although only 20 were involved, it was still a shock when everyone found out we had been sent packing by fucking Ipswich.

We got the rest of the crew rounded up but it was too late to do anything about it, as the OB were about outside and moved us onto the coaches. When we set off there was about seventy crammed onto the Yarmouth coach and thirty on the one going straight back to Brum, and true to form after a bad day at the office there was a lot of arguing going on as we headed to Yarmouth over what had happened at Ipswich. Sometimes you have to put your hands up and admit you fucked up and this was one of those days. Twenty of our lads thought they could take the piss and got their hands burnt. It happens to the best of us at some stage.

A crammed coach was a regular occurrence and often it was a case of get on quick or you will be sitting on the floor. Danny once ran a coach to Newcastle and we had 150 on a 54-seater, with some people sitting six to a seat. You wonder now in the days of luxury travel how and why we did it, but in those days a four-hour journey with a coach rammed with three times the amount was common practice, no bogs, no drinks machines, just cheap lager, carrier bags and cans of piss out of the skylight and the sight of people up in the luggage racks for somewhere to sit. But you do what you do for the Villa, the same as lads did for their clubs all over the country. Without sounding like an old bastard, the youth lads today don't realise how lucky they are!

The problems we had with Ipswich and the fact we had a rammed coach made the atmosphere moody among the lads when we landed in Yarmouth. I just knew that it was going to kick off at some stage. It wasn't long before some of us came across a pub with a load of Spurs inside and we decided to steam the pub and went straight in and gave the Londoners a bit of stick. It wasn't a big deal and nobody got badly hurt but as we were making good our escape, police patrol cars began landing and nicking lads who were on their toes. Something like eight got nicked in that incident and throughout the night a few more were pulled in on various charges, the most serious being when a couple were arrested after a jeweller's got looted. Some people's misfortune can be others' good luck and while we all felt for those locked up there was a lot more room on the coach going back to Brum!

Everyone who was nicked got bail except the two nicked for the jeweller's, who ended up in Norwich prison. On the Tuesday afterwards, I bumped into Curl and Buster, two lads who had been arrested in Yarmouth, and they looked in a right state. They told me how they had just got back, having been bailed on the Sunday morning with no money, meaning they had to walk and hitch their way home, which took them over two days. Buster collapsed at West Bromwich. Comically, he said he didn't want to bother the old man to pick him up. (One thing to put right: the name C Crew did not come from such jaunts to the seaside.)

We were in full control of Brum town centre by this time as the Blues firm was in a bit of a transitional period. A lot of their old lads had dropped out and their main firm, the Apex, weren't up to much. They would find themselves a pub in town to use, we would find out where they were drinking, go round, do them and they would move on to somewhere else. This was a process that went on through the whole of that season and while they had no base due to us ousting them every time they settled, our lads had begun using the Hole in the Wall pub in Dale End and that became our HQ.

In October, we played the Blues away but quite simply they weren't at the races and while I don't doubt they had a little firm tucked away somewhere before the game, we never knew where they were. The walk to the ground was uneventful, as we saw nothing that resembled a Blues firm. After the game, the same thing happened on the way back into town, with not a sniff of their firm. The C Crew spent the night in the Hole in the Wall and various spotters went looking in different pubs throughout the night. I would say it was highly unlikely that the Blues had a firm in town that night and the whole thing passed off as one of the quietest derbies ever, despite us beating them on their own patch.

October was a great month and we won five of the six games we played, drawing just one, a 3-3 classic at Old Trafford, where despite us taking a good following the famous Red Army were not playing. At Old Trafford that day there were less than 39,000, a crowd that included 4,000 Villa fans. These are the forgotten years to the Mancs, as if you listen to them they are the most loyal fans in the world and if you can be bothered listening to the drivel they spout very few admit that their home games were anything other than a sell-out since World War Two!

The following month we were away at West Brom, who along with Coventry were the weakest West Midland team firm-wise. We were drinking in the Philibuster boozer opposite the buses that took you from town to the Albion and the original plan was to get onto the buses but somebody decided we should go by train and we caught one from New Street. Now if we had got off at Rolfe Street the Old Bill would have wrapped us up but we went past there and got off at Smethwick West, resulting in a long walk back to the ground. The decision was made to go into the Brummie Road, their main end. We were late and the game had started and we ran to get in. What we didn't realise was that the turnstiles for the Brummie Road and the Woodman's Corner were right next to each other, so thinking it was all the same we went in through both sets of turnstiles, which split the mob in two.

We managed to get at the back of the Brummie Road and let out the C Crew roar but we hadn't got the numbers to give it a good go. It was a pity the mob was split up. The Old Bill got control of it just as we were scaling fences, while the Albion in their best Black Country accents were screaming, 'You Villa bastards,' at us and baying for blood. We had taken the piss a little and they were surprised that the C Crew had infiltrated their home end.

The Villa fans were opposite in the Smethwick End but the police started to take us the other way, which meant they were going to throw us all out. We weren't going to have that so we had no choice but to run across the pitch and into the Villa end. It resulted in the game being stopped as 200 C Crew ran the length of the pitch. It was all shown on *Match Of The Day* and they and the FA made a big deal of it. The sight of someone throwing a corner flag, spear-like, into the home fans did little to help the condemnation of us all but it wasn't really a big deal and we only went onto the pitch because we knew the OB were going to make us pay in again, which before the days of CCTV was a foolish decision and one that they regretted.

A 0-0 draw that day saw our run of five wins on the bounce ended but things were looking good and we were looking down at the rest of the clubs, although Saunders was remaining cautious, saying, 'We have got off to a good start but it's too early to start making forecasts.' We loved the bloke but despite his caution did not want to hear that kind of stuff, we wanted to win the fucking thing, and despite Ron's caution, the fact that we did not have the distraction of a League Cup campaign – we had been unceremoniously dumped out at Cambridge – and no European distractions gave us a great chance in a three-way race with Liverpool and the media darlings Ipswich Town.

The biggest game of the season to date came on November 22; we were top of the league and were away at Liverpool, the reigning champions. Over the previous few years we had a bit of a history with Liverpool and it's fair to say our firm hated Liverpool, a bit like most teams hate Man United these days. The game was an opportunity to go and give it to the Scousers on their own turf.

We knew there was going to be a big turnout for this one so we had ordered four coaches in advance. These were filled in no time and we sent for a fifth, then a sixth and finally a seventh. We were 350-handed and got there fairly early. Stanley Park, the scene of many previous attacks on Villa fans, was empty, with no Liverpool firm in sight. At the time, we very rarely went into pubs, preferring to go on walkabouts looking for opposing firms.

This was the day that we noticed Melvin for the first time. Melvin was one of the coach drivers, a bloke in his forties, and as we charged across Stanley Park he was there with us, loving every second of it. This became a regular thing and wherever we went, up and down the country, Melvin drove us and was always there when anything happened. The bloke must have been in his element, getting paid overtime for working Saturday and then joining in the rowing. Talk about having your cake and eating it. After that day, we always made sure Melvin was driving coach number one, which consisted of all the main lads. A lot of the fares received from the other coaches subsidized coach number one, where not everybody paid. He was very accommodating and whenever we passed opposing firms he would always pull over and let us pile out. On one occasion he even turned round and drove back so we could engage the mob we had just missed. He became an honorary member of the C Crew and made sure that coach one had no passengers whatsoever when it came to the row.

When we got into the ground, they put us into a section in the far corner of the Anfield Road end. By now Liverpool had got a firm together on the other side of the barriers but we managed to get in with them and they gave it up without a whimper. This was a real bonus, as the section they had given had been jam-packed and it was nice to have a bit of room to breathe again.

When we got outside again, we headed to the coaches and went back across the park in case they were about. We got our wish. It became our own little warzone because they attacked us from the front and the back. We were between the railings and battling through them at the zebra crossings on Priory Road. I was thinking we were doing well considering the numbers and unlike earlier years we had a good firm that was holding the line well, something you needed, as if you were split up Liverpool in those days made you pay for it. We had taken some casualties, Benji had got a broken nose from a cosh, but generally we were in good shape.

Then one of the lads turned to me and said, 'Brittle, look what's coming, I can't see us holding this lot off.' I looked up and saw what must have been 200 lads. There was no way we would have been able to hold it – but it was only the other C Crew lads, led by Moses! Yes it was a relief but the Old Bill prevented us turning them over good and proper. Once they saw what we had pulled together, the Scouse police were gamer than the lads and with the help of horses and the big night sticks that everyone will still have nightmares about we were baton-charged back to the coaches and sent packing.

Our form had dipped and we lost at Anfield, then went on to drop a point at home to Arsenal and disastrously lose at Boro, which took us to the return against the Blues during our worst run of the season. It was the kind of game we could have done without, they were mid-table and once again destined to win a big fat fuck-all but they still had the chance to cock things up for us, which no doubt would have been as good as them winning the World Cup, the Boat Race and an Olympic gold in the shot-put all on the same day, such is their obsession with the Villa.

We need not have worried as thanks to Gary Shaw, our home-grown hero who terrorised them that day, December 13 was unlucky for some and the Blues' dream of ending our dream was over. It ended Villa 3, Blues 0, and what a day. Geddis bagged a brace and in the process will never be forgotten; although he was better for Ipswich he will be fondly remembered for this game in what turned out to be our championship-winning season.

A few Noses tried their luck in the Holte, a few were done, most were surrounded by plod and escorted out, don't get the impression that they tried anything spectacular because they did not, it was mainly a case of get down the front, sing and shout, make their whereabouts known and quickly get escorted out, game over, as so much of the 'making a show' is today. In fact many will tell you the Blues invented that trick.

Most of the lads were up for it, as a few seasons earlier they had shown on Aston Park and we had never heard the last of it, so this was a game where liberties were not going to be allowed. The time they showed on the park was another game we had won, we had beaten the bastards 2-1 and too many were celebrating and not with it out of sheer ecstasy, leaving a number of our youngsters outside to get run. Well that was not going to be the case today, even after smashing them on the pitch.

Everyone was out at the final whistle and looking for them, on the park, down Witton Lane, by the Serpentine, up for it as we had been before the game, and out in numbers. From the spouting that had come from the south side of the city about the park incident, this was, from a Villa perspective, a poor showing by them, and bear in mind that the away numbers brought to second-city derbies in those days would be at least 10,000. There were minor incidents on the walk back into town but there was no great showing from the Apex or Trooper firms, who were the pre-Zulu squads. In town it was more of the same and it seemed to us that it was a game that had been played in Birmingham 8, not Birmingham 6.

The night was to be a busy night. Even though all the lads were over the moon with the result, they had been equally disappointed at the lack of a show from their main rivals from across the city. Most of the usual faces were in the Hole in the Wall this night enjoying a *craic* along with a few of the younger lads but the place was by no means packed and none was expecting much to happen until all the boozers in town started to empty, when they knew it would turn lively. At around 7.30, the good-humoured banter was interrupted by the unwelcome presence of a dozen or so familiar faces of the Blue persuasion, who cheekily walked down the stairs, fucking the Geordie bouncer out of the way, and calmly walked up to the bar. One of the cocky twats even ordered a round.

A silence fell on the pub as everyone looked around for confirmation from one another that this was really happening. One recollection is that it 'seemed like the jukebox turned itself off'. One of the Steamers, Mousey, who was seated in the middle of the room with some older heads stood up and said, 'You ain't welcome lads, you're gonna have to go,' and bang, it's off. The place erupted like it was a saloon brawl in the Wild West, not the fucking West Midlands.

Recollections of who threw the first blow are somewhat unclear, some say it was a Steamer, others reckon it was a Bluenose, but there are no arguments as to who did the most damage that night, of which a big part was played by Clarkey.

In all the years of rows I have had, I have never seriously sought to injure anyone badly, bit that feeling changes when we play the Blues. I can honestly say that I have never taken a backward step when I have faced them. This night was no different. Big Sean and H also did their bit, one of the Noses was knocked out cold and spent a few days in the Birmingham General Hospital, another, realising they had fucked up big time, jumped the bar to safety and never appeared until the fat lady was singing, and she didn't sing, 'Keep Right On!'

Respect was given to the Blues lads who came down the stairs, they were obviously game and came in for one reason, but they bit off a bit more than they could chew. Many things have been said about this particular row, the Blues take on it being that they 'didn't have the numbers' and the Villa's being, 'Bollocks, stay out of our pub.' The fact is that while we had numbers in there we also had quality and had it been equal numbers the outcome would have been the same.

A few of the younger lads followed the Blues out of the pub, not for a row but to see if they were okay; apparently they had a couple of relatives amongst the Blue boys who worked on the markets. Another one of the Villa lads realised afterwards that it was his cousin who was 'spark out' on the pub floor. Families, 'eh! 'Who's the black bastard who was doing all the damage?' was the message that came back down the stairs with them.

DANNY

The night was only just getting started. I was with another Villa firm who missed this episode by minutes, and we turned up with information on where the rest of the Blues were drinking. By now Villa were pissed off with the Noses for invading their manor in town but at the same time were buzzing on adrenaline from the row, so we decided it was time to take it back to them.

First stop was the Gilded Cage, a well-known Blues pub just yards from the ramp at New Street. There were probably 30-40 Villa, made up of mostly the youngsters with a few older heads showing them the ropes, and it was up to them to give a few surprise knocks. Once at the Gilded Cage, the bouncers quickly locked the doors. One Blues lad, a big, fat, drainpipe-wearing clown spotted not only because of his earlier infringement on the Holte End, where he had taken a slap and bulldozed his way to the safety of the pitch, but also because of his prehistoric dress sense, was at the bus stop on his own, sensing that this is not going to be his day. In seconds the roar goes up and it was game on as his own firm had finally turned up, allowing him to relax into his ringside seat, grinning like a fat Cheshire cat.

The Blues came running down towards their enemy, bottles flying and smashing yards in front of the Villa lads, who were a bit slow off the mark, with the younger lot unsure how it was going to go but understanding it was now or never. The hail of bottles started to slow as the Blues firm were now right in our faces, fronted by a white kid, black faces yards behind him, bouncing and shouting, 'Villa bastards, come on!' Villa fronted them and one lad close enough caught the first Bluenose with a right-hander, then the boots went in as all the Villa lads followed suit. It was off and the Villa steamed into them.

The Blues were not prepared, everyone was now buzzing and the Blues were backing off, boots and fists were raining into them. Unlike them I will be honest here and say that white kid at the front deserved a George Cross as he was trying his hardest to keep them together. His cries of 'Stand Blues' were falling on deaf ears and they were soon getting backed off. Even the game ones eventually turned and fucked off, no disrespect is aimed at them for that as they had little choice. Drainpipe boy followed suit a bit sharpish and did the doughnut waltz off towards Hill Street, game over for lardy arse, but his drainpipes had come in handy!

Next call was Sam Weller's and then the Grapes yards down the road, both Blues watering holes where Blues were conspicuous by their absence. The word came back that there was a firm from the Trooper at the Viking pub. No one was quite sure why as this was a well-known haunt for those that, well, bat for the other side, if you know what I mean. Villa walked towards the Locarno, turning left onto the Queensway, a dual carriageway that leads to the back of New Street station. Once outside, we noticed a row of Vespa scooters and realised that there was a do on and that the Blues must be downstairs where the music was coming from. A few of the Villa boys went into the main bar area and stood with their backs to the bar facing the stairway, and it wasn't to hide their arses from the other punters. The rest of the lads were staring straight through the massive plate glass window and a barman in a Bobby Crush-style shirt who offered his services with a bemused look was ignored.

It was another one of those listening-to-a-pin-drop cases when a single kid walked up the stairs into the bar and realised it was on top. CRASH ... one of the scooters came flying through the front window. The kid retreated back down but others were on their way up and it was total mayhem. The first Blues lot ran for the door and a couple jumped through the hole that had been a window but were trapped and done in. The second lot got to the top of the stairs to go the same way but were caught from the back as the lads in the bar came from behind. From this point, lads were either getting caned or were rapidly charging through the volley of boots and fists. Some Blues ran towards New Street with Villa in tow, some towards Hurst Street, same thing, same outcome.

Then came the first sound of the siren and the other boys in blue were out of the vans and getting stuck in far more eagerly than the Blues. The empty seats of the van were soon occupied by a fair few boys from the north side of the city, and one from the south, who apparently wasn't keen on getting his head slapped all the way back to Digbeth. It was funny as a lone copper acted as his guardian and headmaster to the others shouting, 'Fucking pack it in you lot.'

Now, we all think that the Old Bill wouldn't laugh at Spike Milligan if they were stoned on a pound of green, but they have

A rowdy gathering of Villa skins, suedeheads and greasers outside the Aston Hotel in Birmingham in 1970

Villa fans invade the pitch at Mansfield to celebrate promotion from the Third Division in 1972. It would take three more years to get back in the top flight.

The legendary Pete the Greek, the terrace veteran famous for such exploits as headbutting a police horse and fighting Millwall's top boy one-on-one.

Fighting breaks out between Villa and Arsenal fans on the pitch at Highbury.

Black Danny (right) celebrates Villa winning the League Championship in 1981 on the balcony of Birmingham Town Hall with the players.

Arsenal away, the day Aston Villa won the League: waiting to board the C Crew coaches, with Danny wearing the shirt Villa player Tony Morley had given him the week before.

The C Crew in Birmingham city centre: black and white united under one banner.

On the march to the Blue House pub, near Everton's Goodison Park ground, on the day we took it over in 1981.

Some of the lads in town circa 1981. From left: Ceedy, Heaffy, Tommy and Roger from Coleshill.

A *Sun* cartoon during the Falklands War suggested
Villa's hooligans could be sent in to sort out the Argies.

After rioting at Anderlecht, Villa were forced to play their next European home
game behind closed doors. This was the view from the Holte End.

Boxing for the Villa: Black Danny (in action, left) was a stalwart of Aston Villa ABC: 'We had a huge sense of pride when we boxed in the claret and blue.'

Other boxers (below) included: (1) Dave Ravenhall, (2) Steven Dalton and (3) Desmond Gallagher, with coach Paddy Riley (4).

The Aston Villa ABC a few years on, including: (1) James Campbell, (2) Leon Johnson, (3) Steven Dalton, (4) Joe Malcolm aka Al Malcome, and (5) Reggie Bennett.

They don't make goalposts like they used to: a spot of ground-wrecking at Southampton (above) and Queens Park Rangers (below).

Main lads Andy Browne (left) and Jimmy Ryan (sitting) at a social function.

Brittle with broken hand, taking a well deserved rest after a hard night's rioting in Brussels, Belgium.

got a sense of humour, sick yes, but they have got one and this night they excelled themselves. They charged the lone Bluenose last, seizing on the opportunity to squeeze a bit of info that might 'help them with their enquiries'. He must have done the right thing by all the arrested parties and for his trouble he nearly got to spend the rest of the evening in a cell with what must have first looked like a pack of claret and blue hyenas. He wasn't to know that he was not going to get any more clips around the ear from the lads, but they had to have their last bit of fun for the night. 'You just fucking wait' and 'Don't you dare fall to sleep' and 'Don't you sit down, stand by the fucking door' was all that rang in his ears and the poor lad had to endure five minutes of mental torture before a grinning copper opened the door, shouted, 'Come on son, out you come,' and released him from his private hell. Indeed the 13th was unlucky for some!

That win in front of over 41,000 fans did not kick-start the season again and we lost our next game at relegation-threatened Brighton, before beating Stoke City. Then we drew on our travels to neighbours Forest and followed that up with losing at Ipswich, although the game saw us dumped out of the FA Cup at the first hurdle rather than lose more valuable league points. The following week saw Liverpool visit Villa Park and whilst it was a game that everyone looked forward to, it was a game which had a massive effect on my life. For all the wrong reasons.

8 THE LONGEST DAY

DANNY

IF THERE WAS a more on-top place in the Seventies and Eighties than Goodison Park and Anfield, especially if you were black, then I haven't heard of it. I can't separate them, I see them as the same firm. Imagine putting Villa and Blues together, that's the size of firm they could pull to awaiting away fans. If there was a big game at Liverpool and Everton hadn't got a game or were at a place they didn't fancy going, they would often form a welcoming committee at Lime Street Station or on the infamous Stanley Park. If Liverpool didn't get you in the ground then, depending on your mode of transport, they made sure they got you outside the ground. You were in their city and you were either leaving with a Scouse souvenir from a Stanley blade or minus your money or clothes.

In 1977, I made my first trip to Merseyside and I went on the football special. It pulled into Lime Street and we were then ferried by buses to Anfield, to be greeted by a mass of red and white. As we walked through the back streets, reality hit home: it was 'Welcome to Hell' for blacks. I would imagine it would be a bit like going to Galatasaray these days.

We went in the Anfield Road end and it was supposed to be segregated but as soon as we got in and tried to get up the winding stairs, all you could hear was a deafening chant of, 'We are the Annie Annie Road end,' and as soon as we saw them they were onto us. They kicked us down the stairs and threw a cup of hot tea straight into my face. I laugh when I see the sign in the players' tunnel saying, 'This is Anfield.' People say it is a sign that intimidates opposing players, well a scalding drink in the face and a kick in the bollocks is a lot worse, believe me.

The Old Bill managed to hold them off but I was sick with fear. Me and two other black lads, who I had met for the first time (one who later became front line, a lad called Powelly in the C Crew), were targeted and abused like we had never been before. The Villa fans were further up the terrace and the Steamers were rowing with the Liverpool lot and doing well. People tell me one of the Steamers bottled one of the Scousers and had managed to move them, which was good news for my three-man tag team.

The game didn't go to plan as we actually won 2-1 but the three of us couldn't celebrate, as we were not sure we could get out of this alive. Us winning had made the bastards even worse. The game ended and the Scousers were in their element, giving three frightened black teenagers just out of school maximum abuse, threatening all sorts and pointing outside. The police were no better and were pushing me and the other two outside but I wasn't having any of it. That was when the police showed their true colours, as they began pushing us towards the Liverpool lads who were blocking the huge terrace exit. They were all grinning and waiting for their prey to be thrown to the pack.

In seconds it started, whack after whack after whack. At first I was doing okay in fending them off but then the pack mentality took over and I was stuck in the middle of what can only be described as wild animals. I was punched to the floor and kicked repeatedly. I felt I was drowning and had to get away from them or I was dead. I remember thinking, *where the fuck are the Old Bill?*

I somehow pushed through them and climbed over the fence and onto the pitch, collapsing onto the turf, where the St John Ambulance men took over. I was taken to Walton Hospital. The nurse there asked me who had done it. I said Liverpool fans but she said, 'How do you know?' and muttered something like, 'They wouldn't do that.' I gave up when she asked me who won and I said, 'Villa, two-one,' and she said, 'No, that can't be true either as Liverpool always win at home!' My day of terror didn't end there, as even on the train home I was bullied by Liverpool fans going back to Crewe. They pinched my scarf, my first ever Villa scarf, and I was powerless to fight back.

I was still the civilian supporter and decided to go to Merseyside twice more that season, only this time it was to Everton. Having suffered at Liverpool I tried different modes of transport to avoid them, needless to say it didn't work. At the time *Roots*, which featured a black slave called Chicken George, was a very popular TV drama. On the second visit, I got recognised coming out and that's when I heard, 'Here's Chicken George again.' I was a marked man and wasn't even involved in the violence then, just a civilian, but times were changing and they became the enemy of mine from that day. As I was turning into a hooligan, that meant they had also become an enemy for the C Crew.

Revenge was never going to happen overnight and I had more bad days on Merseyside before I managed to get even, but on 10 January 1981, Villa hosted Liverpool in what was already being dubbed a championship decider. It was a massive game, last season's champions playing a team trying to win the championship for the first time in many years. It was built up all week in the local and national press and everyone connected with the club knew this was the acid test. If we could beat Liverpool it would give us the confidence to go and lift the title.

Now while thousands of Villa supporters were thinking of the game all week, I had been looking forward to this for a lot longer; twelve months longer to be exact. I had been plotting and planning and telling all the C Crew lads that this was the big one. For me even the Blues game didn't run it close. I had some very old scores to settle with this shower. The days of being abused and battered on Stanley Park, facing mobs of Scousers who were intent on doing 'the nigger' that day at Anfield when I had to scale the fence to get away from them after taking the biggest beating of my life, a beating that had me pissing blood for a week, made this day special. For me it was about revenge, pure and simple.

I had been to Everton twice in one season and had a small bit of payback but since then the abuse had got worse and I have to reiterate the point that this lot were the worst in the country, finding it funny to shout at me, 'Here's Chicken George again.' It was a gauntlet we had to run up there and me and the other black C Crew lads didn't separate Everton from Liverpool, as far as I was concerned they were as bad as each other. However, at the time I would say Liverpool were the most hated side in the country, not just because they were winning everything either; the team had an arrogant smugness about them, they were like the Italians of the Football League, all back passes and shut up shop at 1-0 and surround the ref if anything did not go their way.

Off the field some of their followers were quite simply horrible bastards. Forget all this bollocks about friendly cheeky chappies singing funny ditties on the Kop, some of them would rob you, mug you and cut you without thinking twice. They had the numbers as well, it wasn't a case of a small mob, they seemed to have lads everywhere and you could get caught out anywhere near the ground unless you were in numbers and with a firm. They didn't give a fuck if you were a normal fan, if you arrived in their city you were fair game, as many supporters will testify.

I wanted to hurt these people, but unlike them I was not after their civilians, I wanted their boys – their hooligans. I was long past nicking scarves for trophies, my trophy was to damage as many of their lads as I could, and while I am not going to go as far as to say I wanted to kill somebody, at that moment in time I had built myself up for this game big time and wanted them all to know about Black Danny. To me it was about getting to their mob, the lads who had given me a problem so many times. I wanted to do as many of them as possible and for weeks running up to the game I was building others up to do the same. Many did not need me to encourage them, as they had their own stories to tell from visits to Merseyside and the stories were not pleasant.

At this time in my life, people were noticing me, I was in the front line and almost every week I was involved in a row with Villa and was a permanent fixture at the end of the game on Witton Road by the station. There were lads who pound-for-pound were even gamer than me, and in my opinion Brittle should have been regarded as the main man, but being a 6ft 4in black lad I stood out from the rest and people looked up to me, literally.

I was asked by Clarkey to meet him for a drink in the Hole in the Wall. Clarkey was a bit older than me and I respected him, as he was a black lad who had the same shit I had at numerous places and stood up for himself and defended others. He was a guy I feel never got the true recognition he deserved, because anyone will tell you he was a warrior. I just think he was more sensible than me and was a bit wiser about the pitfalls of football violence. Even now some of the Noses don't know him and I am like, 'You're having a laugh, he is one of our top boys and you ain't got anyone that could touch him.' I met him and will never forget what he said. I just wish that I had taken it on board.

He said something along the lines of, 'Danny, you're a great lad and I love what you are doing for the Villa, but look kid, if you carry on as you are you are either going to kill somebody or get killed.'

I look back and thank him for that but I was at that point totally off the rails. The violence, the buzz of going week in, week out, my team winning and going for the league as well as enjoying the respect of being up there with a top crew who were winning their battles off the pitch, it was a great time and I genuinely felt for two seasons we were as good as anyone on and off the pitch. I was on a rollercoaster and my inflated ego was massive. Nobody could touch me. It was like lads who take drugs and start off on marijuana and find after a while it doesn't give them that high so they need to move on to something stronger, well for me this Liverpool game was that. Run-of-the-mill fighting wouldn't be enough, yes I wanted to destroy them, I wanted to give them a permanent reminder they had met Black Danny and the C Crew.

The night before the game, I couldn't sleep. I actually went to the Hole in the Wall to make sure everyone was up for tomorrow, double checking that the word had got round where the meet was and the time was right. This was not a game where we could afford any fuck-ups. My bird at the time was in the C Crew as it happened and she must have been bored with me, as all I spoke about was what I was going to do to the Scousers.

I woke up early, it must have been about 6am, and got dressed, putting on my baseball jacket and my claret baseball cap, which I had customised with the words 'C-Crew' on the front. I wanted them to know it was us. I got into New Street by eight, as we knew that many of the Scousers mixed football with 'work' and liked to get into city centres early to get a bit of lifting in before the match, so it was important we had the firm at New Street early. The plan was to meet in the Rail Bar and there were loads of Villa lads there before nine, waiting for the quarter past train to come in. As hard as you try, it is difficult to have 100 match-day lads trying to look inconspicuous by all reading a newspaper.

I was hyper. I couldn't stand or sit in the bar. I don't know why I was worried we would miss them, as there was no way they would have been there before the shops had opened. Eventually me, Joycey and one of the other lads went on walkabout, and who do we bump into coming on the station but the up-and-coming main lad from the Blues, Cud, who would become the so-called leader of the Zulus. He saw me, I saw him and without hesitation we went straight into each other. Nobody else was involved. It was a good ruck until one of our lads jumped in. Cud didn't hang about, he was on his toes. There is no shame in that because the kid was on his own. It happens to all of us at some point, the odds are against you and you decide not to place a bet.

One of our lads, nicknamed the General, turned up and told me later that he could not believe his eyes when he looked at the bar and it was rammed. At first he thought it was full of Blues going to Spurs away. He noticed the ski jumpers and the wedgeheads and realised it was our lot, walked in and scanned the room to see if all the heads were there and soon noticed the likes of Brittle, Andy, Lloyd and Moses and knew that although in those days 100 was not a huge firm, this lot would do, as it was the right 100.

A few of us had now moved on, it was not a time to sit and wait in the pub. After that bit of sport earlier, I was tripping and the lads also wanted to get 'C Crew' baseball caps, so we went to the indoor Oasis Market where they customised the caps. It was a popular clothes haunt with young lads. As we got there, from nowhere Cud appeared but this time he had a small firm with him. He had obviously passed the word around that the C Crew were out and about and wanted a little payback for earlier. It was nothing really, we were into them in a flash but because of what we were planning with Liverpool, we were all carrying. They saw the blades and backed off, then turned and ran through the market and headed towards the Cabin pub, with us giving chase.

As we went past, some workers were painting a new shopfront and one of the lads picked up a couple of the tins of paint and threw them at the Blues lot, but they missed the target and landed smack on a bright new Rover car. The occupants, a middle-aged couple, were open-mouthed that there was now red paint all over their brand new car, which was a shame but typical of the kind of thing which happened week in, week out. We left before they started the tears and that was the last we saw of Cud and the Blues that day.

We ended up back with the lads, who by now were sick of me asking them what time it was and then it hit me. 'No gloves, I need gloves, fuck it, I forgot to sort the gloves out.' I said to a couple of the lads that we had to go to Villa Park to get some gloves, as if we walked into a shop near the station and bought them we could have been traced easily. The problem was we did not have the time to hop on a bus because the train was due, but one of the lads was driving and we jumped into the motor and off we went to Villa Park to buy a pair of gloves, with the instructions that everyone should wait for the main firm of Scousers to turn up and not fuck the whole operation up by attacking Liverpool civilians if they arrived before the Scallies.

While we were glove shopping, Brittle was in the station keeping things together. The Old Bill had started to disperse the mob but about ten of the lads doubled back and were still in the station and the Old Bill were not bothered, as they thought they had moved the numbers out of the way. What they didn't realise was that everyone was carrying in this group. Today they tell me that New Street has metal detectors now, well trust me the whole lot of us would have been nicked before we started that day.

The Scousers must have been on community service or the early trains were on strike because they didn't come in on the first two trains, they actually arrived on the 11.15 and there must have been 300 comfortably on it. Now as far as I was concerned, this was their boys, the Scallies in their hooded bubble coats, bouncing down the platform like they were at Lime Street, all wedgeheads and strong accents.

Andy didn't go in the Rail Bar but stood back on the concourse reading a paper along with Tommy and Jamie and watched as the police went into the bar and pushed all our lads out of the station. That left about six of them as the Liverpool lot came through the ticket barrier, and they followed them towards the Rotunda. The Liverpool firm did not have a clue that there were Villa lads in with their mob until my mate's trusty old Mini pulled up with me hanging out of the window. Andy shouted that they were amongst them and the Scousers now realised Villa were behind them and all began turning round. I was surprised because the station was full of police but there was none with this Liverpool firm.

They steamed into Andy's little mob, making that shouting 'come onnnn' kind of noise that goes with a mob when they charge. The six kept it tight and were exchanging blows with them. Andy had a broken arm at the time and was in plaster so he was using that to clump them. Brittle took his monkey wrench out of the back of his jeans and hit the first Scouser and they started to panic, because by now they could see the blades and knew we were tooled up.

I was out of the car, running towards them, screaming insanely to the lads, 'Get into them.' I was in a frenzy of rage. I will never forget the look on their faces when I shouted out, 'So say hello to your old mate Chicken George then.' Their faces dropped and the courage and strength drained from their bodies. To me, rightly or wrongly, they were all sneak thieves with a reputation for lashing innocent people and pillaging city centres. Right then, in that instant, they knew that this time they had made a big mistake. They had picked on the wrong city centre and walked into the wrong firm.

Whack, whack. The first man went down. Out comes the Stanley blade and I'm into them like a madman, slashing and cutting at anything and everybody. The lads said I had gone and my eyes were glazed, they used the words 'indiscriminate slashing' and it was right. It was that bad that one of our own got in the way and was cut by mistake. Jimmy Coley, a martial arts expert, was now in full flow but because of the numbers it was not a case of targeting just one, it was hit as many as you can. He caught Brittle and gave him a pisser on the side of the head but nothing was said as we were all too busy damaging our victims.

Liverpool realised it was just a handful who were at it with them and made a stand, but then the rest of the C Crew by the Mayfair came running round the corner. Now the Scousers were cornered and stood there glued to the spot. At every point there was what must have seemed like 100 Villa all tooled up. They were in sheer panic and were trying to get away from us and find a safe place but they didn't know our manor.

Dewar, a very well-known and respected lad from the Steamers, was on a bus coming from Kings Norton to meet his lot in the Hole in the Wall and said it was carnage, with people laid out on the floor, others running in different directions and Villa lads holding knives up in the air. It was a Saturday morning and people were going to the Bull Ring to shop and it had turned into a warzone, like hell on earth. He wanted to get off and help, although he could see by the looks of it we didn't need any, but the driver wouldn't stop the bus.

By now we had them running everywhere. It wasn't just me who felt hatred, it was a whole C Crew firm. We had totally gone, lost it, we were savage, frenzied. They were dropping all around. The ones who got away ran into shops screaming for help. Lads followed them in to finish them off. There was no hiding place. One dived under a parked car thinking he could hide. It was all happening in slow motion. I could feel the devil on my shoulder. I started to have flashbacks of what they did to me on Merseyside, so much anger and hate in my head. I pulled him by his leg from under the car. He was curled up in a ball, saying, 'Mister, I'm only here for the robbing, I'm only here for the robbing.'

'Fuck off.'

I kicked him about the head and body, yanked him off the floor and said, 'Look at me, you cunt, look at me. When I close my eyes and go to sleep I have nightmares about Merseyside and what you fuckers did to me. Now when you look into the mirror from now on you will remember me.' Then I hacked at him.

Some now looked in a real bad way and there was blood everywhere. I was covered in it from head to foot. Fordy and a mate arrived on the scene. One lad called Ozzie said to them, 'Fuck's sake, you have just missed a butchery and a half, it got right out of hand and a lot of Scousers have been cut seriously. The Old Bill are looking to lift people, just get out of the fucking way.' We had done some serious damage but I don't think we realised at the time how bad it really was and the publicity it would create.

I went home to get changed. Andy and most of the crew from the incident headed to the Ben Johnson pub and holed up in there right on the edge of town. I was told that a few of the lads were pushing knives and Stanley blades down the back of the seats. It was now on top by New Street with the Old Bill, who were forcing any late C Crew arrivals to move on. The word got around that they were looking for a skinny black lad, dressed in a baseball jacket and cap.

Andy, with the other lads from the Ben Johnson, decided to go to the ground to see if we could get at them again. This was a mistake. They ended up at the turnstiles right outside the away end and the Old Bill weren't happy. Their firm was queuing up to pay in as Villa got level with them but there were loads of police there and they were between the two firms. A lot of Liverpool lads were pointing different Villa lads out to the cops, saying things like 'He was there' or 'He's got a knife.' Because Andy's arm was in plaster, he stood out and a few pointed him out. He was grabbed a couple of times but released. The second time he was pulled, the Liverpool lads were almost begging them to nick him and for a firm who had spent years cutting and slashing fans from all over the country, I thought they let themselves down a bit that day by running and crying to the Old Bill.

By now I was on my way to the ground, having jumped the number 65 bus back to Stockland Green where I was living to wash up and change into a new set of clothes. I had put on my long black coat, thinking I wouldn't get fingered for events earlier, though I knew it wasn't any ordinary old row. But still I wanted to have another pop at them after the game.

At the game people were coming up to me patting me on the back saying that they had heard I had stabbed all the Scousers and it was a bit unnerving, as it was from lads who were not there. I said I didn't know what they were on about and that it wasn't me. Yet I have to be honest and say I was buzzing and the thought of all those Scousers going back with some permanent memories of Villa and Black Danny made my day. I watched the game from our usual spot in the bottom corner of the Holte End and we won 2-0 and I thought life couldn't get any better.

All the talk was about after the game and we decided to go back up New Street. We had got rid of our tools and knew the Old Bill would be on our case, as well as the fact that there would be a lot of pissed-off Scousers looking for revenge. Word had spread about the ambush and the amount of Liverpool lads who had been cut was rising by the minute. We knew by the police presence that some of their mates were in hospital and some had given statements, and although I didn't know it at the time, the local Old Bill were looking for me, this six-foot-four black lad, for a total of nine stabbings.

We got to New Street and they were at the escalators inside the Bull Ring. We didn't need any invitation, this was the Eighties and there was no bouncing around, we were straight into them. This time it was pure hand-to-hand combat and we were gaining the upper hand, although they weren't running this time. I was fighting with this Scouse lad, repeatedly punching him in the face, when I felt a copper pulling me away and I was nicked.

They were really interested in a black guy in a baseball jacket and cap. Whilst I was black and skinny, what I was wearing didn't fit their description, so foolishly I thought I had got away with it. I call it my longest day, and I knew I had moved up a level and was smug to the point of arrogance. Nothing could touch me. The C Crew came of age that day. Yes we had had some major rows before that, but I felt we had really learnt that if you have got a tight firm who are so out of control and without fear, you can do the bigger numbers. No one from Merseyside has ever tried to fuck with me since that day.

About a month later, I was at the dole office waiting to get my cheque when the bird behind the counter said, 'I am sorry, could you wait for a moment, there seems to be a problem.' I just thought the usual that it was some poxy mix-up, but after an hour two Old Bill came in and said, 'Excuse me Danny, could you step in here please.' They took me into an office and nicked me. While I had been waiting they had gone to my house, searched it and easily found the Stanley knife I had used on the Scousers still in my bedroom where I had left it as my trophy. That arrogance was my downfall. They had been tipped off by a Bluenose called Mark Conway who had been arrested for the same fight and decided to blurt out my name to save his own arse. He had been walking past New Street when we were at it with Liverpool and got involved; yet all he did was throw a few shapes and get himself nicked. It was around this time that the Blues had printed business cards and leaflets with 'Black Danny, Wanted Dead or Alive!' I suppose it was a compliment and it was the notoriety I had craved but ultimately it was my downfall. I often wondered would Conway have known me without my name being bandied about at Blues.

I got sent down for two sets of three years, one for affray and one for wounding, and the sentences were to run concurrently. At the time, that kind of jail was almost unheard of in terms of football violence but because of the seriousness of the offence they wanted to send a clear message out to all and sundry that it would not be tolerated. I was in shock. I didn't realise concurrent meant to run side by side and I actually thought I had been given six years. To this day I can still see Conway's mom mouthing 'sorry' to me in court. All through the trial he was never in court with me until that day we were sentenced, and while I was going away for years his detective work meant that he was sent packing for a short spell in Borstal.

Liverpool were playing at Wolves a few weeks later and word had got round about the slashings and my involvement and they actually came to the Hole in the Wall pub to try and find me which I will take as a compliment. It's the game where I made my name and I have been told that Spurs the season after I had been sent down were singing 'Danny gone down forever and where's your C Crew' so I suppose you could say I got my notoriety at a price.

Also I have been told before a Blues game at Man City they had a minute's silence in mock honour of me getting sent down but that's typical of how they felt about me. Maybe they thought the C Crew lads would disband after that. They were wrong. Although it was more than just a one-man knife frenzy, I was the only one to be jailed for the attack, leaving plenty to carry on where I left off.

9 CHAMPIONS OF ENGLAND, PART TWO

DANNY

I was overjoyed after the Liverpool game for obvious reasons: I gave those scousers a permanent reminder of who Black Danny was and the home win was the one result when we knew as fans, *hang on, this is serious*. We played them off the park that day, winning 2-0 and like six years earlier when we had inflicted a memorable 5-1 home win on them, suddenly the football world woke up to Aston Villa on the march. It was the start of a run which saw us win seven on the bounce. After Liverpool, we won at Coventry and then at home to Man City. Next up was Everton away and after what had gone on with their mates from across the park we expected fireworks.

As the season wore on, the coaches had become quite well known and both the police and the hangers-on knew we were leaving from the Mayfair. For this game, Andy and Brittle arranged for the coaches to leave from the Ben Johnson, right on the other side of town. There were four coaches but it was hard to tell who was on them as they were already loaded. On the way up, we stopped not far from Liverpool and when everyone got off I could tell straight away that we had a top firm out.

We arrived early with the aim of taking their main pub, the Blue House, and on arrival there were just eight Everton lads in there. They went straight out the fire exit and over the wall. I had to laugh when all you could see left was a selection of drinks, cigarette packets and lighters on the tables. Something gave me the impression they were in a hurry to leave but they shouldn't have worried, nobody would have bothered with such a small number. I didn't go up for a drink but stood outside the door along with a few others, watching and waiting. I was supposedly a wanted man and even wore a specially made badge for the day, proclaiming, 'Scousers run faster than Seb Coe.'

At about 20 past two I could see in the distance that Everton had got a mob together. As they approached the pub, I stepped forward, saying, 'Come on then, I'm Chicken George.' One of my fellow Villa 'doormen' went into the boozer and shouted something like, 'Get outside, they're here.' For a moment it looked like Everton were going to attack the pub but when they saw the numbers that piled out they stayed on the other side of the road. Villa went straight into them but unfortunately the Old Bill arrived very quickly and saved them from further humiliation.

The game ended with us winning 3-1. We had a great following that day and had taken good numbers there; great picture of the C Crew lads on the wall behind the goal. It was a tight game and we were 2-1 up thanks to a great goal from Tony Morley that won Goal of the Season when Villa were awarded a penalty, which we scored. Game over.

The following week my bubble burst and I was arrested for the Liverpool stabbings. Luckily I was bailed and we won another three after the Goodison victory, seeing off Palace at home and Wolves and Sunderland away before United came to Villa Park. It was a game Brittle remembers well and he and Jimmy Coley led the troops with distinction that day

BRITTLE

Before our home game against Man United, some of the lads gathered at New Street to wait for their mob to land. We couldn't get near them, as they were wrapped up by Old Bill, but Heaffy managed to get among them and caught one with one of the best punches I have ever seen, a real beauty. All you could see then was Heaffy, who fancied himself as a bit of dresser, making a getaway in his Paddington Bear coat, bobbing up and down to evade the coppers and the angry Mancs. That was the only action before the game.

United then held us to a draw that they didn't deserve and I was pissed off. It was a vital game for us and I saw it as a point lost. It was going off all the way from the ground down to Witton Island and I managed to bang a few, which made up for the poor result on the pitch. At the Island, we weren't sure where they had gone, as there didn't seem to be many Man U going towards the station. Then someone shouted, 'There they are!' and pointed up Aston Lane. There was Man U's firm walking up to Perry Barr. We began following them, all the lads, AB, Jimmy Coley, Ozzie, Joycey, etc., and the next thing we knew, they came rushing us.

They were firm-handed and I thought to myself, *fucking hell, we've got it on top here*. I shouted to all the lads, 'Nobody run,' and we went straight into them. They were surprised that we stood and after a few bottles Jimmy Coley went flying in with a karate kick and landed in the middle of them, so I went in after him. More followed and it was bang, bang, bang, and they panicked and backed off. Once we'd got them on their toes, that was it. They tried to re-group together but we just kept going and going.

When we got to the lights just before Perry Barr, the OB were trying to block off the road with bikes because traffic couldn't get through, which meant the OB couldn't get to us in any numbers. It was one mad running battle with bricks and bottles flying all the time. There was one copper at the corner and I couldn't resist the temptation so I ran over and booted him off his bike. The OB blocked us off so we had to go round by the Crown and United came out by the old university and we went at each other again. One of their main lads, Black Sam, had a big iron bar but instead of keeping it and using it, he threw it. I was at the front and it landed harmlessly in front of me, so I picked it up and went running towards him to smash him in the face – but at almost the same time the OB landed. *Fuck this*. I jumped over a little wall and they nicked Jamie instead. That was a proper row and as good as it gets.

DANNY

The following week we went to Spurs, parked the coach up in an estate and walked straight to the first pub. It turned into a row before we had bought a pint of overpriced lager. This set off another pub behind it full of Yids and the next thing was we were fighting two lots from different directions. They were game and probably the best opponents we had come across that season. I have said before that Spurs are a good outfit and although our older lot didn't rate the mobs they had from the early Seventies, these could have it all right.

After it was broken up, we went into the old stand behind the away end. Before long a good number of the C Crew were at the back of the stand playing up. I suppose we did fancy our chances. It had been a good season and when some wise old copper who was a mischievous fucker said, 'So lads, you fancy yourselves as hard men do you?' plenty gave him the nod. He asked us how hard and then opened the gates to the Spurs side of the stand.

Thirty lads followed Brittle, who as usual is leading the lads into battle. The Spurs mob by now are not very happy, in fact they are decidedly pissed off, and they start throwing punches and going mental as more and more Villa go in. One lad called Eddie later told me that a guy pulled a blade on him and if it wasn't for Brittle diving on the bloke, Eddie would have been chivvied.

The chief copper was shouting into his radio, 'Who let these mad bastards in?' and they then escorted us back out. To them it looked like we were taking liberties but the fact is the Old Bill put us in there and it was one of those occasions where we didn't have to try hard to get in amongst our opponents; the OB gave us a helping hand.

Off the field was better than on it, as we lost 2-0 and it looked to even the most optimistic lads that the Villa were trying their best to blow the tile. We were still favourites with eight games to go. Five were at home, including a game against Ipswich Town, who by now were the only team with a realistic chance of catching us. But being Villa the general feeling was that we had slippery fingers even if the title race was in our hands.

A home win against Southampton settled nerves and then we went and hammered Leicester 4-2 away, a game when we infiltrated their end. About 50 of us tried to take it by getting to the back of their section. I gave it the old C Crew warcry which was enough to scatter their end! While it was going off, one of our lads lost his footing on a pillar he was standing on and fell onto a copper, knocking him out in the process. Due to the home mob's reluctance to come out and play, he did more damage that day than any of us. The Old Bill were the ones who ended up moving us out and not the Baby Squad.

We were on the home straight and cantering to the title, and with four home games left, bookies were not taking bets. But despite their faith in the Villa, I did not know one person who openly said we would win it, such was the nervy atmosphere when you are so near but yet so far away from one of football's greatest prizes.

We played West Brom in a night game at Villa Park. Albion were a good side, managed by Ron Atkinson, and there was always a bit of needle with the players, probably more than when we played Blues because they were more of a threat. Anyway Albion came with a mob, their old Smethwick lot, and they came up the road from the Handsworth direction. It was a good-sized mob but when they got to Witton Island they literally disappeared into the night as soon as the C Crew appeared. It reminded me of a game I saw in 1974 at Villa Park as a young kid; they had beaten us 3-1 and again at the very same place after the game they were attacked, with Albion on their toes running up towards Perry Barr.

The game saw a capacity attendance of 47,998, our biggest of the season, with a lot of people locked out. Initially the away end was the first end to have the 'gates closed' sign, so some of the Albion went in the Holte End. We followed them into the ground and I was thinking who the fuck do they think they are, but as soon as we had lost the Old Bill we gave them a right slapping, they didn't even make the terraces, we were literally battering them underneath the Holte stands. We had done our job and now it was the players' turn and it turned into a very nervous night but we won 1-0, thanks to a terrible back pass from Batson that Withe gleefully snapped up to poke home. The crowd went wild and it was almost like we had won the championship that night, such was the relief. It wasn't pretty but Saunders' teams were very fit and always kept going when others couldn't keep up.

The following weekend we had no game, as Ipswich were playing the FA Cup semi-final against Manchester City – at Villa Park. We still turned out a firm to find their lads but ended up running into a very impressive Man City firm who were giving it loads in their Manc accents: 'City ain't running today.' I have a soft spot for them because of a very close mate of mine Clive, a civilian and it was me who said to the City lot that things were sweet and that it was Ipswich we were after, but they never showed as a firm, just rosette-wearers and screaming chicks distraught that City had dumped them out of the cup. I was undecided if it was a good or bad thing: yes they were down after losing but now, like us, they only had the league to go for and the following week they were back at Villa Park for our biggest game in 70 years, bearing in mind that if we beat them we were as good as crowned champions.

Ipswich boss Bobby Robson was playing mind games and on April 14 had already conceded that Villa had as good as won the title. Officially 47,495 got in and like the Albion game thousands more were locked out. They were the lucky ones, as it all went horribly wrong. After probably our weakest defensive display of the season, we lost for the third time against our nearest rivals, who were now a point behind with a game in hand. I thought we had blown it and everyone was dumbstruck. Nobody was talking after the game whereas before the game it was like a pre-title party, even though we did try to get into the Witton end to have a go at the mixed-race Ipswich lads that some of the C Crew encountered at Portman Road. I sat in the Crown pub and saw people speaking to me but I wasn't listening, I was just motionless and thought we had blown it. But after the game when a reporter asked Saunders, 'Well you've probably lost the title, how do you feel?' in typical Saunders deadpan fashion he replied, 'Do you want to bet against us?'

That one comment gave everyone a boost. Yes Robson had won the mind game title beforehand but now Ipswich had to hold their nerve – and the following week they blew it. We beat Forest 2-0 and during the second half the scoreboard in the corner of the Holte flashed up that Ipswich were losing at home to Arsenal. The place went crackers. The title was back on and suddenly the pendulum swung back in our favour. It was ours to lose and it was that close I could smell it with just three games to go.

We then went to Stoke City on a Bank Holiday Monday and took thousands, although we did come unstuck in the home end when a small mob of us didn't do as well as the older lads did in their end in 1975. We evened it out at the end of the game as hundreds got onto the pitch and beckoned them to join us after a 1-1 draw. The mood changed as news came through that in the East Anglian derby Norwich, who were fighting relegation, had beaten Ipswich 1-0. From then on Stoke could fuck off, it was party time!

That Saturday we beat Middlesbrough at home 3-0. It was the days of the transistor radio and sweeping rumours, and they soon went around that we had actually won it. I was hyped up beyond belief that day, I wasn't interested in the row, I just wanted to celebrate with my heroes and get close to them, the football fan in me took over the thug in me. I was perched on the small fence separating the Holte End terrace from the pitch and though the police were trying to stop me, as soon as the final whistle went I jumped over them and onto the pitch. The first player I got to was Jimmy Rimmer, our goalkeeper, a player not noted for his sense of humour. Anyway I proceeded to hug him, telling him we had won the league. He looked at me blankly, so I moved on to Tony Morley, our flying winger, and grabbed him round the neck. He was shaking me off, saying, 'Get off me,' and as daft as it sounds Gordon Cowans, the maestro, came over and said, 'Tony, he is okay mate.'

I felt a million dollars but that high turned into an anti-climax as the Ipswich result came in and we still needed a point to do it. I got off the pitch and went into the Witton Lane Stand. The players came out for a lap of honour and fair play to Morley, he saw me and came over, taking his Villa top off and giving it to me. Man I was buzzing.

The next Saturday couldn't come quick enough, seven more days to wait but I wanted it now, and I didn't want to wait. Yes I was up on a wounding charge with the likelihood I was going down but let's live for the moment, jail could wait. The build-up to the game was nothing like I had ever seen before, it seemed to be 24/7 in the media and nothing else was talked about at home or on the streets. Arsenal, our opponents, were still challenging for a UEFA Cup place so their season wasn't dead and they needed to win to ensure qualification.

Arsenal made the decision to allocate the whole of the Clock End to Villa fans. It was a decision that angered the Gooners, as the Brummies were going to be there in force and they saw it as an insult, made even worse when their manager, Terry Neill, said at the end of the game that if Villa won the league and they managed to qualify for Europe we could have a joint lap of honour, allowing the two sets of fans to celebrate. I remember thinking, *Terry, this ain't rugby mate, this is football, and if I was a Gooner I would be saying no way am I letting them fuckers on the pitch taking the piss.* Today it probably has for a Villa fan the same meaning as when John F. Kennedy died in that we all remember where we were that day. The wait was over. After being in the Third Division less than ten years before, here we were on the verge of winning the English First Division Championship. It's not like we were Liverpool or Manchester United, it was hardly likely to happen again in our lifetime. Probably Forest, Blackburn and Everton fans can relate to what I am saying.

So the atmosphere was already set for the day. We went by coach and I was probably the only one sober. Some would say I was miserable but I wasn't, I just wanted to take the full day. This was what I had waited for since I was that kid walking up Trinity Road back in 1972. I think there were suburbs in Birmingham suffering from woodworm as there were that many that came out of it, it was swarming in claret and blue all the way down the M1.

We got off the coach and one of the C Crew generals, Boris, was pissed but then again he liked his brown and mild did our Boris. He walked straight into a haymaker off one of the Arsenal lads waiting for us as we got off the coach. So here we are for our biggest foot-balling day straight into a row and it's bang off. The Old Bill came and stopped it, then it went off again right outside the turnstiles and we caned and ran them.

You have to remember this was an invasion of 20,000 Villa fans on North London and every lad we have ever had from all eras was there. We had heard stories about it going off on the Friday night as Villa fans had travelled up the night before and were taking over local boozers and it was a night of singing Villa songs, getting pissed and getting into rows with the locals. We had every match-day boy and general out so there was bound to be a fight on every corner. Arsenal ain't mugs and I have always rated them from the day their lads came into the Holte End to have a pop, and contrary to what one West Ham book says, they did a lot better than West Ham. They actually got to the top of the Holte before getting run out whereas West Ham only made it to the middle.

I was proud as punch, standing in my newly acquired Villa top that the week before had been worn by Tony Morley. I could hardly breathe with all the excitement and the feeling that we were so close. *Please don't fuck it up, let me have this moment God!* There were that many Villa fans that the Clock End was full and no more could get in, so now Villa were in the side paddocks and also on the North Bank, albeit in small numbers.

The Arsenal firm who normally occupy one half of the Clock End are in the seats and paddock areas and it's not long before they are into a few of our lads. It goes off on the side with a good lot of Villa but only a few 'firm', but we know they are ours from the wedgeheads. Some of the Villa families in there had to escape and were getting onto the pitch, but then 30-40 C Crew lads, seeing we have Villa fans in trouble, steamed straight out the Clock End, into the paddock and into Arsenal.

I didn't bother getting involved, I was focusing on the game but I had a bird's eye view and it was a right row. The lads were really getting stuck into them. It was a bit of payback for their cheek at coming into the Holte a year earlier but this time we are the ones prepared and this is our cavalry defending the civilians. A few of ours got nicked, including Reggie, as the police struggled to control the situation. You then had a small mob of other lads like Heaffy, Groombridge and Sean, no more than 20, who were in the North Bank and you just knew Arsenal's lads were not going to stand for this and that Terry Neill's 'let's all hold hands together' statement was about as likely as Villa winning the league again while Doug stayed in charge. The Villa lads in the North Bank put on a bit of a show and did manage to stand in there longer than most but were nowhere near taking and were escorted out of the end, with young Heaffy getting into the first aid room. It shows though how confident we were at the time: a firm of 20 going into Arsenal's main end and thinking we could handle their numbers.

The game started and before I knew it we were two down and the lads with radios in the crowd are giving us the news that Ipswich were one up at Middlesbrough. The scene at half-time was so tense there were actually outbreaks of trouble among Villa fans who were frustrated at the fact that we were likely to blow it. It was too much to take in. Well, it didn't turn out that way. Yes, we lost, but Middlesbrough equalised and then they went ahead. The scenes on the terraces were joyous, news was filtering through and people were jumping up and down. No doubt the players knew what was going on as well.

I wanted to be first on the pitch but I think Heaffy beat me to it, as he came from his vantage point in the first aid room with no coppers around him. The police were thinking this was a powder keg and even though both sets of fans were invited by the Arsenal manager to celebrate, they were having none of it. Try as the police did, however, they failed and I got on along with hundreds of other Villa – and what seemed like half of the North Bank. We were not running to the players, we were running towards each other and exchanging blows before the Old Bill formed a blue wall stretching the width of the pitch to keep us apart. Due to the pitch invasion there was no lap of honour, so we turned our attentions to the Gooners, who had now gone into the top tier seats after being moved off the pitch. With the championship in the bag I could relax and go about my day job, rucking with the C Crew!

Our lot on the pitch make the first charge into their area. By then they had the better vantage point, as they were in the seats above the paddock, so we were attempting to climb up and get amongst them. Moses and his crew, who went from Witton by minibus, found an exit door which they broke by pulling the shutters down. It led to the seats above and that was it, we were now all going through the door. 'Come on then, Arsenal,' and we were into them. They initially held us off but we now had the same numbers and it was game on. I got to within striking reach of their main lad, Dainton 'Denton' Connell, and kicked him down the stairs and that really was it, we had the advantage and our lads were too strong. We won the league and we won the row that day off the pitch.

As a firm I don't think we got the credit we deserved that season, a bit like the team. Ipswich were the darlings of the media and were hyped up as Champions of the People, the neutrals if you like, and we fucked it up for them. Off the pitch we were top of our division as well and Arsenal on that last day proved it. After a wait of over 71 years, Villa were crowned champions having used only 14 players all season (including three left-backs) and winning more games than anybody else. We were champions on merit and the history books will say: Aston Villa, Champions of England!

The C Crew too was a team effort. Like the playing squad, it would be hard to pick any individuals out, as both had strength all across the pitch or all across the line. We had a bigger squad to choose from but for 42 games that season we managed to stay injury free and all the lads were on show each and every game!

Along with a lot of Villa, poor old Reggie was carted off to the nick, missed the game and was kept in overnight. The Old Bill, being cruel bastards, told Reggie we had lost 1-0 and Villa had lost the title. He didn't know at the time that Ipswich would have still needed to win their game in hand but it had the desired effect on the Villa fans locked up – until they found out next day. They made up for it when the trophy was paraded at Birmingham Town Hall.

A Hero Just For One Day

Now there are times, like the birth of my children, which will always be my proudest moments, but this is nearly up there with them. In fact I can barely explain what it was like. The City of Birmingham had made plans that they would hold a Town Hall celebration and a victory parade, and over 100,000 people took to the streets. Lloyd's old man worked at the council and had got two tickets to the ceremony, and Lloyd asked me if I fancied going. To say I bit his hand off is an understatement. Lloyd didn't go, he preferred to be in the crowd.

I got into the room set out for the players and was helping myself to the champagne before the players and officials had even got there. Then they arrived. Here I am, Danny the football fan, with my heroes, just looking at them in awe and amazement. I was back to being a school kid, not a thug, this was dream stuff. They came up the stairs and Gary Shaw came over to me.

'All right Dan?'

I think, *pardon, did he say what I thought he said?* He knew by my face I was in shock and he said, 'It's okay Dan, I have mates on the terraces that know you.' I later found out he was very good mates with a lad I have met recently who had kept Shawie informed of the terrace activities. I suppose it didn't register with me but Gary Shaw used to stand on the terraces, not a match-day boy but he would know the score.

Then Tony Morley was looking at me and laughing and says to

our manager, Ron Saunders, 'Boss, here he is, the bloke I was talking to you about,' and Ron Saunders was shaking my hand. It was surreal or whatever the words are. After a few champagnes, it was time for the team and Ron Saunders to go onto the balcony and acknowledge the tens of thousands of Villa gathered below and speak to them and show them the league trophy.

They started passing the trophy to each player and the fans sang each name. Gary Shaw beckoned me out onto the balcony and here I am with my heroes and out there are my mates, my battalion, the C Crew – and he passed me the trophy. I held the trophy, almost shaking, glad I'd had a drink to calm my nerves. Then, like the players, I show the trophy to the crowd and I hear, 'Danny, Danny, Danny, Danny,' which builds to a crescendo.

Have you ever seen a black man go red?

It was like we had all merged into one firm: the team, the C Crew, the Steamers. I was living the dream for all the lads and we were all part of the club that day, we felt accepted. That season I missed only one game home and away, which was Crystal Palace due to me being arrested that day for Liverpool. The C Crew had been everywhere, tried at most places to get into their home end or pubs and took it to all of the clubs without exception. The team were champions on the pitch that season but I tell you what, we were also champions off the pitch as well.

10 INSIDE THE MIND OF A FOOTBALL HOOLIGAN

DANNY   **JIMMY**

Jimmy Coley from the C Crew will give you an insight into the psyche or mentality of what we are about. Jimmy won't like me for saying this but he is up there with the best of them and I can't think of anybody else outside the five people behind this book who can give a better insight into the ultimate football hooligan. Jimmy started by saying, 'Look you can ask me any questions you like but I am not comfortable talking about myself. I want to do this for the lads, not to promote myself. I have nothing to prove to anybody. There are certain things I won't talk about and anything you put in I want to check over first.'

What was your childhood like?

Like most kids I knew I was brought up on a council estate. It was tough and we had no money. I am not bleating about it, it was just the way it was. I was a happy kid.

What were your school days like?

If you mean by that was I unruly, didn't I attend school or was I hassle to the teachers, then the answer is no. But I got into a lot of scrapes with other kids, although I wasn't by any means the hardest in the school. I was quiet and shy, still am today, and I don't find it comfortable talking about myself. My interest at school was sports. I loved sports and loved the competitive side of it. I wasn't academic at all but I found karate at the age of ten. That was my big thing.

Why karate?

I don't know, it appealed to me. I loved the training, the control, and I became good at it and got to black belt standard.

What about the weight training?

I was seven and a half stone at school. I built my body up, put muscle on and, combined with the karate and later martial arts, I made sure I could more than hold my own when I went out in the big wide world.

What do you mean hold your own?

It means I don't get fucked with. Look, I come from Kingstanding. It's a rough place, always has been and you show weakness you won't last. I wanted to make something of myself, so as the old fella preached to me, 'If you're fit and strong you will be a match for anybody.' I took those words on board and I won't change from that. It's important that you are able to perform to the best of your abilities.

You come over as polite, in fact other than the way you look your persona isn't the stereotype hardman.

[Jimmy chuckles]. I have told you about Kingstanding, it was rough but the one thing is we never hurt or bully people. I try to have high standards and high morals and that won't change. I am a family man first and foremost. You mess with my family or my friends then you will have a problem. I will have a straightener with anyone but I am not going looking for it.

Do you feel fear?

What type of question is that? Course I feel fear but that's why you have to be in good shape and top of your game and don't show fear on the outside. Anything less than that and you are already in trouble.

Okay, I think I am getting an understanding but it doesn't answer everything. What got you into the Villa?

I was always a Villa fan, the area is a very strong Villa fanbase. Because of the karate and martial arts I didn't attend a game until I was 16. I went down with Robert Pettit, another good lad from our area, and I can't remember the game or first ruck, before you ask. There has been a lot gone on in my life and let's just say there are more significant moments that I remember than what colour boots Brian Little used to wear.

So what attracted you to the trouble at games?

Do you want the toned down version or the real truth?

The truth.

I am a violent person. I am fuckin' deadly serious; I wanted to hurt people who had crossed me and I would use anything to win the battle. I was fighting every game. I wasn't interested in drinking in the pub or celebrating the win. We were there to fight, nothing else, and it wasn't just me there were a lot of serious young men who were on a mission to defend attack and fight the opposition. People were bringing machetes, knives and at Everton away in 81 one very good lad from my manor brought a ball and mace, something from

Medieval Britain, ready to use it but ended up fucking it at the Everton lads. I don't understand some people's mentality, back then it was anything goes and you have to be prepared to go that one stage further than the next guy or firm.

Jimmy, I have watched you in the battle, you don't seem to show any emotion?

That's down to the discipline of the karate training, it gave me self-control on the outside but inside I am raging with anger. I was once classed by a judge as like a trained assassin. I suppose that sums me up.

What gave you the edge?

I don't know but maybe I was prepared to go that one step further. I knew when it was time to go in a fight, I could understand exactly when we needed to make the move. Others would think I had moved too soon, that's rubbish, I knew when to move all right. Look, it's no good going into a fight half-hearted or as a pussy; you have lost before you start. This is one violent game. If you're not prepared to put everything into it, you shouldn't be there in the first place. I felt pure hatred and aggression and a lot of people say this but with me it was perfectly true, when I was in a fight I was in a trance. Others told me afterwards what I had done. You can't just look the part or have the training, you can't put the fight into a geezer, if it's not there it's not there. I had the fight in me. It's no good talking the talk fella, you got to walk the walk and too many talk a good game. You know the types, I have seen them everywhere I have been, from school right up to prison and they will get found out. The mouthy cunts are the worst. It's an old saying but true; watch the quiet one in the corner sussing it all out.

I have never seen you go down or take a step back on the front line.

Like I said, why would I be there in the first place? But it wasn't just me, I don't remember Brittle or Andy taking any back steps either.

When you have blokes like them and Moses, Ozzie, Fordy and Joycey watching your back, then you haven't got a problem. I could pick ten lads out and a firm of 50 couldn't shift that right ten, and I have seen it.

Jimmy, are there any rows that stand out mate?

Well just reading Brittle's bit on Man U at home in 1981 I suppose that stands out for me, even if he describes me as Hong Kong Phooey in it! The truth is that day I was fucking good and more like Bruce Lee, thank you. I took five of their lads out and to me it was a real toe-to-toe with a good firm of their Cockney Reds. Against superior numbers they didn't shift us and when the fighting stopped there was only one firm on their toes and it wasn't ours. I will let Mr Brittle explain it in detail but without doubt that was the best, although Liverpool at New Street was good but that was more about the weapons than the combat. It all goes back to what I said, you got the right front line you can do the superior numbers. You ask Andy or Brittle about how many of us were in amongst them to start with and that tells you everything you need to know about the front line of the crew.

You hit Brittle didn't you in that row?

Not by choice, Brittle just got in the way and when I am going to work, if you are in the line of fire then I am not going to say, 'Excuse me.' I like good manners but there is a place and a time and it ain't in a football row.

What was your take on West Ham in 1980? A lot of the lads see it as a turning point.

I thought they were a very good outfit and I met some good lads afterwards from there through the raves. But I thought we did well after the game, well my firm did anyway, not sure about the others. You saw yourself, they didn't move us in the ground but they were game and were no mugs. Biggest problem that day is we were all spread out, not all together. I was on a coach from the Rose and Crown and not many people in them days were going round Upton Park with baseball bats. We did. But there is no doubt they are the best we came up against and have got a lot of bottle. Maybe our lads started to take things more seriously from that point. I was already taking it seriously.

You mention Kingstanding a lot, it's obvious it means a lot to you.

KS is my manor. I learnt my trade on those streets, it was my introduction to life. There was an incident one time when some of the Zulus decided to try and make a move on North Birmingham. Let's just say they departed with their tails between their legs. You don't fuck about over here, people will stick together, it's a bit like the old East End. People who know the area will know what I mean.

What are your views on the C Crew?

I don't like being second rate at anything, I am competitive, it's in my nature, so if I am going to be part of something I want to win or I don't want to be involved. This was a very good crew. I don't consider any person as real top dog in the crew, if you're making the book out as either you or one of the other lads was top dog I don't agree. We didn't have a leader as such, we had a very good front line and anyone of that front line could be classed as top dog. I felt we took it seriously. The Steamers were in for the crack as much as the ruck, with us it was serious and you have to remember the likes of me and Andy don't drink. I can't have drunks who fuck it up 'cos they aren't on their game. We were there to win, not lose.

The likes of Ozzie, Fordy, Andy and Brittle are friends that are not manufactured, they are real, proper mates and I see us being like that until our dying days. Moses in the early years ran it close as top dog purely for some of the things he did and he held it together. We created an unbreakable bond and I would do anything for them and the lads I met in the C Crew.

Was it around long enough?

No, it disbanded too quick but for a variety of reasons. I got nicked at 19 for armed robbery and then eventually spent four years in the nick. A lot of the others moved on and were doing other things. We had peaked as a firm but in those years we were up there with the best. Not many could touch us.

What happened to you, did you move away from it?

I moved up the food chain. I became a criminal, simple as that. No point glossing it up, I was a hardened criminal. It's like the bloke who is Managing Director, he didn't just get there, he had to work his way up and the football violence put me on my way. I came from nothing, hadn't got a pot to piss in and I wanted to earn money. I wanted the nice clothes and fast cars and big house and I was violent, had a reputation. It was almost the natural path for me to follow.

So what did you move into?

I organised the raves in Birmingham and the Midlands, attracting tens of thousands at some events, and made a lot of money out of it. We had people trying to tax us but it was never going to happen, the likes of lads from Handsworth muscling in but our front line was good, organised, no fuss, we didn't get fucked with. We had an association with Coventry lads and for a time we were living a life beyond our dreams, not bad for a lad from Kingstanding. Some of the lads from the Villa Youth were good earners and we had a good mix of proper Villa lads running things. As for the Blues and Villa thing regarding the so called rave co-operation they know who I am, do you honestly think we went to them with a white flag or truce? The lad came to me. To me it was more than the football thing though, this was big money, serious stuff and I wanted to be the best at it. But it moved me into other things that really did affect my life.

How did it affect you?

In 1994 I was found with 100kg of cannabis and a shooter in my motor by the Old Bill. I had to go on the run for six and a half years, living here, there and everywhere and it was hard on my family. I decided I wanted to clean the slate and wanted a normal life, if there is such a thing, and gave myself up in 2000 and was sentenced to five years.

So what now?

I am 44 now and long past all of that. I have a family and a great wife that I want to spend time with. I love seeing the lads, they are part of my life and always will be and so are the Villa. But football violence and my criminal activities are in the past and it's time to move on with other things, legally and without violence.

11 FOUR ROWS AND A WEDDING, 1981

Sept 12: The Windsor and Man United
Sept 19: Diamond Lil's and all comers
Sept 24: Pollyanna's and the Fewtrels
Sept 26: The Wedding and Blues at home
Oct 3: Knutsford Service Station and Wolves

BRITTLE

Any lad who went to the football in the Seventies and Eighties will tell you that you could have a handful of fights in one day. I am trying not to sound like Uncle Albert from *Only Fools And Horses* but the facts are that the young lads, and the foolish older ones, still at it today are lucky if they have a couple of tear-ups a season. Back then, a day out in London could see us clashing with Blues at New Street before we had even left our own city, fights on the train with other London-bound fans, kick-offs at Euston with London firms heading north, clashes on the tube with everyone and anyone – and it was still three hours to kick-off!

In these days of CCTV, undercover OB with digital cameras and their mates in the force helicopter hovering above, the good old days are just that and if we were still at it the way we were then they would need floating prisons in the Irish Sea to house us all, such would be the amount of people getting nicked. In a nutshell, we used to fight a lot, but despite violence at the football being so common, one month in

1981 surpassed even what we were used to. Believe me, it was a period in our lives which was not for the faint-hearted.

Row 1: Man United in the Windsor

I don't know how we heard, I am not even sure if it was just a hunch, but the word was Manchester United would be using the Windsor pub, which is tucked away in an alley not far from the train station. At the time, the C Crew were using the Hole in the Wall, but the word got round to use the Windsor and 'be prepared', as the Villa motto so proudly states. As we arrived en masse at midday with all the usual suspects, United were already occupying the upper bar of the Windsor, so we settled nicely on the bottom floor. They started coming down for a gander and you could see by the looks on their faces that their little quiet drink was being interrupted. A couple came in and we got talking to them and they were decent enough but the whole atmosphere was like a tinderbox and it wouldn't take much to get it going. You had two firms of twentysomethings on the beer for two hours or more and it only needed a spark and it was fireworks.

That spark was the Soft Cell song 'Tainted Love' which came on the jukebox. The opening line was taken up and adapted by one of the Villa: 'Sometimes we feel you've got to … (bang, bang on the table) … run away,' and with that the bar erupted as 100 C Crew joined in and began bellowing it out. That was our invitation for United to join us and they obliged. In seconds they came piling down the stairs and we met them head-on, glasses going from side to side and then the lot went. Lads were punching and kicking the United mob and tables were going over into them and in all honesty it was a very one-sided saloon fight, as we were doing all the damage.

We all know what United are like, they have never taken a backward step in their lives, have never lost a fight and have ruled England since Churchill passed away, well when you have similar numbers they ain't the same outfit and this proved to be the case that day. United were pushed back up the stairs and remember this was a firm numbering the same as ours but they were a poor lot and the fact that they came off a clear second best blew their myths out of the water. They are good, yes, they have numbers, yes, and they are unbeatable, no! That day they were firm-handed and they went upstairs and wouldn't come back down.

We had done a lot of damage to the pub and when the police turned up it was a bit like the old *Yellow Pages* advert: 'And you wanna see what they have done to the downstairs bar.' It was farcical, we had some of the lads trying to make the place look normal and sitting around as if everything was okay when in reality we had totalled the place. You had the ridiculous sight of lads pretending they were now having a quiet drink, sitting on two-legged stools around a smashed table with cracked empty pint pots in their bloodied hands.

United certainly lived up to the chorus line of 'Tainted Love' that day.

Row 2: Diamond Lil's, Blackpool

Our next row came a week later but wasn't at the place or with the opposition we were expecting. After the events of January with Liverpool on New Street, and the fact that we had gone up to Everton and done a job weeks later, we felt that a return to Anfield would see the Scousers well up for it. Word on the hooligan grapevine was that they would be turning out for Villa and the C Crew, looking to avenge the beating, or shall we call it the cutting, they had taken at our place. Well if they did turn out we didn't see them as it was a total non-event and from that day on we never looked at Liverpool as a game firm ever again. People say they lost their way after Heysel or maybe Hillsborough but for us if they could not turn out for Villa after what had gone on, they were finished.

After the game, coach one with all the C Crew generals on went to Blackpool for the night, where we ended up in Diamond Lil's nightclub at the Pleasure Beach. The events that unfolded that night can only be described as something you will see on the telly watching Westerns. It was a major saloon bar brawl even by John Wayne and Wyatt Earp's high standards and certainly not 'pull a bird' stuff. After much drinking and lads dancing, thinking they were being cool but looking cunts, they focused on being top rodeo riders, as the club had one of those bucking bronco things and, lads being lads, everyone had to have a go on it. It was all going well until one of the lads, Big Jim, got knocked off it and tried to rip the horse out of the floor. Cue the riot. In seconds we had everybody at us. It was C Crew versus all comers and there were plenty, as we had Celtic, Middlesbrough and a Spurs firm in there.

People were flying into each other and knocking each other out while others stepped over the bodies on the floor to go to the next opponent. I knocked some geezer cold and Danny chased the others into the ladies' toilets. I don't know how long this was going on for but it was chaos and I thought I was in heaven. No row goes on this long but when you are in a club with nowhere to run, it is a case of fight or get battered, meaning there were plenty of people to fight.

Danny had attracted the attention of some Blues lads who were up there on a stag night, lads from Dave O's manor – who by the way was himself getting stuck in and enjoying himself. They were obviously pissed off that we had gatecrashed their party and one Nose made a beeline for Danny, shouting, 'Come on then fella, fancy your chances with me?' It would have been rude of Danny to ignore him so he obliged and was into him. This fella kept going down but getting back up and for the life of him Danny couldn't put him away. The fucker was like the Terminator, he just won't go away, until Big Jim told Danny to move out the way and BOSH, hit the geezer with a fire extinguisher straight into his face, knocking him cold, which sounds harsh but he wanted it and he got it. The C Crew were taking on all comers it didn't get much better than that, it was like being the boxer in the old fairground booth who every wannabe is stepping up to fight, only this was a mob with every other mob stepping up to the mark.

The bouncers dragged me into a corner and I thought I was going to get a right kicking but they said they were doing it for my own safety. Fuck knows what that was all about. I did one back out onto the main street and there was a cordon of police there with all the Villa chanting, 'Kill, Kill, Kill the Bill.' I asked everyone, 'Are we up for it?' and they all went, 'Yeah,' so I flew straight into the police – and everyone else went the other way! It was no surprise when they knocked the bollocks out of me and then nicked me. I got 14 days in Walton and then a gate arrest outside the prison and taken straight back to Birmingham, where they gave me another four months.

Row 3: Pollyanna's

CLARKEY

Two days before his wedding, we had Lloyd's stag night and it became the third row of an eventful few weeks. Everyone met at our old drinking hole, the Ben Johnson, and there were 30-40 of us. We were due to play Blues on the Saturday and the majority wanted to go round Sam Weller's pub by the Kaleidoscope on the very small chance of bumping into any Blues.

As soon as we entered the town centre subways, the first row of the night kicked off as a fight broke out between some of the lads in the group. There was nowhere for anyone to back off in the tight space of the subway, it was very much hands-on. Luckily, a few of us managed to break it up before we attracted any unwanted attention and ruined the night before it had started. We managed to get ourselves into Sam Weller's and there were a handful of Blues in there who knew the score and went to the very end of the pub when they saw us. They were well outnumbered so nobody was going to bother bullying them. Instead people kept telling them we would see them on Saturday.

The pub manageress realised what was happening and didn't like the idea of her customers being intimidated, so she asked us all to leave. It was almost closing time anyway and one of the lads had come up with the idea of going to Pollyanna's, a club situated among offices and well away from all the other city centre clubs. We all got in no problem at all but the club was deserted and with no girls to attract the lads' attention, it wasn't rocket science to work out what would happen next. Before long a handbag was stolen and the door staff eventually found it in the men's toilets, minus its contents. For some reason, Danny was singled out as the main suspect.

DANNY

I first noticed something was wrong when two doormen came up to me and accused me of taking the bag. I thought, *you can fuck right off*, when they asked me to leave. No way was I going out of there for something I hadn't done. All the lads were spread out all over the club at this stage and a few of them had seen what was going on and came over to see me, asking if I was okay. Then the whole thing started to get heated as voices were raised.

The club was owned by Don Fewtrel, one of a group of brothers who almost had a cartel of the Birmingham clubs at the time. Legend has it they were the ones who had run the London mobsters the Lambrianou brothers out of town in the Sixties when they arrived for a confrontation with well-connected Aston pub landlord Colin Lawler (RIP), who had slept with one of their women. The Fewtrels were not mugs, anything but, and mixed with the likes of the Broadhurst family, Johnny Prescott – the boxer not the overweight MP – Andy Gray, who at the time was a top class playboy and footballer, not a gobby TV frontman, and the band Duran Duran; in fact anybody who was anybody in the city was a friend or acquaintance of the Fewtrels. They were part of an elite few who ran Birmingham back then and you didn't make enemies of these people, well most didn't. They were tough but smart, above board in their business dealings and were very successful entrepreneurs.

Whatever they were, they had not come across the likes of us. While they were used to handling the odd drunk or lairy teenager, even a stag night that decided they could take on the doors, they were not ready for an organised football firm. As voices were raised and the doormen were struggling to get me to move, unbeknown to us they had phoned their network of clubs and sent for reinforcements. The doormen realised I wasn't going anywhere and one of them grabbed me, so I knocked him away and said, 'Get your fucking hands off me.' In the struggle, I hit him. Now this wasn't the days of professional doormen with their martial arts, CS gas and stab vests, it was dickie bows and haymakers and the guy reacted like a street brawler. The powder keg exploded and the whole place went up as all our lads joined in, with the rest of the door staff along with a handful of the Fewtrels' friends coming from the foyer on hearing the commotion.

We were in a middle of a free-for-all and what was a quiet night in Polyanna's resembled yet another Wild West saloon. The sheer number and force of the lads backed the Fewtrels' mob into the foyer and we went to town on them, as they couldn't hold us. The foyer got trashed as much as the doormen and we were like a raging fire that no one could put out, in fact the fire was spreading as others decided to go for the optics. There was breaking glass and watered down spirits everywhere.

I had done what I wanted to do and went and found Lloyd, who was completely gone and didn't know what day it was, let alone that it was his stag night. We agreed he was entitled to a night off. As we all piled outside, yet more reinforcements arrived and the group who we had given it to inside came out for another go. I was looking after Lloyd and took no further part in the events outside, which was a good job as things took a turn for the worse. Clarkey was not so lucky and paid a big price imaginable for his involvement in the incident

CLARKEY

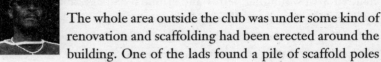

The whole area outside the club was under some kind of renovation and scaffolding had been erected around the building. One of the lads found a pile of scaffold poles and pudlocks and we helped ourselves to them, unleashed the pudlocks at the doors and went into the doormen outside, leaving bodies in our wake on the floor. We should have left it there but we had got the scent and it became like a football row; we wanted to take all of them out. By this time they had obviously realised we were no silly boys on a piss-up but were organised and dangerous, so they barricaded themselves in, leaving their mates outside. We rammed the doors using the poles as battering rams but couldn't budge the doors and soon police came from everywhere. We all scattered and headed back down towards the Cathedral at Colmore Row, dodging in and out of parking meters as we ran. I was outpacing the copper chasing me but just when I thought I had lost him the old-style Sweeney police car pulled up in front of me and two coppers grabbed me with their best Jack Regan impression: 'You're nicked son.'

I was told it was for drunk and disorderly and I was cuffed and put in the back of the car, which drove round to the back of New Street Station next to Sam Weller's, where I saw my mate Check handcuffed. The car stopped and they put him in the back with me and while I was pleased to have some company I felt sorry for Check, as to get that far away before getting nicked he had obviously given the cops a great run for their money.

When we were taken to the station it turned out that five or six had been nicked and we were all sat in reception waiting to give our names and hand over our belongings. We were having the crack and joking about whether our fines would be £10 or £20 when Don Fewtrel came in. He pointed at me straight away and said, 'I want him nicked.' He did the same to Check and the same to one of the other lads. Although he hadn't got his hands dirty himself, he had obviously witnessed the whole thing and wanted the lads who did the damage banged up.

I never heard any mention of D and D again and was eventually charged with wounding, affray and criminal damage, and sentenced to 18 months in prison. The trial was a joke, they even brought in a scaffolding pole carried by three blokes and had the jury and judge believe I had on my own used it as a weapon. Strong as I am, Geoff bastard Capes I ain't.

For a so-called hard man, Fewtrel had gone crying to the police and asked for us to be charged. I lost all respect for him. I was also not best pleased when, while I was on bail, a car full of blokes drove slowly past my parents' house, which upset my mother. My dad wasn't impressed or intimidated and one time he chased after the car with a machete, which made me howl. What I didn't howl about was the fact that just two weeks before the European Cup final I was sentenced and missed the greatest night in my club's history.

The Wedding and Blues

DANNY

Lloyd's wedding was on Trinity Road, less than half a mile from Villa Park, at two o'clock on a Saturday afternoon – the day of Villa v. Blues! Now this was the days before the wedding organisers were considered as part of the package and God knows whose idea it was to have it then; I can't think it was Lloyd's but what a predicament, you just knew it wouldn't go to plan. There were a lot of us in there in suits and one of the lads even donned a little claret and blue number. Just after the service had started, another 30-odd lads came in from the Crown and Cushion in Perry Barr, having made sure they had their match-day liquid refreshments but causing the service to be held up for a minute or two.

Once the service had finished, we went next door to a hall hired for the reception. But while everyone was congratulating the bride, the lads were telling Lloyd hurry the fuck up because 'the game starts in half an hour and them cunts will be en route'. The 30 lads didn't hang around, were off looking for Blues very quickly, a firm of wedding guests up for the row. The rest of us, mainly the ones wearing suits, began to get itchy feet and it was obvious the speeches weren't going to be made before kick-off. We got together and all agreed that we had to get to the game and at one stage even Lloyd said he was going with us and the honeymoon was over before it started, but someone talked him out of it.

At around half two, we all began slipping out of the reception and we must have looked a right sight walking down the road 20-twenty handed in suits. As we got to the crossroads, we came across the Blues firm being escorted towards the Witton End of the ground and they couldn't believe their eyes when they saw us all suited and booted. 'What's with the suits?' came the inevitable question and there was a fair bit of verbals going on before the OB moved them on. After they had gone, there were leaflets all over the floor that looked like confetti strewn across the pavement. I picked one up and read the headline: 'WANTED – DEAD OR ALIVE, BLACK DANNY.'

Meanwhile back at the wedding, Lloyd had done a great job in covering for us all but even he was stuck for an answer when the speeches began and the shout went out for the best man, Buster, to make his speech. Buster was by this time in the ground cheering the lads on. In fairness you can always get married again but Villa v. Blues you can't miss!

Row 4: The Subway Army at Knutsford

The final row in a mad few weeks was with Wolverhampton Wanderers and if it weren't for problems on the motorway we would never have met them. We were at Leeds United and they were playing at Man United. We would normally have gone via the M1 but it was closed and we ended up on the M6. Our coaches stopped at Knutsford Services and as the lads were getting off and either going into the toilets or getting bits from the shop, we noticed Wolves on the bridge upstairs. They had also noticed us but in fairness to them they had only one coach and we had the numbers. But they also had a certain Mr Quintine, who was their main lad and probably one of the best if not the best I have ever come up against.

We flew into them on the bottom of the stairs and were fighting on the bridge. I am not going to pretend it was a major row because it wasn't but we had a result against inferior numbers. They had one bloke that kept them tight and he didn't back off, he stood his ground and held them together. Armed with a weapon he had picked up, he held their line and we couldn't put him away. We should have annihilated him but this guy proved he was as game as they come and was a warrior. I can't deny I saw myself in him that day, he reminded me of myself and the numerous times I had found myself in the situation he was now in, heavily outnumbered and trying to hold things together. In my case it was usually on New Street Ramp surrounded by Zulus. This day he had done the same job, in fact possibly an even better one than I could have done and most if not all of our lads would give Wolves a lot of credit that day.

We were all nicked as we got back onto our coaches and taken to the nearest police station. I since heard that the Wolves lot were allowed to carry on. Luckily, nobody was charged and our coaches were allowed to carry on to Leeds. When we landed, it was about half three and we sprinted to the ground. A small mob of Leeds hanging around outside the away end had the shock of their lives when they saw us hurtling towards them. In truth we were just rushing to get into the ground but it was a nice bonus to chase that lot off in the process.

We had had four rows and in between a wedding on derby day, and again I'm trying hard not to sound like Uncle Albert but there are lads who have been going to the football for ten years and not seen that much action, they have well and truly missed the boat. I'll tell you something else, it took its toll and I think we were entitled to a rest after that few weeks, but what a time it was.

12 CHAMPIONS OF EUROPE

(When you had to win something to get in it!)

BRITTLE

Only a handful of English teams have won the big one, or the 'Big-eared One' as we prefer to call it. The European Cup is indeed the biggest prize in club football and in 1982, twelve months after winning our domestic championship, we achieved what we all believed was an impossible dream. I mention winning our championship, as that is important, as today teams can win the European title despite finishing as low as fourth in their own league. Today the competition is more like the 'Super League' that the crooks at UEFA strive for. In 1982 it was called the European Cup, and we fucking won it!

Sept 16	FC Valur	Home	W 5-0
Sept 30	FA Valur	Away	W 2-0
Oct 21	Dynamo Berlin	Away	W 2-1
Nov 4	Dynamo Berlin	Home	L 0-1
March 3	Dynamo Kiev	Away	D 0-0
March 17	Dynamo Kiev	Home	W 2-0
April 7	Anderlecht	Home	W 1-0
April 21	Anderlecht	Away	D 0-0
May 26	Bayern Munich	Final	W 1-0

That little list is how we did it, yes it was unspectacular, yes it may have been boring to watch but look at the 'goals against' column, check the names of the players who played and then do your research on the manager who steered us to the final after our messiah left us in the shit after a silly argument over a rolling contract. You will then have to agree that it was one of the greatest ever achievements by a British club side in Europe.

FC Valur

A draw against little-known FC Valur from Iceland was like having a bye into the next round. We hammered them 7-0 on aggregate and the only thing noticeable from the trip to Norway was the smell of fish. One of a set of brothers from Aston had gone there and this is what he thought of it: 'It was a tiny place holding no more than 3,500, equivalent to somewhere like Colchester. We were trying to watch the game and keep warm at the same time. It was freezing. All you could smell was bloody fish from the fish factory next to the ground and the beer was ruddy expensive. There was no trouble and the only problem was explaining the smell of fish to the missus when I got back!'

The Iron Curtain

Our next two games were both against opposition from the old Soviet Bloc, Dynamo Kiev and Dynamo Berlin. Now these weren't places that many English travelled to. For one thing, getting through immigration and obtaining visas wasn't that easy and them damn Ruskies weren't exactly welcoming to the West. The lads said it was especially on top in Berlin and if it wasn't for our Army lads who were based over there who came to support the English team, we would have been turned over. It was the old Communism v. the West thing.

It wasn't a place either where Western teams usually won yet we did Berlin in their own backyard with two wonder goals from Tony Morley, and Jimmy Rimmer even saved a penalty. It was one of those places that wasn't welcoming and we were glad to see the back of, but after three games that weren't very attractive for the common lad to travel to, Anderlecht, which was far more accessible and within our price range, was ideal.

BRITTLE THE BATTLE OF BRUSSELS

On April 2, Argentina on the orders of General Leopoldo Galtieri, invaded the Falkland Islands, which were under British sovereignty, triggering a war between the two countries. Thus for the first time in nearly 40 years, our country was at war. This was five days before we were due to play Anderlecht in the home semi-final of the European Cup. There was only one English club left in competition and that was Aston Villa, my team, our team, and we were representing our country in more ways than football.

Our boys were going to fight a war and some would come back in bodybags. The sense of patriotism amongst us was immense and we felt we had a duty to do our bit, if you like. It might sound odd but no other club up to then had been in Europe in the days of football violence and represented its country whilst at war. Whoever we had drawn in the semis, we would have taken more or less the whole firm as the European Cup had now become a realistic target.

As soon as the draw was made, one of our lads, Gaz H, started making plans to go over to Belgium and got his hands on a load of tickets directly from Anderlecht. By the time of the first leg, Gaz had been to Belgium, purchased 300 tickets and was selling them like hot cakes. I think by the end of the game that night, the 300 tickets had been sold. We won our leg 1-0 courtesy of a Tony Morley special that was followed by a legendary one-fingered salute celebration to somebody in the Trinity Road upper stand, and the second leg of the tie was to be played two weeks later at the Emile Verst Stadium in Brussels. The management, players and supporters of Anderlecht were certain they would turn the game around in Belgium whilst any Villa fan who dared to travel was told that they would be in for a warm reception from Anderlecht's 'notorious' mob, The 'O-Side Hooligans', a firm so fucking notorious that they never turned up at Villa Park in the first leg.

As far as most of us were concerned Belgium was a bland country, a nation famous only for making chocolates and getting sexual pleasures from young children. So if the O Side hooligans were waiting for us in here the land of the sweet-toothed paedophiles, they were not going to be disappointed. We were the Villa and Brussels was destined to be our oyster.

The vast majority of the lads had booked to cross on the midnight ferry from Folkestone to Ostend on the Monday evening, with the rest travelling on the Tuesday. The Monday night lot went down to London in two groups, the first that morning and the second in the afternoon, with everyone meeting in London around teatime. Most had been on the piss all afternoon and there was a real holiday atmosphere amongst the lads as we boarded the train to Folkestone. My mate Jimmy Ryan had been through a bad run of games where he had been nicked about six or seven times and on one occasion was due in two different magistrates' courts at the same time. Jimmy had attended one court and I attended the other one and posed as him, as we knew he was only going to cop a fine. With the European Cup gathering momentum, Jimmy had decided not to turn up for any more court dates while we were still in the competition, as he knew he was only going to get so many fines before they sent him down.

On that Monday, Jimmy was due to sign on in the afternoon and went to the office early in the morning, as he explained he was going to Belgium. Now whether the police were planning to nick him that day when he signed on or whether all ports had been alerted anyway, we will never know. What we do know is that there were three warrants out for Jimmy and we were amazed when he was allowed to board the ship without getting nicked.

We settled down for a drink and were in top spirits, and then the inevitable happened. A few strange faces surrounded us and Jimmy's European adventure was over. We were in a group playing cards and Jimmy had won the toss and was the dealer when two plain clothes police officers announced themselves and told him he was nicked. I got up and told them that they weren't taking him anywhere but Jimmy told me not to bother, as he was nicked fair and square, believing he wouldn't be going anywhere other than into the office to sign bail papers before returning to the card school. I left it on the condition that I could be the dealer!

Jimmy was mortified when instead of being given bail papers he was taken overnight to Coventry under police escort and told he was in court the following morning. He was delighted to get bail even though he missed the semi-final but was brought back down to earth when he noticed that his trial date was set for May 26, the day of the final. So while Villa were winning the cup in Rotterdam, Jimmy watched the game on his own in a pub in Moseley while all his mates were over in Holland. He was yet another one who paid dearly and missed Villa's greatest night.

This put a downer on everyone, as we were all gutted for Jimmy. As the boat pulled out of Folkestone and the bar opened, the party started going again as people began to hope that maybe Jimmy would get bail and catch up with us the following day, not knowing that he was history. As the drinks flowed, things began to get a bit out of hand all over the ship and it wasn't long before the casino was closed, followed shortly afterwards by the bar. Somebody climbed up a flagpole and took the flag, replacing it with a Villa flag, which was the straw that broke the camel's back as far as the captain was concerned. He announced that the boat was turning round and heading back to Folkestone. I don't think we had been on board for an hour and after some negotiations and the return of the flag, the captain agreed to carry on to Belgium.

On another ferry, the Rose and Crown firm were on their way to Brussels.

FORDY

We were in party mood, for many of us it was our first time abroad and we were full of high jinks, good mates together. On the ferry were some loudmouth American GIs, this lot were drinkers and I don't know how it started but it was down to the booze and they were trying to take liberties. I was C Crew but we had our own firm within the firm and were running coaches from the Rose and Crown pub, if you like, who long before the C Crew were always down the ground early doors getting up to no good, as any aspiring young Villains would be. We had been fed on stories from the likes of Rob's and Doc's brothers. Kev C was also someone older than us who we grew up around, forever giving us the tales about the Quinton stars, the Kingstanding firm and the older Erdington boys like Amy Smith and his lot. To us young 'uns at the time it was exciting and everybody our age seemed to be getting into it. Later we were to find out that so was every urchin in every city in England.

I don't remember what started it but it went right off and our boys didn't fuck about when it did, we got stuck into these loud-mouths, and it must be said they had some big, fit lumps with them. We always seemed to be fighting older lads in the scrapes we had outside of football. As this row came to its conclusion, the Yanks were screaming and diving all over the shop and then caught sight of Sparra and Doc throwing their cases into the English Channel. He was like that Sparra, you could be having off with anyone and he would always end up doing something totally off the wall.

I remember one Saturday after a game, our lot were having a night out at some rugby club over Sutton way. There must have been ten of us having the crack and playing up with local birds, kids in a sweet shop thing. A couple of the lads in there took umbrage but we were causing no harm really. We knew it was going to be on top at some point so we stayed right until the lights came on after last orders and then all decided we would move away from the club and out by the main road, and if we were followed by these lads they could have it, but we were really not looking for it. We casually walked towards this gully and I remember looking back and there were all these lads about 100 yards behind, probably about 15 or so. We got onto the main road and waited, these lads came out, saw us but now looked unsure, then every one of us steamed in. It was bedlam for about five minutes before these lads ended up on their toes.

After a while we were walking up the road when this car pulled up. A couple of geezers jumped out and one big fucker came at us with a baseball bat and went for Fonzo, our resident boxer and someone you should seriously not piss off. Babe Ruth swung his bat at Fonzo and in one movement Big F grabbed the bat with one hand and sparked the geezer with the other. *Strike!* The other fucker ran for first base, then we heard the engine turned over and there was Sparra leaning out of the driver's window. 'See ya tomorrow, lads!' He wheelspun down the road, his only problem being that the geezer's nan and grandad were in the back. He even apologised to them for leaving them both in the middle of a field before he was on his toes. Barmy cunt.

The Yanks on the ferry was the first little incident in what was to be a top trip for the boys.

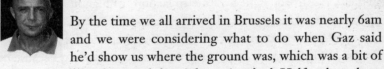

BRITTLE

By the time we all arrived in Brussels it was nearly 6am and we were considering what to do when Gaz said he'd show us where the ground was, which was a bit of a trek with all our bags and the night we just had. Half an hour later we got to the ground and I would compare it to the standard of our old Fourth Division at the time, at best. The walls were low and lads began climbing in and before long everyone was on the terraces and the first chant of 'the C Crew' was heard. People began scaling the fence onto the pitch and a couple of lads broke into the dressing room area and came out with a few balls and tracksuits. We soon got a game underway and although the nets weren't up and it was 50-odd a side it was a great crack.

I pissed myself when I noticed one of our fat lads trying his hardest to get over the fence so he could join in. Then we saw an old man running along the terracing with his fist in the air, shouting angrily in Belgian. This was as funny as our fat lad, as he couldn't get onto the pitch either, and we carried on with the game. Somebody then appeared with a couple of dogs and we decided to call the game a draw and make a quick exit. That tells you what the security was like, a joke.

By this time Brussels was beginning to wake up and we saw a café open right next to the ground and piled in. It wasn't long before the police landed and began looking in people's bags for any of the stuff that went from the dressing rooms. Luckily they didn't find anything and no one was nicked. Some of the wedgeheads amongst us decided to go on the rob and rifled the foreign shops, taking the Lacoste, Tacchini and Fila. We were only doing what the Scousers had been doing a few years earlier but it set us apart from the rest of the Midlands in the fashion stakes and earned us all a few quid as well. The police didn't seem to bother and if the lads were hungry they ended up robbing food as well and bring it back to the pub to eat. Like inside the ground, security outside was lax.

We left and headed for the city centre. It wasn't long before we came across what the English call the Stock Exchange and this became our headquarters for the next few days. The Stock Exchange was situated at a crossroads right by a metro station, with another couple of bars opposite. After we had all got our digs sorted out, we took advantage of the all-day licensing hours, which at the time did not exist in England. The locals stopped using the bus stop outside it because of all the abuse they were taking and the fact that it was swimming in piss.

The local skinhead girls found the Villa boys a major attraction and it didn't take long for one of our lads to cement Anglo-Belgian relations. To cut a long story short he ended up moving in with a Belgian bird and stayed there for another six months. There was no real trouble leading up to the game, the police left us alone and we never saw anything from the Belgians, the only fighting was with a small group of North Africans and it was nice to give them a slap and nice to hear more of our lads had done the same. As the night wore on our numbers were swelled as the Tuesday ferry began to arrive and the drinking went into the early hours.

Wednesday came and throughout the morning the Stock Exchange filled up for another day on the piss. All the songs were belting out: 'Holte Enders in the Sky', and to the tune of the 'Young Ones' by Cliff Richard, 'The C Crew, yes we are the C Crew, and the C Crew never run away, we'll stand and fight the shite in blue and white, the C Crew are fighting today.' If ever the words of a song were true then that was it!

As the day wore on, lads began to head to the bars near the ground. The biggest problem was finding one they could get in, as the boozers were that packed. Most Villa were now going to off licences and buying cheap wine and drinking it on the streets. The Belgians didn't know how to take us which led to a few little incidents, which in turn led to a few battle charges from the truncheon-wielding police.

As more and more Villa lads began to arrive, the police were finding it hard to keep a lid on things and eventually were forced to retreat, leaving us to carry on drinking, although a couple of lads got nicked in the process. They didn't want Villa lads drinking on their streets and their heavy-handed approach was leading to a rise in tensions. It didn't help that most of the Villa mob was half paralytic, not just pissed. I have never seen a firm as drunk in my life. Some couldn't stand up and it was a recipe for disaster.

We got into the ground and were among the Belgians. It was crazy, there was no segregation. The bulk of the Villa fans were to our right side and going round the first part of the terrace behind the goal. We were directly behind the goal. It's fair to say that the majority of lads had been on the piss all day. Nobody has ever been sure what started it off, but it wasn't long before a fight broke out between some of our lads and the police, which quickly developed into a mass brawl. Huge gaps opened on the terraces as the fighting got out of hand and the police were soon bashed out of the end.

The terrace did not seem as full as it had been as a lot of the home fans had moved out, but gradually more and more Villa fans began climbing out of their section to join in. By this stage the teams were out and the match was about to start. Another squad of police came running round the side of the pitch, to an ovation from the home fans, but the loudest cheer they got was from us as they reached our section. One of the few Belgians left turned to me and said, 'These are our special police.' I wish I could have seen his face when two minutes later they were on the retreat.

The game had started but behind the goal things got completely out of control. There was something about the Belgian police that made them look vulnerable, I think it was the silly cloth caps they wore as opposed to helmets, and they all looked so young. Another squad of them came running round to us. I saw my Belgian friend again and he said, 'These are our *very* special police.' I had to laugh as they looked worse than the first lot. The Belgians by now had moved back to another section and were booing us, as were the Villa fans in the away section.

During the first half, an off duty British soldier from West Germany ran onto the pitch wearing a claret and blue polo shirt and the confusion he caused resulted in the game being held up for six minutes. This was followed by cheers of 'Argentina, Argentina', and given the Falklands War situation I don't think they could have chanted anything more insulting. Our soldiers were risking their lives to help people who had been invaded, just as our soldiers had done for the Belgians 40-odd years previously. Villa began climbing into the Belgian section next to them and it cleared in no time. This was the first time we had had a proper confrontation with the Belgians the whole trip. A few people had gone over the fence at the front to get out of the way and a few Villa followed them. A couple of Villa fans went onto the pitch just as Anderlecht were attacking and the referee blew up to stop the game. Anderlecht would later appeal to UEFA to try to get the game replayed because they were denied a chance to score by the invasion.

Most of the Villa team came over and tried to calm things down, though at this stage most of the fighting had stopped as the Belgians had moved back and their 'very special police' had formed a double line in between us and them. The Villa fans in the away section started singing, 'You're the scum of Birmingham,' at us, to which everyone laughed and stuck two fingers up to them. On the pitch the Villa team were holding Anderlecht and we even had a good goal from Peter Withe ruled offside and Gary Shaw went close when he hit the crossbar.

When the referee blew his whistle for the end of the game, there was a scene of wild celebrations as we realised we had made it to the final of the European Cup. One giant knees-up continued outside the ground with still no sign of the O-Side Hooligans who, like their 'very special police', weren't very special at all. We made it back to the Stock Exchange boozer and we were just enjoying the night, but the police were wary of what might happen after a day and night of trying to halt a series of Villa fans charges at the chocolate-lovers. The Old Bill were outside the pub in large numbers and unlike the previous two nights when the pub had stayed open until the last man standing had had enough, the pub closed very early that night. There were also no Moroccans or North Africans mooching about that night either, as opposed to the previous two nights, which was a pity.

The next day, as everyone began arriving at the station for the journey home, we saw that we had made the front pages of every morning paper over there. One headline read, 'Villa Gorillas,' which still makes me smile. A total of 88 fans were arrested and 20 people had been injured and had to receive hospital treatment, some of whom were police. I don't think we knew at the time just how our antics were perceived back in Blighty.

When we arrived back in England, we realised that every English paper was full of the story as well, but no one mentioned the provocation of the Belgians with their 'Argentina' chanting. The ground was piss-poor and it was far too easy to climb from section to section. The police were clueless and completely unable to control our lads. That night we got away with murder and it was like being at school with no teachers supervising. Three years later in the same city, at an equally piss-poor ground the Heysel Disaster occurred. Well I doubt you will find a Villa fan who was at Anderlecht who was surprised at the events in Heysel.

Villa were eventually fined 50,000 Swiss Francs and had to play their next European game behind closed doors. Our next home game against Notts Forest also had a public announcement asking us to behave ourselves. That made us laugh. We knew that it had put us on the European map and for us it was a job well done.

BRITTLE
SHE WORE A CLARET RIBBON IN THE MERRY MONTH OF MAY

Date: 26 May 1982. **Venue**: Feyenoord Stadium, Rotterdam. **Match**: European Cup Final. Teams: Aston Villa versus Bayern Munich.

Fourteen years before, we had been on the brink of going out of business. Now here we were, at the very first attempt, playing in a European Cup final against one of the giants of European football. We had to pinch ourselves to prove we were there. Bayern Munich had won the European Cup three times in the mid-Seventies, beating the great Leeds side in 1975, and suddenly my club, who were novices in terms of Europe, were to play them. Nobody was giving us a chance before the game, all the talk was how these seasoned European campaigners would brush aside the English team that had finished only mid-table that season. We had lost our manager and had a caretaker manager in charge who had only ever been an assistant and a scout. The team wasn't littered with internationals like Bayern. So what chance had we got?

After all the trouble in Brussels in the semi-final, Aston Villa took total control over ticket sales and transport for the final. Nobody was allowed to travel or buy a match ticket other than from the packages the club were organising and they also announced that no supporters would be arriving in Rotterdam until four hours before the kick off, while apologising for the small minority who had spoiled the trips for the vast majority. While that vast majority travelled on the organised trips after being allocated 14,000 tickets for the final, however, the small minority had other ideas.

On the Monday before the game, the ten o'clock ferry from Harwich to the Hook of Holland was packed to the rafters with most of the C Crew who were looking forward to a couple of nights partying in Amsterdam before moving on to Rotterdam for the game on the Wednesday. The crossing took most of the day and the ferry arrived at the Hook around teatime. Ten of our lads had been over since the Saturday and had travelled to Rotterdam on the Monday to sort out tickets.

As the train pulled into the first station, which was Rotterdam West, the ten lads boarded and everyone was pleased to hear that there were loads of tickets and that you could just go up to the ground and buy them. The other thing they told us was that they had had some problems with a load of Moroccans and one of the lads, nicknamed Joe Jordan, had had his head split open with a machete by one of them. He also told us that he knew the club they all used.

As soon as we arrived in Amsterdam, we were shown the club and arranged to meet in the three bars opposite it as soon as we had got digs and ditched our bags. Within an hour, there were 250 C Crew drinking in the three bars. It wasn't long before we went over to the club but 250 of us had no chance getting in and the doors were quickly slammed. We had no choice other than to try to smash our way in, as these cheeky cunts needed to learn a thing or two, and it ended up with the whole of the front getting totalled.

It was only a matter of time until the OB turned up and sure enough a couple of vanloads appeared, sirens blazing. The road was busy, with about four lanes and a central reservation, and as the cops landed outside the club, the C Crew moved to the other side of the road and bombarded them with the remains of the armoury. Unfortunately it began to go wrong for us as all three bar owners had seen what was going on and had locked their doors, leaving us on the streets as more police vans arrived. There was a lot at stake, as nobody wanted to miss the final, so we decided to do one in the opposite direction to the police, who were now charging at us with batons shouting, 'English go home.' Unfortunately a few of ours did get nicked, including Joe, and they were all held until the Thursday and joined the long list of well-known faces who missed the game.

After that, there was no more trouble and it was then a case of a couple of days on the piss. On the Tuesday night, another ferryload landed, bringing the rest of the firm including most of the Steamers.

On the day of the game we made our way to Rotterdam and plotted up at a big 'Double Diamond' pub on the main road. It was blazing hot and most people were happy to sit in the sun and drink. Nobody wanted to get nicked this close to the game and as there were no Bayern Munich fans around where we were. The atmosphere by the ground wasn't anything like Brussels and you even had a 200-a-side football game between Villa and the Germans, although it did get a little out of hand when one of the lads, Johnny Thorne, decided to kick a German lad up the arse. I can't remember the result but I'm sure we lost that one on fucking penalties!

There was a good 100 C Crew right in the middle of the Germans' end – you can see it on the video of the game, where there is a small Union Jack smack in the middle of them. It was one of the rare occasions when to us the trouble was secondary to the game. We realised that we had come close the game before to getting Villa chucked out of the competition and now we were here we wanted to enjoy it. What amazes me to this day is the lads who got that pissed and slept on the central reservations and missed the game completely.

As the two teams came out it was very emotional, seeing the Villa lads standing there all in white with the national anthem being bellowed out from the stands. Ten years before we'd been in the Third Division. I saw lads with tears in their eyes and it was hard enough to stop the choking in my throat, never mind sing the anthem. *Come on lads, do it for me, the lads, the Villa and your country*.

The game started tentatively but our hearts were in our mouths when we lost our keeper Jimmy Rimmer and had to bring on Nigel Spink, who had only ever played once for the first team. It didn't take Spink long to be tested and his first save brought huge cheers from the Villa faithful behind him. If he was nervous he didn't show it and continued to look assured and made a string of fantastic saves. We got to half-time goalless and despite the amounts of alcohol I had consumed and the spliffs beforehand, I sensed history was in the making. We just needed a break.

The second half was very much like the first, we struggled to create any clear chances and the Germans looked more likely to score but we were working our bollocks off, closing them down, harrying them, and if only we could get our flair players in to it we would have a chance. That opportunity came on 67 minutes and is without doubt the most famous incident in our footballing history. Gary Williams was in possession and played the ball into Gary Shaw. He turned and shook off the defender and played it inside to Tony Morley, who twisted and turned the full-back inside out and crossed the ball into the penalty area and from no more than a few yards out. The ball bobbled up and ...

As if in slow motion, with 14,000 holding their breath in the ground and hundreds of thousands back home watching open-mouthed, like the scene in Fever Pitch *when they are on their sofas watching Michael Thomas score against Liverpool, the ball bobbles up and Peter Withe sticks out his leg and it hits his shin. The ball hits the net – and the thousands in the ground and the millions watching television sets let out an ear splitting YESSSS and Withe celebrates, tangled up in the goal nets with his trusty Villa sweatbands, arms in the air. It's ecstasy time. People are going wild and the whole Villa contingent can sense we are on the verge of greatness.*

Every time the ball was cleared upfield or played in the German half brought us that few seconds closer to the end of the game and a few more chomps on fingernails that were now down to stumps. Then the Germans scored – but the sigh of relief could be heard back in Birmingham when the linesman flagged offside. Brian Clough in the telly commentary assured the watching millions that it was offside. The Villa fans were whistling reminding the ref for full-time, *come on blow the fucker will you*. And then the moment came. The whistle was blown.

From Rochdale to Rotterdam in ten years, from Lockhead to

Withe, a journey that started so long ago. Words cannot explain how it felt or even come close. I don't care if you have just had a threesome with Kylie and Danni Minogue the feeling was a million times better. Our country at war, millions watching, praying we would win, and old men who had followed Villa all their lives, did they ever think they would see their club win the European Cup? They might have dreamt it, but win it, never.

As Dennis Mortimer lifted the cup up a huge roar went up and people were crying with joy, hugging each other, shouting, screaming, in total disbelief that we had done it. Paul Breitner, who had tried to slate the Villa and English teams in general before the game, saying how they were a superior side, was a desolate figure on the pitch. Fucking tough!

It may never happen again in our lifetime, it may never ever happen again in Villa's history, these things just don't happen again unless you're Liverpool. It has to be one of the greatest moments in their lives: ASTON VILLA, CHAMPIONS OF EUROPE. As the team brought the cup, Tony Morley in the red Bayern shirt he had swapped – *that* I wouldn't have done – was doing his Gazza bit, dancing with the trophy perched on his head in a lap of honour to cries of 'Rule Britannia' from the crowd and 'Are you watching Ron Saunders?' It was magic. I didn't want it to end, I wanted more, if I'd had my way they would still be on the pitch now.

It was hard not to spare a thought for Danny, Clarkey and all the others who hadn't made it that night. They had done as much for the Villa as any of us and it must have been hard for them listening to it on radios, but in our hearts they were there with us, they had always been with us and tonight was no different. That is how I felt but the lads who missed it obviously felt different.

CLARKEY

I was in Winson Green prison at the time and the biggest thing I can remember is when Villa scored, the whole prison erupted.

DANNY

I watched the match on TV even through I was grief-stricken not being there. I did attend the FC Valur home leg match before I got sent down. I did feel as if I was part of the success that night. But I was a lonely figure in my cell, listening to Tony Butler on the BRMB sport show. It was a far cry from the season before, when I had held the championship trophy aloft in front of thousands of Villa fans chanting my name.

BRITTLE

Back in Holland there was no accommodation in Rotterdam and after a night's partying and celebrating we had no choice but to get our heads down for a couple of hours until the early morning train to the ferry port. There was a central reservation on the road leading away from the station and it was quite a sight with a few hundred Villa sleeping along a couple of hundred yards of this grass verge. The police kept shining their headlamps into us, which would piss everyone off, and then at about 4.30am we were woken by chants of 'Bayern' as a mob of Germans were making their way to the station. They must have had the shock of their lives as a mob of angry Englishmen jumped up out of the darkness and charged at them. It wasn't so much that they were Germans (although that didn't help), it was more because the noisy bastards had woken us up. We didn't see them again and I'll never know if they got their train.

Most people were totally wrecked by the time we got back into England, but the feeling was there and stays with me to this day. We had achieved everything we had dreamt about and for most Villa fans it was the greatest week of our lives. Unfortunately there was only one way to go from there – and the same applied to the C Crew, if nothing else to prove we had conquered Europe together!

13 WE HATE THE BASTARDS IN CLARET AND BLUE

DANNY

The one thing the whole of the Midlands agrees on is that Aston Villa are the biggest club in the region. However you measure it, whether by history, tradition, number of trophies won or simply support, it's Villa by a country mile. Ask anyone in the Midlands who doesn't follow Villa who they hate most and I guarantee if it's not us we will be second after their derby rivals. So naturally, with all that jealousy and the short travelling distances, Villa have had some lively times against their near-neighbours. With the help of some of the main faces from the Steamers and C Crew we have detailed events and opinions on our Midland rivals.

West Bromwich Albion

Most people assume that our real rivalry is Blues, but certainly in the 1960s it was the Albion, probably because as a club they were relatively successful, were in Europe before us, and when their striker Ronnie Allen scored to send Villa down to the Second Division he did a lap of honour, fuelling a real hatred between the supporters.

There were numerous incidents in the Seventies and Eighties in which they came off second best and Villa supporters treated a trip there as a day out, almost a day at the seaside, maybe that's why we use to sing 'Oh I do like to be beside the sea side' and the brass band played 'Fuck off West Brom'. The firm Albion have now is very different to the ones we encountered then and most agree that they are a lot better than Wolves or the Blues now, but back then, well judge by some of the accounts our lads give.

D.DUB 1974/75 SEASON

It was considered the norm then to go into the Brummie Road end of Albion's ground, the main standing area for home fans. It was almost a tradition for Villa and while the police did their best to stop it happening, you could guarantee that every year some Villa would slip the net and get in. The secret was always to try to go in there in ones, twos and threes so as not to attract any attention, then all firm up when inside.

This particular season, a pal and I had gone in on our own but got sussed out downstairs by a few Albion. We were spotted straight away and I copped a right-hander full on the nose, which started pissing with blood. There was an old bar there, which was more like a cattle shed and wouldn't have looked out of place at St Andrews, and as it was on top my pal jumped over the counter. I wasn't far behind him but not before I had got a couple of digs in myself. For some reason it was like we had entered the 'forbidden zone' and not one Albion fan followed us. A lot of insults were exchanged while we hoped we could hold out until the police came.

I don't know why but the bar was unsupervised at the time, so we both helped ourselves to a bottle of beer, it would have been rude not to. Unfortunately I soon needed a piss but there was no way I was going through that lot. It was then that I had a brainwave. I tipped a bit out of several bottles and pissed in each one. *That's good enough for the Albion fans*, I thought. Soon after that, a couple of coppers did indeed arrive and we went round to the Smethwick end, where the Villa contingent were all standing.

That wasn't the end of things though, because when they opened the gates 15 minutes before the end, we all went out in small numbers and went round to the Brummie Road end. We regrouped outside but Albion wouldn't come out to us, so we charged in at them. Pete the Greek was magnificent as he charged up the stairs at them on his own, and none of them would go near him. We may have lost the game but we won the psychological war and that was the start of us having the upper hand over them.

CLARKEY

For the home game later on in the season, all our lot met in the Shakespeare in town, 80-100 of us. What often happened was that the people who used to have to come through town to get to Villa Park would stop off and drink in town and the people who lived on the other side, like Erdington and Kingstanding, would drink by the ground, though obviously there were exceptions to this. We got the train as normal to Witton station and when we got off the train, somebody said that Albion were in the pub across the road, the Witton Arms. It turned out that a lot of our lads were in the lounge but Albion were in the bar, with a few standing outside. Our trainload charged across the road at the pub and Raggy glassed the first one. The few that were outside ran back in and they bolted the doors behind them. Albion were shitting themselves and wouldn't come out. As was usual on that side of the ground, the police weren't far away and it didn't take long for them to land and move us on.

Villa won the game in style 3-1 and were still right on course for promotion to Division One with only a few games left, and we were all in a good mood. By the time we all got back to Witton station, Albion were on the platform. The police managed to keep them on one half of the platform and us on the other and when the train came,

Albion got onto the last two carriages. Bizarrely, only a couple of police got on the train and they went right to the front by the driver. The train was packed solid, as you would expect after a local derby, and Villa wasted no time in going into the Albion and it soon turned into chaos. Windows began to smash and Albion were backed into the last carriage and for obvious reasons couldn't go any further. It was hard to fight properly as the aisles on the train were so narrow and you ended up with people climbing all over the seats to try to land a punch. One Albion lad at the front of them was trying to fend off all the Villa with a large triangular sheet of glass that had come from one of the windows. How he didn't cut his own hands I will never know.

At Aston, two minutes away, the train made an unscheduled stop. In those two minutes it had been wrecked and Albion were at sixes and sevens. As soon as the train ground to a shuddering halt, Albion were off but Villa came at them from all directions. They got absolutely battered and began running all over the place. Some went down the tracks back towards Witton, some jumped across to the platform on the other side, some ran out of the station and some simply got kicked all over the platform. D.Dub had a real bonus as he spotted the bloke who had given him a bloodied nose earlier in the season and made sure he gave him a bit of stick.

When we got back to New Street the police were waiting and had blocked the whole platform off. It was so one-sided it was untrue.

BRITTLE WBA AWAY, MAY 1982

After our exploits a season earlier at their place, we decided to try again and carry on what was almost an annual Villa ritual of going into the Birmingham Road. Forty of us paid into the Brummie Road end and made our way up to the back corner about 20 minutes before kick-off. The scream went up, 'Fuckin' Villa,' and we went straight into them. All the usual suspects were there: Andy, Jimmy Ryan, Jimmy Coley, Fordy, Joycey, etc. Albion backed right off and I suppose a lot of them couldn't even see us through the crowd so didn't know there was only 40 of us. The Old Bill were on us almost straight away and got us all down to the front, with Albion all coming back round us now the police were there, but they couldn't move us before the OB came. We were thrown out and had to pay again into the seats on the side, where there was a mob of Albion next to us all game with police in between us. Yet again, once we got outside where there were no police, Albion were nowhere to be seen.

CLARKEY ALBION'S SECTION FIVE

This lot are a different proposition to their old firm, certainly very active and have acquitted themselves well when we have come up against them. They are best known for the battle at the Uplands pub in Handsworth in August 2004, a major row which led to several dozen from both sides being arrested. Albion arrived at the pub tooled up, and when Villa came out to meet them, the brawl that followed was largely captured on camera. Whilst the majority at the Uplands battle were lads from a firm called the Villa Hardcore, some of ours, albeit not many, were involved and one of the Steamers, along with some very good lads, held the line for a long until the Hardcore leader arrived on the scene. The younger lads know him better than they do our lads and it seemed to galvanise the rest of them, even though Albion were the ones carrying weapons. One of the main lads involved in that fracas faced an Albion lad wielding a metal bar. In trying to protect his head, he raised his arm and apparently you could hear the bones crack as the bar met his arm. Faced with that, all he could use was his belt. He wanted the lad to drop the bar and have a straightener with him but he wouldn't oblige.

Of all the West Midlands firms we have come up against in the Prem, Albion have been the most impressive. Yet having spoken with heads from the Steamers and the C Crew, it is difficult finding anyone who rated the older Albion lot. Maybe there are some who think otherwise and I'm not saying we haven't had lads who have copped a kicking there, but in general they were poor.

Wolverhampton Wanderers

DANNY

Now these are a different kettle of fish. I and a lot of others have a lot of respect for the old Subway Army, which I rate above the Zulus in their prime, and one particular individual called Quintine is a true warrior. He could have it, as I found out in Knutsford service station [see Chapter 11].

The first row I encountered with Wolves was in 1978 at Villa Park, first game of the season. It was by Witton station, where the Wolves lads were waiting for the trains back into Wolvo. I went down there as I normally did to see what was going on and to get at the away fans. I could see all the old Erdington and Stockland Green lads like Peter Asbury, David Owen, Brian Desmond, Amy Smith and the Kennedys, so I knew they weren't going to wave them goodbye without some sort of parting gift.

We got across the road from them and said, 'Take a walk lads,' and fair play to them, they were happy to oblige and a mob of theirs walked away from the station and onto Electric Avenue, a side road away from the station. It didn't take long for it to turn into a full-scale row and what amazed me was how we all managed to fight and run that long – it literally went on for 25 minutes, with each mob seemingly gaining advantage before the others regrouped and came back. A bus window got put in by Wolves and a few match-day boys got off the bus and joined in but most on board were Villa civilians who wanted to get out the way of it all. There was no Old Bill and the row carried on to the Yew Tree pub and it was a good one with no side really claiming any win.

Going to Wolves could be a rough ride in much the same way

that Forest was in those days. The subways around Molineux were the subject of many tales in terrace folklore.

We had the battle at Knutsford and a few on either side took real kickings but Wolves were looking for revenge, so we knew there would be a welcoming committee for us when we next went. It was 1983, a Sunday and the first Midlands derby to be shown live on national television. We took a firm but not as big as I would have liked; it was one of those places you needed numbers and a good front line. We got to the ground and sure enough they are waiting for the C Crew and it kicked off right by the dual carriageway but it was running battles with nobody getting the result.

Then came what has to be one of the most surreal moments for me. We went in their new stand, the John Ireland, nearest to the subway – and they put us next to Wolves. I am not joking, we sat there exchanging stories and pleasantries all in full view of the police but nobody was playing up. They said to me, 'Danny, you're okay mate, we don't want you but want it with the rest of the Villa.' I replied as anyone would, 'Sorry lads, ain't leaving my lads, if it goes outside then it goes.'

It certainly 'went' outside, with one particular Villa lad, Dave 'the Rave' Ravenhall (RIP) causing a lot of damage. It was another good row but again it was a score draw with the OB drawing their truncheons to stop all the fun. I have no particular liking of Wolves but looking back they were a very good firm and could hold their own with most at their place.

I also remember on one of my scouting missions on semi-final days at Villa Park seeing a massive mob of Wolves obliterating Arsenal on Aston Park, which was no mean feat as Arsenal were also a tidy firm back then.

MOSES

For me there isn't a lot of difference between Wolves and Albion. I was only on the scene for seven years or so but in my time neither were up to much, although I did get nicked at Wolves. I think it was the 1981 season away and after the game there was a bit of a row and I was focussing on this geezer with bleached red hair. After a bit of a stand-off we were into them and the Old Bill were straight in and looking for people to nick. I tried to play the innocent bystander caught up in it all and put my hands in my pockets and tried to walk, not run, away.

The police, though, focus on me and despite my protests nick me and for good measure throw the odd 'black bastard' verbal at me while I am in the cell. That probably did it for me. I was incensed because it seemed the police wanted a scapegoat so chose me. I have said before the posse I used to go the game with was me and 19 good white lads so I am hardly anti-white. In fairness to the lads they supported me. I didn't want to be sent down for something on this occasion I hadn't really done. Yes there were lots of other occasions when I was lucky not to get sent down but this wasn't right.

I rallied the lads from my area, all the old Villa lads, mates who I went to school with and had been on the front lines with, and we hired a 52-seater coach to go to court. These guys were going to be my 51 witnesses. They didn't even get through the courtroom; the judge threw the case out. I was overjoyed, especially as I had fucked up them Wolverhampton coppers who thought it funny to give it the black bastard bit.

I said, 'Right lads, I will buy you all a drink,' and we ended up going into Wolverhampton town centre. That one drink turned into a session, I suppose we got a bit rowdy and would you believe it word got round Wolverhampton that Villa were in their town on the piss. They then go on a recruitment campaign for the day and after being on it for most of the afternoon we end up with the Subway Army paying us a visit and it going bang off. No one was taking a back step and no one got nicked even though the police quickly descended on the pub and gave us an escort out of town. Ironically I did more damage in the pub than outside the ground for what I get nicked for.

Yam Yam, who has links with Wolverhampton (hence his nickname), gives his opinion of the new Wolves lot:

For the one Premiership game at our place they couldn't even muster 50 lads. I was very surprised and disappointed by Wolves and they really had no excuses for not turning up. At one point, we were organising people to go into Wolverhampton later on the night via the metro to try to get some action, but the police sussed what was going on. The return at their place was a non-event. We tried to evade the attentions of the Old Bill and went to Bilston to a local snooker hall but they were onto it. I knew who was in that Wolves firm and who was in Villa's and it's that old cliché, they wouldn't have lived with what we had out that day, but that's my opinion. It proves to me how difficult it is these days and the penalties just ain't worth the risk.

Coventry City

DANNY

If we didn't rate Albion then Coventry was like a walk in the park, yet having worked there as a doorman I know it's a real rough town with some very bad estates. But when Villa went there we just seemed to overrun the place and met little opposition in comparison to other places. The biggest problem at Coventry was the walk back to the station; if you weren't fit it could be a serious problem to your general health and that summed them up.

The year we came up, 1975, Villa seemed to have more in their ground than Coventry. We were in the big, uncovered end and the place their lads occupied, the West End. So Villa were in two out of the three sections and were taunting them with, 'You are surrounded.' In 1977, the week after we had won the League Cup at Old Trafford by beating Everton after two replays, we took 15,000 to Highfield Road. To say we annihilated them is an understatement and the local press was full of it. It felt we had taken the town and was a throwback to the Third Division days.

The worst problem I ever had at Coventry was off Blues once

when they came there to meet us and the Zulus got the better of us. In 1981 we went again early and all met up in their boozers, the Market Tavern and Silver Sword. We literally took the piss. Cov came for a look but couldn't do anything about us; we did as we pleased around the town and caused more damage to property than to their firm, as they just wouldn't have it with us.

No more than ten Steamers went in their end the one year and Cov couldn't budge them. The Greek and my old sleeping partner Groombridge were fighting for what seemed to be all through the game. We were enjoying the entertainment although Groombridge did lose his faithful sheepskin as it got cut to ribbons.

There were other games, like a night match in 1978 when two different mobs of Villa went into the Coventry end and did very well before the police shifted them. Both were escorted out to a heroes' welcome from the large spion kop end but it tells you everything you need to know about Cov back then.

FORDY COVENTRY AT VILLA PARK, 1992

I was drinking with Gaz and Brittle in the Little Crown in Perry Barr. It was my turn to get a taxi to the ground and meet this kid to pick up some cheap tickets. I decided to nip round and have a pint with all the Rose and Crown lads in the Yew Tree. It was about 1.30 and the bar had a really good atmosphere, Rob and Doc were at the pool table, there were a few Coventry lads in there, banter was going but there was no bad atmosphere at all.

I got my first pint and I was talking to Joey the Bat when this minibus load of Coventry lads walks in the boozer. The atmosphere nosedived. They were led by a big lump wearing a bandana. Bang, it's off, the bar is like a battlefield and me and Joey the Bat are into them with the rest of the boys. Unfortunately one of their lads ended up cut real badly, it was impossible to know who did what but this bloke needed nearly 100 stitches. The Coventry firm picked the wrong pub to look for trouble.

I was outside when the police landed and was nicked along with Joey and taken to Steelhouse Lane for forensics after I'd had my head stitched. Other lads like Doc ended up having wounds stitched, so you know it was a proper tear-up. The problem I had with all this, same as Joey, was that these lads came into the boozer for the row, they copped it big time, it was us or them. I do feel sorry for the kid who got badly cut but I never glassed him, it was just madness in a flash. My problem was, the same geezers who came looking for it turned grass. I was given police bail, the same as Joe. I then got the early morning call about a month later and charged properly. They was talking 'attempted murder' at one point. Fuck me, I'd got hold of a pool cue but that didn't warrant what they were throwing at me.

I was taken to New Street Station to be identified; my solicitor gave me the cue to follow this group of blokes and walk towards the escalators, where the witnesses would be. There were five of them at the top and one at a time they came down and looked us up and down. I was picked out five times out of five and was down the stairs. I finally got done for wounding with intent and I received three years. I am not sure how they did Joey but he was charged with the same, also getting three years. Would I have done the same to those Coventry lads and picked them out? Would I fuck.

I do think that getting away with supposedly headbutting a copper before the Liverpool game a few years earlier did me no favours, because I walked on that charge. Like all of the other lads in our firm, at some point or other it was going to catch up with me.

Derby County

THE GENERAL THE FORTY-NINERS

We had hired a double-decker bus that went from the Crown and Cushion in Perry Barr to Wembley for the England v. Holland World Cup qualifying game in 1988. There were 44 on the bus and as it was a midweek game, we set off early. We were on the beer and whizz from the time we got on it and for most of the day. We got to London early and ended up in some boozer by Baker Street, where Derby seemed to be giving Chelsea the runaround and basically were taking liberties. We didn't get involved; most of the lads were intent on getting pissed and just watched these Derby lads, who seemed to want the whole place to know they were on the England scene.

We started to make a move to the station at about seven o'clock and these cunts were still larging it when we got to the underground and thought they could do as they pleased because of the numbers they had. I turned to the others, including the likes of Fordy and Gaz H, and said, 'Fuck it, let's have these cunts.' With that I gave it the gob, 'Come on!' and we ran into them, jumping the turnstiles in the process. At this point there was no more than half of our crew and they had a good 60, I know that for a fact because the Old Bill who pulled us said, 'Are you lot mad, there are sixty of them.' It wasn't a major confrontation and no one got nicked but it set the tone for later. The police arrived quickly, I think Derby's playing up earlier and trying to get a name for themselves had alerted them so they were in the vicinity. They split us up and put us on separate trains into Wembley.

Nothing really happened at the game other than the wankers let a two-goal lead slip. I love my country almost as much as my club so I was pissed off that we hadn't won the game. As usual at Wembley, getting out of the coach park was a nightmare and we were stuck for a couple of hours, which didn't help the mood. On the way back we were laughing about the Derby lot and thought what a cheeky bunch of cunts, when the lads decide they want a piss break so we pull into the Watford Gap service station.

Would you believe it, the same Derby lads are on the services, two coaches of them. We now number 49 because we had met five Albion lads who were sound and they had hitched a ride home with us. Everyone was thinking the same and was roaring and we flew into them. Their first coach was about to pull off so I instinctively picked up a slab of concrete where they were doing repairs to the service station and fucked it through the window. It ended up on the driver's lap. That stopped the coach and now they had no way out of it and had to make a fight of it.

We had a right good crew and the lads were hyper and bang up for a row. The Derby lads, who outnumbered us two to one and had been playing up all day, couldn't handle it. They were scrambling over each other to get away and Villa lads were dragging them off the coach and battering them. I don't think they could believe what we were like. From an outsider's view it must have been total carnage. We wrecked the coaches and everything on them. It was a hell of a row but it was very much one way, there were bodies all over the services and they were theirs. Lads like Fordy and Gaz H were doing plenty of damage and the Rams were getting their arses kicked. There was a ready-made pile of weapons because of the building work so bricks and even a waste paper bin went into them and how somebody wasn't killed I don't know.

They managed to get themselves together, got the injured back on their two coaches minus the windows, and made their way back to Derby before the police pulled them over on the borders of Derbyshire and took the injured to hospital. It made the national papers and even GMTV next day, which showed the service station and the wrecked coaches. I knew I would be fingered for the slab so I went back into the toilets to wash my hands and get rid of the dirt. Luckily I had the vision to talk to two cleaners in there and say, 'I've had to get away from that out there, I don't want to be involved or get arrested for anything.' They assumed I was innocent, must have been the baby face, and agreed that they would stand as witnesses. They even gave me their full names just in case.

We made it to Corby before the police caught up with our double-decker and escorted it to Birmingham. We decided to get the coach to drive towards the Castle Vale area and then do a runner, every man for himself, knowing that some would get nicked. The driver was a relative of one of the lads and probably one of the few not to get involved so he knew the score. It didn't go to plan, however. The cops did stop us at Castle Vale but split our group into two and took us to two stations in Daventry, where the coach driver gave a statement to the police identifying the slab thrower. That's when I called in the cleaners' names at the service station, who were true to their word and said I was in the toilet at the time trying to avoid it. Thank you for that!

A few of the lads did get nicked for it which was a pity but it was a right good tear-up and a result for the old C Crew lads.

Leicester City

BRITTLE THE BATTLE OF FILBERT STREET, 1977

You were guaranteed a row at Filbert Street and there has been a lot of history with them, probably stretching back to the day they more or less relegated us to the Third Division in 1970, and in 1977 there was a riot at their place. I was there that day with Jimmy Ryan and it was obvious that things were going to kick off, as Villa fans were in the section reserved for away fans in the corner of the Home end, a split stand where, due to the numbers we had taken, Villa overspill were now going into the next section. At the same time, other Villa were in the opposite end stuck in that poxy corner bit. All through the first half there was banter and the shouts of 'what a fucking shithole' from the thousands of Villa that had gone there, and people were goading each other to come over into each other's sections.

In the second half, Villa fans started dismantling the wooden refreshment stand and tins of paint and pieces of wood were thrown to and fro. One Villa lad went a stage further and, along with four others, scaled the fence and jumped into the Leicester end swinging a red crate round and a plank of wood. Another unfortunate lad trying to scale the fence was left with his arm impaled on it. That was the cue for the rest of the Villa to get involved and the Steamers joined in, which was the signal for Villa fans at the opposite end to run the length of the pitch to also join the action.

It was classed as a riot. I have seen a lot worse but here was an end completely cleared, the Leicester lads were on the pitch and Villa were milking it for all it was worth. The adrenalin was flowing and it could have turned really ugly for a nothing game. The referee had no option but to take the players off, as hundreds of their lot were now on the pitch behind the goal. Villa captain Leighton Phillips and John Gidman came over to us pleading for calm but we were winning 2-0 and enjoying ourselves taking the piss.

After the game there were a lot of running battles, as the home supporters weren't happy at all with us taking their end. Villa went on the rampage and it went off all the way back to the station. In one incident by a car showroom, Villa were giving chase to this Leicester mob who have bitten off more than they could chew. Realising it was well on top and that we were not in the mood to end our party, they sought refuge in the showroom but that wasn't going to save them. One of the lads picked up a scooter and threw it straight through the window. The Old Bill struggled to control the number of Villa who wanted to get involved and for every fight they did prevent there was another two they couldn't. It was a lovely sight as the trains pulled into New Street Station to see the pink *Sports Argus* headlines, 'Villa fans riot.'

I mention in the Introduction and there's no doubt about it, I took my biggest hiding there, and got the nickname 'Frag', in the Nineties. We had some good results there but like anywhere you can get caught out if you're in the wrong place at the wrong time.

DANNY KEYSTONE COPS, 1987

In 1987 we had been relegated and the following season we got off to a sluggish start. We hadn't won a game by the time we played Leicester and the team needed a lift. Before the game we ended up drinking in a pub in their town centre. Clarkey and Brittle were there and we had a good little firm but it didn't take long for the Baby Squad to find us. They came straight to the boozer and beckoned us out. I will always give Leicester credit, if you're in their town they will find you. But on this occasion we had quality in our firm and whilst they had numbers we ended up putting them to the sword. Unfortunately Clarkey got nicked in the process.

At the game our firm went in the seats on the side. Having got off to such a disappointing start to the season, when Mark Lillis scored the relief got to me and God knows why but I ran on the pitch and jumped on Lillis, along with the Villa players. Mark Walters, a local lad playing for us who I knew through the old Aston area, was trying to calm me down but it was too late. A policeman came on to get me off and without realising he was on me I spun round, accidentally taking him over my shoulder. The copper tumbled, his helmet came off and he cracked his head on the concrete perimeter and was out stone cold.

I stood in front of all the Villa lads with my arms raised, acknowledging the cheers, which obviously antagonised the Old Bill. The rest of them dived on me and I get swamped beneath the bodies, arrested and taken away. They ended up taking me to the nick past Leicester lads who have been arrested and who are shouting, 'Danny you're a wanker,' the usual banter. I ended up slapping one who put his head out the cell at just the right height. While I was out of action, the lads were doing very well after the game and by all accounts gave Leicester a proper hiding by the hospital.

When it went to court I was charged with assault and they were looking to ban me from every football ground in the country. Thankfully my defence was a lot better than the copper, who was never going to make a gymnast.

The older Steamers have differing views about Leicester's older lot. D.Dub and Granny both think they were not up to much but others who had run-ins did rate them. In their Baby Squad days Moses will confirm that Leicester was a moody place to go and you could always get a row there.

MOSES

I recall going there one game and being refused entry at first because I had a walking stick due to an injured leg. After much persuasion, the police did eventually let me in. For some reason we were in the seats that day and the Baby Squad were right next to us. It didn't take long for it to go off big time and I was in the middle of it, using the walking stick, waving it round like a madman and trying to hit any of them who came near me. That was another game I was lucky not to get nicked at.

Nottingham Forest

MOSES 'VILLA, VILLA, CAN YOU SWIM.'

The old Villa lads came badly unstuck at Forest in the 1973/74 season. Villa tried to get into the home end and did very well inside the ground for a while but after the game they didn't keep together. Villa is a club that other Midland mobs would turn out for in force and Forest had every lad out. After the game they bashed Villa from all angles, I suppose you could say we were ambushed. It was also the day one of our lads got thrown in the Trent. The story became terrace folklore and was to circulate around Birmingham for years. The poor bastard couldn't swim either.

We swapped divisions and didn't play for a few seasons, then under Cloughie they came back up and we ended up having to play them twice in 1977/78 at the City Ground. The first game was on a Saturday and despite everyone going up there winding each other up – 'Have you brought your water wings,' etc. – a lot fancied having a pop at them. I went with the old Perry Common and Erdington lads and we were all determined to go in the Trent End. That's exactly what we did. We got in early and the Steamers were also present. There were over 100 Villa in there and due to sheer numbers they couldn't move us. The police formed a line between us and Forest, who were fuming but couldn't do anything about it. All they could do was spit and throw bottles at us.

Lads from the Steamers like D.Dub and Raggy admit that going to Forest was always lively but they said in the Seventies they didn't travel in numbers to Villa Park and were almost a totally different firm to the home one.

Stoke City

D.DUB STEAMERS AT STOKE, 1975

We played at Stoke City in the 1975/6 season after we had come up from the Second Division. It was the year of the balloons and we must have taken 7,000 up there, filling the large open end. We had gone up by private coach, arriving in Stoke early doors, and were queuing outside the social club underneath the Boothen End at quarter to eleven. As soon as they saw us they opened early and began serving. We had a good three and a half hours in there and when we left, nobody could be bothered walking round to the away end so we all paid into the Boothen. We must have been sussed as we went in, which wouldn't have been hard as we were hardly keeping our voices down after a good drink in that social club. When five or six of us went for a piss just before half-time, we got quizzed in the toilet. A couple of the lads who were with us were half-Asian and one of them was in the bog at the time.

'You lot are Villa,' said a Stoke lad. 'I know you are because you're a Paki.'

What the Stoke lad hadn't realised was that everyone in the bog at the time was Villa and a couple went back to the rest of the lads to warn them that it was about to go. As the rest of the lads came out of the bogs, loads of Stoke were waiting for them at the top of the stairs and began to go down at them as they left the toilet area.

Forty of us came behind them and fucked them everywhere, they were well confused.

The OB landed on us but decided that we could stay, so we watched the second half in there as well. Just after half-time, Plug bumped into us. 'Oh there you are,' he said. 'We had heard you were in here.' God only knows how he had heard or where he had come from but he had found us and we watched the rest of the game without further interruption.

DANNY TONY MORLEY'S PLACE IN JEOPARDY, 1983

This game for me was all about the look on Tony Morley's face. It was our European Super Cup season and we were cruising 4-0 when about 20 Stoke came on the pitch from the Trinity Road, trying to do nothing really, it was a real token effort. But as they were running up the touchline to get to the Stoke section in the North Stand, Joey the Bat from the C Crew decided to get involved, jumped onto the pitch and raced up the touchline. This was in the second half with the game still going on. Tony Morley had the ball and Joey went past him. Now this bloke has 32 convictions for football violence – you have to ask if he can run that fast why did he ever get caught? Morley must have known then that his days were numbered seeing Joey outsprinting him and not long after he was sold. The police shepherd them away and I think Joey escaped another conviction but was thrown out the game for his little shuttle-runs.

The plan afterwards was for an arranged meet on Aston Park, so we left the game early and got the high ground, a good 70 of us. I was saying, 'Just hold it lads and wait,' like them old films with the bows and arrows and they can only reach when they are within striking range. Stoke appear and I am still saying, 'Hold, hold, hold it,' but no, we get a few who break through who can't wait, the premature ejaculation ones in our firm. When they go, the rest follow and we are now running down the park into the Stoke firm, who are on their toes. Not a punch was thrown in anger and I was fuming. We'd had the chance of a right good punch-up but we blew it by being over-eager. I hadn't long been out of nick and was itching for a good old tear-up and the new boys in the ranks fucked it up. It was no result for me, a complete waste of time.

STU 'GOODNIGHT CHARLIE BROWN'

On Saturday, 24 October 1987, we were due to play Stoke City away. Villa had begun to get their act together on the pitch after a poor start to the season and the fans were optimistic about a quick return to Division One. There would be another massive Villa following at Stoke and a large hooligan element was guaranteed.

Very early on the day of the match, about 70 Villa lads met at The Crown and Cushion and made their way to Stoke in a series of vans and cars. A few more were picked up along the way, so there were probably about 80 in this firm. Everybody had arranged to meet just outside Stoke so that all the vehicles could travel into the city centre together. The plan was to get into one of Stoke's main pubs before they did and then wait for them to turn up and for the sparks to fly. The Villa parked up at a pub in town which I think was called the Talbot. The pub was just opening up so everybody steamed in and waited for Stoke to show.

Sure enough, before long Stoke started showing up in twos and threes. They were gobsmacked to find the Villa boys in there and ended up down the road in a place called Charlie Brown's. Stoke eventually rang the pub Villa were in to say they were coming down and a little while later about 70 of them came up the road. At the same time, another van full of Villa had turned up and they were also making their way towards the pub. There were only about 15 of them, but Stoke decided to run at them anyway. The Villa in the pub saw what was going on and started to come outside but the bouncers locked the doors after only about 20 had made it. Villa were outnumbered outside by about two to one.

A big fucker at the front of their mob came bouncing up to our lot, giving it loads. Within seconds, some Villa fan ran in and hit him and he went down like the Titanic. Stoke saw their main man on his arse and froze. A couple of Villa lads started spraying gas and cries of 'Youth! Youth! Youth!' could be heard as they ran at Stoke. Stoke backed off and a few of their lads who had frozen got a right kicking. Two Villa boys even caught hold of a Stoke fan and gave him a 'leg and a wing' through a shop window. Stoke cleared off and the police rounded up the Villa and took them back towards the pub. It was fortunate for Stoke that the Villa fans in the pub hadn't managed to get out but as it turned out they had not been needed.

The police eventually got all of the Villa together, now numbering the best part of 100, and escorted them towards the ground. Stoke did not seem to have much else to hit the Villa with, and you have to remember that this was only a part of our mob. A lot of the other Villa lads that day had gone by coach and train, so everybody knew that we would have a massive mob together after the game.

Their ground was a sea of claret and blue. The attendance was 13,494 and Villa took well over 7,000. It was like a home game for us and the atmosphere was brilliant. The Stoke fans were very quiet and some looked intimidated. The game itself was a load of bollocks and ended up in a 0-0 draw. All the talk through the match was about how Villa were going to hit Stoke after.

The game ended and we had a very large mob assembled. The Old Bill tried to keep on top of the Villa lads but there were too many. A good 300 managed to escape their clutches and headed for deepest Stoke territory. Villa landed bang in the middle of the city centre yet all we found was one little firm, who saw the Villa and had it off on their toes straight away. Villa roamed around looking for someone to fight and all they could see were pockets of Stoke running down side streets. This was their city but they just rolled over. They didn't even try to handle the Villa.

The police finally managed to get the Villa under control and escorted most of them to the train station. There were, however, still the best part of 100 lads parked up by the pub in the city centre. They made their way back to their vehicles under police supervision. The Old Bill made sure that the Villa boys then left the area, but it turned out to be not quite so straightforward for one bunch of lads. A van carrying about a dozen had been broken into and the tyres let down. Inside the van, in felt tip pen it said, word for word, 'Unlucky Villa look like a long way home.' It appeared to be the work of an illiterate schoolboy. Apart from the tyres – which they hadn't even slashed – the van was in good enough condition to drive. The lads agreed that in hindsight parking there had probably been too cocky a thing to do. It was the only way that Stoke could get one over on Villa that day.

A couple of police stayed with the Villa fans by the van. One of the officers sent for a pump to get the tyres blown up and remove the Villa boys back to Brum. Inevitably, after a while about 30 Stoke turned up and started to hang around the edge of the car park. They had found some bottle now everybody else had gone. For us this was the best part of the day, a dozen Villa and 30 Stoke, yet they did nothing. They didn't seem to have it in them to have a go, yet the two cops would not have been able to stop anything. A few verbals were exchanged and then a police van pulled up and Stoke left, again.

The Old Bill hadn't been able to find a pump so they towed the van, on flat tyres, to a nearby garage. The tyres were inflated and the fans were escorted out of Stoke. That was not quite the end of events, however. A couple of vans and several cars full of Villa met up and went back into Stoke later that night to try to cause more havoc. They drove around looking for Stoke and found a few groups here and there, who were promptly sent packing. They must have had claret and blue nightmares for weeks to come. It was late on Saturday night when the police finally escorted the last load of Villa vehicles out of Stoke.

The following January, Villa went to Man City and won 2-0. A rumour went around that Stoke were going to turn up for a revenge attack on us. The Villa had a big mob out that day but didn't bump into any Stoke. We don't know if they showed up somewhere or not but we would not have been hard to find. We expected Stoke to have a go when they came to Villa Park in the March of that year, but for whatever reason they didn't. The active Villa lads of that time always felt that Stoke were a little bit in awe of them.

All that said, a couple of ours have got a lot of time for Stoke and saw firsthand what they are capable of. Fordy and Coff were up there a lot in the late Eighties. Fordy recalls their top boy Miffer (RIP) as a genuine character of the football scene and someone that deserved respect. He shared some great times with him and his boys on many occasions, like the row in a boozer in Burslem with Port Vale when Fordy took more than a few bruises from a baseball bat-wielding, lunatic Stoke-hater, who obviously didn't know that Fordy wasn't one of Stoke's boys. 'I thought I was going out for a good night out so I wore my best whistle,' said Fordy. 'Next thing I know, I am in the middle of a brawl with Stoke's main enemy. But kindly Miffer and the boys let me soak in a nice hot bath above a nightclub they were running. Cheers lads.' He also witnessed what happened at St Andrews when there could have been a full-scale riot with the Blues: 'I don't think the lads from the Seventies and probably the early Eighties had the same impression from their accounts, but Stoke were a firm to be reckoned with, no doubt about it.'

14 THERE'S A CIRCUS IN THE TOWN

BRITTLE

All football fans assume that their local rivalry is more intense and more bitter than any other, but in England probably only West Ham and Millwall run the Villa-Blues derby close. To understand the rivalry and hatred that exists between the two teams, you have to go back a long time. This isn't something that has sprung up in the last 20 years; it has probably been in existence as long as they have gone without winning a trophy. Unlike the other derbies, the Birmingham clash has never lost its atmosphere or its intensity, despite the number of times we have played each other. Even midday kick-offs have failed to take that away.

When Villa were winning trophies in Europe, they were winning the Atari six-a-side at the NEC. When we were winning League Cups at Wembley, Small Heath, as Birmingham City were originally known and as Villa fans still like to call them, were winning the Leyland Daf and Autoglass Windscreen trophies. They are the biggest under-achievers in the history of English football bar none and have been a constant source of ridicule. When things are looking bleak at Villa – which is not unknown – we console ourselves with, 'It could be worse, we could be Blues.' What other club blames a gypsy's curse for everything, and in an attempt to rid itself of that curse, tries various bizarre things from bringing exorcists in to painting the soles of the players' boots red? You couldn't make it up.

We have always classed them as inferior to us and football-wise have never taken them seriously. They really have no argument so they resort to telling anyone who will listen that Villa have a crap firm, have never done this, never done that. Well for a firm they say they don't rate, they certainly give us a lot of coverage in their books. Some of the things they have written are beyond comprehension, almost juvenile mixed up in all that bitterness, but let's not get the facts in the way of a good story, hey? Their hatred definitely clouds their judgement and they seem to suffer from selective memory, so we will try to jog their memories with a few facts about events that they seem to have overlooked.

The night of 16 September 2002 and the City v. Villa game saw the biggest football-related violence off the pitch for probably over a decade on English soil, part of which we cover in detail in the final chapter. The return leg at Villa Park saw scenes in a ground many hadn't seen since the Eighties. Now the rows go back to the late Sixties and probably before, and you could write a whole book on just Villa-Blues fights. There are enough press clippings in circulation to fill 20 scrapbooks. They were by all accounts more organised than Villa in the late Sixties and made three attempts to take the Holte End. They never succeeded but if the truth be known, on one occasion the police presence stopped them doing it. These were the days, though, when even West Ham had their main end taken by Man United (in 1967) and it was a regular thing for visiting supporters to wander into the home end. If you got in early with numbers, you could take it.

We all are in agreement that during the 'hooligan years' from 1984 to probably 1987, the Zulus were far more active and organised than Villa. They certainly got recognition nationally and the riot against Leeds in 1985 brought them the notoriety they craved. It has always been about numbers with them, and in that period they certainly could turn out a decent firm. We give them respect for that. However, there were untold numbers of incidents when our lads were picked off in ones and twos or when out with their partners. Whenever we have played them on match day, it has been a different story.

The Internet warriors might believe the hype but the truth is we have the local knowledge and the past experiences to go on and don't rely on fourthhand information from nobodies. We haven't become the attention-seeking whores our neighbours have become over the years and nor will we try to sensationalise minor results, but here are just a selection of past incidents. Now let's get it right.

Paul Ali, an old Villa veteran, was at one of the very first major battles between Villa and Blues.

PAUL ALI THE BURLINGTON ARCADE MASSACRE, 1971

During the Sixties, as gangs began to attach themselves to football teams, Villa had varying degrees of success against their nearest rivals. Where we always seemed to come second best to them was on the organisational side. For games at Villa Park, Blues' mob would always come onto the Holte End. Their end was the Tilton Road, which held 12,000, the Holte holding 28,000, so if you got in there early it made a difference. Sometimes Blues came from the left side, sometimes from the right, and after the initial toing and froing the coppers would always get in the middle and form a wall around the Blues mob, who would then stay there all game. Once the police wall was formed, many more of what we would call 'barmies' these days would go and join the Blues mob making it impossible for anyone to shift them. The old Villa skins got onto the Tilton Road and occupied the bottom part of it one season but it wasn't any major result. As time went by it was far more difficult to get into home ends and you had to be a little bit more inventive than just turning up early.

After a couple of seasons of not playing each other when we dropped down into the Third Division, a pre-season friendly was arranged at Villa Park in August 1971. For once we were determined to be organised and word got out for everyone to meet in the Parisian pub, which was opposite the Windsor in Needles Alley in Birmingham town centre. We didn't have an organised firm back then but all the different pockets of lads turned up other than the Quinton crew, who oddly never showed on that occasion. The Quinton were a hard set of lads and were probably a little more sinister than the rest of the Villa. They were as proud of their area as they were of their club. It wasn't uncommon for them to be tooled up and unfortunately one Blues lad from Selly Oak was killed during a row with them around that time.

Inside the Parisian we had somewhere in the region of 100 lads. Blues' haunt at the time was the Gilded Cage, less than 200 yards away on the other side of New Street. At around two o'clock, a shout went up from within the Parisian that Blues were making a move, so we all went outside into the alley. There was no sign of any Blues, so we all headed down the alley, across New St and into Burlington Arcade, which the Gilded Cage was more or less opposite. As we walked down the arcade, Blues appeared, about 200 handed, and the ones at the front seemed surprised to see us and very hesitant, stopping in their tracks. Our mob charged forward, bombarding them with half of the glass stock from the Parisian – and in those days the beer glasses were the jug type which were much thicker and heavier than today's 'sleeve' glasses. The Blues piled forward and some braver blokes got to the front but they couldn't cope with the onslaught of beer glasses and bottles in such a confined space and were trying their best to dodge the artillery as we got in amongst them. They were at sixes and sevens as they ran back to the Gilded Cage. Not all managed to get back inside and as the doors were locked they ran along the shopping precinct towards the back of New Street station. The Villa mob concentrated on the pub, beckoning Blues to come outside, but no one would and the ones shut out simply stood and watched from a safe distance.

When the police finally arrived, we went back the way we had come and it wasn't until we were right the other side of town on Corporation Street, past the law courts, that they caught up with us and began nicking people. The reports in the papers claimed a baby had been thrown from its pram, which was a complete and utter load of crap, but it is fair to say a lot of shoppers were caught up in the fight. At the game, Blues came in the Holte as usual but got another hiding as the adrenalin flowed amongst the Villa mob high on the earlier victory.

The battle became legend at Villa and is commonly known as the 'Burlington Arcade Massacre'. It was our first major result against them.

CLARKEY THE BATTLE OF THE WINDSOR

Without doubt the best row I had with Blues was in their pre-Zulu days. It was with the Steamers and must have been about 1978. We were all in the Windsor, which all the usual faces used in those days, especially on match day. It was between two alleys smack in the middle of Brum, with entrances at the front and back. It had three levels and we would occupy the middle-floor bar.

On this day we were playing Blues at home and drinking on the first floor as usual. There was around 80 of us and out of them we had about 50 rowers. Foxy was downstairs with a few of the Steamers and clocked a firm of 50 strangers walking up to the middle floor. They came into the bar and it was as if the jukebox had been turned off, there was an eerie silence for a second as everyone waited for them all to come in.

It was Blues and they hadn't come in for a drink. It immediately kicked off and we backed them back down the stairs quite quickly, where Foxy and his crew were clumping them as they came down. I thought they had gone on their toes but as I got outside into the alley they were there and not moving. I must admit, the 50 Blues were very good and it was obvious this was their firm and they weren't carrying passengers. Whoever they were, it was very hard work shifting them. They seemed older than us, veteran rowers, and I was caught up with one bloke who wouldn't go down, he just kept coming back.

All of a sudden one massive fat bloke, most likely the pie-seller on the market who ate his own stock, grabbed me in a bearhug and was squeezing the life out of me. He was strong, a bit like Mick

McManus of wrestling fame at the time, and I could not free myself from his grip. I was frantically trying to nut the back of my head into his face but it had no effect. All of a sudden I saw one of ours, Fast, who was free and shouted to him to help me. The bloke I had been throwing punches at and who wouldn't go down was in his element and kept running in and giving me a dig. Fast came straight over and smashed the fat bloke in the stomach and for a split second he loosened his grip, allowing me to work free. I turned and gave the fat bloke an almighty dig, which finished him off. I found out later that Fast hadn't punched him but had stabbed him and I felt a bit guilty about banging him after that.

We had managed to get ourselves on top by this stage and there were bodies lying all over the place. The row was vicious and had gone on for some time and it was on those occasions you looked at the lads with you and knew you were part of a top firm who wouldn't leave your side. When the police finally arrived they came from both sides of the alley, blocking any escape. Most of us ran back into the Windsor, straight through the pub and out of the back door which led to another alley. We ended up at the Old Contemptibles near Colmore Row, another boozer we used at the time, and kept a low one.

I would say fair play to the Blues that time, they were old skool and came up to row, not to shape. They came off second best in the end and it was their bodies on the floor in the alley. We took a couple of casualties, as you would expect, but the result was ours. It had been proper toe-to-toe and from that day I classed myself as a Steamer. At the ground it was funny watching the same Blues lads coming past the Holte Pub looking worse for wear, with bruised faces and bandages.

ANDY ST ANDREWS, VILLA IN THE KOP

February 1982 and tensions were running high. Ron Saunders had left the club and switched sides to the Blues, so as you can imagine from him being the messiah he was now a Judas bastard. Up until that year, whenever we left town to go to their ground we either had the police with us (nine times out of ten) or they picked us up on the way. I had thought for a while that something new was needed and at that time my sister was running the Peacock in Highgate, an inner-city pub well away from the usual haunts in the town. I told my sister that on the Saturday Villa were playing Blues and that myself and a few mates would be popping over on the morning of the game for a drink.

I began to tell people on the Wednesday before the game where we would be meeting and come mid-morning on the Saturday 'a few friends' totalled around 200. My sister later told me it was the best day's takings they had all year.

BRITTLE

As we got out the pub, I stopped everyone, got on a car roof and gave a short but precise speech: 'Everyone stick together and keep quiet. We are going in their end.'

Here we were with the right numbers, no police and one mile from their ground. It was our best ever chance of getting into their kop. The early stages of the walk were a doddle, but once we crossed into Camp Hill the pressure was well and truly on. As we got onto Coventry Road, within spitting distance of St Andrews, we were landed on by the Old Bill. One of our lads, Jordan, knowing we had been rumbled, broke into the Blues anthem 'Keep Right On' and others quickly joined in, with those who didn't know the words just humming along. It must have been one of the most half-hearted efforts ever made to sing a song but it worked and the police gave us an escort straight to the kop turnstiles.

As we queued, I heard one copper say to another, 'I'm sure this lot are Villa you know,' but by then it was too late, as our lads were beginning to get in. We were still quiet and casual as we waited until everyone had got in; Andy even sat down on the steps. We were now by the big clock and the Blues around us had sussed that we were Villa. It was only a matter of time until the police did the same but the C Crew were in. Someone shouted for us to go as not all the Villa had got in – the original plan was to all get in and then walk quietly up to the back of the kop but once we got sussed we had to make a split decision to charge, otherwise we'd have been wrapped up by the coppers.

We steamed right across the kop, with people parting and making huge gaps as we went towards them. A Villa fan in the Tilton Road described it as a tidal wave rushing across the terracing. I'm not claiming I'm Moses but you get the picture. Cud and his mob came across to us and had a go. I went in first and they grabbed me down and I was taking a few kicks until Jimmy Coley and a few others bailed me out. We then ran them straight across the kop. Halfway along there's a fence and that's where their firm was.

Jimmy Coley grabbed me and asked, 'Are you with me?' Of course I replied, 'Yeah,' so we went up the terrace and flew into them, and after a bit of hands-on they scattered. Another firm of Blues ran over from the seats but didn't have the arsehole to come over our side of the fence. Twice I was grabbed by the OB and dragged out to the back and twice I went straight back to the front line again and back into them.

The police finally realised what was going on and managed to get us surrounded right in the middle of the kop just as the players were out and warming up. Everyone thought they would get us onto the pitch but when they eventually got us out, they threw us outside.

Once we were out, we were singing and dancing on the street as they took us round to the Tilton, while Blues watched us from inside the ground. We knew we had done them that day and they knew it too. By the time we had reached the Tilton End turnstiles it was 20 past three and the turnstile operators were beginning to cash up for the day. A certain lad called Jimmy casually leaned over, snatched the day's takings and sprinted away from the ground with the turnstile operator attempting to give chase, shouting, 'Stop, thief!' This was enough to alert the police who at one point managed to grab Jimmy's leather jacket but he slipped out of it, leaving a copper holding it.

Having lost the police, Jimmy continued running but slipped on a bombpeck, stopping him in his tracks. A caring St John Ambulance guy came to the rescue and Jimmy explained how he was running from Blues. They cleaned him up and put him into the ground free of charge, where he checked the takings and found he'd cleaned up, with £800 plus free entry to the ground. After the damage he'd done to Blues on the Kop earlier on, this was the perfect ending, and just when he thought it couldn't get any better someone gave him his jacket back at the end of the night.

ANDY

There have always been comments from Blues about how early we went in there but as we were taken out that day, the teams were out warming up on the pitch so we weren't early at all. We took a massive liberty, made sweeter by the fact that Saunders was signing his new contract on the pitch that day. For all their hot air, they have never done anything to match that at our ground. The Steamers had their results against Blues at pubs or outside the ground but the C Crew that day took it a step further and did it in the ground on their manor.

STU VILLA VISIT THE KOP AGAIN

After a few seasons playing in different divisions, 1987/88 saw Villa and Blues renewing old rivalries and it was as intense as ever. After a fairly uneventful game at Villa Park earlier in the season, other than Blues going in the Witton Lane seats, shouting 'Zulu' a few times and Villa making efforts to get at them via the Holte terraces, nothing of note happened. But at their place on December 12 it was very different. Tensions were running high, there was bad feeling between both sets of supporters and it was inevitable that something would give on the day of the match.

The Villa fans arranged to meet at the Rocket pub in Duddeston, an area not that far from their ground but far enough away to avoid police attention. The day started off with Villa lads breaking in to St Andrews and painting 'AVFC' on the pitch. It almost caused a postponement of the game and was the first paint that place had seen in 50 years! We had a good firm – I know everyone says that but it's true, a good 150 and no passengers – as we made our way through the back streets of Digbeth hoping to take Blues by surprise. The Villa made their way along Heath Mill Lane towards High Street Deritend, and the Old Crown, famous for being the oldest pub in Brum, was in focus. The Blues had a few scouts out but they must have had a shock when they saw this little lot. They had no more than 20 outside the boozer and they were on their toes up the road as we continued to march up.

There were Blues inside and some were frantically trying to lock the doors. Villa were all over the pub in seconds, the windows went through and some lads started spraying gas everywhere. The Old Bill were soon on the scene and the Villa made their way towards St Andrews with the police too close for comfort. It was the usual intense atmosphere as you would expect for a derby but the Villa were also playing well and had a chance of promotion, so it wasn't a game with nothing on it other than local pride. The Tilton Road was heaving with Villa and the two sections allocated to us were full, so 60 Villa fans who couldn't get into the away end actually paid to get into the kop.

The roar went up, Villa were now amongst them and were also running across the no man's land separating the two sets of fans to get at the Blues, who were backing off. No one is claiming we took the kop but you have to say it was Villa taking it to Blues on their patch and whilst in 1982 the C Crew's raid was planned, this wasn't, it was due to sheer weight of numbers in the travelling support. It got covered on the *Star Soccer* on TV on the Sunday and all the press coverage was about Villa fans causing trouble, as it was going off in the game until the police regained control. The match itself saw Garry Thompson score two great headers and we beat them 2-1.

Fighting in the Holte End with Arsenal's Gooners. The vast end held 28,000 spectators and was often a target for infiltration by rival gangs.

At Knutsford Service Station on the M6 motorway. Wolves's Subway Army are in the walkway in the top right of the picture, while police have formed a line at the bottom of the stairs.

Co-author Paul Brittle, C Crew stalwart and main Villa face.

Clarkey of the Steamers, probably the first mob to bring together groups from different areas of the city into one outfit. He has been following Villa since 1968.

Some of the Villa lads in high spirits at the Wembley Hilton on the eve of the 2000 FA cup final.

Albion fans praised for pitch invasion restraint

Villa fans in terror ambush

COACH ATTACKED ON M-WAY

Parker drives | Moseley win with belt

VILLA FANS IN BATTLE OF M6

Cafe is 'ripped apart' in clash with United

Soccer shootings: Villa fans bailed

Villa fans bailed

THE 'FRIENDLY' FANS RUN RIOT

by JOHN SCOTT

Escape in car crash

YES...IT WAS US

Villa fans' pitch battle story

Headlines of crowd trouble involving Villa over the years, including Glasgow Rangers at home in the mid-Seventies and the notorious trip to Anderlecht in the early Eighties.

BIRMINGHAM Evening Mail

THE AFTERMATH

Villa battle: 65 in court today | Rees probe on 18-hour wait | Howell: Rule by a drunken mob

Police chief calls for a 'fail appeal'

YOU NEED NOT BE BALD

Man dies in karate fight

Big police probe starts after the battle of Filbert Street

Evening Mail Reporter

A FULL SCALE police inquiry was launched today into the battle of Filbert Street where 23 people were hurt and 17 arrested in violent clashes between Aston Villa and Leicester City fans.

At the same time officials of Leicester City football club were hurrying out their own investigation.

Anderlecht seek match replay

'KICK VILLA OUT OF EUROPE' CALL

Double-decker headache!

Deep trouble

Andy Brown (left) and Jimmy Coley, staunch friends and two of the most formidable lads you could ever encounter.

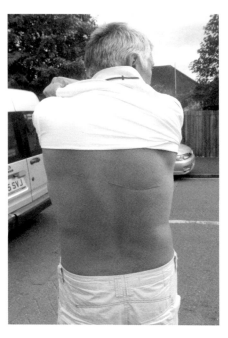

An old Steamer bearing the scars of a violent run-in with Portsmouth's 6.57 Crew. He stood against them but was slashed across the back so badly he could have died.

Black Danny with Villa's own God, the centre-half Paul McGrath.

A gathering of the lads outside Club Sensations, scene of the now famous speech by Yam Yam at the start of this book.

Main contributors to *Villains:* (from left) Andy, Sean, Danny, Brittle, Dewar (obscured), the General, Clarkey, Jimmy Coley and Pete the Greek.

CLARENCE HOUSE
LONDON SW1A 1BA

From: Jamie Lowther-Pinkerton Esq, M.V.O., M.B.E.,
Private Secretary to Prince William and Prince Harry

Private and Confidential

26th February, 2007

Dear Mr. Brown,

Prince William has asked me to thank you very much for your letter of 13th February, and for the copy of "Villains – The Inside Story of Aston Villa's Hooligan Gangs". As a loyal Villa supporter, The Prince will be interested to read the story of the Club's problem with hooligan gangs over the past decades.

His Royal Highness was touched that you should think of sending him your book, and sends you and Paul Brittle his best wishes.

Yours Sincerely,

Jamie Lowther-Pinkerton

Mr. Danny Brown

By Royal Appointment? Not exactly, but Villa fan Prince William sent this appreciation to Danny Brown after receiving a copy of the original hardback edition of *Villains*. Nice one HRH!

Outside the ground you could cut the atmosphere with scissors and being a winter's day it started to get dark, adding to the tension. Villa stuck together and we made our way to Lawley Middleway, where we managed to shake off the police and walked up past the White Tower pub by Duddeston. The Zulus were behind the boozer in Windsor Street South. Both firms knew where the other was and if we continued our paths we were due to meet somewhere along Great Brook Street.

The two mobs finally had each other in their sights. Villa charged and yells of 'Youth, Youth' echoed down the road. Blues stood across the street and one of them was waving what looked like a baseball bat or a big stick. Villa got to within 30 yards of the Noses and they dropped everything and ran. Some couldn't get away fast enough and got a kicking. They say their front line has never been broken, well this Zulu front line had more holes in it than a Ken Dodd tax return.

The police arrived and rounded us all up and we headed back to the Crown and Cushion to celebrate. The local press reported it as the worst violence that the city had ever seen and there were numerous arrests. It was a good result for the Youth that day and showed again that despite the hype, on match day it was a different story. We ain't Palace and we ain't Blackpool!

However, the day didn't finish there for one of ours, Reidy, for more than one reason. It had started off well with a 2-1 win and promised to get even better with his works Christmas party in Leicester that evening. During the course of the night, Reidy and a Bluenose workmate got talking to three Leicester fans and the conversation soon got around to football hooligans. The Leicester lads started giving it the big 'un, saying how Villa and Blues were fuck all and they had never rated Brummies. The inevitable happened and Reidy and his mate gave it to the Leicester gobshites.

After the fight had finished, Reidy went to the toilet to wash their blood off his hands, leaving his Bluenose mate alone at the bar. When he came out of the toilets, he found the Nose surrounded by a dozen Leicester lads. Adrenalin took over and Reidy ploughed straight into them. In the course of the struggle, one of the Leicester fans sank his teeth into one of Reidy's ears and bit it off. Naturally, Reidy let out a scream and when he did everything seemed to stop, with the Leicester lot backing off. Reidy went for the lad who had bitten him and proceeded to kick the shit out of him while the other Leicester fans looked on.

Reidy and the vampire from Leicester both needed hospital treatment. The police had been called in and both lads were set to be charged. Both decided that they would not take things any further and the police let it go. Reidy just wanted to get home and eventually turned up at Birmingham Accident Hospital with his ear in a shoebox. He spent five days in hospital and later needed to have a synthetic rubber ear fitted.

For some reason, the word got around that some Blues fan had been responsible for Reidy losing his ear in a knife attack. This was total bullshit; nothing could be further from the truth. The fact is that Reidy only lost his ear because he was trying to help a Bluenose who was about to get a kicking. Hopefully, this puts the record straight and leaves Reidy with the proud title of Villa's own Vincent Van Gogh.

To end, I must offer a word of warning. If ever you are out drinking with Reidy, be careful to keep one eye on your pint. If you fail to do so, you may end up with a rubber ear in it.

BRITTLE THE HAT-TRICK: GARRISON LANE, 1993

Even after the results of 1982 and 1987, we were still having to listen to the Zulus, who were living on a well-worn reputation. Not having played them for six years, it was time for a local reminder. It's all about pride. I put the word around that for this evening cup tie we were to meet beforehand at the Ben Johnson pub, but trouble was going off all day. The first off was in the Sack of Potatoes, where 30 Blues walked through the pub with 20 Villa. That riled me. If they were looking for us, don't worry, they would find us soon enough.

People were coming into the Ben Johnson in dribs and drabs, mainly due to work commitments, but come 6.30 pm we had a mob of around 350. We walked past the fire station and Aston University with no police in tow. My only concern was how we would be able to avoid the Old Bill with this many. We must have passed three or four boozers en route to Small Heath and each one was full of Blues but only a handful would come outside, only to get whacked. I got everybody together and we made a move towards the ground. We walked past the Cauliflower Ear boozer and I don't know what happened but someone put the window through, something stupid really but it got everyone excited. The downside was that the police came and rounded everyone up.

About 50 of us made a break, got away from the escort and carried on towards the ground. As we got to Garrison Lane by the park, their firm – and there are no two ways about this, it was their firm – came steaming down the hill at us, throwing bricks, bottles and glasses. I shouted to the lads, 'Fucking get into them, nobody runs.' It was all our lads so no-one was going to leave us anyway. We were straight into them and the first geezer I reached had a flick cosh, one of those with the ball bearings at the end of it. He tried to hit me with it but I put up my arm and blocked it. I took it off him, got him up the wall and did him. That was more or less it then, their arseholes fell out of it – and that was before the main firm got there and we ran them up the hill. By the time the main firms landed, they had tried to break away from the escort and we all hit the park. It was game over by then as all the horses caught up with us.

ANDY McDONALD'S/ROCKY LANE, SEPTEMBER 2002, AFTER THE MAIN EVENTS

What happened before the game is covered in detail in Chapter 17, but this is the account of what happened afterwards and is relevant to this story. During the day I had told everyone that I didn't want them landing back at the club (Club

Sensations – see final chapter) afterwards because I didn't want to bring it on top for the club. All day long I had left instructions with the staff on how I wanted the doors closed at all times, I didn't want parked cars outside, etc., etc. I wasn't planning to go back there myself but town was shut, and after the shenanigans on Rocky Lane before the game they had closed Lichfield Road as well, where a lot of the lads usually headed for. In the end I decided to go back to the club after all. When I got there the place was very quiet with just four or five Villa inside, a few regular customers and some dancers.

I was in a staff meeting when I heard a loud bang from the foyer, which I now know was the front doors being slammed shut by my doormen. Now all day I had been on edge about the club in the evening, as I had planned to stay out with the firm, but as soon as I arrived back there I relaxed. The sound of the door slamming changed my mood. What I now know had happened was that despite leaving instructions with the doormen to remain inside the club and keep the doors shut, one was standing outside. A Blues spotter approached him and asked, 'Any Villa in there mate?' The doorman told him there wasn't and off he went. Less than a minute later, 70 of them appeared. A quick-thinking doorman inside the club grabbed this person standing outside and pulled him back in, and at the same time managed to slam the door.

At this stage I obviously had to leave the staff meeting and go to the foyer. By this time the doors were being battered with all sorts and a couple of panels went through. They started putting arms in and trying to undo the latch holding the two doors together, so I began to cover the latch with my arms. More panels went through and they were able to bash my hands and arms as I struggled to hold the doors together. At the same time, I heard the shout of 'We're in,' and guessed they had broken into the cellar, which leads to the main club area. I sent one of the doorstaff to the door that leads from the club to the cellar and luckily he got there before Blues did, as they came up the stairs and tried to get in. My only regret was that I had not been on that door at the time because you can only come up the stairs one or two maximum at a time and it would have been a great chance to get the first half a dozen or so in, shut the doors and give them a beating they wouldn't forget.

The Old Bill eventually arrived after what I would guess was 20 to 25 minutes. They took away the CCTV footage of the incident, which they still have.

WELCOME TO VILLA PARK: THE ROYAL OAK 2003

The return game at Villa Park later in the season was one shown live on Sky and a Monday night affair, resulting in another long day ahead. This time around we tried a different approach, keeping our lads in different places. The younger lot plotted up in the Barrel on Summer Lane Newtown but the Old Bill got wind of it and landed on them, closing the pub and splitting them into smaller groups. Our lot were in the Erdington, Kingstanding and Sutton areas and my same small group of 15-20 were again on Broad Street. We had been in contact with Blues at various times throughout the day and at one stage they had asked about a row just with the firm that had done the business at McDonald's [see Chapter 17] but that never came to anything.

I was wearing a new Villa tracksuit top and kept going on walkabout through town, as I wanted as many Blues as possible to see me and know that I am Villa. One of the lads with us, Ginger, also got restless and went off looking for Blues. At around a quarter to five, four of us got a taxi to the Adventurers pub where we had decided to meet, as Blues couldn't commit themselves to anything. The minute we got in the cab, the phone rang and it was Ginger, claiming to have found where Blues were plotting up. We had told the driver to head for the Adventurers before Ginger's call but now he was telling us he was in the Royal Oak, a pub in Lozells. He had been on a mission all day and we talked for a minute or so before deciding we would stop off on the way and pick him up.

When we got to the Oak, we parked outside and D.Dub got out

of the cab to make a call to some of our lads. I got out too because I didn't want him out there on his own. Now in the book *Zulus*, they state that 'Villa landed' at the Royal Oak and try to turn what happened into some kind of result for them. They fail to mention the fact that it was the grand total of four Villa who landed in a black cab. D.Dub was walking up and down talking on the phone while I went up the bar door. A bloke standing outside told me not to kick off and I told him I was sweet. I noticed a few heads peering round the corner from the other entrance to the pub; word must have spread that something was going on outside.

With the coast looking clear, Blues decided to come out of the pub from the door furthest away from me and began to fill the pavement. D.Dub finished his call and made his way back to the taxi.

One bloke stood in front of him said, 'Are you Villa?'

'Yes,' he replied.

The bloke didn't know what to do, so he asked him again, 'Are you Villa?'

D.Dub made a split-second decision to chin him and caught him with a right-hander that lifted him clean off the floor and laid him out. As soon as this happened, another bloke jabbed a broken bottle into D.Dub's face. The taxi driver panicked and drove off and the next thing I knew I was facing about 20 of them.

'Andy Browne?' someone asked.

'Yes,' I replied.

I started trading blows with a few of them directly in front of me until they got behind me as well and grabbed my arms and neck. I ended up on the floor while one of the lads got D.Dub into the taxi and bribed the driver £50 to go back and get me.

We were taken to Dudley Road Hospital. There I remembered that I still had 15 tickets for the front row of the Trinity Road Stand, right next to the away section, and I sent the lads back with the tickets for the lads at the Adventurers.

It hadn't worked out as well as the time we met at the club and maybe I fucked up a little by being out and away from the lads all day when I should have been focussed on other things. Me and D.Dub were seen by the doctor at around 10.30pm and then I went back to my hotel and D went home.

GINGER

After the total nightmare of what happened to my two pals, which was my fuck-up, I was seething and wanted to take it out on any Noses we could find. I ended up going to the away end before kick-off with a lot of other Villa lads and waded into Blues who were by the Witton end. There was sheer panic in their ranks and they were scrambling to get away as the Villa dished out the slaps to all and sundry. Word had spread about what had happened at the Royal Oak and Blues were now under the cosh. The Villa stewards, on police advice, ended up opening the North Stand sections just to get the fans into the ground and out the way of the Villa mob. It was stupid really, I could have got nicked from the CCTV, but like a lot of people I was past caring.

The one thing that sticks out in mind as we were on Witton Lane was the number of them that came on coaches. Coaches for a three-mile journey? And it wasn't just scarfers, it was lads on them. I left there to go to the Adventurers, where there were hundreds of Villa mobbing up both inside and outside. It was pointless trying to get in there as you couldn't move, as word was that they were coming there. We then received a call to say they were coming across the park. We made our way up there and caught the tail end of their firm but after an exchange of verbals they ran down towards the Trinity Road before the Old Bill surrounded them.

Inside the ground, I haven't witnessed an atmosphere as hostile as those first two games against Blues in the Premiership for a very long time. It was evil. It must have been great television and maybe the rest of the country now realise what a Villa-Blues game is like. The rumours as usual were that they had bought tickets in the Villa end and were going to make a big show. There wasn't a Villa fan in that ground who wasn't pumped up and talk about spotters, we had 35,000 that night.

Anybody who had strayed into a home section and was daft enough to make himself known was attacked as all our barmies entered into the spirit of things – it was a wonderful sight. Villa supporters themselves ended up on the wrong side of other Villa supporters as it was indiscriminate at times. Even the Birmingham coaching staff got attacked; Keith Bertschin took a few punches in the Trinity Road and tried to get help from the police, who admitted it would be best if he left, as they couldn't guarantee his safety. It was the first time I've seen people in corporate boxes take a leathering as the silly twats were celebrating and goading Villa fans when they scored. They had the shock of their lives as Villa lads vaulted the balcony into the box while others stopped stewards and the police from getting up there to protect them. We were told Blues fans ran into the corporate lounges and took refuge in the toilets but the Villa lads followed them in and did them good and proper. I blame the ones who own the boxes for inviting them in; they should have been battered as well and banned from Villa Park.

In my seat in the Trinity Road I could see Blues fans in the corner balcony boxes leaning over and goading Villa fans. I felt a little better when they got showered with coins from the Holte End and had to retreat inside for their own safety. If somebody jumped up in the stands there were 20 Villa jumping on them and in the Doug Ellis and North Stands upper a few of theirs were severely dealt with. Two in the Doug Ellis were kicked down the steps. The stewards had no chance of controlling it, people were long past caring as that red mist descended on us all. The whole ground was a tinderbox waiting to explode, there wasn't a hiding place anywhere for any Nose who strayed from his own area. Everybody was straining to see if any Blues had dared to come into the home areas and unfamiliar faces were asked, 'Are you Villa?' That caused even more trouble as Villa would row on Villa, the tension of the night was getting to everyone and on the pitch our own players lost it. Villa had two players sent off with Dion Dublin headbutting that prat Robbie Savage, who rolled around as if he had been shot.

The night got to everyone and we were woeful on the pitch, losing 2-0. Who in their right mind agreed to make these two games 8pm kick-offs? It has to go down as one of the craziest decisions ever made by the police and they will never take that chance again. You also had in the Doug Ellis Stand a young mob of 150 Villa hooded up trying to get at Blues in the next section, all in the full view of a national television audience.

Anyone who has witnessed it will know how you feel when you lose a derby, but after being in the top flight for 15 years and basically taking the piss out of them for that long, it was even more humiliating. For youngsters who hadn't witnessed a derby, let alone lost one, the feeling was indescribable, the lowest of the low. After the game, with tempers and passions running high as Blues celebrated a Premiership double over us, there was a riot on Witton Lane, where the old bill formed another line to prevent hundreds of Villa getting at the Blues. They baton-charged Villa all the way back to the 'Ads' pub. There must have been 400 Villa lads, and with the atmosphere of a derby day they took out their frustrations on the Old Bill, resulting in a lot of meat wagons getting damaged and the police taking a severe pasting, with several injuries. This went on for a good 30 minutes and the police were panicking. People talk about certain events being 'a throwback to the Eighties' but I doubt the Eighties saw anything like that. Certainly Villa Park hadn't.

A few weeks after, when the police released photos of people they wanted to interview about that night, you realised the spectrum of people who had been involved. One guy looked like a pensioner in the mugshots, but then it had gone from a firm-on-firm row to every normal fan getting involved. For some who had never experienced a derby or had forgotten what it was like, those two games certainly brought it all flooding back. The local radio stations were full of Noses complaining, saying they had never seen hatred or felt intimidation like it at a football ground.

I think after that episode and the number of police that got hurt, they made it their mission to clamp down on the Villa hooligan element, or as one copper allegedly put it, to 'take us out of action'. You could argue they have done that to a certain degree because our older lads won't take the risks anymore and many of our younger lot have been convicted and banned.

BRITTLE ZULU FABLES

When we first met to discuss writing this book, it was unanimously agreed not to bother responding to the crap the Zulus said about us in the book *Zulus*. Since that meeting, a second book has come out which upset Danny in particular. Jimmy then read the first book and wanted to say a few words and finally Andy decided to break his silence over the cheap shots taken at him, although you will notice that Andy has not stooped to their level and has as usual spoken with great dignity.

JIMMY COLEY

I read the quotes in the *Zulus* book about the rave scene and the Hummingbird incident, where they claim to have gone in and thrown their weight around. I was in there that night and no drinks were bought them and no friendships were made. Do they think people would believe this just because the guy they talk about, Garry Lyttle (RIP), is no longer with us and cannot defend himself? I don't want to get into a slanging match but here was a lad who was a proper stand-on kid who had respect and morals, something they wouldn't understand.

They talk about a pal of mine, Andy Browne. Andy is a true friend and I've never met a straighter, more loyal man in my life.

This no-mark talks about him as if he is in his league. Andy is strictly Premiership whereas the other guy is Vauxhall Conference.

The Apex or the Zulus? For me there is no difference, the same guys really when I was at it, other than it gave them a chance to run round town on a Saturday afternoon shouting 'Zulus' at people doing their shopping. I haven't seen any evidence of any major row with their lot where they haven't been turned over by Villa, and they know it. They took their rows to the lower divisions and caused havoc at places like Blackpool and Nuneaton. What does that tell you?

ANDY

When I first started work on this book, I wasn't going to mention the Zulu book, but after reading parts of it for a second time I've decided to make a few comments.

Whereas I will give the likes of Cud a certain amount of respect and also people like Dougal (their last man standing at McDonald's), I don't understand why someone like Walton was fronting their book, but then again he's always talked a good fight and they say that bullshit sells.

We want people to read this who may well have been up against us at various incidents we mention and to say, 'Yes, that's how I remember it.' Sometimes the truth doesn't sound that impressive but we want it told right.

DANNY MY INTERVIEW FOR *APEX TO ZULU* BY DAVID GEORGE

I gave you an exclusive interview and my blind trust that you would give an accurate word for word account has rebounded on me. You live in fantasy land, mate, and you twisted the words to suit your propaganda machine. I have read your deposit in your book on the C Crew, and take your bullshit deeply. Remember what you said about jumping me on the ramp, when you were 15? Why didn't you mention in the book the other 20 heads you had with you when you attacked us. I don't remember me or my missus running that day. Do you?

Also remember that line you said about what it was like for me being the only black face following Villa home and away. Come on kid, you and I know what's going on. Stop your Machiavelli bullshit. The old school football world knows the C Crew had a firm full of black lads in it. You didn't even ask me that question, let alone mention it, so why lie? I remember you fuckers from way back in the Seventies, when Cuds and your brother were among only one or two black heads down St Andrew's. When the Apex and the Trooper dressed like something out of Sham 69, the Blues were a firm based on racist skinheads who hated blacks or anything not white Anglo-Saxon. No Zulus around St Andrew's in those days!

It wasn't unusual to see calling cards with the words 'Nigger Danny wanted Dead or Alive, BCFC' stuck all around Birmingham. Believe it or not, it wasn't a problem for me, I loved the attention. It meant I knew where I stood with those Bluenose NF sympathizers. The other bullshit doing the rounds is that me and Cud have done business together. Sorry storytellers, not even the United Nations peacekeeper Kofi Annan could cut us a deal. We have never done business together, we see each other round town now and again and we have respect for each other but that's as far as it goes.

After I became one of Villa's top boys, Blues really noticed me and knew the C Crew were the real deal. Like I said in Chapter 1, my reputation was always built on 50 per cent facts and 50 per cent storytellers. You can portray me as you wish, I couldn't care a toss. Everyone knows the facts about the C Crew and accepts we were the first multi-racial football crew in Britain. We don't need to write a book to illustrate the facts, as we all know the truth. The only reason we have written this is to put the record straight and leave a true, accurate account of the best football team and firm this city has ever seen: Aston Villa FC and the C Crew. I was one of a select band of top boys, maybe not the hardest but game as fuck, which never played the numbers game, never bullied or hurt a civilian football supporter.

BRITTLE

People talk about the demise of the C Crew and the end of the Steamers and how we disappeared off the scene. It is true that numbers-wise we were absent for a few years, as lads started making money or began families or whatever, but for most of us Aston Villa and what goes with it remained close to our hearts, as it will to our dying day. Eventually the Steamers and the C Crew ended up merging into one firm probably dubbed 'our older lot' by the younger lads.

There has always been in-fighting at the Villa, from the Quinton mob rowing with the Kingstanding and Erdington mobs, who in turn used to row with each other, to the problems with the right and left sides of the Holte End, to the Steamers and the upstarts in the late Seventies who went on to become the C Crew. Then the Villa Youth clashed with the C Crew and there was even a pre-arranged ruck between these two sets on Aston Park after a local derby with Blues. Just as they were about to get it on, Blues were spotted coming across the park and all differences were put aside to have it with our neighbours.

It's not as if this is new and it's certainly not unique to Aston Villa. You will always get personality clashes and people not getting on when you have such large groups and gatherings but let's get it right; we all share the same love and passion – Aston Villa.

We have entitled this chapter Joint Operations because the following accounts were joint efforts from lads of the Steamers and the C Crew who bonded together after years of fighting side by side and formed new friendships. This chapter could have been the biggest of the book because for the past 20-odd years we have been side by side as one firm.

CLARKEY POMPEY PLAYING UP, 1983

At Villa Park there were two main places to get at away firms at the time, either Witton Station for the train lot or the Serpentine coach park for the coaches. The visitors arriving in cars were taken care of in the main by the Aston Tramps mob, who specialised in picking off stragglers, the ones and twos. We knew Portsmouth's main lot had brought a number of coaches and once the game finished we ended up meeting their coach mob head-on in Witton Road as they were going back towards the Serpentine. It was a very similar row to the Sheffield Wednesday [see Villa Youth chapter]. It was nowhere near as long as that one and not as tasty but it involved a number of running battles along the length of the road. They had brought a good following and we were finding it difficult at first to get them to back off but the breakthrough came when some of theirs ended up in the neighbouring Asian gardens. As quickly as that happened, the Old Bill got between the mobs, forcing us apart.

After that, a good firm of main lads, numbering 20, left the rest of the firm and were drinking in the Manor Tavern just off Lichfield Road, which is the main drag from Aston to Birmingham town centre. We were quite pleased with our night's work and feeling we had the better of the skirmishes. Villa Sam then came into the pub to tell us he had bumped into Portsmouth by Park Road and told them if they wanted it, he knew where some Villa were. Sam told us there were about 35, maybe 40, but they were armed with bricks and that we needed to get round the back of them, not meet them head-on. He also told us they were by the old Ansells brewery, which is now a Mercedes garage.

We left the pub, walked across Lichfield Road and up Victoria Road, which is on a slope going towards Ruskin Hall. We tried to meet them head-on but they had a high vantage point and we became easy pickings. Doing exactly the opposite to what Sam had advised us, we just ran into a hail of bricks and from that moment we didn't have a chance of any result. We did have a stand-off and did manage to get into them but we just couldn't avoid the bricks, there was no hiding place to dodge them. Lads were getting their heads split as the bricks were hitting the intended targets and we were struggling to hold the line. Every time we tried to advance, the bricks would rain on us.

We backed off to the point we were on our toes but one of the Steamers wasn't running, he was standing firm, ending up in no man's land. He was attacked with ferocity by the Pompey lads. They should have dealt him a kicking and left it at that but they didn't, they went to town and cut him all the way across his back. We realised that he was on his own and went back for him and carried him back to the pub, literally holding his back in, as the cut made was that clean the skin of his back was wide open, as if he had been skinned. It was horrendous; I have never seen a knife do that much damage.

He was in agony and when we had got him back to the pub the gaffer was giving him whisky, anything to try to numb his pain as we waited for the ambulance. At one point I thought he might die. The lad is one of the gamest lads from the Steamers but he has specifically asked for no mention of his name in this book, which we will respect, but people at the Villa who know him will agree he is a top front line soldier.

Portsmouth's 6.57 got the result in that incident and credit where credit is due, it was in our manor on our streets, because we made a tactical error of Custer proportions. But they get no credit for what they did to one lad. Ginger from the Steamers was with another Villa firm that night battling Pompey on the other side of the ground and they fared better than we did but as I always say it just depends who you run into on the day and who you're with. It sometimes just doesn't go your way.

BRITTLE OK CORRAL, *AKA* EVERTON, 1984

Aston Villa and Everton have played each other more than any two clubs in the history of English football, and there is no doubt that over the past 30-odd years this fixture has had its share of off-the-field incidents. Most Villa will say there was more history between us and Liverpool, but we have had some notable battles with the blue half of Merseyside. 1984 saw one of those nights, when a pub fight descended into a scene reminiscent of the Gunfight at the OK Corral. We were in a transitional period as a Villa firm but for the odd game could still turn out a decent firm. This was a Milk Cup semi-final against Everton, with a chance of some silverware.

We started out early for a night match, something like 2.30pm, with most getting tucked into the beer and generally in good spirits. We arrived in Liverpool around five-ish, parked up the coach and found the nearest pub, which was the Blue House just around the corner from Goodison. Now three years earlier the C Crew had been in there and taken the pub with little resistance. This time it was mixed, with Everton and Villa civilians in there early doors. The atmosphere seemed relaxed but you could sense it was going to go as the lads with us started to play up and the real Everton lads coming in weren't too happy about an '81 episode developing.

With more and more coming in, the place erupted just after six o'clock. Who started I don't know, but what followed was one of the best pub brawls I have ever seen. Both sets went for it. Ashtrays, bar stools and glasses were used, it was a full-scale riot. While this was going on it set off another pub called the Winslow up the road and exactly the same thing happened there. So now you had two different mobs of both sets of fans going for it hammer and tongs.

The gaffer in the Blue House was trying to restore calm but got attacked and hit by a bar stool and then the window went in. Both sets of supporters were getting hit by missiles and one of our lads, Ginger Joe, was out for the count as a flying glass hit him. The row worked itself onto the road and there was a battle outside, with the pub's contents used as ammunition. Villa supporters dismantled the pool table and actually took that into the ground but certainly not to carry on playing pool, it was being thrown to and fro with the Everton supporters who were giving as good as they got.

The atmosphere was pure evil as the two lots battled it out on the street but the Liverpool coppers eventually waded in, arresting 28 people. During the game it was a case of 'duck' as the pool balls came whizzing past and to make matters worse we were robbed of a stone blind penalty that would have given us a fighting chance in the return leg.

Now while I think we probably shaded it before the game Everton certainly had the better of it after, they were more organised. One mob of Villa were turned over on Goodison Road in what the Old Bill described as a pitched battle, with six Villa suffering from the Scousers' favourite friend, the Stanley knife. Compared to events you get in this day and age this would be classed as a riot. It was ugly, violent and it took no prisoners.

THE GENERAL JUVENTUS, EUROPEAN CUP, 1983, HOME LEG

Villa were the current European Champions, had just won the Super Cup and were still a very good side but we now faced a team who boasted three World Cup winners from the 1982 Italian side, plus two of the best players in the world in Michel Platini and Zbigniew Boniek. It drew a capacity crowd of 48,000 and saw a lot of Anglo-based Italians making the trip from around the country. It was the quarter-final, the tie of the round and probably the biggest game in Europe that season, never mind England.

Ozzie had just come out of borstal, so as you do me and Brittle took him out on the piss all day. Oz was a little out of practice so he turned in at five, leaving us to go to the game. Me and Fraz, as I call him [see Chapter 13], went in the Witton End, which was where all the Italians were. A lot of people that most likely were Noses were also in there just to see a European game, well they ain't likely to see one at their place, are they? Nothing really happened even though the bastards were one up within minutes of the start, but when the second one went in it went off in the Witton and the atmosphere changed, although I didn't really see a mob of them in the ground.

Afterwards Fraz wanted more beer and fucked off to the pub but I was pissed off we had lost and fancied a row, so ended up with about another 40 Villa lads, some of whom I knew, others I think were just heading home and got caught up in it. We met a mob of them on Village Road and we steamed into them. I got a good dig in on the one but then felt a sharp blow to my stomach. I knew straight away I had been stabbed because I had been stabbed at Wolves only a year previously so I knew the difference between a punch and a knife.

It was a winter's night so it was dark and I don't think anybody was sure who was who. The truth is as soon as they gave it the Zorro bit with the blades most of the Villa in that crew were on their toes. I was stabbed along with Shana and Sam; in fact eleven Villa got served up that night. The dirty bastard not only stabbed me in the gut, which he couldn't fucking miss by the way, but I later found out he had stabbed me eleven times in the head, as the doctors who stitched me showed me the scabs. His blade actually broke on my skull, as he couldn't penetrate it. For a while it shook me up. Having the row was part and parcel of match day for me but being stabbed twelve times was totally different. Shana was very lucky, he had bent down to pick up his deerstalker and got stabbed in the heart (right ventricle). Not many survive being stabbed in the heart but he did.

It was a bad night for the Villa and a total letdown. We can argue that most of the front line weren't there but we had 40 lads looking for it and we got turned over on our home patch. I heard later that another firm of Villa had given it to the Juventus lot after the game in the Serpentine but the ones I was with were done good and proper and I have the nine-inch scar to prove it.

The Sun ran a story a few days later: 'Villa thugs get what they deserve'. Very patriotic. The kid who chivvied me was a hairdresser from Surrey; well he was a bit over-eager with a blade so I can imagine what his haircuts must have been like. I didn't make the away leg as I was still in hospital but word had got round what had happened and the lads went out there to get some revenge.

LLOYD AWAY LEG

This was a trip into uncharted territory for the C Crew and some Steamers. The plan was go to the FA Cup quarter-final at Highbury on the Saturday and then go direct to Italy from there. Arsenal was a big game in itself but we really wanted to avoid trouble or getting nicked, just keep a low profile, as Juventus was the one we were all looking forward to. We knew what to expect after what happened in the home leg with eleven of ours getting stabbed and this was definitely another level on from previous European trips.

Danny hadn't read the script, in fact for much of the trip he was, let's say, a bit hyper and certainly ring rusty, having just come out of the nick. Danny was an organiser in the very early days and whilst others were getting pissed in the pub and waiting for the other firms to land he was off and about doing the spotter's job. He wanted to take control and was headstrong and sometimes thought he always knew best. Well things had changed and he readily admits that during those 18 months away a lot had changed with the firm. There were a lot of new kids that had joined up with us, like Dezzie and Patterson, plus a lot of black lads from the Birchfield and Perry Barr areas. Patterson came in very handy as he organised the bent rail tickets for everyone to travel on. This was another progression for the firm as we had to make the most out of the very little money we had in the Eighties.

At the Arsenal game there was very little trouble beforehand but inside the ground just before kick-off a few Arsenal got into our side. Danny, on hearing this, forgets he is still on licence, forgets we are all telling him to keep out of trouble, and forgets how much he hated prison life and goes flying in – and gets himself nicked. Fortunately for Danny he was taken away by the Old Bill but God must have been smiling on him as they let him go after the game. This is the bloke who was sitting in his cell reading about Villa in Anderlecht, which was making national and international news, and had listened to all the stories off us about our trips abroad, so you would have expected him to wait till we had at least left England before kicking off.

He had heard of Villa lads robbing abroad, bringing back the fashions you couldn't get in the UK and the money lads were making from flogging the gear. The C Crew were selling clobber all over the West Midlands and even the Noses were buying stuff. What better way is there to earn money than watch the Villa in Europe and partly funded by a robbing spree? Danny had this vision that he was Che Guevara or William the Conqueror leading the troops into battle. I'm not saying it wasn't a buzz at home but this was something else. At that time there weren't many English clubs playing abroad so we felt that, along with the likes of Liverpool and Forest, we were carrying the flag. It was another league up and the previous season's exploits had given us a taste. Danny wanted to be amongst it with his lads, conquering new pastures, yet here he was putting the trip in jeopardy.

The game ended and we lost. Now if we hadn't had Juventus on the agenda we would have a proper tear-up with Arsenal but we had a big European trip in our sights. We made our way to a pub called possibly the Shakespeare, by Victoria Station. I was having my first beer when I looked out of the window and saw what must have been 300 lads gathering outside. We had a total of 26 travelling with us and not all of the 26 were in the pub at that time, in fact less than half were. I said to the lads, 'Here we go.' To this day we don't know if they were Arsenal or Chelsea or whoever but it wasn't us they had come for – in the pub was a small group of ten lads but game as fuck and it was them this mob were after. They didn't need to be asked to go outside, they just flew out the pub and into 'em. It was good pre-trip entertainment but it wasn't our row and we didn't want to fuck the trip up. I just hoped the likes of Danny and Brittle would behave and not get involved and thankfully this time we didn't need to put the leash on them.

We got the train to Dover and then the ferry to Ostend, where there was a bit of a domestic with me and a lad over a bird we were both interested in but no other action other than drinking on the ferry, a bit different to the last time en route to Anderlect where one of the lads was shafting a bird in a cabin with us cheering him on. You look back and wonder how the fuck you can drink that much, how you get through non-stop drink for five days. We lived on a liquid diet and as soon as we got off the ferry it was straight into the boozers. It was just booze and more booze. This was new to some, especially the ones who hadn't been to Europe before, with 24-hour pub openings, not close at 2pm for an English siesta.

I think at this point we were getting a bit lairy and all the old songs were coming out but the reputation of Villa supporters in Belgium from last season had made their police wary. Asking a load of pissed up English lads to keep quiet was never going to work so they ended up drawing their guns on us and gave us a good-old fashioned baton charge, maybe a bit of payback for Anderlect the season before.

We headed towards Paris on a night train and when we got on the sleeper most of the lads, if not all, were lagging. With that came all the usual high jinks: letting off fire extinguishers, people going to sleep and having eyebrows or moustaches removed, people setting fire to each other, just stag party stuff but even worse when you're that age with not a care or responsibility in the world. Arriving in Paris we were sick of sleeping rough on the trains and we all agreed it was about time we got some digs. We found a place in the city centre and then the oddest thing happened. Melv from the Steamers suddenly started spouting French and I mean not the pidgin French but fucking fluent French. Seeing is believing and here was Melv, a battle-hardened self-appointed leader of the Steamers, sounding like some compere off the Eurovision Song Contest talking to this French guy about rates for rooms. He did save our skin later that night when all the C Crew lads were pissed and playing up in the hotel bar which ended up with the owner pulling out a gun, waving it at us and telling us to behave as we are throwing bottles at him. Melv got a knock on his room and came downstairs to smooth it before telling us to 'behave and fuck off you wankers'.

Next day the funds were very low and Victor from Newtown decided enough was enough and trapped back home with his pal. Our next stop was Dijon in northern France and by now we were getting pissed off with carrying our sports holdalls around, so we headed to the station to find some lockers. Brittle opened a locker up thinking it was empty only to discover it was full of heavy duty knives. Now I don't know if it was some butcher's bag but whatever, he helped himself to it. Brittle opened the bag up and dished out the knives to the lads, as we knew what awaited us in Juventus. The Italians were the masters of the knife, as we had witnessed two weeks earlier, so it was a blessing.

These were the Eighties, the early Thatcher years, and Birmingham as an area was suffering from high unemployment. People were hardly awash with cash. To travel in those days on a shoestring required you to have your wits about you and we were no different to any set of English football lads travelling abroad. Sometimes desperate measures were needed. Only Brittle and Patterson had any money and they were the ones paying for the beer but they were good at this robbing lark, experienced campaigners. Myself and Danny weighed in with a few bottles of whisky and brandy compliments of the top shelf of some unsuspecting off licence. Meanwhile one of the lads, Chelsea Paddy, had one gallon too many to drink and started to attack people, getting himself arrested, so we lost another of the crew.

We then made our way on a sleeper train to Turin, where we met up with three West Ham lads who had gone over to rob. They filled us in with stories from their older lot, the ICF boys who had been in the European Championships in 1980 with England in Turin. The game has been well documented but it was the night of the long knives and a lot of English got stabbed that night. Most were caught out thinking they could do as they pleased in Turin, unfortunately it's not that type place and is certainly not a city for tourists. Turin isn't Milan, if anything it's similar to Birmingham as it's the centre of their car industry and an industrial city, tough, uncompromising and full of little lowlifes who would think nothing of stabbing or slashing Johnny Englander. These wideboy London lads were as good as gold and we were glad of their assistance in the end.

At 6am we were knackered and all slept in the station waiting room using a couple of flags as sleeping blankets. This alerted the Juventus fans to our nationality and they walked past giving the cutthroat signs. While the lads snored away Danny became morning watchman; he couldn't sleep and was worried that if we were all asleep they would chivvy us up.

We hadn't come with the official party so didn't have tickets and they weren't selling them for the away end, so we had no choice but to get tickets for the home end. We knew the little mob we had we couldn't afford to split; we had to stick together, so we avoided the touts and went to the ground to get tickets. I knew it was on top and tempers and nerves were frayed but it didn't help when we bumped into some scousers who were talking to a few of our lads. When we got back Danny heard the accent and said, 'What the fuck are you doing here? You're fucking dead, I will deal with you later.' The Scousers were only there on the rob and I think by now they realised who Danny was. Danny blamed them for everything from the beatings and abuse he took in Liverpool to going to jail for slashing a few of them, and they were soon on their toes out of it.

We got on the tram and met up with a few of the others from the Norton pub who had travelled a day earlier. We got our first sign of what really awaited us as there were now 25 of us, including the three West Ham lads. Some Italians saw us and were at us straight away flashing blades. Quick as a flash the London lads sprayed them with gas and that was them out of action, coughing and spluttering. We followed it up by going through them.

From what we had heard a few of our normals had taken a bit of a bashing and whilst we also heard about a bit of an off at a pub when some of ours did very well, this was a place you really needed safety in numbers. We got to the ground and they were searching everybody for weapons. We still had Brittle's little stash with us and whilst some were unlucky others managed to get away by putting the knives down their fronts. Amazingly nobody was getting nicked, they just took away the knives that they found. The thing is, they were finding guns on the Italians so you can tell it was pretty serious and wasn't going to be a place for the faint-hearted.

In the ground we made our way to the front. We had put our flags in carrier bags – we weren't that stupid or brazen – but we stuck out anyway. It was two hours from kick-off and the place was jumping, the ground was already half full with Juventus singing and people bouncing up and down, waving huge Juve flags. I wondered what it would be like at kick-off. I said Danny was ring rusty and as usual he couldn't keep still so he went off to get a programme and a pizza. The rest of us began to get noticed and the wagons were circling. It must have looked like an old Western with the Indians surrounding the cowboys, and we didn't have any wagons to turn over for a shield. Danny walked back with his pizza totally oblivious to the scenario unfolding.

Their lads were dressed in red flying jackets and there were hundreds of them, with loads carrying and flashing blades at us. What chance did 20 have against a whole end who hate anything English? There were 65,000 there that night and I wouldn't mind betting that other than 1,000 or so Villa, the majority were evil knife merchants. Whatever you hear about the Italian hooligans in a row is true, you can forget hand to hand combat – with them, it's all tools. It's funny how things like this aren't mentioned when people talk about what happened at the Heysel Stadium.

I began to think there was a very good chance of some of us not getting out alive. We just didn't have the numbers. People began opening their coats showing us knives that they were carrying, with some openly holding them in their hands.

The police sussed what was going on and came in and escorted us out, putting us in with the rest of the Villa fans in a caged pen. Oddly there was an Italian amongst us who was trying to revive Anglo-Italian relations; he was a Torino fan, Juve's staunchest rivals, who shared the same ground at the time. He taught us how to say 'Fuck off Juventus' in Italian. It had the desired effect as they went mental and began prodding the cage with six-foot poles. Some fucking ground search!

All game the atmosphere was hostile as we spent 90 minutes trying to protect ourselves from bottles being thrown at us as well as the poles. The game finished and would you believe it the red flying jacket mob were now circulating at the top of our end. It was totally on top. They had the numbers and they were looking to cut any English they could. Danny, on his first European trip, led the charge and with the lads behind him we ran them out of our end and onto the streets. The Villa official coaches were parked right outside to take the normal travelling fans back, so we asked for a lift to the station. They could clearly see what was happening but knew we were the scum they didn't want to associate with, or to put it politely we were 'not in the official travelling party'. Eddie was arguing with the Villa's official corporate compere, or in layman's terms Doug Ellis's arse-licking side kick, and Eddie gave him a backhander. At that point we knew we were on our own.

We were standing by the coaches, at the most 20 of us, and we saw Juventus. There must have been 300 of them in the road. I turned and said, 'Here they are lads.' I said it very cocky as if we were about to engage a firm of similar numbers, I suppose it was a double bluff. It was then that we had a stroke of luck. Never mind the police, this time they had got the Army in and they came to our rescue. I'm under no illusions here, we were fucked and some of the lads would have been going home in bodybags. That is not an exaggeration. If you have got 300 blokes who won't throw a punch but are tooled it's pretty obvious that you are going to get cut and with their numbers we would have been cut bad.

It would be great to say we ran them but the fact is the Army had them on their toes. Danny was that hyped up he decided to enrol in the Italian Army for the night and ran with the soldiers chasing after them. For our own safety we were then taken in armoured vehicles back to the railway station, with all these mad Italians hollering and shouting abuse.

Now some of the lads are buzzing like it's a good day at the office but it was so on top that if you stand back and think about it we were lucky to get out alive.

Who do we bump into at the station then? Danny's old scouse friends who he had promised to deal with, so me and him are into them but could they run. We chased them down the rail tunnel, the rest of the lads were pissing themselves when they saw the two Liverpool lads looking blacker than me and Danny when they emerged from the tunnel.

To the 20-odd lads who made it, including the three West Ham, if medals for bravery were being given out, trust me a George Cross would have been awarded for every single one of us that night.

DANNY VITORIA GUIMARAES

After Juventus I had got the Europe bug and even though it wasn't the European Cup, only the UEFA, it was still Europe and I wanted to make up for lost time. We agreed to go as a joint firm of Steamers and C Crew and while it wasn't the full firms, just 30 of us, I thought if it was anything like our Italian visit then it would be a good one. The meet was at New Street Station but for once I was late. I couldn't believe there was nobody else there when I arrived; I had missed them. As I stood planning my next move, I spotted a lad from the Steamers, Groombridge. Now this was a frightening guy, scared of no man and someone you simply could not beat in a fight, he would just keep coming back until he won, a terrace legend. He had also happened to try to stab me a few years earlier over a Villa domestic. I was thinking, *great, the one bloke out of the 30 who you don't want to be on your own with*. He didn't really like the C Crew lads; I think he looked upon us in the early years as pretenders and trying to take over. Anyway, I had no choice but to get on with it, so we caught the train together to Victoria Station in London. We were only about an hour behind the lads on the earlier train but in the days before mobile phones they had assumed we weren't making the trip.

We got to London, then a train to Dover and a ferry to Paris and travelled by train to San Sebastian and on to Lisbon. We were trying to catch up with the lads but with neither of us getting any sleep I couldn't relax so I didn't drink although he did. I wanted to stay alert in case he might turn after a beer. We arrived at Lisbon and by this time we were knackered and needed sleep, so we managed to find some digs. Just my luck, the only room available was a double with a double bed. I thought, *what is going on, please God, I have paid my price for New Street*. I slept with one eye open, him snoring away with an arm sloped over me at times. It might sound funny but at the time I believed I was rooming with Charles Manson.

Next day we found the local whorehouse and asked some British tourists who happened to be sampling the delights if they had seen a group of Villa fans. They told us they had seen some on the coast in Estoril. We travelled up there and found our lads in the boozer, surprisingly not the whorehouse. I was glad to see them and could relax and have a drink, and we all had a bit of play-up in there before some silly Portuguese fool got a bit trappy and it ended up going off. Brittle had got hold of a gun and pulled it out before all the locals joined in and that seemed to calm things down a bit. Brittle being Brittle had come out to Portugal on police bail but needed to go back to sign on, so we had a whipround to send him back but he was never going to be able to make the match.

We got back to Lisbon and caught the main train to Porto spending a night there and got yet another train to Vitoria. I say train, it was a bit of a Casey Jones effort with an old wooden floor and people getting on with goats, chickens and one woman breast-feeding her baby. It certainly wasn't something you see in the travel brochures. When we arrived, I bumped into a Benfica fan, we got talking and he gave me some advice I didn't take: 'If you want trouble you will get serious trouble here but if you are quiet no one will bother you.' We found out later that Clarkey with his crew had missed the game, typical Clarkey, he thought it was an evening kick-off but it was in the afternoon so they missed what we were about to encounter.

At the ground we got split and ten of us, including Groombridge, went in their main end. I was lagging from the all-day session in the bars. I can't drink at the best of times but was just going with the flow and enjoying Europe. I stood on my own at the back of the end with a big Villa flag singing fuck knows what but I was enjoying myself, typical Villa on Tour stuff in Europe. I banged away on the back of the end, shouting my head off all through the first half with no one bothering me. All that was to change in the second half.

My sleeping buddy, Groombridge, was in the middle of the end on his own. He wasn't into the singing or making new mates and instead decided to kick it off by lumping this Portuguese bloke standing next to him. The mood changed within an instant and a gap appeared but now blokes were wading into him. I spotted it all and with the fact he was Villa, one of us and in trouble, I knew I had to help. I didn't think about anything and was pissed anyway, I just jumped off the fence and felt like Superman as I flew down the terraces, pushing people away to get to him.

I pulled people off him and got well stuck into them, hitting anything and everything like a man possessed. According to Hicky, who was suffering from food poisoning at the time, I disappeared under a mountain of bodies. We later found out that Groombridge had hit this geezer who was a gypsy and was part of a big Portuguese gypsy firm that lived in the mountains. We had disturbed a hornets' nest and they weren't happy.

Three of us were now getting seriously hurt – me, Groombridge and Gary Harwood (RIP) – with Hicky trying to pull these mad fuckers off. I sobered up quickly and managed through sheer survival instincts to get away, with my old Benfica friend shouting, 'I told you don't mess with these people, run, run!' I got to what I can only describe as an old bombpeck-type fence that had barbed wire all around the top of it and could hear the Benfica kid shouting, 'Jump, jump.' I went from Superman to Spiderman and scaled the bastard.

It was a relief to get over the fence and when my leg gave way as I hit the ground I thought it was just from the jump. But I could see the old gypsy in red cleaning his nails with a knife and realised I had been stabbed in the thigh. The pain was unbearable. I lost consciousness and was taken round the pitch with my jeans soaked in blood, out of the ground and straight into an ambulance. I was also minus a few teeth, seven in fact, so it was a proper job and I looked like Villa's Elephant Man. I was annoyed with myself for drinking that much and putting myself in that position.

Thinking I was on the way to hospital and feeling sorry for myself, I was surprised when the doors were flung open and Groombridge and Harwood were thrown in. I thought, *I am in a fucking nightmare here*. Outside the hornets nest we had disturbed were screaming, hollering and banging on the sides of the ambulance. It was mob rule and for a minute I thought they were going to turn the ambulance over.

Thankfully we got to the hospital for me to get stitched up and the others to get attended to. Like the walking wounded we eventually limped out, only to see a mob of these mountain gypos baying for our blood. The mob advanced towards us and we had no choice but to hobble back into the hospital to seek refuge. This has now turned into our own Beirut, a scene you might see on the news from some Middle East hellhole. It's 'Death to the English'. For our own safety the police were called and they put us in a taxi to get us away from the mob, who were shouting for our heads, and to the safety of Porto.

When we got out of the taxi, this fella shouted to me, 'English English,' and showed me the paper. We had made the front page of their national newspaper and in the process taken a beating of a lifetime. They say if you can't beat your opponent stand there and take your punishment, which Groombridge, Harwood and I did. I have had two trips to Europe and nearly got killed at both occasions, no complaints!

BRITTLE SPURS: THE TRILOGY

By the time the Premiership started, football violence had changed and in the Nineties fights tended to be on a smaller scale. It was very difficult to get mobs of 250 or even 100 from A to B without being picked up by the police, and while the mobile phones have played a big part in organising rows, they have also prevented rows as people tend to be sloppy when they are in earshot of police spotters.

What happened at Spurs in the early Nineties was about smaller numbers. In April 1992, we were away at Tottenham. At that time I was spending a lot of time in the East End and had made friends with a few old ICF lads, so a trip to the Smoke suited me. There was 15-20 of us in the Park Hotel on Park Lane before the game, having a drink and minding our own business. I was with Godds and a few of us popped out to put a couple of bets on. Unbeknown to us, a group of Spurs had spotted us and called it on. The rest of our lot came out of the pub, put Spurs on their toes and then went back inside and carried on drinking. It was nothing to write home about and to be honest if they hadn't started anything it wouldn't have bothered us in the slightest and the incidents that followed over the next two years would never have happened. But it set the tone for far worse incidents and was the start of some nasty business with the North London lot.

Not long after that game, I was sentenced to three years for supplying E's and missed the corresponding fixture down there the following season.

CLARKEY

The 1992/93 was Big Ron Atkinson's second in charge and Villa were on fire. By November when we were away to Spurs we were top of the table and playing some awesome football. The Spurs game on November 21 fell on Micky C's birthday so a few of us went down on a 15-seat minibus for a bit of a piss-up with him. We landed down there at around noon and having heard about Brittle's little altercation the previous season, we made a beeline for the Park Hotel, where we had arranged to meet up with another group on a 15-seat minibus who were travelling down from the Little Crown in Perry Barr.

When we entered the pub, there was a group of Spurs lads sat around a table in the middle of the room but apart from that the place was empty. The Spurs lads all drank up and left not long after we had landed and then a few Villa arrived who were living down that way, including an old face from the past, Melv. About an hour later, the Perry Barr minibus turned up and our numbers were now about 35-40. We had a quiet afternoon's drinking with no sign of any Spurs before making our way to the ground in dribs and drabs.

I was beginning to think that all the talk before the game about Spurs having a pop was just that, talk, when I saw a load of them pile out of the pub in front of us, the Olive Branch, and attack the Villa lads who were level with that pub. None of us was walking in a group, just in ones and twos, and the lads who were attacked stood no chance and were demolished. Those of us who were behind the altercation grouped together immediately and went forward in the direction the Spurs had gone. The OB were soon in amongst it and there was a lot of verbaling going on. All the Spurs were telling us they would see us in the Park Hotel at half past six and that the match-day Old Bill left the area at six. We didn't need much persuading and we made an instant decision to go back to the Park Hotel after the game.

The game ended 0-0, with Villa playing them off the park but unable to get the goal that their performance deserved. We ended up back in the Park Hotel with more or less the same group from before the match, the 30 on the buses and a handful who were based down there. The pub had pretty much emptied of football fans by around six o'clock and one or two locals had begun to come in, as the karaoke was set up for the evening's entertainment. By this time, most were becoming bored and rumours started to fly around that Spurs were in a pub called the Northumberland Arms. Quite a few of the lads wanted to go and find this pub, do a job on them and then get going back to Birmingham, but we didn't get around to leaving the Park. Then, dead on 6.30pm, all hell broke loose.

Our 40-odd were spread out all over the lounge, a group were playing pool at the front, some were sat at tables, a couple were stood by the back door near to the toilets and a couple were stood at the bar waiting to get served. At exactly half six, a group of less than ten came through the front doors chanting, 'Yids, Yids, Yids.' At the same time, some came through the back doors and some through the bar. They also lined the street along the side of the pub and began putting every window through. The ones that came through the bar began throwing bottles and glasses through the bar area and at people standing at the bar in the lounge.

Joycey was at the bar and caught a bottle or glass straight in the face. It broke on impact and tore his eye. In the meantime, the lads playing pool at the front had got the Yids who came through the front door back out again and there was a lot of banging on the door as they tried to get in and we tried to get out. The same story happened at the back door, where our lads had swiftly dealt with the Yids who came in.

While all this was going on, all the windows along the front and the side were going through and various objects were being hurled into the pub from outside. I don't think many, if any, escaped without getting cut, there was glass flying everywhere. Pool balls were being hurled through the broken windows but most were simply sent flying back in and people were smashing the remains of the windows with tables and chairs in an attempt to get out at them. I have been in several pubs where the whole place has gone up but in terms of flying objects and glass nothing compares to that night at the Park. It's a miracle there were not many more serious injuries.

The whole thing seemed to go on for half an hour but I guess in reality it was more like ten minutes. Those who have been involved in these kind of things will tell you that ten minutes is a very long time and although it became a stalemate, with Villa unable to get out and Spurs unable to get in, the pub was an incredible sight when the police landed. The carpet was a sea of glass and it was like walking on a layer of peanuts or crisps, crunch, crunch with every step. There wasn't a chair or table left intact, the optics and everything else behind the bar had been obliterated, there wasn't a window left and the front door was hanging off. I think the karaoke may have been cancelled that night as well. It was a mad experience even though not a lot of hand-to-hand fighting had gone on. We were there to go feet and fists with them but they decided to throw things through the windows from a safe distance.

The funny sight of the night was when one of them got a bit too close and Big H planted a beer tray on his head. The bloke wobbled all over the place and the whole sequence looked like something out of a Tom and Jerry cartoon. The bar staff re-appeared from their hiding places and informed the police that the pub had been attacked from outside so we were free to go. Unfortunately Joycey had a serious eye injury and kept in hospital down there for five days before being transferred to Birmingham, where he spent a total of three weeks. I am happy to report his eye was saved. Joycey said afterwards, 'My mate Frank was also in hospital and through my good eye I watched the bump on his head grow and it was like watching a cartoon, about the only thing to fuckin cheer me up.'

BRITTLE

I soon got to hear about what had gone on and what had happened to Joycey and was told that plans were in place to visit the pub again the next time we were down that way. That was something they didn't get round to but by the time we drew Spurs away in the quarter-final of the League Cup the following season, I was back on the streets and raring to go.

The whole thing about the Park Hotel had now become

common knowledge and even on the way down there, when we stopped off at a motorway service station, 'the Park Hotel' seemed to be the topic on everyone's lips. Sure enough, when we got there the pub was heaving, jam-packed full of Villa. The OB were taking no chances this time and there were meat wagons, police horses and cars all the way round the pub. I thought that if anything was going to happen then it would be afterwards, but I was wrong.

As we left the pub heading towards the ground in a constant stream rather than a firm, a mob of Spurs came towards us from the direction of the Olive Branch. We clashed in the middle of the road briefly before they were sent packing and some police from the Park quickly wrapped us up.

We ended up winning the game 2-1 and had reached the semi-finals. Everyone was ecstatic but as soon as we got outside, there were running battles all along Park Lane, despite the number of police about. When we got back to the Park, the Metropolitan Police were again all around the pub and wouldn't let us near it. I'll never know if they opened it that night. A large group of Villa gathered outside the pub and eventually we decided to head back towards the Olive Branch.

We had only gone a few paces before we came across Spurs' mob but they failed to hold it together and scattered as we went into them. I chased two Yids across a forecourt and managed to trip one of them but as I went to kick him, I fell over him and ended up on the floor myself. As I lay there, two Villa fans came over and started booting me. 'I'm Villa,' I growled and they stopped immediately. By this time, Spurs had disintegrated and the police were all over the shop.

That was the last of our little sequence of run-ins with Spurs in that period. They had been told to come to Perry Barr when they played at Villa but they never did.

OLD HABITS DIE HARD

I can't remember the exact game but it was around 1983. I went into the Windsor after the game and while I was at the bar waiting to be served, two blokes noticed the 'AVFC' tattoo I have across the back of my hand. 'What's that stand for, Aston Villa fucking cunt?' said one clever lad, who turned out to be an Everton fan. *Ahhh*, I thought as I got my drink. I wanted to kill the pair of them there and then, not just give them a couple of digs in a crowded bar.

I went away from the bar and over to a table where Jimmy and 'Mr X' were. I explained how I felt and we agreed that the best way to get them away from the pub to somewhere a bit more quiet was to invite them to a 'party'. I had a flick knife on me that one of the lads had given me to hold onto earlier on and I tossed a coin with Jimmy to see who could have it for this pair. Jimmy won and unfortunately for the two Everton lads, they lost.

I went over to them and started talking with them. We had already planned to take them to a quiet car park at the back of the pigeon park, a landmark in Brum town centre.

'Do you fancy a party boys? We've got a nurses' party to go to just round the corner.'

Almost at once they replied, 'Yeah, yeah, we're up for that.'

We got them over the pigeon park and were walking down this dark alley when all of a sudden we began to hear music. I got up onto a ledge to investigate. To be honest, I was that pissed I thought there actually was a party. All of a sudden I heard 'click' and knew Jimmy was out with the blade. Nobody seemed to take any notice so I heard 'click' again. I thought, *fuck this*, jumped off the ledge, grabbed one of them and smacked him in the face.

'Aston Villa are fucking cunts, are they?'

With this, Jimmy came in swinging and jabbing the knife around. I copped a thrust into my arm which cut it wide open and Mr X got stabbed in the back of the neck, one Everton fan got stabbed in the stomach and the other Everton fan got a stab wound which punctured his lung.

It wasn't going to take Sherlock Holmes to work out who had done the two Everton lads, so when the police started showing them pictures of known Villa hooligans it wasn't going to be too long before Jimmy and I got collared. The next time Jimmy went to sign on, sure enough they were waiting and he was nicked. I decided to go on my toes for a few months. I stopped signing on and went to live with my then girlfriend at her mum's house in Harbourne.

Eventually they found out I was living there and went round and kicked the doors in, only to find I wasn't there at the time. When I finally turned up and was walking towards the house, the window cleaner shouted to me, 'Paul, don't go down there, the Old Bill are waiting up the road to nick you.' So I turned round and went straight to the gym Andy was running at the time, which was not far up the road. The window cleaner sent my girlfriend up to me and I sent her home to find out what was going on and told her to phone me to let me know. When she went to the phone box, her mum told the Old Bill that they'd probably find me at the gym up the road. The next thing I knew, they were all inside the gym.

'Mister Brittle, can we have a word with you?'

I got twelve months and Jimmy got 15 for it. It proved how very difficult it was for us to just show the other cheek and walk away, they had insulted us and we couldn't let it go.

ANONYMOUS I ENJOYED THE PARTY SO MUCH I BOUGHT THE PUB

We had West Ham on Boxing Day 1991 and I had a few pals coming up from the East End for the game. We arranged a party for the night at the Little Crown pub in Perry Barr, which was our base at the time. The Little Crown had a lot of Villa memorabilia on the walls, only they were pictures of the lads in action rather than the players. The gaffer of the pub was called Frank, a Villa fan who had become a mate of mine. In the daytime, Franny had a fall out with one of the lads, who ended up putting one on him. Franny then decided he was shutting the pub, he was fed up of the hassle he was always getting and this was the final straw.

When we found out after the game that the pub was shut, we phoned him and asked him what he was doing. He told me he had

had enough and didn't want to know no more. I said, 'Fair enough,' and put the phone down. A couple of hours later, we were sat in the Crown And Cushion across the road when one of the lads suddenly said, 'Fuck this, we'll break in, charge everybody five pound on the door and whatever money we make we'll give to Frank the next day and tell him it's a leaving present.'

The lad went across the road, onto the roof and broke into the pub. I got the Alsatian dog, put him in the living room and made sure the door was shut. I noticed a red light going off and thought the place might be connected to the police station, so I went back over the road and stayed put. Once 20 minutes had passed and there was no sign of any coppers, I announced to everyone that we were having a party in the Little Crown.

If I say so myself, it was one of the best parties I've ever been to. I put doormen on the door, I got staff behind the bar, I got Buster as the DJ and charged everybody a fiver in. It was rammed. At first we were just drinking the bottles but they soon ran out so we had to start on the draught and it became every man for himself, as people didn't want to play barmen all night. By two or three o'clock in the morning it began to get a bit silly as everyone was pilled up, coked up or pissed and they started breaking into the machines. At first I tried to stop them but then I got off my head myself and I said, 'Carry on.' All the optics went, I saw people getting into taxis at five in the morning carrying bags of spirits. The place was rocking, everyone was dancing and people were coming up to me telling me it was the best party they'd ever been to. Someone asked me where Frank was and I said, 'He don't know about it.'

The next day I got a phone call about four o'clock. I was scared to answer my phone but did so eventually. My mate told me I had to get myself back down to the pub, as Frank and his missus were there. When I walked through the doors it looked like a bomb had gone off; the place was destroyed. Frank's missus was devastated, sitting in the middle of the pub. Every machine was turned upside down, cigarette machines were ripped open.

Straight away I've gone, 'Whaaaat the fuck happened here?'

Frank said, 'I thought you was a mate.'

I told him, 'This wasn't supposed to happen.'

I think we only took about £800 on the door. The police thought it was an insurance job and tried to do Frank for that. In the end, I told him to let me know exactly what the damage came to and we'd pay for it, which I did and ended up losing a couple of grand on it. I paid for all the damages out of my own pocket and then I bought the pub two months later. I want it to be known that I never did any of the above with the intention of buying the pub but what a night, though very expensive for some.

 ## CLARKEY LEEDS UNITED

On the way to reaching the FA Cup final in 2000 (least said about that the better), we played Leeds United at home in the fifth round. The game was live on TV, with a 2pm Sunday kick-off. The landlady of a pub near Villa Park that we used to use then offered to open up for breakfast, so as a one-off our usual group of around 15 met at the pub at 9.30am, having a good breakfast as well as a good four hours on the lash. The game was a humdinger with us eventually winning 3-2 thanks to a spectacular hat-trick from Carbone. At the time Leeds were the up-and-coming challengers to Man United and Arsenal.

All our lot were on a high and on the way back to the pub we decided to pop into the Adventurers, which is the first pub behind the Holte End as you leave Villa Park. At the time, Andy worked on the door there as a favour to the landlord, so it wasn't unheard of for us to pop in from time to time to say hello. We bumped into Hicky on the way and he had told us of a mob of Leeds who had walked down this way before the game, giving it loads from behind a police escort. We didn't pay it much attention, we were on a bit of a roll and if the truth be known we were more concerned about how many deep the bar in the 'Ads' was going to be.

FORDY

One of my closest pals, Pete, was outside the Ads on his mobile, unaware that this Leeds mob, numbering 30-odd, were now on the car park and looking for Villa. Pete, seeing that they were targeting him, tried to get out the way and the only gap was over the cars parked outside the pub. They were on to him before he could get away and he got pushed onto the floor.

I don't think anyone realised for a minute that Pete was stranded outside, the door was shut and he had this Leeds mob on his case. The first lads out the boozer were the two doormen at the time, Martin Breen and Andy Browne, and they and I went straight into them. Martin didn't realise it was Pete on the floor, picked up the '2 for 1' meal sign and bashed it over his head before Pete said, 'It's me, you prat.' Martin is a good Irish lad and as hard as nails; I winced when I saw him hit Pete with the sign. The manager of the pub, Tommy, remarked later that Pete was a great advert for the pub's Sunday meals, as the force of the blow had left the sign imprinted on his back.

Pete was just getting his senses together when from behind the Leeds mob came one of our old pals, Stevie Norton, a really top lad who sadly passed away at the age of 44. (A gathering of over 500 people attended his funeral and as someone remarked afterwards, 'The Lord Mayor wouldn't have a turnout as good as that.' That shows how much esteem he was held in and even the Noses came to pay their respects.) Stevie went flying into the Leeds lad and now there was five of us battling with them before the cavalry came.

CLARKEY

Just as we got our drinks, the shout went up, 'Leeds are outside.' I couldn't see out of the window from where I was standing but I immediately thought about Andy, who would have been just outside the front door. The whole pub tried to empty out through the only door and it became a bottle-neck. By the time I got out, Leeds were on the back foot and across the car park with most of the pub in pursuit as they headed up towards Lichfield Road. They came across a pile of newly delivered fence posts on somebody's front lawn and to their credit they armed themselves and came back for another go. A lot of firms would have carried on running in that situation.

We formed a line and as I glanced to my right and left, I saw that the whole line consisted mostly of our lot who'd had breakfast in the pub together earlier, plus the likes of Del, Jarvo and Pete carrying his '2 for 1' meals sign on his back. It went off all right, with the fence posts being swung and our lads gradually getting them off the Leeds one by one. Leeds began to back off as we got the upper hand but they had left a man down and with all the crowds still streaming past from the ground, many passers-by went to town on him. One bloke who was walking past with his son picked up the post that the Leeds lad had dropped and began beating him relentlessly as he lay on the floor. Other people began laying into him but he was motionless and making no attempt to cover his head.

We were still going hammer and tongs with the other Leeds, who to their credit were trying to get to their mate. Big H saw what was happening to the lad on the floor and went and stood over him, telling all the Villa fans to back off. The Leeds were still trying to reach him but couldn't break the Villa line. Davey B had taken a pole off one of the Leeds lads and was using it himself when another guy crashed a pole onto the top of Dave's head, opening it up. I heard the familiar sound of police sirens coming from behind me and the fight began to break up. Everyone began dropping the poles, with the Leeds lot going in the direction of Lichfield Road and the Villa lot heading back towards the Adventurers. A couple of Leeds lads went to pick up their mate and Big H turned to head back to the Ads himself when one of the Leeds crashed a post down onto H as hard as he could. H told me afterwards that he felt paralysed. I turned round and saw him bent double, with his hands on his knees and the two Leeds lads carrying their mate away. H was fuming over their cowardice, especially after he had gone out of his way to save the kid from a further beating. H vowed afterwards that he would never help anyone again, but knowing him as I do I would put big money on him doing exactly the same thing again if he was in that situation because that's the way H is.

We went back to the Ads and had a quick drink before heading back to the pub we'd started in. We were still in there going strong when Davey B appeared with a freshly stitched-up head after a visit to A & E. It was a good day all in all and Wembley and our holy grail the FA Cup was on the horizon. Sadly after beating Bolton in a penalty shootout in what was like a home game, as there were almost 40,000 Villa in the crowd, we then played Chelsea in the last ever final at the old Wembley, and it was one of the worst ever finals to be played there. We went down for the weekend taking the train on the Friday and then to the game on the Saturday in style in limos and it was a real party atmosphere, but sadly once the referee blew his whistle the team completely let us down and don't think I have ever got over it, you ask most Villa fans of my age and that performance / result was probably as low as anything we have ever encountered. Some of the players that day were a disgrace and soon after it was like rats leaving the sinking ship as they were asking for transfers, wankers!

Off the field there was a small altercation at the Hilton Hotel with their lot after the game when some silly cockney cunt sprayed CS gas into a bar where women and kids were and I understand they got a beating at some social club up the road beforehand, but it was a very quiet day on the fighting front. Most Villa were elated to just be in an FA Cup Final; it was a real carnival atmosphere with people dressed up as claret and blue Vikings holding the old Villa player Chico Hamilton up on their shoulders to some terrible claret and blue suits before the game. People were more interested in taking photographs than taking a swing at a Chelsea lad. After the game we were that pig sick no one was angry, more empty than anything.

ANDY

On the subject of cup finals, I would like to mention an incident before the 1996 League Cup final against Leeds United. For the day of the game, somebody had organised a Villa meet in a club about five miles away from Wembley. I arrived there on the morning and didn't like the place at all, there were some good lads in there but I couldn't understand why we were so far from Wembley. I had visions of Leeds being all over the place by the ground with no Villa about, as we were all in this social club in the middle of nowhere.

At the time I was going through a lot. Paul [Brittle] was a couple of years into his sentence, I was looking after the Little Crown and there was a pile of problems all round. When I look back, I think that what happened next was the result of a build-up of all the problems and stress, a relief from it if you like. Whatever the reason, about ten or 15 of us left that club straight away, only to be told that there was no train line to Wembley. Taxis were few and far between and our best bet was to hop on a bus to the ground, which we did. A couple got off on the way, leaving about six of us by the time we got off near the ground.

There were crowds about now so we were walking on the road to save a bit of time and just as we had passed a tube station, a group of Leeds came out from off a train. As I looked round at them, my impression was that they were all lads, not wearing any colours, and they were looking at us in a way that made me think they were going to start something. In my mind, I made a split decision to have a go at them before they started on us, and I jumped over the barrier between the road and the pavement and went towards them. Pete Moore was with me, as he has been many times, as well as my good friend Steve Barnes (RIP). They backed off a bit at first but they kept pouring out of the station. By the time they'd all got out, it looked like there was over 100 of them and after a time it was on top. I got pulled down to the floor, managed to tuck my head in and took a bit of a leathering, which does you no harm every so often.

I got up, brushed myself down and saw the Leeds mob heading

in the direction of the ground. At this stage I wasn't sure where Pete or Steve were, so I jogged up the road to catch the tail end of the Leeds lot up. I started again at the back end of them and quite a few punches were traded before some of their lads stopped it, telling everyone that it was over. A few of them began shaking my hand, they were a good firm and it was a good day out.

After I'd left them and walked round a corner I bumped into Steve, who had ripped a fence up and was heading back towards them. I told him it was finished and we went on to the game. I must admit, I was very sore on the train home that night but thankfully we had won the cup which made the journey a little bit easier.

16 BOXING IN THE CLARET AND BLUE

DANNY

I come from a family who were more into boxing and cricket than football. We always took an interest in the noble art, so much so that our parents named both my brother and myself after boxers: Floyd after Floyd Patterson, while my middle name is Ray after the legendary Sugar Ray Robinson. Growing up, most lads would remember their fathers telling them stories about the great footballers of the past, but I can remember as if it was yesterday my father telling me stories, stories that took my breath away, about the great old boxers, like Jersey Joe Walcott, Joe Louis and Rocky Marciano, to name but a few.

I've always thought of myself as a bit of a boxing buff and over the years I've collected lots of memorabilia, which includes a photograph taken with my all-time hero, the great Muhammad Ali. My good friend Joe Egan has also introduced me to some legends of the ring. The truth is, there has always been a strong boxing connection in my family because Donovan 'Razor' Ruddock, the Canadian heavyweight champion who fought Mike Tyson twice for the World Boxing Championship, is actually my cousin. So it would be fair to say that it was in my biological make-up to box.

When Floyd started boxing, it seemed natural for me to follow him, so aged eleven, off I went to Aston Manor Amateur Boxing

Club, which was on Yew Tree Road, Aston. This old boxing club was originally formed in 1908 and has a long and proud tradition of producing some very fine boxing talents. These included F. Lench, schoolboy ABA champion, P. Riley, lightweight MCABA champion, and Don Broadhurst, who was featherweight ABA champion and Commonwealth gold medallist. Maybe I thought at the time that I was going to be one of the best, if not 'the' best boxer, they had ever produced!

I had three stints at the club, the first being when I was a wide-eyed schoolboy and just wanted to box like my idol, Muhammad Ali. The second was as simple as this: I wanted to get fit and to learn the boxing skills that would hopefully give me the edge on the terraces. This decision came about after a West Ham game in 1980, we all knew after that little taster that we had to wise up and get serious, we had to take our front line to the next level if the C Crew were ever going to compete with the big firms, and it had to be done. The final stint was to learn the trade of boxing, turn professional, make something of myself and to earn some serious money. Unfortunately the latter never happened! I am not saying that boxing appealed to all of us, as there were some who where very successfully into martial arts and weightlifting. Then there were others, like Jimmy Ryan and Heaffy, who would never have been able to fight Queensberry Rules, but for some of us it was exactly what we needed to move the firm forward.

During 1977, Paddy Riley, who was our coach, thought it would be a good idea if we changed our name, so we were now Aston Villa ABC and our 'home' moved to the Holte Hotel. For me and the other lads, it was a great feeling knowing we were training there in the colours of claret and blue and fighting in the name of ASTON VILLA. The sense of pride was huge, even though some of us were out and out football hooligans. Every time we had a boxing show, we would send Aston Villa FC complimentary tickets, and each time they would be returned, along with some poor excuse as to why they would not be used. During a testimonial year for one of the Villa players, they decided to host a boxing show of their own, and held it at another of Birmingham's boxing clubs. What a kick in the teeth that was when ours was on their doorstep. The only footballer I can ever recall attending our boxing shows on a regular basis was ex-England captain Bryan Robson.

There were some good lads at our club during this time, such as Lloyd Johnson, Reggie Bennett and Dessie Ryan. Big H and Buster had gone to box for Birmingham City ABC, as this was seen as a stepping stone for them to progress into the professional ranks. In 1984, Buster did turn professional and was sparring with the likes of Lloyd Christie, along with the great American Donald 'The Cobra' Curry, who was at the time WBA welterweight world champion. Buster was a very good technical boxer who should have won a British title, but he didn't have the much needed discipline to go with his natural talent. Dave 'The Rave' Ravenhall was one of Villa's and Kingstanding's finest terrace lads, now this kid could box or fight, take your pick, he could have it. His dad was at his wits' end with him, as he was always in trouble and he would literally fight anybody, win or lose. Anyway, his dad went to see Paddy and asked him to take Dave under his wing and try and straighten him out, which he did, admirably. Dave took to boxing like a duck to water and in 1981 he went on to win two Midland light-middleweight titles, that's how good he was. He could have gone on to become ABA champion, but events outside the ring ultimately affected him realising his true potential.

I have known heavyweight Joe Malcolm (aka Al Malcome) since the 1970s, when we were about ten and were growing up together on the streets of Handsworth. We had sparred together as amateurs and even though he wasn't a Villa fan, he had a huge sense of pride when he fought in the claret and blue. In 1983, hard-hitting Joe went on to become Midland super-heavyweight champion, and in June 1989 he became the first boxer to fight future Olympic gold medal winner and future world champion Lennox Lewis on his professional debut.

Being a notorious football hooligan, you would assume that I would have been more suited to the fighting style than the boxing technique, but without sounding too 'braggadosious' (a word of ours), I was always the boxer first, with a good upright style who kept his opponent at the end of a long-range jab, but had a good right cross if they came in too close. There were a lot of good lads fighting at the club, some of whom weren't Villa boys, such as Steven Dalton and James Campbell, who both came from Stockland Green, Erdington. Even through they were juniors when I boxed, I still remember them well. Steven was an upright, skilful, slippery customer with a good left hook. James, on the other hand, was an all-out fighter who would try to take your head off at the earliest opportunity. In 1983 he got to the semi-finals of the ABAs. Steven and James were both at my side in the infamous Sunday Bloody Sunday row in July 1998 at the Lyndhurst pub [see Final Word]. Steven's bravery that day is legendary, so much so that he was invited to take a bow by the man himself, Mike Tyson, at a banquet show in Birmingham. It's just a pity that these two lads never followed their mates down the Villa, as they would have made excellent football hooligans, and would have been top of the tree.

In my third and final stint at the club, I was the father of two boys and I thought that there might have been a chance that I could have made a future for us by turning professional. I wanted to be more than just a notorious hooligan and was looking to somehow get out of the football violence. It seemed like a good option at the time, I was more than a bit good with my fists, so why not put them to some good use? The story that I am going to tell you is about the lads who fought for Aston Villa ABC on that eventful night at the Alcan Plate on 1 October 1987, that night my two sporting worlds well and truly collided. My trainer, Paddy, asked me if I felt ready for my first fight. My reply was an instant yes, I was at my physical peak, I had trained really hard and felt more than ready to show the world Danny the boxer. Everything had been confirmed for the Alcan Plate Sports and Social Club, Kitts Green, in a show organised by the Birmingham Irish ABC. Kitts Green was and still is a predominantly Blues area of the city, in fact, it seemed like it was a breeding ground for Zulus, who at that time were multiplying at an alarming rate. But the last thing on my mind that night was football violence, this wasn't a Black Danny on the terraces thing, this was a Danny Brown in the ring thing. I wanted to box that night, not to have a row in the car park.

When I got there, I noticed that I was last on the card and due to fight a Trevor Small from Kingshurst. It turned out he was the older brother of Bryan Small, who was to play for Villa. We hadn't been there long when I started to notice a few Zulus in the crowd. I saw one of our boxers, Leon Johnson, talking to another boxer called Antonia, so I went over and asked Leon if there was a problem. 'No,' he replied, 'there is no problem, Antonia is just someone I know from my old manor.'

Just as I was going to warm up and put my kit on, I noticed that the arena was now filling up fast with Zulus. Even Stevie Wonder could see that actually there was a problem looming, and a big one. This was then confirmed by Leon. Antonia had told him that the Zulus were there just for me. He went into detail about what they were going to do to me (I shall spare you the details) but basically they wanted my head on a plate. Well, my mind was set. I had trained long and hard for this fight, I was totally focused and wasn't worried about what might happen to me after the fight, I was here to box and box I was going to. I went to get ready, and was warming up, shadow boxing, when my cousin Stretch came in and said that they had got the call. 'We know what's going on and we have your back covered, now go out there and box.'

I came out to a crescendo of boos that got louder and louder as they announced my name. There must have been seventy or eighty Zulus there, all hurling abuse and chanting, 'Danny is a wanker.' There were three two-minute rounds, the first of which was pretty even, but during the second, everything I had trained for went straight out of the window. I got hit by some really silly shots and then I started showboating to the taunts from the crowd, really unprofessional but the abuse just got to me. The referee stopped the fight on a technical knockout. I had lost. The Zulus went berserk, baying for my blood. Still chanting, they rushed the ring and bottles and glasses were coming at me thick and fast. The rest of our boxers, including Sean Davis, Michael White and Paul Casey, all stood on; even though we were hugely outnumbered, not one of them ran. Fighting was breaking out all over the arena, complete mayhem!

Paddy got hold of me and said, 'Danny, no, this is not why you're here, let's go.' Then Stretch pulled out a machete and shouted, 'Do you want it lads? Well you can fucking have it then.' With that, the brave supermen were on their toes. They went from bad boys to pussies in ten seconds flat and were falling over themselves to get away, jumping over tables and chairs, heading for the nearest exit. It was then I realized what Stretch had meant when he said that he had my back covered, a big fuck-off machete turned out to be a good deterrent.

Paddy was trying to get me out of the way and back into the changing rooms but seeing my mates fighting on my behalf, I just wanted to be amongst it. Those bastards had just ruined my big night and I wasn't going anywhere. Due to sheer numbers and the amounts of bottles that were being thrown, it was fair to say that they got the better of us, I would have much preferred their top twenty-five lads against our top twenty-five and then let's see who would have come out on top but that was never going to happen because it was mob rule along with the numbers game. It was utter chaos. Some folk were worried that I could have been killed.

I was still kitted up, gloves included, when Warren Bonner opened the door and shouted, 'Danny, for fuck's sake, let's get out of here, I have a car waiting, let's go and NOW!' I wasn't in a position to argue because the Blues really were taking over the asylum. I was taken away for my own safety to the Little Acorn pub in Erdington. It seemed my days on New Street ramp were now just the same in the boxing arena, I was the number one target and it was a flashback to the day at Villa Park in 1984 which is covered in the Villa Youth chapter. It was something that the likes of Brittle or Gary Lyttle could relate to, these lot hunt in packs and wanted my scalp. There were no hard and fast rules how they achieved it, it didn't matter if it was ten or twenty onto one, it was something they could boast about, how they got the result over Black Danny. The numbers involved were incidental, their logic would simply be that they had done Villa's main boy, something they could spin round south Birmingham for the next ten years.

Another Villa boxer who was at ground level that night was a lad I had trained and sparred with, a very proud Irishman from Belfast called Martin Breen, I have the utmost respect for him, in and out of the ring. Martin isn't a Villa fan, in fact he follows Celtic and I'm sure anyone who witnessed any of this fights against Howard Clarke, who went on to fight Fernando Vargas for the World IBF Light-Middleweight Championship, would admit that if anyone deserved to be called a Celtic Warrior, then it would be Martin. He had thirty-two amateur fights and won the majority of them but, being modest, whenever asked he always replied that he had won one and only lost thirty-one! Martin has a heart of a lion and is another who could have really gone on to another boxing level, but his liking for a good night out didn't mix well with the training. Like all athletes, the long periods of disciplined training that you have to put in does affect your social life and I can't blame anyone for deciding after a while that enough is enough. I was glad to have him on my side that night. The following is his version of events.

MARTIN BREEN

The first thing I have to say is that I was never part of any football firm, the team I follow is Celtic, but when I came over from Belfast and settled in Aston, I did go to a few Villa games with my pals, and a lot of my life has been spent in and around the Aston area, both socially and professionally. That night still feels like yesterday to me. Although I knew that Danny was a football hooligan, it was something that we never talked about, and so the last thing I expected was the melee that happened that night.

I could tell that there was a different atmosphere from a normal boxing night, as there were large groups of lads who were not just pissed but angry pissed. I had gone over to some of our boys, Sean Davis and Michael White, and said, 'It's going to kick off.' One of our lads had come prepared as he was carrying, but coming from Handsworth that was the norm, so it wasn't especially because the Blues were coming, because none of us knew they were. When it did kick off, I was standing with a group of lads which included my two good mates, Casey and Carmichael. There was just a barrage of glasses and bottles being thrown, it was like a shower of glass coming our way. Now right in the middle of this and refusing to budge was Carmichael's dad, Charlie (RIP). He was a very good friend of our family and this man in his early sixties was having none of it. To give you some insight into Charlie, I'll tell you a story that typifies the man to a 'T'.

Charlie was a big brave man, a real character, who in the middle of the Belfast Troubles came over to Northern Ireland to pay his respects to my father, Dan, who had sadly passed away. Charlie was from Barbados but once in your company you felt as if you have known him all your life, a real larger than life character who had the habit of cheering you up when you were on a real downer, what a guy. When he arrived at our house, everyone was there, including my dad in his coffin. He knocked at the door and my young niece ran off to answer it. Moments later she came rushing in and said that 'Desmond' was at the door. That wasn't her being intentionally rude, I think she was simply stunned that there was a black man at our door and the only black face she could relate to was Desmond the barber from the TV sitcom *Desmond's*. Charlie was unmoved when we asked him about travelling over and if he'd had any trouble. He looked at us almost incredulously and told us that nobody, but nobody, could have stopped him from coming to pay his last respects to his dear friend Dan Breen. Three days later, everyone in my local pub knew the name Charlie Carmichael and he was being treated by all like a long-lost friend. People were buying him drinks, he knew more of the locals than I did, but that was Charlie all over.

So, when fifty-plus Blues were throwing bottles and glasses, this guy wasn't moving for anyone, not one inch, despite all of us shouting at him to move, and quickly does it. Not a chance! The problem we had that night was that we hadn't got the numbers. The lads who were there were quality but they were spread all over the arena, we just weren't organised – but we wouldn't be, would we, because we weren't expecting a row.

The Blues were banded all together and were throwing whatever they could get hold of, but what they hadn't banked on was Stretch, aka Crocodile Dundee, who pulled out a machete. It was then like the first hurdle at the Grand National, the Blues were falling over themselves to get away, breaking tables, chairs and probably bones in the process.

I thought that would be the end of it, I thought that they would have gone after 'Dundee' had fronted them out. A few of us got into our cars and left, truly believing that the brawl was over, but apparently it wasn't. I have to give Danny credit, it took balls for him to get into the ring in the first place and fight to rules, knowing that there was a crowd of bully boys baying for his blood, but he did it and he did it admirably. There were a few known Villa hooligans amongst us that night but the majority of us weren't football lads, though we could fight with anyone if we had to.

I loved boxing, and while I was boxing I was having the best time of my life. I have, over the years, seen some football rows, like the one with Leeds at the Adventurers pub, where I used to work, but for me what occurred that night at the Alcan Plate was pure and simply out of order.

DANNY

To be honest, I should never have boxed that night, but we all know that hindsight is a wonderful thing. My focus and discipline had gone, I was way too busy watching the crowd when I should have been concentrating on my opponent. It wasn't Trevor Small's fault, in fact he was almost apologetic about the outcome, it was a total farce. The event made it to the Thursday edition of the *Birmingham Mail* and I think we all knew that there would be an investigation. There was, and the Amateur Boxing Association decided that I could only box outside of the Birmingham area, or at the Holte Hotel. I don't think Bluenose Robert McCracken had all these problems after his troubles at the NEC, did he?

I went on to have another ten fights, winning eight of them, so I suppose you could say that I was a half decent boxer, and like the Villa, I won more than I lost! My heartfelt and most sincere respect goes out to all the Aston Villa boxers who stood by me at the Alcan Plate, you all know who you are – THANK YOU.

In 1995 I was approached by an ex-Aston Villa boxer, Paul Wesley, to lead him out into the ring for his fight against the above-mentioned Robert McCracken for the British Light Middleweight Championship, but after the fiasco at the Alcan Plate, I decided that it wouldn't be in his best interest and could possibly only hinder his performance. On the actual fight night, anyone who witnessed it would tell you that Wesley outboxed McCracken but was robbed of the British title, and that's not being biased, that's being a genuine boxing fan. McCracken was a good boxer and has his Lonsdale Belt to prove it. Wesley went on to have a vibrant professional career, fighting boxers who had won European and World titles, including Chris Pyatt, Howard Eastman, Steve Collins, Sumbu Kalambay and Paul 'Silky' Jones.

My dallying with the noble sport didn't end there. I and both my sons, Daniel and Marcus, all have very strong personalities and I have always taught them to be precise and well polished in everything they do. I would never have forced either of my boys to get into the ring, after all good boxers are born not made, they need to have a particular psychological make-up. When Daniel was twelve, he decided he would like to box. I decided to take him to Frank O'Sullivan's gym in the city centre. Some people couldn't understand why I hadn't taken him to my old club, Aston Villa ABC, but I thought it would be better that he wasn't under my shadow and maybe if he was out of the area completely. One thing I am glad about is that Daniel is an Aston Villa fan through and through, just like two of my other children. There was never any fear of him changing his colours.

The gym was used by Robert McCracken on our first visit there and I came across my brother Popeye, who at the time was McCracken's minder. Due to a family domestic we hadn't spoken for a couple of years, nothing to get too excited about, it was just the typical sort of stuff that goes off in families from time to time. Anyway, the one thing that sticks out for me was the number of Blues who said to me that if they had known that Popeye was my brother, blah blah blah. Well, my retort to that was that I had earned my stripes off my own back and that I didn't need to trade off my brother's name, he is his own man and I'm mine.

My brother loves to wind me up about him being a Zulu, but the truth is he is a Manchester United fan (tut, tut). He has been to a few away games with the Blues but it's a strictly business relationship with them. And for the few idiots who think that he or I would ever go up against each other, just remember, blood runs a whole lot thicker than water. This was proved by my cousin at the Alcan Plate, when he stood up to superior numbers. I have never doubted that my brother would do exactly the same for me, and more importantly, me for him.

A roll call of lads who fought in the claret and blue:

D. Ravenhall (R.I.P.)	L. Johnson	R. Bennett
B. Singh (R.I.P)	A. Malcolm	F. Brown
A. Robinson	S. Robinson	A. Keeley
L. Davis	Leroy Davies	D. Gallagher (R.I.P)
S. Dalton	J. Campbell	J. Reynolds
M. Breen	P. Casey	J. Carmichael
M. White	S. Davison	M. Pinnock
D. Ryan	S. Garfield	R. Lynch
J. Fellows	P. McCormack	C. McCormack
M. McCann	L. Henderson	M. Stanford

17 VILLA YOUTH, PART ONE

STU WAS ORIGINALLY a young C Crew lad who moved on to a new firm called the Villa Youth. He gives his version of how the Youth came together and some of their days out.

STU

By 1984, a number of lads from the C Crew were no longer as active as they had been. There were various reasons for this, but notably a lot of main heads had received prison sentences and the C Crew name started to drift out of use. Lads who had been younger members of the C Crew and were now ready to play an even bigger part in the hooligan element of Aston Villa moved into the so-called new firm.

Quite a few of the lads had tried to come up with a name for us to carry out our antics under. We seemed to have everything from the Zombies to the V.R.A. (Villa's Republican Army – the suggestion of Dave Ravenhall). The problem was that no one could come up with a name that everybody agreed on. At the end of the day, a name is just a name, and whatever we were called we were still Villa.

One of the younger lads from Kingstanding came up with the Villa Youth, originally for the younger element of our hooligan following. However, this name stuck, and became the banner that Villa hooligans would fight under for several years. In no time it started appearing in graffiti attacks all over Brum. It was funny how many teams then went and called their firms after something relating to a younger element. They know who they are!

The odd thing is the Youth name lasted a good eleven years, probably longer than any other name for a Villa crew, although the Hardcore name is not far off. Even in a major row the Hardcore had with Chelsea when they turned them over in 2004 at Kings Cross, one lad was said by the courts to have shouted 'Youth!' as he steamed in and he was probably 40! Old habits die hard. Villa were really starting to get it together again. We had some good lads and some solid youngsters coming through and we were taking it to a lot of places home and away.

HELLO DAD, IT'S NOT ME ON THE TV

We began the 1983/84 season with QPR away and the first game to be played on their plastic pitch. Jeff Taylor ran a coach from the fire station in the town centre but 109 Villa boys turned up and the driver refused to take us. The police arrived and half the lads had to wait for another coach. It was quiet before the game but as you would expect for a first away game the Villa filled the standing away end and a firm went in the seating section. The seats were full of QPR and it went off, with Villa steaming across at them. It would have been a really good row but the Old Bill were onto it quickly, forming a position between the two sets of lads. Throughout the rest of the game there were a lot of taunts exchanged and it looked certain to kick-off afterwards.

One of the lads, Windmill, or the 'Silver Fox' as he is more affectionately known these days, got captured on TV and the row made the BBC News. The footage was then used in a Conservative Party political broadcast. His old man was sat watching it, moaning about the hooligans on view, when he noticed his nipper right in the middle of the action, windmilling away. Just as he shouted, 'Is that you?' his son scarpered out the house, before his old man could go into full rant at him .

The game itself saw Peter Withe score but it was not enough to prevent a 2-1 defeat and the lads left the ground intent on a tear-up. There were quite a few police outside but 50 Villa lads were able to make their away towards the home end. They soon bumped into about 30 QPR who were full of mouth but couldn't back it up. As soon as Villa ran at them they scattered. After the police had rounded up the Villa and everybody was on the coaches, Rangers decided to show themselves again. Behind the safety of the police they started to mouth off, all 30 of them. We had seen more lads at a Sunday League game.

A few years later, in 1986, they had a little mob next to the away end who kept dishing out all sorts of threats towards the Villa fans and singing, 'Where's your famous Villa Youth?' The Villa were laughing at them and to be honest they looked like they were on day release from a mental hospital. Again they turned up after the police had put everybody on the coaches. The last coach pulling away was one of Jeff's and full of nutters. There were just a couple of motorbike cops behind it and about 20 QPR and giving it their usual mouth.

All of a sudden the driver slammed on the brakes and Villa started to pile out of the emergency exit and the main door. QPR ran all over the place. A couple of them got whacked and then more police turned up. Villa got back on the coach and the police escorted them out of the area. As far as Villa lads were concerned, if QPR fans had been in the film *The Warriors* they would have been the Orphans.

THE TRACTOR BOYS

Last game of the season and the glory days seemed a long time ago. We were in the midst of mediocrity. It might be all right for some clubs but not us. Maybe we had been spoilt. The only thing to look forward to was a trip to Ipswich and the seaside, and the added prospect that either Small Heath or Coventry were set to be relegated. If we had the choice, of course, we'd prefer the Noses to go down but Coventry were annoying, like a fly you just wanted to twat.

We were always going to take a good following and it was no surprise to find a lot of Villa drinking in Ipswich town centre. It seemed strange that we could roam from pub to pub without any of the locals making a show at all. As kick-off approached, we made our way to the ground and most of the lads were pissed off that Ipswich were nowhere to be seen and most went into the ground but 50 of us were determined to find some action and hung around. We tried to get in their end but were sussed and fucked off by the police. It was the same story with the seats; perhaps if we had been wearing wellies or chewing carrots we might have had more luck.

We had just made our way round to the Villa end when about 100 Ipswich came out of nowhere, running across a car park towards us. Most of the lads had switched off and all of a sudden it was right on top of us. Where the Wurzels had been all day I don't know, but they were here now. Villa backed off about ten yards and regrouped and Ipswich ran at us, but surprisingly stopped short. They just didn't have the bottle to go in.

That bit of hesitation was all we needed. About ten of us went into their front line and then almost before it started Ravenhall ended the whole battle with one punch. He was a hard fucker, Ravenhall. When we he was in the nick he graduated to minding for one of the Krays, and when he hit you, you knew about it. This punch was probably the hardest anyone there had ever witnessed. Worzel Gummidge hit the deck and for a few seconds it was as though everything had stopped still. He was spark out on the floor and we all thought that he had gone to meet the great haymaker in the sky. The Ipswich fans froze, Villa ran at them and they backed off. Then the police came with dogs and batons and Ravenhall and Skinhead Neil were put in the back of a meat wagon. I don't know what happened to that Ipswich lad but I bet he wished he hadn't bumped into Ravenhall that day.

As for the game, we lost but didn't really care, as Blues could only draw at home to Southampton. We still needed Coventry to win for them to be relegated and a player they had loaned to Coventry, Mick Ferguson, only went and scored the winner, to send his employers down. You couldn't make it up. At the end of the game the Ipswich tannoy announced Blues had been relegated and it was carnival time in Rio, the place went wild. We went to Great

Yarmouth that night and had the customary run-in with the locals but unlike some didn't attack the donkeys.

The future was looking bright off the pitch and we were all looking forward to the 1984/85 season.

COVENTRY AT THE BALLET

The first game of the new season saw us play Coventry at home. Coventry have been on their toes more times than Rudolph Nureyev at the ballet. They had put the word around that they were going to bring a big firm to Villa Park; *yes, right, we've heard it all before.* The day arrived and we had lads in town, a mob in the Witton Arms to cover Witton Station, and the boozers on the Lichfield Road were full in case any of them got off at Aston Station. We had all met up early and then played the waiting game.

Eventually about 15, yes 15, of them got off at Witton Station. Before they could even leave the platform, just a handful of our younger lads ran at them. Some things in life never change and Coventry took straight off along the side of the tracks, heading back towards town. A few of our young lads, the ones who were not laughing, chased after them for a while, but these Coventry fans were like Roadrunner on acid. For all I know, they are still running now.

We thought that they must have more than this, and indeed a little later they did turn up with a larger mob at Aston Station. Villa landed on them from everywhere and most of them ran back into the station, looking for the safety net of the Old Bill. The ones that didn't make it got kicked to bits. The police intervened and built a blue wall around them. At the match, Des Bremner scored as Villa won 1-0, so it had been a pretty good day. On Monday, 27 August 1984, we were due for our first away game of the season at Stoke City. The boys were in good heart and we couldn't wait.

THE BIRTH OF THE YOUTH: STOKE CITY, 1984

About 70 of our main firm went to Stoke on a coach run by Jeff Taylor from the Bromford area. He had been running coaches to games for some time and if you wanted a laugh and a good punch-up, this was the way to travel. The coaches would usually go from the Bromford pub and pick up in town. Jeff's regular crew came from Bromford, Shard End, Kingshurst, Chelmsley, Castle Vale and Erdington. For bigger games, lads would come from all over Brum and extra coaches would be hired.

Stoke was an evening kick-off and Villa continued their good form, with two goals from Mark Walters and one from Peter Withe giving the boys a 3-1 victory. The attendance was 12,605, which doesn't sound a lot but gates had fallen dramatically in the mid-Eighties. Hooliganism was widespread and many fans stayed away. English football was on its arse.

After the game, Villa got together and managed to shake off the Old Bill. They went in search of Stoke's main lot and there were some isolated scuffles before the police rounded everybody up. There were about 300 Villa and most were escorted back to the train station. Our lot headed back towards the coach, with the Old Bill in tow, but we also had somewhere in the region of 50 extra lads who had decided that it was not time to go home yet. They told the police they were also on a coach, even though they had travelled by train. All in all there were about 120 of us.

When we got back to our coach it was the only one left. Everyone started to get on and the driver was doing his fruit. There were about 100 on there and we were crammed in like sardines. Everybody was fucking around and singing and chants of 'Youth! Youth!' filled the little air that was left inside the coach. The police were still hanging around and the driver was adamant that he wasn't going anywhere until the correct amount of people were on. Obviously he was in the right, but he hadn't moaned on the way when there were 70 of us on it. He must have thought that he was in for a good tip off all that lot.

The Old Bill were trying to clear everyone off the coach and our lads were getting pissed off. A few of them started to vandalise the coach, and someone tried to set fire to one of the seats, not the smartest thing to do on reflection. The driver was understandably fuming and kept telling everybody that he would leave us all there.

Next thing you know, one of our lads grabbed the keys from the ignition and said, 'If we're not going anywhere then neither are you.' He then ran off the coach and threw the keys into a nearby river. Everybody was pissing themselves laughing and now the coach driver appeared to be in the same boat as us.

After that it was chaos. It was getting later and later and there was still a large mob of Villa in Stoke. The police knew that they had a problem on their hands and they wanted to get us back to Brum as quickly as possible. There were no more trains that night and no replacement coaches could be obtained. All the Villa were fucking around and the Old Bill seemed to be running out of ideas. After what seemed an age, a fleet of police mini-coaches turned up. We were told that they were used to carry either riot police or the police brass band!

We found there were still a few musical instruments on board some of them. Before you knew it there were whistling and clanging noises everywhere. By now the Old Bill had lost any sense of humour that they may have had, and before the Villa Youth Philharmonic Orchestra could find its feet, their instruments were confiscated. We had an escort all the way back to Brum and it was nearly 5am on Tuesday morning when we were dropped off at the Crown and Cushion in Perry Barr. What a night. You would think the Old Bill would have been a little more grateful after all the extra overtime we had got them.

The papers the following evening were full of our exploits and I still have not a clue how the coach driver got home. One major thing to come out of this incident for me was how it popularised the name of the Villa Youth. Everybody knew who they were now.

CHELSEA

The following Saturday, we played Chelsea at Villa Park and won 4-2. After the game, about 30 of them walked up past the Holte End, keeping to themselves. With a lot of police around, Villa quietly followed the Chelsea, blending in with the scarfers. Chelsea walked past the Aston Villa Leisure Centre along Aston Hall Road and the police cleared off, obviously thinking we were all Villa. Chelsea walked under the railway bridge and it turned out they had a couple of minibuses parked down a side road. The 30-40 Villa following them made themselves known. Chelsea were surprised and a dozen of them took a beating while the rest ran off, but they didn't know the area and a few got trapped. To be fair to the Villa lads, they knew they'd had a result and there was no need for any bullying, so they backed off and left the Chelsea until the police turned up. It was refreshing to see that at least some of the hooligans had a sense of decency.

THE GOONERS

In January 1986 , Villa were in the quarter-finals of the League Cup against Arsenal. A supposed meeting of firms was arranged for Aston Park after the game and we had a decent mob assembled. We were all on top of the hill concealed by the trees and the darkness of the night. Arsenal eventually turned up and stood at the bottom of the park, seemingly wondering where we were. We didn't give them long to think. One of our lads fired a flare in their direction and we all charged down at them. They ran off down Trinity Road, with a few standing until we got within 30 yards of them. They then decided to run too. One or two got caught and took a few digs before the police steamed in with horses and dogs.

As we had drawn the game, we were left with the prospect of a replay at Highbury. The mode of Youth transport seemed to be Jeff Taylor and his coach and we took a good crew, with the biggest challenge of the day being the London rush-hour traffic. The jams beat us and we ended up arriving very near to kick-off. Danny led us round to the back of the North Bank but there was no sign of Arsenal and the police sussed us out and back to the away end. That was it, although with a crap side we managed to win 2-1 to go through to a semi-final against Oxford United. There was some trouble at Oxford in the second leg and whilst them cunts were celebrating after the game having beaten us 2-1 we couldn't just let it go and ended up running them until the old bill restored order. Truth be known I think most of their lads were probably in party mood and weren't really making any show as it was them going to Wembley not us.

LUTON AND THE MIGS

The usual suspects of the times, like Smiffy and Skinhead Neil, went by coach to Luton and we arrived very early, parked up and headed for the town centre. We all piled into a pit of a pub, I think it was called the Dutchman, and waited to see if Luton would show. We were joined by about another forty Villa who had made their way by rail and car, making in total a good 100 of us in the boozer.

Before long pockets of Luton started to show up. They saw Villa had taken the pub and fucked off but as we left the pub about thirty Luton were hanging around.

Luton started giving it the verbals from a distance but didn't hang around too long to let us get close to them.

We made our way to the ground without encountering any further Luton lads and attempted to get in their end. The only problem was we stuck out like a sore thumb and it wasn't very well organised at all. The Old Bill moved us on but about forty of us managed to get into the seats right next to their main end.

We were giving it loads and annoying every Luton supporter in earshot yet surprisingly the police didn't move us.

Luton went 1-0 up and the fun started, with scuffles breaking out until the Old Bill decided that enough was enough and moved in, escorting us to the Villa standing area. At the time we were a very poor side and went 2-0 down but just kept singing our Monty Python song, 'Always Look on the Bright Side of Life'. We were shit, might as well enjoy ourselves.

A small mob of us managed to evade the police, who seemed everywhere after the game, and we started to walk down some side streets. We hadn't a clue where we were heading. Then by chance we turned a corner and bumped into a good 80 Luton. It looked as if we were fucked. We stood in the middle of the road, spreading ourselves out to make it look as if we had a bigger mob, but we had to back off. The opposition had a four-to-one advantage and we didn't fancy our chances. In the adverts the makers of our expensive designer trainers claimed they would enhance an athlete's performance; this was a good time to test the theory. We were heading backwards and within moments the Old Bill were around us and Luton ran off, leaving the officers to get us back to the coaches. It was a pity we hadn't bumped into them before the game with the numbers we had, as every fucker knew where we were.

DANNY

Now for my part I thought that, as a firm at the time, they lacked enough of the older lads and were not like the C Crew, where we had a very good front line and if some didn't turn up others would fill in their places. I always felt with them they would turn up one week and not the next. Maybe it was the rave scene that affected it, too many hugging each other and interested in earning money, rowing at football was no longer a priority. So I suppose it was no surprise that for a period the new Villa lads were out of their league with the Zulus. It was probably like that for the Blues' Apex firm with the C Crew, when they just weren't in our league.

Zulus were now on the rise and were on a major recruitment campaign with the New Street ramp black lads, who were in it for the robbing as much as the rowing. Even worse, some Villa black lads defected to them. These are lowest of the low in my eyes. You can change your bird or your car but not your club, but they did. Some living in Nose areas couldn't stand the heat and that's why I respect the likes of Heaffy, Lloyd and Dave O, they were in the heart of it but not once would they think of defecting to the enemy. It was difficult if you were a known Villa face in town at the time and we had always had problems late at night. Brittle and me especially were forever battling at bus stops or on late night buses or simply walking around town where they had scores of lads looking for Villa heads. Their numbers had swelled and we no longer had the same lads patrolling the city streets; while our new lot were too young and learning the ropes, they simply had the numbers. At times it was men against boys and as harsh as that sounds, to Villa lads for a time that's what it was like.

The Youth had some bad run-ins with Blues, like the game they cover in the book *Zulus* about them attacking us at Coventry Station, it's 100 percent true what Cud says in that they did call it on and he waved his troops into ambushing the Villa Youth. I hold my hands up, I was on my toes with the rest of them as people were literally clambering over each other to get away, whilst the Zulus were laughing as they attacked and CS-gassed our lads. We were turned over good and proper and whilst there wasn't anybody from the C Crew other than me, the Zulus took full advantage and did what was in front of them.

Another time was 1985 when they beat us 3-0. Before the game I was with the rest of our lads in The Crown by Perry Barr and we just didn't have the numbers. I was restless and walked from there right up towards the away section, where Blues had a large mob of their main lads. They noticed me but not until I had walked past and then you get the 'Danny, you wanker' and 'that's Black Danny'. My pace stepped up and I walked with them in pursuit up Witton Lane towards the Holte End. When I got to the Holte a big mob of Villa Youth were congregating and then the Zulus carried on marching and said to the Villa, 'Look, it's not you we want, it's Danny.' I watched as they came through and they were getting closer and like so many times before I was the scalp for them, as in their eyes I was the main lad. I still can't get my head round the fact that they don't even know some of the main faces at Villa now?

I am now by the turnstile watching as the Zulus march past the Villa Youth saying, 'Look, it's Black Danny we want, no one else.' These fuckers had ex-Villa heads in their firm; even lads from Erdington were standing with them. To this day I can't understand it. Why? Why? Why? Ya born a Villa fan and you die one, end of! These turncoats are like the Italians in the Second World War changing sides. I was sick to the stomach looking at them. Have these wankers got no shame?

I stood there and watched as they got closer and closer. In their eyes I was still top boy and they wanted my scalp. All on my own, no Brittle, no Lloyd, no Andy or Jimmy, no C Crew front line to even up the odds, or even Steamers. I only had my pride and my balls and I wasn't going to break them for that scum.

'Come on Danny boy, let's take the walk.'

And take 1,000 kicks off you cunts? I said, 'Good odds hey, fuck off.'

It was hard seeing them jog around Villa Park without no Villa firm taking them on. I stood my ground, didn't run, what else could one Christian do against the Roman Empire?

SHEFF WEDNESDAY AND RELEGATION

On Monday, 4 May 1987, we needed to win to have any hope of avoiding relegation but we lost 2-1 to Sheffield Wednesday. After 12 years back in the top flight, winning the league championship, European Cup and Super Cup, we were going down. It was heartbreaking but all of us saw it coming as soon as Doug Ellis appointed the likes of Graham Turner, who dismantled the European-winning side and replaced them with players who couldn't lace their boots. We then ended up with that great tactician Billy 'Bingo' McNeil who had the distinction of managing two relegated clubs in the same season. He had one tactic: give the ball to Mark Walters, cross it and bingo, goal! Trouble was, it didn't happen; it never happened. We were terrible for most of the season.

The Sheff Wed game drew a paltry 15,000 but gates all around were down then in the wake of Heysel and apathy reigned supreme. Wednesday took a severe battering at Witton Island and even some of their civilians ended up getting whacked. I started to detect the old days of three years before coming back. For me, we had better rows with Wednesday than we did against their more notorious local rivals Sheffield United and a couple of incidents stick in my mind. The first, which is covered in the Steamers chapter, saw Villa take their huge kop end in 1975. Wednesday's kop had only ever been infiltrated once before, by Manchester United so it was no mean feat.

That was the promotion party day from the old second division so I suppose it was justice that the same club we won promotion against, then relegated us. The party mood of twelve years earlier was now funeral atmosphere, from one extreme to another. The second incident came when we played them in a League Cup game the season after our relegation. We lost again and there was an almighty row with them. They were definitely up for it and brought a sizeable firm that came up from Witton Lane after the game to the Holte End. They brought it to us and it was a battle royal that the old bill struggled to contain. Their numbers filled the road while ours outside the Holte steadily grew. No one could move and no one was moving. Those fans who needed to get down to Witton Lane to get home were unfortunately caught in the crossfire but all it did was stoke up the atmosphere. There is nothing like a night game in the winter, pitch black, lads with no colours and not sure who is who. It puts the fear into some and adrenalin into others.

Lads who had come out of the Trinity Road side of the Holte came steaming across the old bingo hall car park at the back of the Holte to join our numbers and this wasn't a one-minute row and wasn't contained to the main road either. It spilled off into the side streets and the Wednesday lads, seeing we had broken their front line, tried to seek refuge in the Asian houses by the ground. Up to that point they had done well but we eventually got the better of them. Whilst that season as a firm we had really got it back together, they gave us one of our toughest tests, but a lot of the younger lads were now coming of age.

So here we were, relegated. We had one last game left in the old First Division and it was Manchester United away. By the end of that day I knew by the firm we took that we were back on the scene and could be a credible force again.

MANCHESTER UNITED 1987

I always think of United's firm as one of numbers. Of course they have some good lads and you can't argue they travel, but same numbers they ain't as special as they would have you believe and when you have been front line with them a lot will agree. This was a game we decided to treat as a relegation party and I don't mean the fancy dress brigade that come out, I mean a match-day boys' party and that's what it was.

We had arranged to meet in a pub opposite Piccadilly Station. It was an old Tudor building but I cannot remember the name. We had gone by cars and minibuses and you could tell as soon as you got in the pub it was going to be a good turnout. It wasn't long before we received news that the Manchester scouting system was working and one of our scouts said, 'They're here.' We didn't have time to finish our first drink and it was the shout of, 'Get out the boozer,' as I didn't want them attacking it and we couldn't get out.

United did steam the boozer but we had a good 100 lads and were up for it. After a bit of a battle we got the better of them before the inevitable Old Bill arrived and surrounded us, not them. The Old Bill didn't want Villa in one big mob moving around their city centre so they split us up into small groups. They took me and Brittle and the lads we came up with, numbering about 20, into some pub outside the city centre. We stayed till about 2pm and then got taxis into Old Trafford, walked through the tunnel and went into the seats, which were in an area reserved for United fans. I looked around and it was like three years ago, we now had all the old boys back and the Youth were coming of age. We were all together and it was a good crew, we were proud to be Villa, we were going down but we were going down with a bang. All the old Villa songs were sung throughout the game and it was a throwback to our glory days when we were the top team in the country and Europe.

The majority of the Villa support were in a different position to our firm and all through the game you had the United fans saying, 'Get them out, they shouldn't be in here.' But we now have got 150 in there and it's full of match-day boys. There were a few skir-mishes through the game, nothing major, but at the end of the game we made a beeline for a mob of theirs and they did a runner across the seats.

Now I knew it wouldn't be as easy outside. I had taken my younger brother, Tony, to the game. Like a lot of black lads at the time he had started to get into it; it became a fashionable thing for black lads to go down the match, unlike in the Seventies, and a lot of his pals followed the Blues but he had no choice but to follow the Villa. The problem he had was, because he was my brother people expected him to be like me; he didn't have to serve an apprenticeship like others. When the row came on it was assumed he would just get involved and that it would come naturally, as it was in his genes. I didn't really want him in it, he was already getting the harassment off Blues lads about being my brother and rather than just bang 'em out or have at least a straightener with them he would end up arguing with them, but you can't get away with that every time.

I said to him, 'Right, you ready? They will be waiting outside so no hesitating, no ifs or buts, straight in. Watch what I do and follow me.'

He said, 'How do you know?'

I said, 'Trust me they will be waiting. Now are you ready?'

He said yes but I looked at him, he was nervous and jumpy. I had seen that in the pub before when United steamed it but now I could see he hadn't got the eye of the tiger. This was totally alien to him and wisecracks wouldn't help him. He once tried that at Arsenal with a load of black lads who were trying to intimidate us. I wanted to get in amongst them, he wanted to reason with them, but that's another story.

We are outside and true enough United are waiting and there is no hesitation, we are into them and throwing punches. I have to grab Lloyd as he sparks this kid and pull him back into the Villa crew as the Old Bill are looking to give him a tug. It's now 2 mobs at each other and the police are having to use horses to keep us apart.

I look around and now United have mobs everywhere, they are

behind, in front and to the side of us and it's back to the numbers game, but this time we have 150 lads who ain't the same as 1985, we have a back line that's as strong as the front line, we are strong all the way through. We hold our own but we are taking it to them.

Now I don't care who you are, if you have 150 lads and it's strong then you can have 500 against you, it's going to be hard for them to beat you. This was a firm nobody was going through. Ask anybody who was there that day, we did very well and were the best firm we have had out in years credit where credit is due the Youth lads and their generals like Little and McCann did very well, they came of age. There had been some infighting between the two sides but that was over and forgotten, we were united as one and gave them a problem right on their doorstep. The lads were buzzing, singing 'always look on the bright side of life' in black humour at our defeat on the pitch and many with cuts/bruises. I am convinced that's where the Mancs hijacked the song from.

I knew then that we were back on the map and the second division would see a new Villa and the likes of Millwall, Leeds and our neighbours Birmingham would see a very different Villa firm to the last three years. The Old Bill escorted us now back to the rest of the Villa fans and wanted us just out of the city before we could cause any more mayhem, but the day went to plan and it was nice to sign off from the first in a bit of style off the pitch.

I was buzzing, think most of the lads were buzzing and we had got a result against the odds against the supposed super firm but the only one not feeling like that was my brother. He had a look of a relief on his face, the look of someone who was glad it was over, not a match-day boy who had enjoyed it. I knew then he hadn't the stomach for it and if he stayed around in Birmingham he would be an easy target because of his name. He had an opportunity to go to live in the States not long after that game and I made sure that he took it. He lived there for seven years.

Some of the Youth lads ended up going to Rhyl in North Wales high on the adrenalin of their activities but had a lot of trouble getting into the clubs due to the amount of facial injuries they had.

BRITTLE

We were already relegated by the time the last game of the season came round. We were away at Man U and loads of people were going to go, lads and scarfers alike. We travelled up about 100-handed; all good lads on an early morning train to Manchester and started off in a pub not far from the station, which if I remember right was called the Pink Flamingo or something like that. Word obviously went round the city that we were there and it wasn't long before Man U paid us a visit. Someone inside the pub shouted, 'United are on their way,' and I thought they were talking about 50-strong. No chance, there was at least a 150 of them, they were a firm and a half.

At first we couldn't get out of the pub as there were that many of them outside but the pub had two doors and while some Villa were still blocked in one door, some of us got out of the other door and attacked the side street, where there were more United. This was when we realised how many there was. I thought, *fuck*, but we went straight into them and they broke up a little bit and then began running. We ran them all across some waste ground but they would not stop running, all they did was throw bricks and bottles but they stayed on the back foot. We ran them into the city centre but that was where it stopped because the OB landed on us.

They put us all in different meat wagons and dropped us in different parts of Manchester. Ours dropped us in Moss Side, thinking they'd teach us a lesson but we were loving it. There was only ten or 15 of us and the first pub we saw we said, 'Right, let's hit that fucker.' The cops thought they'd done us a bad favour but we were well up for it, thinking this was an even better buzz. Nobody troubled us, the locals were half all right with us and we had a good crack.

We got to the ground and met up with everyone else. We weren't in the away section, we had tickets for the seats on the side and were all in with the United fans. At half-time I got talking to some big lump who was giving it loads, saying, 'You want to watch yourselves, it's dangerous here.' I told him, 'That's what we're here for man, we're here to have it off.' He told me that it was nothing to do with him, he was just trying to help, and I told him not to worry because we were there for trouble.

When we came out of the ground, guess who was at the front of all the United. The big lump from half-time. Me and D.Dub had gone out on our own and it was moody out there. United were all over the place and we thought, *whoah, let's get back in and get every-body together*. I told everyone that it was well moody outside and that when we got out I wanted everybody to stick together, no fucking about, just go straight into them – and that's what we did.

I still don't know who it was but one of our lads came forward and took out my mate from half-time, his nose was gone every-where and he went straight down. That was it, we all went into them and United shit it, all on their toes again. The OB came in on horses and it was only when they had made a cordon round us that United came rushing back like they'd done us, but by then we'd already run them across the Scoreboard car park and I mean proper run them.

At this stage all the away fans were still locked in the ground so there were no Villa to help us. The OB took us round to the away end and kept us outside until all the Villa fans came out but that was really the last thing we wanted, because we wanted to get back amongst them. We got escorted back to the station and caught the train back to the city centre but we got off at the stop before and went into a couple of pubs. We let the word go round that we were there again and sure enough they found us again. They tried to rush us but we did them for a third time and yet again they ended up on the back foot.

I realised that day that things had turned full circle for us. Three years before it probably would have been us on our toes but we had come a long way and were seasoned rowers, whereas the United firms we had met were a couple of years behind us. We were tight, we all knew each other and could all trust each other 100 per cent. Any lad from any team will tell you that this is more important than numbers and that is how it was that day.

JOE JORDAN SECOND DIVISION, 1987/88

So the Villa were in the Second Division and with a new set of lads, along with some C Crew veterans for certain games. We were getting our act together again. Hull City away early in the season went bang off in the seats, which was the shape of things to come, and once again being the biggest club in the division meant all other teams were turning out in force for our visits. One top away match that season was Huddersfield Town, who steamed Villa as we left the open end, which left a bit of resentment. After Barnsley away, a firm travelled to Huddersfield and exacted revenge. Huddersfield at first thought our mob were Man City, who they had played that day, but soon recognised the chant of, 'Yoof ,Yoof,' and we evened the scores up on their patch . Another notable game that season was Plymouth away, when Brittle, against the odds, led 30 of us into their whole mob, running them for ages across some park outside the ground.

Other games that season saw a huge C Crew presence and we really wanted to have a go with Millwall on their manor. We had a firm of 300 there but they were one of the few teams who didn't have it together that year; their boys were in a transitional period in much the same way we had been three years earlier. It was disappointing given the history between the supporters that our only chance to really get it on with them saw nothing happen.

The last game of the season, when we clinched promotion at Swindon Town, saw the home side give Villa a ridiculously small allocation of something like 2000. Those without tickets made sure they got in; they kicked the doors down. It could have been another Hillsborough as the morons didn't even open an empty section to let us in, despite the crush.

FORDY LEEDS, LEEDS, SO GOOD WE WENT THERE TWICE

We played Leeds United twice in a matter of weeks, once in the league and then in the FA Cup, and as a firm a lot of the old boys were out to play and were having fun again. We went to the league game in minibuses and there were a good 100 lads but nothing much happened. On the way home a dozen of us stopped off in Huddersfield looking for a row and found it, with Dezzie copping a right hiding. Not a wise move. It had worked after the Barnsley game but taking twelve lads against a whole town wasn't exactly thinking straight.

The cup game was a different affair. We went in a convoy of minibuses and cars, 80 C Crew and 60 Kingstanding Youth. We met up at the service station just outside Leeds, then went to a pub not far from the ground and sent our two spotters out on the road to find our playmates. There was no one about so we moved on, parking the vehicles on their main car park. We had a very minor rumble with some of their Service Crew but they didn't have the numbers at the time.

The C Crew went in the seats behind the goal and the Youth, led by Gary Lyttle, Aaron and Gary Morgan, went in with the rest of the Villa following. The General got talking with some Leeds and we arranged to meet them on the car park afterwards. When we got there it went off, two mobs into each other, but our lot weren't budging. Leeds were wasted on that car park, they didn't stand and we expected better of them. A copper on a horse radioed for back-up with the words, 'This Villa lot are running havoc with the Service Crew and if we don't get some assistance they will be going through the rest of Yorkshire.' He was in a flap and was the only copper there at the time on horseback. If you think it sounds dramatic they were his words, not mine.

The Old Bill rounded us up, put us into our vans and cars and gave us an escort out. A hundred yards up the road, D.Dub and the Steamers were getting stuck in to Leeds. Pete the Greek was amongst it and the police let a dog on him. Now Pete always seemed to have problems with police animals, they just annoy him, like the horse he punched at Albion or the horse he headbutted against United, so the dog must have known what to expect and took no chances getting in first biting his leg. I can't say who but somebody shouted to the copper 'get the dog checked for rabies.'

We were escorted as far as Huddersfield with the police thinking we would continue back to the Midlands. Wrong! We turned back and were told Leeds were going to be in a pub called something like the Prince of Wales by the main train station. We parked up under a viaduct and walked into the town. We must have taken them by surprise, especially when we gassed the pub so they had to come out, and as they appeared we attacked them. The truth is that gas causes as much disruption to your own side as to your enemy and we had some of ours spluttering away but we were giving it their lads inside the pub as we went in. The windows went in and unfortunately Kev C (who is another lad with a million Villa stories) put his arm in the main window, severing an artery. He was in a bad way but thankfully was okay after treatment in Leeds General.

The Old Bill got hold of us once again and this time they weren't taking any chances and took us halfway back to Brum. It was without doubt a good result for the two crews that day, even though we took a few nickings, like Gary Morgan (RIP).

DANNY

Let me put the record straight about the Villa Youth and say they did have a very good set of lads. Because their name would be about for longer than the C Crew, even now I get asked if I was part of the Youth. In the beginning they were a little naïve and didn't have the numbers and I thought when they came up against the Blues they just didn't stand a chance. Credit where credit is due though, they stuck at it and got it together. Some moved on and into bigger things; we can't mention them by name but they know who they are and total respect to you lads. You were part of our social history and were about in my day so we have acknowledged your exploits for the Villa.

18 VILLA YOUTH, PART TWO: NORTH BIRMINGHAM

RUSS

I was just one lad who was part of a golden era, the early Villa Youth. Maybe we were not renowned for what we were doing on the pitch but it was the Villa Youth era and no finer set of mates could you wish to be standing side by side with. I am never going to claim I was a top lad nor am I ever going to claim the Youth were in the same league as the C Crew, because we never were, but we had our moments and I would like to thank Danny and Paul for giving me the opportunity to tell the story of the North Birmingham Youth.

I was taken under the wing of a lad called Manners, a good pal of mine even if the cunt constantly is on the wind-up and cranks me up relentlessly. Nevertheless, he was the lad who got me into it and I thank him for showing me the ropes. I was originally taken down the game by a friend of the family and unfortunately the first row I ever saw was a mob of Villa being run by Blues around 1978, on Trinity Road. Not long after that, I watched a Villa mob getting stuck into Everton outside the Witton End, with a house brick missing my head by inches as it thudded into the white van selling hot pies. I got home, thought for a minute that it could have killed me, then thought, fuckin' hell, I like this football violence stuff. There was no reasoning about my thinking but all football lads will know that feeling, the buzz! I was hooked and like the other lads I enjoyed the row as much as, if not more than, the football. Villa was my club, it was in my blood and I am proud to have played my part in it.

In later years, I was with Villa lads who got separated from an escort coming away from the Albion's Hawthorns and took a proper shoeing that day off their black lads in a side street off the main drag, Soho Road. Some of them later defected to the Small Heath lot. Manners was with me that day along with Sean, a good lad and best mates with Manners, when we got turned over but fair play to Sean he stood on for me and, being the older lad, stopped me from getting the belting of my life. Manners, though, couldn't resist cranking the life out of their lads and that after all of us were a very distinct second best on that occasion.

My take on it is very much the same as Stu's in the previous chapter, but I want to state that when it started it came from the Kingstanding and Erdington areas. There were no more than forty original members, it was never in the hundreds like the C Crew was. The Villa Youth in my opinion were iconic and all younger than the main firm. It was a very young firm, period. After time, yes, there were more than a few hundred or so who would claim they were Villa Youth. You probably get that in most firms, with lads claiming they are firm, but the truth is it started with forty young lads and grew from there. We had to do things differently when the C Crew frontliners left to go to pastures new. We were at a loss. Suddenly we were left to front a firm on our own and we seemed just like rag-arse kids. At one point I wondered if we should call it Ken Dodd's fuckin' diddymen, we seemed to have so many lads barely above 5ft 5ins.

Kingstanding has quite rightly been mentioned as the core of the Villa Youth and it's very true that they were the leading players, but lads from the Wyrley Birch and Falcon Lodge, Witton, areas of Brum and Drake's Drum, Beggars Bush pubs were also very prominent in the firm. I think the Youth, albeit not in name, were actually at it probably a year or two earlier than 1984, almost like a splinter mob from the C Crew, although I suppose my lot were a few years younger than Jeff Taylor's mob and we were certainly doing our own thing. We started off small, trying to get publicity with small results and even going round areas with spray cans, spraying 'Villa Youth' with a definitive 'E' or 'KS' or 'S' after it for the area you came from: Erdington, Kingstanding or Sutton. Even then it was still very tribal between areas and we all know what Kingstanding is like as an area, but like them we Erdington lads are very proud of our patch and Erdington and Kingstanding are still the mainstay hardcore areas of Villa fans. We even one night plastered the doors of the old Tilton Road with 'Villa Youth'. It might seem childish now but it was the thing of the day back then.

There were some very good lads in that firm, too many to name all of them. Probably the main guy at the time was Brendan McCann, who was awesome in a row. I never saw Brendan, who was a great lad, lose a row. He was up there with the best of the C Crew. There were times in those early days when I wondered if we would be able to cut the mustard when we came up against Blues, as so many top lads from the C Crew were not as active as Blues, except when we played them. Would we get turned over? I shouldn't have worried, because in 1983 we did hold our own, and in the row I was involved in, by Dale End, we got the better of them, like so many times before – even if it was hilarious to see some of ours, who had been into a shop to get ice creams, of all things, then using the cones as weapons, jabbing away at them frantically. It wasn't the case all the time and Blues did get results, of course they did. But on match day it just seemed to galvanise Villa lads. It was the pride in us. I cannot ever remember Blues coming onto my manor, Erdington, for instance, and turning us over. The last time they tried it was around 1979 and a mob from two pubs in Alum Rock, the Pelham and the Brookhill, got turned over by Rob Dunne's lot from the Roebuck. That's about as much as I can remember of them on our turf. These were the stories of our manor and we wanted to follow the lead of the older lads and we were proud of our roots.

We were a resourceful mob. We hadn't got the numbers of some of the bigger firms of the day, so we had to be a little bit more inventive, and the planning/organisation was key to our ability to get results. You also had the likes of Billy B, a crafty geezer and good to have in the firm. There was also a splinter firm who deserve a lot of credit, the VYA, some of whom were younger brothers of the lads, like the Coyles. They were as game as fuck and quickly became part of our firm. The positive thing is, we were bang at it, week in week out, and didn't hide. We worked at it and built up a good reputation where others got to hear about what we were doing and wanted a piece of it. I have picked a few incidents that highlight what the firm was about. While there are far more, these stand out in my mind.

Leicester City in 1984 was one of my first away games. For me this was a defining moment, one of those where you learn from experience and become somebody who has been there, done that. There was fighting before the game with their boys and it was tremendously exciting and a great crack. Anybody who has been to Leicester will tell you it's lively and for me over the years it was my favourite away ground.

That day, one battle stands out. It was a row in the town before the game. Some of the younger lads were a little hesitant, we didn't run but we were spectating at times as opposed to getting front line. The Baby Squad were throwing bottles at Villa but Villa were standing their ground. The police then landed and gave us an escort, but a respected face of Villa's firms during the hooligan heydays who was a bit older than us, Black Roger, turned to us and seemed a little miffed. 'You young 'uns wise up,' he said. 'If you wanna be part of this then start fucking shaping up, get in there and battle!'

Those words I have never forgotten and after the game we remembered them. We went for Leicester without hesitation and got the result as their lads were run everywhere. As I say, always a lively place and more often than not the Zulus were waiting for us at New Street Station, so the action never ended there.

I remember the Arsenal League Cup game in 1986 that Stu covers but what didn't get mentioned is the night before the game, when three of us, myself, Billy B and DJ, got hold of untold crates of empty milk bottles (how we got them is another story). We hid them in the bandstand in the grounds of Aston Hall and agreed we would ambush Arsenal, thinking they would have the bigger numbers. On the night of the game, with the Arsenal firm being escorted to the ground, two of us, including a good friend of mine, Gary Morgan, RIP, managed to evade the attention of the Old Bill and infiltrated the escort. We told them where the meet was after the game. Now there was never any fear of taking a belting, as there was too many police in the escort and anybody would have got nicked straight away for trying anything, so we got in amongst them and said, 'If you fancy it, meet us on the park afterwards.' The old school gates bit, eh!

It went to plan. The Arsenal lads were game but we had the ammunition and hit them with everything we had. It was a case of 300 green bottles sitting on a wall, along with a flare that was let off straight into the middle of their firm. They got slaughtered that night. Everyone knows Arsenal could pull a firm and in their prime they were as good as most but that night the Youth were a little bit more clued up and we got a good result.

But the truth is, we were better in smaller numbers. There was less chance of getting picked up by Old Bill and as we had fought together there was a trust between us that no-one would get on their toes. It doesn't mean to say we were always victorious and sometimes we didn't have the numbers to counter the bigger firms. Man United, for instance, in 1985 at our place literally took the piss afterwards. We couldn't muster the numbers and weren't organised to combat what they had out.

Wolves in the League Cup game sticks out as one of those occasions where a tight firm can do the business. We had all been in the Crown in Perry Barr on the day as Gary Morgan had come out the nick that day and the firm was out celebrating his release. Twenty of us decided to go to the game and caught the train from Perry Barr, leaving Gary and the rest to stay on the piss. When we got off the train, we were on a hill by some traffic lights. There was a group of black lads and it's the old cliché but there was double our number. I am not sure to this day if they were Wolves or Townies like you would see around that time in Birmingham town centre, but they looked as if they were up for it.

Eddie Corkhill (RIP) took charge. He told us to spread out in the road to make it appear there was more of us, as they would only be able to see what was in front of them as opposed to what was behind us. I had seen Eddie do this countless times, he was a game little fucker and mischievous when he got going but he was into them and the rest of us didn't need an invite. We followed his lead, we were not going to run from these mugs. A close mate of mine was in and had grabbed some geezer by the strap of his camera hanging round his neck. He was swinging him round and the other lads were taking pot swings at him and he was going back and forth, taking a leathering left and right. I think I was the only fucker out of our lot on the floor. Now and again it would have been nice to win one but at least I was on the winning team, even if I was losing my own personal battle.

Maybe they weren't used to a mob of football hooligans or maybe it was the case that we were twenty lads who knew we would stand on for each other, but very quickly we got the upper hand. They could see we had plenty of bottle and they didn't fancy it, as soon as a few of theirs were on the floor their arses fell out. They were on their toes very quickly and we were buzzing but one of the lads, Eddie Faye, was a bit more cautious about things. He was smarter than the average bear and said, 'Listen, we got the result, quit while we are ahead. The place will soon be swarming with Wolves and we ain't in numbers to back it up.' So me and a few of the others decided we'd had our fun and didn't even bother going the match. Sure enough, as Eddie warned, we had just got on the train to go back and finish drinking with Gary when loads of Wolves arrived and, no, we wouldn't have lived with what they had out that night. But the Youth did very well earlier.

It was a valuable lesson learned. Yes, we didn't stay around for further action but worked on the adage that we had got a result against all odds and to try and do it twice was asking too much.

STU THE BATTLE OF MCDONALD'S

This is what the Youth refer to as the Battle of McDonald's, years before the better-known event at another McDonald's [see Chapter 20] but also with our local rivals Birmingham City. The season 1985/86 was the nadir of English football. The Villa's average crowd was 15,000 and Blues was even worse, averaging 10,000, though their claim is that half of them were football hooligans. Fair play to them, even if they have lived on their reputation longer than the Rolling Stones have.

We arranged to meet in the Cabin pub in town before the game but that day we were a bit light on numbers. Some of the older lads had decided to do their own thing and we probably only had forty in the boozer. We had the usual main faces of the Youth from Kingstanding and the Bromford but we were really a young firm and I think deep down we all knew that we were going to have our work cut out. There were no mobile phones back then so we decided to take a walk round Sara Moon's in Dale End, another one of our haunts, to see if we could pick up any more numbers. They were on top of their game, one of the most notorious firms around, and this was when every tabloid newspaper was running exposés on football violence, so the entire country knew about the Zulu Warriors. My mind flashed back to the days of the C Crew battles with the Noses and how I wished we had some of those lads with us now. We got to Sara Moon's but found there were only about 20 Villa boys in there, mainly from Chelmsley Wood, Kingshurst and Shard End. The one plus point was that there was a handful of older lads there and, more importantly, Groombridge, who as everybody knew was totally fearless and fantastic in the battle. We had a couple of pints but in all honesty I don't think any of us felt like drinking too much as were all suffering from P.M.T., or pre-match tension! About 15-20 were standing outside the pub with roughly 40 more Villa Youth inside and that was it, our mob for the day was no more than 60.

We saw the Noses appearing over the horizon, or to be exact, coming into the High Street by the side of the McDonald's. Even the Noses admit there was 150 of them. Our lads piled out the pub but we were well outnumbered. All the roars and the 'come ons' started and shoppers started to flee for cover. Cries of 'Zulu' went up and they were bouncing up and down, giving it loads. Some old bloke walking past Sara Moon's with a shopping trolley said to one of our lads, 'Lulu, Lulu, what are they shouting Lulu for?' I could laugh about it afterwards but at the time I had more pressing things on my mind.

We let out our shouts of 'Youth, Youth, Youth' in defiance and this was it, it was right on top, in front of us, and we had to deal with it. The familiar faces of their main boys were staring at us, angry, contorted faces, and they were baying for claret and blue blood. We were the Villa Youth, just our way in the world of football hooliganism, taking over where the C Crew had left it and we were trying to get a reputation. At the time the Zulus were well established. We had been getting results but on a smaller scale and this was a big test for us.

We might have been game as fuck and eager to impress but we did have our secret weapon – Groombridge. About 40 Noses actually came close enough to kick it off, with the hangers-on in the background, bouncing around and shouting. They even threw the odd missile, surprise, surprise. It started going off and luckily a couple of their lads got put down quickly and Groombridge went into overdrive. Bang! He put one of their front liners down and it certainly sent the Blues into shock. Their front line started to back off and we pressed home the advantage by advancing into them. When those at the front turned round to run, it panicked the rest of the Blues and they legged it up the high street. We were in pursuit and a few Noses fell over, taking a kicking. Before we could totally humiliate them by running them the length of the town, the Old Bill landed and wrapped us up.

We were totally jubilant and chants of 'We are the famous Villa Youth' and 'We're the pride of Birmingham' filled the air. Me, Jeff, Smiffy and Duggan jumped up and down, hugging each other and laughing our bollocks off. Against the odds we had done the business again. A lot of our younger lads came of age that day and the Kingstanding boys were top notch, as usual. That day showed us we could compete and we blew the Zulu myth wide apart. The major credit though has to go to the old hand, Groombridge. He put the fear of God into them and no-one fancied it with him.

Without a doubt they had underestimated us and paid the price. I don't think they could believe our numbers and the fact we didn't run. To be fair we were outside the boozer and nobody could have run even if they wanted to, but the result proved that what we lacked in numbers we made up for it in quality, and we were not going to budge an inch. Fair play to you Blues, you gave us credit for that one in your *Apex to Zulu* book although you reckon there were far more than 60 of us. There weren't, but on another day your superior numbers would have turned us over. The trouble was that Blues took a few early hits and it snowballed and they folded. Let's be honest, this was a totally unexpected result for us and we will never forget the battle of McDonald's and the day we broke their hearts.

THE PROMOTION SEASON

Towards the end of the 1987/88 season, in the old Second Division, we were taking thousands everywhere, probably because there were new grounds to visit. As the season went on I started driving to a few aways, Reading for one. We got to the ground and I saw the familiar figure of a lad we knew from the Crown and Cushion pub nick-named, for some reason, Chequebook. He was a printer and had decided that Villa's allocation of tickets for the ground wasn't enough, so he had thoughtfully provided a few more, sold some and was giving the rest away.

Then came Millwall and the firm we had out there passed into legend – I've talked to London lads who'd heard all about it – but Millwall were nowhere to be seen that day. They might not have been organised at that point but they're supposed to have hundreds of ordinaries who'll fight anyone. They played us in the old First Division for two seasons after that and although we didn't travel with such numbers again, I'd have thought they'd come looking for revenge but they never did. It's a pity we didn't get the chance to have a dance with Millwall, there were a lot of lads who had gone there with a point to prove and it was a real downer.

Then we played a couple of daft home games. Stoke were up first, and in their book *Naughty*, Mark Chester says there was a big off in the Witton Lane stand. I'd like to ask him how they managed it, because that stand had Perspex screens running top to bottom and a line of stewards and police dividing the supporters. All that happened was that a few of our kids came in the stand when the gates opened, as they did every match, and started singing. If that's Stoke's idea of a battle, how did they get their reputation?

Shrewsbury came next and nobody expected anything. They brought a couple of thousand, which was all they were getting at home then, and later that night we heard they had wrecked the Vine pub on Lichfield Road, which was at the time a pub that accommodated home and away fans before the game, certainly not a lads' pub. The then-unknown English Border Front had gone into this empty pub early on and wrecked it. It made all the papers and I suppose they'd class it as a result. The landlord, Colin Lawler (RIP), and a family of Irish lads, the Boyds from Aston – all three of them – stood against 100 cowards with some silly bird who stood on the bar taking photos of their firm attacking four lads and two women. Maybe their dads had told them of Villa in the old Third Division taking their town, never mind the ground, but they were a complete load of tossers.

After looking dead certs for promotion a few months earlier, we'd started to lose our way a bit and went to the last match of the season, at Swindon, with no more than an outside chance of automatic promotion. We needed Bradford City and Middlesbrough to both lose at home otherwise it would be the play-offs for us. Even though we could have taken thousands down there, Swindon only gave us half of one end and a few seats. The other half of the end was a members' area, and we didn't know it at the time but their police were utter bastards. You had to be over a certain age to be a member there and a few weeks earlier the police had gone in and arrested anyone who couldn't prove they were old enough.

Tickets were snapped up immediately and, again, Chequebook had decided to help. Villa had asked Swindon to increase their allocation and been turned down, so the papers were interested in the story and had reported forgeries circulating throughout Birmingham. I was having a drink in the Drake's Drum in Great Barr early that week when I saw Chequebook, who asked me how I was getting there. I think he'd been angling for a lift so I told him I hadn't decided. Even if I did drive there was no way I was being associated with him that day. As it happened, things went perfectly. Everyone who had a ticket got in, even if about 300 of them had the same serial number, plus Villa kicked in the doors. In truth it could have been another Hillsborough, as the end was crammed and probably housed double its safety number.

Although Villa only drew, Boro and Bradford lost, so we were promoted! A few lads who had got into the stand piled onto the pitch and carried Graham Taylor shoulder-high over to the away end. Some of us tried to climb the fences but those bastard police wouldn't let us. One of them hit me on the foot with his truncheon, and as I jumped back down onto the terrace, I put my hand on the fence. He hit me again, on the hand, and I've still got a small scar. He was a very brave man, hitting out when he was behind a fence, and even after all these years I'd very much like to have a word with him, one to one, and him without his truncheon and riot shield, about that afternoon.

Graham Taylor, with the class we came to expect from him, turned down a civic reception because he said that finishing runners-up was nothing to celebrate. This was in contrast to the rabble we share a city with, who would celebrate the very same thing at the Council House the day after someone had been killed at their hovel. I think it was John Major who first talked about a classless society, but that lot had no class years before. A couple of years later, I was talking to a PC from Queens Road who knew the score a bit better than his colleagues. 'We knew all about the tickets,' he said. 'If there had been a problem we'd have been round Chequebook's house next morning but it all went off okay so we couldn't be arsed.'

PAUL

I was originally in the C Crew and later went on to the Villa Youth, but following Aston Villa has been a passion all of my life. I have followed them for over 30 years nationwide and in Europe. I have not been involved in any hooligan activities for over 15 years but in my time I have been glassed, slashed and had my nose broken twice, plus the usual half a dozen arrests, but that was all part of it in those days. I also made some great friendships which have lasted the test of time. One of those friendships was with two Stoke fans who me and my good mate Andy met at Stoke rail bar after Villa had beaten them 3-0 in November 1982. These two were big fuckers and from that day became good pals.

The next time we went to their patch was March 1984. We went early and met them in the Talbot pub, taking overnight bags with us with a change of clothes for the customary night out. We had a few beers and decided to move on to another pub called the Wheatsheaf. As we got up to leave, we noticed a big police presence outside the pub and as we approached the Wheatsheaf one of the dog handlers asked if he could look through my bag. I asked him why and he told me some Villa had raided a sports shop down the road, which was the norm back then even if people keep saying it was only the Scousers that did it. Villa were dab hands at it, emanating really from our trips into Europe when we flooded the West Midlands with the latest hooligan fashions of the day.

As I opened my bag to show him, the dog he was holding just attacked me. He sunk his teeth into my thigh and I fell to the floor in agony, screaming for the handler to get the fucking dog off me, but he couldn't control him. The dog just carried on savaging my leg, so Big S, one of the Stoke lads, grabbed the dog by the jaws and threw him off. The Old Bill stood there useless and open mouthed, the bastard dog had torn my leg open and ruined my jeans. The police bundled me into the back of one of their vans and off to A and E, day over for me.

Our next visit there was October 1987, which Stu has covered in the previous chapter but I had a different view of the day from inside the enemy camp. That season was great as we were visiting places that we didn't normally go to and the Youth was establishing itself as a credible firm. Me and Andy drove that day, as we were going straight to Blackpool after the game. We met the Stoke lads in the Wheatsheaf, as Villa were already in the Talbot. It was only about 11.30am but the pub was busy with a lot of moody-looking Stoke lads. We got a lot of looks but no grief because of who we were with. You have to give Stoke respect, they left us alone and there certainly ain't no bullies in their firm from what we encountered.

We moved on to another pub called Charlie Brown's and later found out this was their main boozer. It was full of lads but again we were treated as guests. Me and Andy knew Villa would bring a decent-sized firm but didn't expect to see it. We were chatting amongst our little group when a young lad came running through the door and shouted, 'They're here!' At that, they upped and left the bar – but within a minute they were all clambering to get back in with the Villa firm in pursuit. They may tell it differently but we were there. Andy and I were quietly chuffed. Who wouldn't be? But we were glad the Old Bill were straight onto it, otherwise we might have got turned over by our own. One of their lads even said to Andy, 'Fair play, quality firm.' We were treated well and invited to sit with them in their end, which suited us as we wanted to get away straight after the game. We sat behind the goal in what was usually the away end and Villa were allocated the whole side, which was rammed full with what must have been 7,000 Villa fans. It looked incredible, although the game finished goalless. We missed the fun and games after but if you speak with most that day they will tell you it was one of the best days out for the Youth, against quality opposition.

Huddersfield in 1987 was another new ground to visit up North and as usual we met on the Crown and Cushion car park and travelled in a convoy of cars and vans, with the usual suspects like Stu, Carl, Dunc, Andy and Kev, a good 80 of us in total. The weather was awful, it was teeming, and Villa were allocated an open standing end. For once we used our brains and sat in the stands with a lot of other Villa.

Just before the final whistle, the Huddersfield mob started moving from their big kop on the side and around behind the goal. We knew what was coming. They exited on the same side as us and it kicked off as soon as both sets of fans hit the street. They bombarded us with bricks and bottles. They were no mugs and right in the middle of it were the Old Bill on horses going mental to try to stop the trouble. A lot of our lads got nicked, including our driver, but fair play to Huddersfield, we went to bigger clubs that season, even Millwall, and they didn't show.

The police moved us on away from the ground and we headed up the Leeds Road into the town centre. We were on one side of the road, they were on the other, with the law in-between. As we hit the town it was a busy Saturday afternoon, full of shoppers, but both firms met head-on again and this time it was fists and boots flying in from all directions. I homed in on one lad and gave him a few shots around the head, then a whack around my ear took me off balance, so the lad in front took his chance and twatted me right under the left eye. It hurt. The adrenalin was pumping and I ran at him, he could see I wasn't amused and he had his best chance, so he turned and ran.

At this stage we were getting on top and some of their lot were bottling it. Some even stood in bus queues pretending they were ordinary shoppers. The police turned up in force and swarmed over us and we scattered in different directions to avoid more getting nicked. I ended up in a small firm of about 15 and walked around a few bars but there was no action to be found, so we decided to find the local nick and get our driver out. We were told he would be let out on bail with the others. We went to the pub opposite and got a few beers, chatting with the locals and not a hint of aggro. Some of the lads got restless and wanted to move elsewhere, so on the way out I went the bog and as I was on the hand dryer I couldn't hear a commotion going on outside.

As soon as I opened the door, someone smashed a bar stool over my dumpling. I stumbled but instinctively ran for the door, only to find the bouncer had bolted it. I ran back but being on my own had nowhere to go, I was trapped and was running around the pub trying to find a way out. The locals started to lay into me and I was in the shit, big time. They were kicking the crap out of me, punching me, hitting me with bottles, even the birds were having potshots at me. I was hanging for dear life onto somebody's jeans when thankfully the lads realised I was missing and came back for me. They kicked in the door, and the bouncer in the process, and then the law landed. I was carried outside caked in blood with bits of glass sticking out of my head. The Old Bill asked me to identify my attackers. They were all rounded up and it was obvious it was them but I didn't identify them as it wouldn't have been the done thing. Huddersfield were paid a few more visits that season by the Youth. I have to say it was another cracking day out but I ended up on my tour of the town's A and E departments for my involvement.

Crystal Palace away in 1988 was another huge Villa turnout and saw lots of little rows all day. The biggest was in the seats above the paddock. It was a scene they later used in the film *The Firm* with Gary Oldman – it was us in the shots at Palace but unfortunately we didn't get paid for our activities, now immortalised in the original football hooligan film and still one of the best. Saying that, I don't think Bex or Yeti would have been a match for the lads we had out that day.

JEFF TAYLOR BROMFORD TRAVEL COMPANY

I started running coaches when the C Crew disbanded and ran them for a number of years. Kingstanding and Erdington Youth were doing their own thing but we needed to accommodate the lads from all the other areas, primarily my mates from the Bromford. The lads from Kingstanding and surrounding areas quite rightly get their just recognition, they were full of good lads, but for a long time our crew were more than doing our bit to get the Youth on the map. Bromford is an area on the edge of Erdington in North Birmingham. It was originally a racecourse and when the housing estate was built most of the roads were taken from the names of the famous horses that raced there. The estate was built in 1967 and was really an overspill for people who lived in Aston and Erdington, with a minority from the Washwood Heath area. A lot of the people that moved from Aston came out of houses that were being demolished on the Lichfield Road. The old Aston houses were nothing special, in fact a lot had outside toilets and I suppose they would be classed as slums, but try slagging off anyone from Aston and you will get a lecture and a thick lip. It is probably the most famous area in Birmingham and the likes of Summer Lane and Lichfield Road are landmarks, legendary areas that the Birmingham historian and Villa fan Carl Chinn has dined out on for the past twenty years or more!

However, when those people moved to the new Bromford estate, they would think that they were moving up in the world. The Bromford seemed almost posh in comparison. What it did do was to foster a togetherness and everybody seemed to know everybody, which created the bond and trust you get with close communities that aren't awash with money. The local comprehensive school in the area was Hodge Hill secondary, a real throwback, a hard school and primarily full of Villa supporters, like the Jones and Bell families, the Smiths and the like. If they ever did a count of how many people had been expelled in the late Seventies or bunked off school to watch the Villa, I think you will find it running into nigh on 100-plus.

It was a school where you had to stand up for yourself and it was 100 per cent football, day in, day out. It shared intense rivalries with other schools like the Burney Lane and Alderlea Comp, an all-boys school where they had one of the best rows that a school playground has ever seen. In 1978, in the middle of a teachers' strike, Alderlea came to Hodge Hill mob-handed, led by one Noel Blake, former Villa trialist and Blues legend (cough) who was a man in schoolboy uniform. So as you can see, we had our Villa–Blues rivalries even back then. They also had a few good football teams over the years, in which some of my generation went on to play for local clubs, like Alan Ollis, Dave Feenan and Derek Duggan. The school was full of the hardcases of the area, young, white and Afro-Caribbean. It is now almost 100 per cent Asian and has lost its original identity but that's how multi-cultural Birmingham is these days, never mind Hodge Hill school.

The Bromford is now something like the estate you see on the TV programme *Shameless*. It is criminal how it's ended up, it still has some great 'salt of the earth' people but it is also full of scumbags, with the subways havens for muggers and druggies. Having said that, I am proud to say I was brought up on the Bromford, there was a real good spirit, a togetherness, and it was a real strong Villa area.

It was only natural that we would run coaches from there. The Bromford lads, led by Del, were the ones who withstood an onslaught from Blues lads in 1987 at St Andrew's, when they were in the upper tier behind the goal opposite the Tilton. It was possibly the only result the Zulus got that day but even then the dummies attacked their own. They were mad times. I seemed to spend most of the week ringing round coach firms in readiness for the away excursions, even blagging coaches from as far away as Stoke to transport my boys as local firms cottoned on to our activities. These were the things you had to do if you were a football thug, as the police were onto our little escapades and wanted the Bromford Travel Company shut down!

Our coaches were not little quaint trips to the seaside, bring a packed lunch, it was to watch the Villa and have a row, simple as that. In short, the rules to running a trip were: book a coach, fill it with lads, get to the game, get in, get home! Sounds simple, doesn't it, but it never was. We originally started picking up people from my manor, the Bromford pub, then the main fire station in the town centre and then Harry Parkes's sports shop. Harry Parkes was a famous Villa player, then a director, and was a supposed Villa man but when he couldn't seize control of Villa he defected to the unwashed and in turn lost thousands of customers as Villa fans boycotted his shop, the turncoat.

We saw it all during those years: windows falling out of the coach, coaches getting burnt out, taking two coaches to the game but coming back in one, police stop and searches, losing lads along the way, getting nicked, losing keys to the coach and getting stranded, mass brawls at service stations, sometimes not even with other football supporters. There was sex on the back seats, rivers of beer flowing down the aisles, pissing in bottles when you had no posh loo on board, getting lads to pay for the coach with their gold credit card, fighting with the locals as the Old Bill just stood by and watched – and that was just one day! Me and Smiffy often felt like travel agents, deciding if we were going to Blackpool or Great Yarmouth after games. It was a great time in our lives, even if the football was shite.

Danny and Lloyd started to come on our coaches, so I suppose our notoriety was growing. I laugh now when I think back to Ipswich away. Me, Danny, Stu, Smiffy and a few other hardy souls decided to go in their main end. Danny was actually saying, 'We will get done here,' then when we got in he forgot all about that and we ran into them and cleared the back of their end. People might say so what, it was Ipswich, you can come unstuck anywhere. Ask the likes of Arsenal or our own C Crew about Ipswich a few years earlier and they will tell you it isn't all plain sailing. The C Crew around their prime got well and truly turned over trying a similar tactic at Bristol City in their main end, as they tried to infiltrate it and take it. Not everyone got through but the ones that did, like Heaffy, Ozzie and Eddie Norton, took a hell of a beating. It was all part and parcel of the game we were in. We had great times, didn't always win the rows but one that really sticks in my mind and gives me a lot of pride is our coach trip to West Ham – who ain't no fucking Ipswich.

West Ham was never a place for the faint-hearted. I was running a coach that day from outside the Harry Parkes sports shop in Brum town centre. It was a 52-seater and on it were my pals, the Bromford lads, Smithy, Faz, Young Dugs and Tony Smith. The coach was mainly full of misfits, normals, fashion disasters, old C Crew from the Crown at Perry Barr, a good few lads Stu had brought along and some original Youth, so it was a mixed bunch. We had also picked a few scarfers up in town who had been going down by train. I don't think they realised what they were getting themselves into. Of course we had our trusty driver, Wilf, to chauffeur us. Wilf had been driving us up and down the country for a few months and ended up getting involved in a lot of the scrapes with us. He was funny, Wilf; when we were all having the rows in the service stations, he would be busy himself helping himself to loads of boxes of chocolates which we all used as peace offerings to our old ladies or girlfriends when we returned from our excursions. And all because Wilf loves Milk Tray, eh!

On that day we had only 35 on board and we had already left town late after a run-in with the local Blues tramps in the town. It put us behind schedule and we didn't get into London until three o'clock and then were in the thick of the Saturday afternoon traffic. We didn't actually get to the ground until 3.30pm. Wilf spotted a firm of about 30 barrow boys outside the ground and decided to pull up 50 yards up the road. Straight away I felt that rush of fear, the trepidation, the buzz, and my heart skipped a beat. Wilf would do things on the spur of the moment and though we were in no rush to have a row, it was too late. The coach doors opened and a few of the lads got off, the rockers and punks in our crowd, to beckon their lads for action.

All hell broke loose on the coach as one of our lads, let's call him Darren, froze with panic at the front, seemingly not knowing what to do. Panic just took over him and he would not move from the doors, but Smiffy seized the initiative, grabbed the young youth and chucked him over the seats. We are now off the coach and in equal numbers on their turf. We hold our line. Me and Stu are walking towards their lads and my head's thinking, *West Ham at West Ham with a bunch of Villa misfits, thank fuck for the Bromford lads with me*. To the left of us are the local shops and people going about their Saturday shopping and the Cockneys aren't sure what's in front of them. They start to hesitate and up goes the call of, 'Youth, Youth, Youth.'

It's on top, there is no messing about and right in front of me are my lads getting right in, it's like some wet dream vision, I am in ecstasy, in the moment, battling for the Villa Youth. There are now bricks and the obligatory traffic cone raining down on us and I am dodging them as we advance forward. And then with 20 seconds of the old windmill we are still having it and I am still on my feet with my arms flying in all directions. I am in the middle of the high street and cars are pulling up and trying to get out of our way and then a bus pulls up and more lads appear. I look back to see four lads on the floor but there isn't time for Florence Nightingale acts of mercy. I am now looking at a sight that I will treasure and keeps me glowing in my old age of fortysomething, the sight of the locals on their toes and my bus of Villa misfits getting a major scalp.

As one, the Villa lads move forward and another small ruck breaks out by the shops and maybe it was with the young Mitchell brothers of the time but now we are making our way back to the bus. The walking wounded are picking themselves off the floor with their ripped clothes and bloody noses and great big smiles to go with it. This is a West Midlands firm who didn't get to Euston Station, run about waving their arms, shouting and singing, and get nicked for being loudmouth wannabes, this was a set of lads up for a row on one of the most notorious home patches in Europe, never mind London.

It had been a good five minutes and there were no Old Bill and we had done more than well, we had been fucking marvellous, gladiatorial almost, but that was as good as it got, because by now the hornets' nest had been stirred and they were gathering in numbers by the gates. There are now 40 grizzly East Ender types and they are coming towards us. We break into two groups but it makes no difference, our young firm takes a kicking. Let's just say they weren't best pleased with us taking liberties on their manor earlier. There are no heroics now, we are on our toes, and before I know it I am in the bus garage behind the ground looking for salvation.

When I got back to the battle scene there is total chaos, bodies everywhere, and all around are Old Bill in big numbers. It's not a good scene as three ambulances pull up and the police have got 20 or so lads against the wall with the dogs snarling at us. We got collared and slammed against the wall but it was not just us nicked, there are a fair few West Ham as well. Some of the wounded are in a very bad way and are getting treated by the ambulance crew. One of ours looks serious with a head injury, it turns out he got hit over the head with a work sign used as a battering ram by the West Ham boys. He actually ended up in the local hospital for a number of weeks, thankfully making a full recovery.

Wilf now appeared, without the coach but with a notebook in one hand and a box of chocolates in the other. He took down a list of injured and nicked just like a copper. I looked at Smithy and the sight all around us and he just looked up and said, 'Not good Jeff, but not bad. Not bad at all.' We knew we had been in a row and we knew we had done well and to confirm it, the unthinkable happened. Like two great sparring partners, bloody but not beaten, we got a pat on the back from our respected opponents that you could dine out on for years. The police escorted us into the game as the second half kicked off and to our surprise, as we walked into the away stand, a section of the lower-stand West Ham fans stood and clapped us in. It was a fantastic feeling, the opposing fans clapping us in after a right tear-up. Not many firms go down and have a tear-up at West Ham. Definitely something to tell the grandkids.

BRITTLE

Some years later, and maybe not as youthful as they once were, another very good set of old Villa Youth from North Birmingham were plying their trade in London in what goes down for many of those lads as their finest moment fighting in the name of the Villa.

GARY M ARSENAL 1996, OUR FINEST MOMENT

It was the semi-final of the League Cup and Villa were flying that season under Brian Little. We were in the latter stages of both of the domestic cups doing well in the league and playing decent football. Dwight Yorke was on fire and all around the team we seemed to have confidence and were giving anybody a decent game. It was a good time to be following the Villa.

The League Cup was a two-legged affair and we had drawn Arsenal, with the first leg at their place. All the old lot were going down. You no longer got the allocation you did say in the early Eighties and they put you in that shitty corner bit at Highbury, which was a crap view. You ended up coming out the ground underneath some houses and walked beneath some old boiler hanging her best drawers out on the washing line. Fucking odd considering the marble floors of Highbury and all that, but nevertheless it was still one of my favourite places to go, a place steeped in football history, a bit like Villa Park. That night cemented my thoughts on Highbury as some of us would say it was our finest moment. The Stoke battle was good and the results against Blues were always satisfying but this was different gravy.

We headed out from the Golden Hind pub in Kingstanding. I went by car with Aaron, Gez and Ian, the others went by minibus and cars. We had taken a call from the radio station king Beebo [see Holte Enders in the Sky] who told us that all the Villa were meeting in the Highbury Barn boozer. We arrived in North London, parked up and got to a boozer which seemed adjacent to the Barn pub and we got inside. Our crew was already in there, the likes of Big George, Micky C, BG, Lee and of course Big Phil. There were 30 at most. There was never a hint of trouble, in fact it was quiet, with a good drink and a semi-final to look forward to. Arsenal was never an easy place to go to but we had got some good results there over the years and fancied ourselves again, so the atmosphere was relaxed and we were in good spirits, with the pre-match warm-up comedians, Lee and BG, keeping us amused. We could see the odd lad coming in to the toilet and leaving but we were having such a laugh that nobody was paying any attention, we didn't think anything of it at the time. That mood was about to change and what happened would go down in Villa folklore. It was the row for some that would end all other rows.

It must have been 30-40 minutes before kick-off when I decided to go back to my car to get something and noticed a police car up the road. When I got back, it had gone. Our lads were now coming out of the pub and I noticed shopkeepers were pulling their shutters down and they even bolted shut the door behind our lads. It was surreal and seemed like they all knew something that we didn't. We were now on our own and I can clearly remember saying to Aaron, 'It's on top here.' Then there appeared a big mob of Arsenal, a lot more than us with a good three-to-one advantage. Arsenal have never been anybody's fools and they didn't hesitate, they came charging into us and we were startled and on our toes for a short way.

Then came the fightback. No doubt Big Phil, George and Micky C led the resistance and we took it to them. People were grabbing anything and everything to defend and attack, it must have been bin day in Highbury because everywhere was bins. Gez and Ian grabbed some big blue breadbasket and were pulling away at it, trying to wrestle it from each other to use against the Cockney boys. It was frantic stuff and no one was left out of the row. Normally you only get the front line fighting and the rest as back-up but we had no choice, it was all of us jumping in to do our bit. It was toe-to-toe and how we managed to hold our own against superior numbers I will never know. It's true they backed us off a couple of times and at one point had got us down some side road but our adrenalin and the fact we all knew each other gave us some sort of edge.

We now had the bit between our teeth, even though Big Phil had taken a hell of a whack with some road sign over his head, with blood streaming down his face. It just seemed to make us more determined to make a stand. We actually had them backed off twice in that row and I can still hear one of theirs saying, 'Don't run, there's only a few of them,' to his lads. It was a battlefield. There was debris everywhere and the shopkeepers and pub owners obviously knew what was going to happen and didn't want their premises being trashed. The traffic was at a standstill and one woman driver (there's always one!) had panicked and in the melee of fighting bodies had clipped Aaron, but George did his best Starsky and Hutch impression and rolled over the bonnet, rescuing Aaron.

It was a hell of a row and I don't think any words are going to do it justice, it went on for a good ten minutes and that is a hell of a long time with no Old Bill and fighting superior numbers on their manor. I wouldn't say we done them, I would say it was a draw, but a score draw. We had come from behind and had a bloody good second half. We got to the ground bloodied but feeling pretty damn proud of ourselves. In amongst us is Big Phil who was bandaged up and looking like Terry Butcher in that famous picture playing for England in Poland, bloodied but victorious.

In the summer, Micky C was on holiday and bumped into an Arsenal lad who was there that night called Walshy. He recognised Micky, saying, 'You were with the Villa lot at the Highbury Barn.' He gave a glowing reference to our lads. That night I think they underestimated us and we had got a wicked result on the pitch as well, coming back from 2-0 down to draw 2-2, a bit like the Villa Youth beforehand. For numbers against, there won't be many better performances than that against top-class opposition.

BIG PHIL

Arsenal Away, Tuesday, 14 February 1996, the League Cup. Can't keep track of who the sponsor is now, let alone back then. Villa in the semi-final, a midweek game down in London – only one thing for it, a week's holiday! We were going in a minibus from the Crown and Cushion. I met G and we got to the pub just before noon. The gaffer opened the doors and let us in – sound familiar? A few drinks and the usual good laugh and it was time to set off for The Smoke. We had arranged to meet some of the lads at a pub someone working down there had found near the ground – the Highbury Barn. Before we left, some chipped in for a little bit of gear to help us through the day. Things must have been a little barren at the time because we ended up with a couple of speed pills and quite a bit of change. Next stop, off-licence, and then off we go.

The usual crack, with pisstaking all the way down until we got down to about Milton Keynes. As expected when you've been in the pub and drinking cans all day, the bladder gets a right good workout and a few jimmies are the order of the day. Danny M, who was driving, had missed the turn for the services so everyone was moaning at him to stop for a piss. We all piled out and began watering the roadside daisies. I had just finished and was putting the little man away when G gave me a massive shove and I somersaulted down the bank – arse over tit is the common expression. I climbed back up the bank like Worzel fucking Gummidge. The lads were roaring except one – G had got a little bit of shit poking into his pants, I don't think he thought I'd see the funny side. I didn't at first, but a few miles down the road, when we'd finished pulling brambles out of my head, face and the brand-new Boss jumper I'd treated myself to the day before, I calmed down a bit.

We got to London and near to the ground and the mobiles started to ring. *Where are we, where are you and where's this pub?* There are quite a few Villa about looking for boozers, we've got our pub sorted and we just need to find it. Mission accomplished and we're back on the pop. We were having a cracking day, now don't get me wrong but Arsenal or the Gooners hadn't even come into it as far as I was concerned. We were all good Villa lads and the fact we were there on their manor speaks for itself but I would go as far as to say at that time we were all more into gear and a Saturday night than football. Anything other than Blues for me was down to the younger lads, I'd got a kid on the way and I suppose I'd settled down a bit. Whether it was drink I don't know but the fact was that there was our van and maybe two other carloads with us in a pub full of Arsenal and it didn't matter – we were on our way to Wembley!

As match time approached, we started getting ready to go, and I suppose it was only then that it dawned on me. Due to the banter and the craic, call it what you will, I and I'm sure many of the others had been oblivious to the pub filling up with Arsenal. I walked out of the door and it didn't look good, there's 80-100 Arsenal waiting to meet us. I turned to Gaz M and said, 'You'd best get the others, we're going to fucking get it here.'

Arsenal have come straight up to me and a kid in a red coat is stood in front of me. Bang, I've got it first, a black kid has come over the top and either hit me or cut me with something and I'm now getting slapped by a few of them and all I can see is my blood splashing back up off the road. I get myself free of these and there's only one thing for it – keep going forward. Carter, George and G, well in fact to a man, everyone is having it good and proper. We're well outnumbered but giving a good show, every time Arsenal come we stand up to the task. There's no way with their numbers that they're going anywhere but I'm sure we made them think about it. The air was full of missiles and the street full of soldiers battling, there are bottles and bread crates going everywhere. At one point G had appointed himself logistics manager for Allied Bakeries and cleared a stack of about ten crates Frisbee-style into oncoming Arsenal. Then it stopped. I don't remember any Old Bill. In true sporting fashion, it was just a case of an imaginary whistle went, there was no shaking of hands but we just set off to watch the game. Both sides had done their bit for a hard-fought draw, now let's see what the players can do.

On the way to the ground Danny M appeared with a plaster – he'd been in the shop and bought me a plaster! – I've never forgotten that, that's a mate. The fact I've got a wound like a cunt and he's got a tiny plaster were irrelevant. He'd bought me a plaster. The game starts and we're 2-0 down before people have stopped staring at me and my head wound. Why, oh why do I follow the Villa? At half-time I decide I've seen enough and potter off to the medical room for a quick check-up and get an injection and a turban

– *great, let's start the staring again.* Needn't worry, it's as if the Villa have taken example from our performance. They pull it back to 2-2 and the job gets done.

After the game there was no repeat performance but the walk back past the Highbury Barn showed the road still covered in debris in a fitting tribute to what had gone on before. That will all be long gone now but I got my own memorial from a top row, six stitches from Good Hope Hospital in Sutton Coldfield the following morning, right smack bang on top of the scar. I would like to add my own roll call of honour for the lads who were there with me that day who deserve a mention for their heroics, and my apologies to those I forgot but blame that fuckin' bump on the head for the memory loss: G, Carter, Mags, Danny M, George, Bunny, Steve Turner, Young Alex, Micky Small, Ozzy O'Hare.

DANNY

I wanted to track down some lads from the opposition to give their view on fights with Villa. I spoke to Cass Pennant and Bill Gardner, for instance, about the Upton Park battle in 1980, where Cass was raving about one of our black lads doing a hell of a lot of damage. Unfortunately it wasn't me! It was more likely to have been Big H or Clarkey that day. It was interesting to hear Cass talk about Villa being one of the first firms of black and white lads fighting side by side. I also spoke with Ginger Bob from Millwall about rows with Villa, like the 1974 episode and the Youth Cup semi-final at our place. And I spoke with my old adversary Quintine about our battles with Wolves in the Eighties. Whilst some would argue that people are going to be more polite now, I don't see it that way, these are guys who tell it as it was.

I was eager to track down a lad I had heard a lot about, a lad who had become famous for his activities with England and had made Sunday national newspaper headlines. A lad who certainly wasn't shy coming forward and, as anybody who has met him or talked with him will know, it was fucking difficult getting a word in edgeways. But there is no doubt he is a very respected head of the Gooners firm. The lad I tracked down was Ian Davis. Now this is no ordinary football hooligan; like some of the major players in the C Crew he went on to do other things. Ian was the minder for the Pet Shop Boys and was also a main organiser for Ronnie Kray's funeral, so putting it in 'London speak' he certainly isn't a mug and is more than qualified to put his point across. He was with Ali Jobe, the lad who led Arsenal into the Holte End in 1979 and another well-respected face on not only the London circuit but also nationwide. This is Ian's story, with Ali's input, of that night.

IAN DAVIS THE GOONERS' VIEW

Before I agree to this interview, if your accounts from your lads are bollocks and it's all hearsay then I ain't fucking doing it, simple as that. I have been on the front line, been in the national press, and feel I am qualified to give an honest account from someone who has had it with the best of them. The only reason I want to do it is, it was a fucking good tear-up and I would like to pay credit to one of the best non-London firms of the times that came to us. It's in our top five all-time rows, outside of the London ones. I have had some other rows with Villa, like '81 when they brought huge numbers for the game, they won the League and we were ready in big numbers ourselves. We clashed on the pitch before and after the game and my view is there wasn't a winner. It would have been fucking mayhem though if the Old Bill hadn't got in between us that day.

Here's my version of 1996. We were totting in the Highbury Barn and we took a phone call that your lot had been in the Gunners pub. We had all our main boys, Dainton (RIP) and our main lad Ali Jobe, more commonly known as Black Ali, and all the top boys of the time. We came up the road along a concourse and saw your lads in front of us. Now I ain't going to give you any bollocks, we had a lot of good lads with us but also some fucking idiots, but the firm we had was a good 100-strong. No fuckin' messing, we went straight into yours and I went 'bosh' with a road sign over some cunt's head. We had your lot on your toes to start with but fair play, game little fuckers, they came right back at us. It was a right old tear-up and it was carnage as things were being thrown and people generally getting stuck in to each other.

You know in a football row what it's like, no cunt wants to admit anything or give any credit to the other firm, but let me tell you, I don't know who the fuck these lads were but there were no more than 30 of them. It was going for a good ten minutes and in a football row that's like a lifetime, anybody who has ever done a bit will tell you that. The difference is, all your lads were top lads, they weren't hanging around, they were standing on and gave as good as they got. I have seen Man United come with hundreds to Arsenal and get fuckin' bashed everywhere and yet, with your lot, a small group did very well against a bigger firm of ours.

Nine times out of ten, as any mug will tell ya, the bigger numbers will smash the fuck out of a smaller number but this day was different. I ain't no lover of any club other than my own, but credit has to be paid and I would say categorically Villa are one of the best firms outside of London ever to come to Highbury, for that row alone. Others from your area like Birmingham have done sweet fuck all at our place and I don't rate them. Wolves are another, although they are a better firm than Birmingham.

Is it ok to put your name in?
Yes, no problem.

19 CHARACTERS FROM THE VILLA PARK TERRACES

BRITTLE

The terrace characters are as famous to most Villa supporters as the old footballers. Everybody has stories about certain people and I suppose we will get accused of missing some out, as we did with the hardback version of this book. It is difficult trying to please everybody. What we have done with this chapter is tried to cover some of the terrace characters that we missed in the original, and let's start with an absolute fucking nutter!

WE'VE GOT A WEREWOLF, YOU AIN'T, YOU AIN'T

Of all the supporters going down the Villa in the Eighties and early Nineties, the most famous, even better known than Nigel Kennedy, was Werewolf. I can remember Villa fans singing to Southampton away, 'We've got a werewolf, we've got a werewolf, you ain't, you ain't!' He revelled in it and loved the attention. Boris Karloff eat your heart out. He wasn't a hooligan, but everybody was frightened of him. The reason was that although he was harmless, you were always scared that if you got too close, you might catch whatever it was that made him act like that.

He looked barmy. His face had bits protruding where they shouldn't and he had wild, sticky-out hair, but the dead giveaway was his clothing. Werewolf used to wear old clothes that belonged on a tip, topped off with a fluorescent workman's jacket that had painted on it 'WE HAVE GOT A VILLA WEREWOLF' and a children's police helmet. He carried this bag round with him, and every time he went to go in an away ground, crowds would gather, because we knew the police would search him and we knew what was going to happen. The bag was full of scarves – Villa, Liverpool, Tranmere, Hartlepool, Celtic, Rangers, Hibs, whoever – and every time he pulled a scarf out of his bag he waved it around and sang a little song. The police would usually give up after about three scarves and let him go in, with the rest of the bag unchecked. Werewolf could have taken a nuclear weapon into the ground and they'd not have known, provided it was hidden below the first three scarves. One time though, I think it was at Boro, a steward made Wolfie take every scarf out of his bag and at the bottom there was a large, heavy object. The steward must have thought he'd made some big discovery and insisted that Wolfie showed him what was left inside the bag. It was a cabbage, a fucking cabbage. Why? I don't know. To make it better, or worse, Wolfie waved the cabbage round all through the match.

There are numerous stories about Wolfie, though none about him pulling a bird, but one that sticks in my mind is him going to an away match and coming back to Villa Park and finding it funny to get hold of a Villa lad and a pair of handcuffs. He handcuffed himself and the lad to a lamppost but he hadn't a key to get him away. They ended up having to call the fire brigade to free the bloke, who was now terrified. Imagine being handcuffed to the Werewolf all night – it doesn't bear thinking about.

Back in the days of terraces and strict segregation, the young wannabe hooligans from the home team would usually stand on the other side of the fence dividing the supporters and shout threats towards the away end. Usually, the away fans would do the same, but when Wolfie was around we would always get him up against the fence. Whenever the Ipswich Junior Youth Casual Battalion, or whatever they called themselves, were screaming what they were going to do to us after the match, Wolfie would answer back in his own, unintelligible, language. It always worked – they were always stunned into silence. Wolfie's old man looked like an older version, except for the bag, the scarves and the cabbage. He used to sell programmes down the match and drive round town on Saturday nights selling the *Argus* and the *Sunday Mercury* round the pubs.

All good things come to an end, and Wolfie stopped going to the match some time in the mid-Nineties. There was a story that the Villa sacked him from some job he used to do, seat cleaning or something, so he turned his back on the club and went off to St Andrew's. So it wasn't the silver bullet that got him in the end, it was that graveyard for old football players and supporters with no hope. I suppose you could liken him to a modern-day version of the Elephant Man, a freak of nature, and he certainly found his circus at St Andrew's. They welcomed Wolfie with open arms, and it says a lot for him that he managed to stand out in that particular human zoo.

But like Ron Saunders, Wolfie's heart was never really in the Blues and he soon left, off to Walsall on a free transfer. With the lower gates at Bescot and them not taking many on their travels, Wolfie had the opportunity to really stand out and he made the most of it. One particular adventure, at Fulham in their pre-Fayed days, made the big time as Robert Elms wrote about him in his *Times* column. Wolfie's last appearance at Villa was a few years ago, when he turned up to a night game in his old fluorescent jacket and began directing traffic on Witton Lane. Luckily, the police led him away before he could do any damage. Wolfie recently has made a more prolonged return to Villa Park and brought a guest, well a bird. Not sure where he picked her up from, maybe one of his full-moon outings, but he is back.

GEORGE KINGSTANDINGS'S FINEST

I can't really separate the lads I am going to describe, they came in a package and what a package they were. As areas go for Villa, this was one of the most notorious. I think the word is insular, well in their thinking it was. Let's just say the lads from Kingstanding in the Seventies were a proud lot, almost arrogant, but boy could they row.

The first time I came across them was in a pre-season friendly in 1970 after the World Cup. We were playing Albion and I was just an innocent young anorak going to watch my team. Albion were the team of the moment in the West Midlands, two divisions above us and Villa were in decline, it was in our Third Division days. As you would expect, they brought a following. Nothing happened during the game but after was very different; these were the days of the old Villa bootboys and I watched, bemused, when a pack of some 60-odd Villa came round the corner decked out in high-leg Doc Martens, sta-press jeans and Ben Sherman shirts. These shirts were claret and blue with the braces to go with them. For a young buck it looked impressive and even more impressive was the way they got stuck into Albion. I later found out it was a Smethwick mob of Albion and they were all over the place, they actually got run the length of Witton Road, round the island and back towards Perry Barr. There was hardly any Old Bill about and the Villa were doing as they pleased, they basically had the run of the place. It was heaven for a football hooligan and the lads were in their element.

The Villa firm in question were Kingstanding and right at the front were the likes of Wally, Stan, Ken G, Dave Gillette, Sucker, Venny and Herman, nicknamed that because he looked like Herman Munster. There were no backward steps taken from this lot, it was just get stuck in and fight, and it was a sight I was to see a lot of times as I got older and started to run with them. I was really from Erdington but my mates were from Kingstanding and, despite my allegiance to my manor, I have to say nobody was finer at that time than these boys at the Villa and that includes the more renowned Quinton Stars of that generation.

They were a strange bunch, almost creatures of habit. They drank in five pubs in the area: the Charlie, the College Arms, the Crossways, the Hare and Hounds and the old Kingstanding. Saturday was the day when all of the football hooligans from the area came together as one. One of the surrounding areas, Great Barr, saw a lot of their lads attaching themselves to Kingstanding and they almost classed themselves as honorary KS lads, joining the KS Villa on match days. Kingstanding is a pale shadow of what it was back then. In those days it was very much a Villa area and no-one fucked with it, but they sure fucked with other areas. There are numerous times when they went into other areas just for a row, it was part of their make-up, and it wasn't about Villa v Blues, it was area on area. When I talk about creatures of habit, this lot rarely drank in Brum town centre and that may put some myths to bed in the process. They always stayed local, maybe straying to the odd function or pub just outside the area but in the main drinking locally. When asked where they came from it was Kingstanding first, not the city of Birmingham, and they wanted the world to know it.

For a while they would congregate in the top right-hand side of the Holte L block and made sure everyone knew who was based there with the old, 'Kingstanding, la la la.' They had a long-running feud with other areas, especially Erdington, who occupied the left-hand side of the Holte K block. Some of the fights were brutal. In fact because it was rare for away fans to travel to Villa Park other than the odd game, the police spent more time monitoring the activities in the Holte between these two mobs than anything else. That doesn't mean that if Erdington lads were getting attacked by opposition supporters that Kingstanding wouldn't stand on with Erdington, because they would, but make no mistake about it, the two areas didn't get on and I was smack in the middle of it.

I got my first personal taste of football violence when Villa went to Port Vale in October 1970. We took a good following and even got in their end. It was surprising that Stoke were also there, not to help Port Vale but just looking for the row with the Brummie invaders in their town. While Villa seemed to do well in their end, causing the Old Bill to loose the old police dogs onto the terraces, I got a bloody nose outside, off either a Stoke or a Vale lad.

Now I wanted to be part of a firm that could dish it out, not take it, and so I ended up running with Kingstanding, later to be known as the Witton Warriors by some people. The older lot's antics brought others into play from the area and you had the younger lot joining the fun like Baz G, Horricks, Sadler, Chris K, the Mal twins,

Smiffy, Tommy H and Foody. They were then followed by the likes of Stan Anderson, Bicky, Danny L, Maurice T and Coop. Their match-day meeting place was the Witton Arms and for all you visitors in the Seventies who were met by the waiting home firm, more than likely you ran into the lads I have mentioned. Others would join them like the Greek but in the main they were the Villa Park welcoming committee. Smiffy was big mates with the Greek and even when Pete went on to the Steamers, through their friendship and both being as nuts as each other, they provided the link between the two mobs.

While the Steamers came from all parts but in the main South Birmingham and drank in the city centre, the Kingstanding lads were still very territorial about where they drank and now where they stood on the terraces. The majority of KS lads eventually moved into the Witton End and for six seasons terrorised the away supporters, maybe not winning all of the battles but they made sure that the opposing supporters were given a taste of Kingstanding hospitality. They couldn't take the constant grief off the police in the Holte about their altercations with Erdington and Quinton mobs and decided that the old grass bank called the Witton End was their new terrace home.

Three games stick out for me in the Witton End with Kingstanding. One has been covered already, against West Ham, but the others are Bristol Rovers and Nottingham Forest. Rovers, fair fucks to them, attempted to take the Holte and nobody was doing that back then, but they ended up getting fucked out onto the pitch and escorted into the Witton End. Now what the lads liked about this was there was no segregation and it was relatively easy to get it on and see some action. The Rovers lads must have been congratulating themselves, even thinking they had created history and got off rather lightly, well that thought couldn't have lasted long as they got absolutely bashed from pillar to post as soon as they climbed into the Witton End. They ended up in the old Trinity Road lower terrace for safety.

The other game was the revenge game against Nottingham

Forest, who earlier that season fucked one of our lads into the Trent and proceeded to give Villa the full works, a right going over. This was different. We didn't attack them at Witton Station, we waited till they got in the Witton End and Kingstanding let them walk past and waited till they were all in. The Forest lads went to the top of the Witton terracing and the Kingstanding came from both sides and underneath them. As the fists and boots went into them they were all over the place. They were demoralised and, with nowhere to run other than down the steep grass bank behind , they were falling over themselves. Some actually left the ground. It was a classic attack and total payback for the game at their place. The police did regain control but the damage was done and whilst everyone was out for them after the game, it was Kingstanding who had done the initial damage.

When travelling to away games, a lot of the Kingstanding lads used the coaches that Rosco ran with his Sealand Air enterprise, but it wasn't long before they started to run their own coaches from their own manor. One trip was to Manchester United in 1976. We both had been promoted and there had been a few incidents with them the season before. Let's make no bones about it, they were the pioneers of football hooliganism in that decade. The Red Army were notorious, travelling everywhere, and it was their antics that led to new police control, the caging-in of fans and the segregation of supporters. Every time they were in town, every Tom, Dick and Harry turned out for a pop and they could handle numbers, don't worry about that – there were thousands of them. Newspapers and media coverage of the Red Army arriving on the football specials, showing them marauding through cities and towns causing havoc, sent shock waves to their next opponents. The 'Bay City Roller mob' was my abiding thought, they all looked the bloody same, clones of each other, but there is no doubt that the rest of the country was doing the same, just not in their numbers. Added to the name of United, it provoked media frenzy. Villa had done just the same in the Third Division without ever getting the attention that United were getting in every Sunday newspaper, week in, week out.

Kingstanding had history with their Cockney Reds. We bumped into them on New Street Station, with us travelling in different directions to games, and ended up having it with them on the platform. Make no mistake, the Cockney Reds were not a secondhand firm, they also had numbers and for a long time they were the ones doing the business for United in London and were cocky Cockney bastards. It was a nice little off but a few of ours came off a little worse and were gagging to get back at them. So when somebody suggested running a coach to Old Trafford, we expected the full firm to go.

Maybe it was their reputation that put a few off or some just couldn't be arsed, but we hired a twenty-nine-seater coach and twenty-one made the trip. We went from the Crossways pub, where we started off on Friday night, ending up with a lock-in which went all the way through the night until the coach arrived at 9.30am to take us. Of course we loaded that up with crates of booze to take with us. At the time there was some lad from Manchester, a United fan as it happens, who was living on our manor and drinking in the Crossways. He told us exactly where the Cockney Reds stood in the ground, the United Road stand.

So twenty-one of Kingstanding's best decided to go in there and take them on. And we did. It lasted all of two minutes – even that may be an exaggeration, to be honest – but we went in there and made a stand. Then we got well and truly fucked. I think they were shocked at first to think anybody would dare come onto their holy ground, they were arrogant cunts, it was like 'We are United, nobody would dare do that', but we did. The Old Bill thankfully arrived and got us out but not before we were pelted with coins, meat pies, cans, anything they could get their hands on. The police were as shocked as United that somebody had dared to have a go in there.

We were told to leave the ground for our own safety at 4.15pm, some twenty-five minutes before the game was due to finish, as they couldn't guarantee us safe passage. We took their advice, thinking let's not push our luck, only to be met outside by a huge mob of their lads. I wouldn't like to guess how many, let's just say thousands. You couldn't see anything but red and white bootboys. We knew that we had bitten off more than we could chew and it was a case of, let's get back to the coach, hopefully with all our limbs intact. One of the lads asked a copper for an escort back to the coach, his reply was something along the lines of, 'Tough shit, you shouldn't have come in the first place.'

We had to get to our coach by the cricket ground and everyone was taking a panning. There were that many of them they were like red ants and I wonder now how we got back in one piece. Imagine running that gauntlet! Somehow we did get back to the coach and for some reason it gave us all a buzz. We went onto the coach and grabbed the empty beer bottles, two apiece, and went back out to confront them. For a very brief moment there was a stand-off and they were hesitant, as the first ones knew they were going to cop it, but just as they made the move the police came to our rescue.

The buzz it gave the lads was immense and these were some of the same lads who had survived the Millwall Cold Blow Lane episode in 1973, with one of ours, Dave Gillette, being a bit of a hero that night. Word got round about it, the coach numbers increased and we started to go to certain games with the objective of doing the same thing as at United, because nothing was ever going to be as on top as that. We had taken a liberty and got away with it, well, we were still alive to tell the tale. The Twenty-one Musketeers did well and set the standard for the rest to follow.

For Stoke City away in 1976, we hired a bigger coach, a 52-seater, but our bloke couldn't count and 78 got on it. The plan was to get into the Boothen End and give them some grief and we felt that with bigger numbers we could make a real go of it. We got to Stoke and sure enough went into the Boothen End 20 minutes before kick-off and paid in ones and twos, thinking we would all get to infiltrate the end and give it a proper go. So far, so good, but as soon as we got to the other side Stoke were waiting. They had sussed us and every fucker that came through was pummelled. We just couldn't get enough of us through to make a stand. There was no option, we were hurdling back over the turnstiles and through the emergency exits. Not quite the cunning plan but the Old Bill were ready to nick us, not Stoke.

The old Baseball Ground was a funny place. The terraces were very close to the pitch, well mud heap is a better description than a pitch, and it was a real old football ground with a great atmosphere. Back in those days, Derby had a really good side and won the League twice. It was a footballing town and had its fair share of lads. There had been some high profile rows at Derby, with Man United and Chelsea causing mayhem and our neighbours being involved in a pitch invasion there in 1974/75, when a lot of Blues ended up in a bad way.

At the time, there were countless incidents up and down the country of young lads doing what we were doing. Most of the trouble was inside grounds. Jimmy Hill was having a field day on *Match of the Day* about a Chelsea–Palace game and somebody doing a kung fu kick in the middle of the terraces, you had darts being thrown and young lads were busy in the workplace or metalwork class making weapons for the match. They go bananas now if a bloke throws a plastic bottle on the pitch but back then you had six-inch metal stars and even petrol bombs. It was a recipe for disaster.

The then Minister for Sport, Dennis Howell, a Villa fan as it happens, attended the Derby match and was brought onto the pitch to address the fans. Due to the sheer amount of Villa that were at the game, our side of the ground was full, so we went in their part, which was the other side of the fence to the Villa lads. A lot of Villa will remember the game for the guy dressed as a Viking and us giving our best rendition of 'The Villa, the Villa' to the tune of the theme to the Kirk Douglas/Tony Curtis film *The Vikings*, which was popular at the time. So there we are in their end and before we knew it we ended up battling with Derby's mob right in front of Howell. We didn't give a fuck and when he got on the pitch and through his loudspeaker said we were a disgrace, there was nothing for it but for one of our lads, Arivo, to chuck a 'party eight' bumper can at his head. A few got nicked and by now our reputation was going before us, so much so that all the coach firms were banned from taking anybody from Kingstanding.

Times were changing, it wasn't the same for the lads now that segregation and caged pens had been introduced. It took a lot of the fun out of it and when the Villa reached Wembley after an epic three-game semi-final battle with QPR, which we won at Highbury, we ran a couple of coaches for probably the last time. It was 1977 and you couldn't get a ticket for love nor money. The Villa were playing football none of us had seen the likes of before, it was the Little, Gray, Deehan era and in the end we had to beg an extra 2,000 tickets to try to satisfy demand. It didn't, because Villa had another 2,000 on the car park of Wembley that day that couldn't get in to see us play Everton, and the attendance was 100,000.

Now the lads liked a drink, and a day on the piss watching the Villa plus a row was well the norm and nothing to beat it. We parked the coaches at Marble Arch, went to Piccadilly for a beer and landed in the same pub as the Scousers and there was no trouble, we went on the piss together. After a fairly insignificant goalless final whose main moment was when one of the band lost a spur at half-time and the game was held up while they played hunt the spur, we returned to the Cockney Pride pub in Piccadilly.

We met up with the same Everton and there must have been a good 150 between us in a pub in the middle of London and no one seemed intent on having a row. That changed because out of nowhere came a London mob, some say it was Chelsea, some Millwall, fuck knows but they didn't come to shake hands with us, they went straight for it. Ironically it was Villa and Everton together. We were hardly bosom buddies but we stood side by side against a very game London mob and without it sounding ever so corny, the proverbial Wild West pub brawl broke out.

The place was getting trashed and people were using anything and everything to defend and attack with. Then the fruit machine got turned over – and the Scousers reverted to type. As the machine toppled over, they stopped fighting and were literally on their hands and knees, scrambling for all the 50p pieces on the floor. It was hilarious. The cheeky cunts were even saying, 'Move out the way, la,' as they were picking up the money and pushing our feet off the coins. They were more bothered about the money than the Cockneys throwing beer glasses at them. The KS lads were left to do the fighting and while they were working there were tens of lads on the floor but not one from an opponent's blow, all in the name of the most famous Scouse tradition of all, robbing!

The Metropolitan Police arrived and luckily the Cockneys got the blame while the Scousers were grinning from ear to ear, counting their shekels. The Met wanted us out of there and away as quickly as possible, so everyone, including the Scousers needed to get to where the coaches were parked at Marble Arch. Before they could even think about fucking off with the money, we said, 'Come on, you pay for the taxis.' And so they did: 20 black cabs. And every one paid with the 50p pieces from the fruit machines.

Thinking our day was over we said goodbye to the Robin Hoods and made our way to our coach, only to find that one of ours, the worse for weather, gets on the wrong coach full of these big Australian lumps. Now I very much doubt they were tourists, they may have been watching the egg-chasing, and our night didn't end there because now we were in a free-for-all with this Aussie lot. It was a right old end to a funny old day and maybe after that game it fizzled out for the lads. The days of that Kingstanding lot as a firm at the games just died but after seven years of action those lads deserve recognition as one of the best firms in Birmingham in the Seventies. The days of no segregation, stand where you like, limited policing, hit who you want, fight all day if you want, were coming to an end. Today is totally unrecognisable from those days.

Kingstanding was full of characters and full of hard men and even thirty years later the area is still revered for the antics of those lads. Whilst the area will never be the same, as things have changed, it still retains the reputation, through folklore and the lads who still live there, as a one-off area in Birmingham. There really nowhere like it.

20 McDONALD'S ISLAND

CLARKEY

We hadn't played Blues since 1993 in a competitive game and before that in a league game since 1987, and both clubs had seen a lot of change in this period. They suffered relegation to the Third Division twice and we won a couple of League Cups, played in Europe regularly and as usual we were lording it over them. When they got promotion at Cardiff, their rabble was full of what they were going to do to Villa when we played them and the usual hype and spin was doing the rounds. You have to remember a lot of the younger fans of both clubs had never witnessed a real local derby so many weren't sure what to expect.

To say tensions were building in the city would be a gross under-statement and even though the robbing bastards were charging the extortionate price of £35 a seat for Villa fans, tickets were like gold dust because a lot of the older lads wanted to come out of retire-ment for this one. We had to beg, steal or borrow to make sure we had tickets for the right lads and the 'normals' didn't end up with all the allocation. It was important that we had the right lads there, people who could be trusted to stand their ground if it came on top and not let anyone down.

ANDY

I was happy to be involved in this night's events and in the weeks leading up to the game the hype on and off the field was building. The leader of another Villa firm approached me and asked what our plans were for the Blues game and we had a long chat. I kept in contact with him leading up to the game but had my concerns over the meeting place that was being bandied about for two weeks leading up to the game. I thought it was common knowledge way too soon and that would mean only one thing, the Old Bill were sure to know about it. I kept thinking back to 1982 and how well it had worked when we approached the ground from Highgate, and seriously considered using the Peacock again. In the end I decided to open the club up for the lads to drink before the game. The club is situated just up from Highgate on Moseley Road and is about 15 minutes' walk from the ground.

We kept it quiet until the day and began letting other lads know on the morning of the game, with the word going to just the Steamers and my firm, the C Crew. The game was being shown live on Sky TV, whatever possessed them to have a live Blues-Villa game on a Monday night at 8pm I do not know, and they didn't – or maybe did? – know what they were letting themselves in for. This wasn't your Everton-Liverpool derby they were used to on Sky though. Some will always argue about their own local derby being passionate but you have to witness the Birmingham one to appreciate it. I think somebody sent a letter into a national paper explaining the rivalry and for those watching to get their kids to bed before the 8pm watershed, a pisstake but not far off the mark. You have to wonder how many booked a day off work or just didn't turn in because both firms were out drinking most of the day.

The meeting place bandied about for two weeks was O'Reilly's on Lichfield Road, opposite the HP sauce factory in Aston, and it was where all the Hardcore lads began to gather. About ten of us spent the first part of the afternoon tucked up on Broad Street and I had agreed to speak with the leader of the other Villa firm at 3pm. As it went we didn't leave Broad Street until three so we got a couple of taxis straight to O'Reilly's. We didn't stay for a drink, I just went over and told him I was opening the club and our lot were meeting there and he was welcome to bring his firm there. He told me that once everyone had landed they would be over. We then went to the Adventurers pub, where another small firm were drinking, to tell them that the club was open. From there we went back to open the club up.

People began landing at the club from around 4pm and by 6.30 we were about 100-handed, the vast majority being aged 40-plus. Blues must have known we were in there, as someone took a call from one of the Zulus shortly before Rocky Lane exploded saying they knew Villa were in there. At around 6.30pm the phones started to go off in the club as reports came in of a major altercation on Rocky Lane between Villa's Hardcore firm and the Zulus. At around 7pm, with everyone who was going to be there now *in situ*, Yam Yam made his Churchillian speech, which is reproduced at the front of this book. It certainly roused the troops, though some lads didn't fancy it and left to go by car. We made the move about 7.15pm and all the way down Moseley Road we were making sure we kept it tight. Certain faces were acting as shepherds and some were behind the mob as we walked to Camp Hill, crossing Camp Hill towards the Iron Bridge. Some Blues came in with us by mistake but we weren't interested in them and let them on their way. That's one thing Blues would never have done and that's where we differ.

As we approached the island at Coventry Road by McDonald's restaurant, a large group of Blues came towards us. A lot of them had bottles of beer that they began hurling at us. We still kept it tight; nobody charged in, we just kept walking slowly towards them; the front line was very strong and was going nowhere.

CLARKEY

Andy covers the day in more detail but it certainly was another good day at the office for Villa. I had already seen a few of their lads on mobile phones loitering about the area at around six o'clock but saw them off without much resistance. I don't know who they were or whether they relayed the message where we were to their main group. The objective was to go firm-handed onto their manor. If it came on top we would deal with it and that's what we did.

When we had got within spitting distance the guy who was fronting their firm was Dougal, a bloke I had been introduced to previously who was a friend of a friend. I shouted to him to leave it out and he changed his direction and got out of my path. I was glad about this because I wouldn't have wanted to knock him out but if he had continued coming in my direction I would have had to. Whilst Dougal might have thought he had got off lightly, he had effectively jumped out of the frying pan and into the fire by placing himself in H's path. Another black guy came towards me who I didn't recognise but to be honest he didn't last long. I later found out this was Barrington, a professional cage fighter, and when I heard this I was very disappointed as I would have expected a lot more from him.

A couple of ours took a few slaps as we kept on advancing forward and as we got to the main Coventry Road a few of ours on either side began breaking away to go at the Blues who were to our sides. By this time the Zulus were on the back foot.

After the cage fighter was out of the way, and unbeknown to me at the time Dougal was also down, they folded and we advanced. I focussed on a big skinhead who I decided I wanted but he just kept backing further away.

They were well and truly destroyed by now, and were tripping over themselves to make sure they weren't at the front as we came towards them. Once we were wrapped up by the police, Blues began to regroup and started to give it loads, knowing full well we weren't able to get anywhere near them. A few token bottles were thrown at us and inviting outstretched-arm gestures were made but it was all for show. More police began to arrive but the damage had been done, on their manor.

The police plan was to escort Villa's Rocky Lane firm all around the inner city, taking them to the ground way after kick-off so as to miss any confrontation with home fans. Now here we were 200 yards from St Andrews, on the main route to the ground, with home fans all around us. The Zulus now started getting brave, much to the amusement of most of our firm, and we were treated to a show of jumping up and down on the spot shouting 'Zulu!' in the misguided belief that they were scaring us. We were held by the island until no end of police vehicles arrived and they had stopped all people from approaching the ground. We were then slowly taken up the road towards the ground, escorted by officers who formed a ring around us by locking arms. We were crushed together like sardines. There were also two lines of police vehicles, another line of police on the other side of the road and then finally the Zulus, who were doing plenty of shouting and general shaping, while most of our lot were laughing. Five minutes earlier, when there were no Old Bill, they would have been happy to run off into the sunset, leaving their own people lying on the pavement. I told a copper to let us out for 30 seconds and we would soon clear the Zulus for him, but needless to say he didn't take up my offer.

The next day, I had both Cud and Dougal on the phone to me and both said, 'Fair play for the firm you had out.' The other thing I noticed next day was that the whole of the back of my legs were a mass of bruises from the truncheons when the police waded in to break it up. The funniest thing I heard was when one of the lads from my local told me that the cage fighter was going round telling people we'd had hired help. That night they underestimated the Villa, they were under the impression that Villa's lads consisted of the Hardcore firm only and thought that was all they had to worry about. The shock on their faces seeing a firm of their old adversaries and a front line they had encountered so many times before – for example, 1982, '87 and '93 – had come back to haunt them, maybe they thought we had retired or didn't exist anymore. They had even invited guests from Coventry at the island with the intention of putting a show on for them and showing how the Zulus give it to the Villa. It didn't go to plan. It was never going to happen on our watch. In their book *Zulus* they look to recover face and change the events to suit. They state they were at the Island with their kids, though they can't even get the numbers right between them and try to out-exaggerate each other.

The day itself heralded retirement for a lot of our lads. We had proved our point. They have never done anything like that at our place and after the two incidents that night it's most likely it won't happen again, certainly not for our older lads anyway. The night showed that Villa can pull quality as well as quantity and I don't think Blues knew what had hit them, as Villa firms came from both north and south Birmingham. They may think they deserve an open-top bus tour around the city for a draw on Rocky Lane in a 30-a-side stand-off, but overall there is no doubt who had the result.

For most of us who have been battling with Blues for almost 30 years, and witnessed the Apex to the Zulus, the events that unfolded that night came as no surprise – you can go back to the Burlington Arcade Massacre, the battle of the Windsor, the kop pisstakes or their humiliation on Garrison Lane, the results have always been the same. We have listened to the same old tired excuses from them: we hadn't got the numbers; we couldn't get the taxis; it was the police we ran from, not the Villa; you were all tooled up; it wasn't our real firm; we were with our kids; you landed too early; you landed too late; you had another firm with you; you had hired help. The one thing that has never changed from the Burlington Arcade episode right through to McDonald's Island, is that they never admit to losing and it will always be the same from them, they have 'never' been done or run. I suppose if they keep telling themselves that then they will begin to believe it.

DANNY, BRITTLE, ANDY, CLARKEY and PETE THE GREEK

Our final say, as we call it a day, is that when it mattered and when we needed to stand up and be counted, we were never left wanting. Our legacy is this: The Steamers and the C Crew have nothing to prove to anyone.

Our message to the Blues is simple: for more than 30 years we turned out quality firms for you and not once have you pulled off anything that resembles a result against us. For all your hot air, your 'Villa this, Villa that' and your idle threats, just remember one thing … actions will always speak louder than words.

21 HOLTE ENDERS IN THE SKY

BRITTLE

The most important part of this book is the list that appears near the front of friends and loved ones who are no longer with us. NOT ONE of these people will ever be forgotten and we have listed a few memories of some of the lads below. For obvious reasons it has not been practical to include everyone but here is a selection in alphabetical order. Let's start with a real character of the airwaves, a lad who was one of the regulars on the local football phone-ins:

DANNY BEEBO

Beebo was one of the C Crew lads. He came from Great Barr and he hardly ever missed a match, home or away, even when the Crew started to fade off the scene. After we stopped running our coaches, he would travel with a group of lads from the Crown & Cushion in Perry Barr. Like the rest of us, he was a passionate supporter and wouldn't hear a bad word said against the Villa. If one of the players was doing badly you'd get a few of the crowd starting to moan but Beebo was always telling them that we should get behind the team. Anyone who said that we didn't care about the Villa, only about the violence, should have met Beebo.

There was a local radio sports personality (cough), Tom Ross, who had taken over from George Gavin, now working for Sky, and was doing the Friday night phone-in on a radio station in Birmingham, BRMB. That other Blues celebrity supporter, Jasper Carrott, used to use it in his stand-up comedy routine, where one of the guys ringing in would say in the broadest Brummie accent, 'What about the Villa, Tone?' and Tony Butler, the founder and the master of the phone-ins, would say, 'What about 'em?' The reply was, 'Thanks, Tone,' the point being that more than a few morons used to ring in and let's say Blues supporters cornered the market in it, despite the spin from Carrott!

Well Tom Ross started to get calls from this guy with a heavy Asian accent named Ashok. Ashok would say he was calling from the 'Drakey Drum' and would usually start off by talking about the Villa, then would quickly end the call taking the piss out of the Blues. Ross, who made no secret of the fact that he supported Blues, would usually go along with Ashok, probably glad that he was talking seriously for a change, then Ashok would start laughing at the Blues again and Ross would be speechless. 'Ashok' was, of course, Beebo, putting the voice on, and everyone who knew what was going on would listen every Friday to hear him get one over on Tom Ross. Beebo brightened up a lot of people's Friday early evenings. The phone-in, which was generally from six to seven o'clock, got people chuckling and was another Villa fan getting an opportunity to take the piss out of the Noses. Ross must have had his suspicions that Ashok was really somebody else but he was never sure and Beebo played it to the full. If you remember the Indian accent Peter Sellers used in films of the Sixties and Seventies then you will get the picture of Beebo in full Ashok mode, and you know what, Beebo was better.

Beebo carried on going down the match and nobody ever had a bad word to say about him. Then one morning he was found dead at home, presumably from heart failure. He could have only been in his thirties, and when someone you have always known and who is only as old as you are dies like that, it makes you wonder what's around the corner. Beebo's funeral was a full house as almost everyone who knew him turned out to pay their respects. To his credit, Tom Ross was there as well. I like to think he appreciated that he'd been beaten by a better man and the Friday night phone-ins are a lot less interesting since Ashok left us.

MICK BISHOP PETE BISHOP

I was asked to recall a story about Pete that could be used in this book. Pete and I were around right from the start of the Steamers, although we were mostly there for the laughs and the drinking. We both worked behind the bar in the Hole In The Wall and the Imperial Hotel. There are many stories to tell but one that comes to mind is the Barcelona trip in 1978, which is told by Foxy elsewhere. After we had booked into the hotel, we all went down to Coco's disco next to the Rosamar Park Hotel. Once Melv had smashed the Spaniard, all hell broke loose outside and it wasn't long before the Spanish police started turning up and began lashing out at everyone. Me, Foxy and Pete made a run for it round to the side of hotel, where we found the terrace doors to the restaurant open, so we slipped in. The room was in total darkness and as we crept through we stumbled across a table full of booze and wine. All three of us sat under the table and had a right good session as we got stuck into most of the contents on the table. After about an hour and a half we simply strolled back round to the hotel when all was quiet.

Later that same night, Melv came up to our room for a nightcap and decided to phone the reception to tell them exactly what he thought of them and the Spanish police. The following morning, me and Pete were kicked out of the hotel and had to find, and pay, for somewhere else to stay – cheers Melv. They were great days and great memories. Pete Bishop died in 1998. Pete's two sons, Mick and Jamie, both in their twenties, are now as passionate about the Villa as their dad was. RIP Pete.

PAUL ALI GEOFF BROOMHALL (BOOTS)

I first met Geoff in 1968 after we had lost 1-0 at home to Preston. This game became the catalyst for the protests against the board in what transpired to be a big turning point in our club's history. After the game, a couple of hundred mainly younger fans streamed out of the Holte End and began demonstrating outside the directors' entrance on Trinity Road, chanting, 'Send the board to Vietnam.' After a sitdown protest, the demonstrators marched into town en masse and on the way I got talking to Geoff . We ended up outside the Post and Mail building, which guaranteed us big publicity in the papers. As the whole thing gathered momentum, it was announced in the papers that a meeting was organized at Digbeth Civic Hall. I met up with Geoff and about ten or so others but when we turned up at the Civic Hall, we were almost frowned upon by all the older blokes who were organising it, which really pissed us off, as we felt we had started the ball rolling after the Preston game. From then on me and Geoff became really good friends and would go to Villa games together.

In those early days, Geoff was a greaser with hair down past his shoulders and would knock around with all the greasers from the Glebe. The skinhead craze was just coming into fashion and one Saturday about six of us went into town to get our hair cropped. Geoff was with us but he had no intention of having his hair cut. It was hard to find a barber who was prepared to shave our hair, as the old crew cut was the shortest any of them would do, although we eventually found a barber in Digbeth who said he would do it provided we agreed not to come back and complain. As we walked back through town there were five skinheads and Geoff still with his long hair – it was like the parting of the waves as people continually moved out of our way. A few days later Geoff turned up on my doorstep and was unrecognizable in sta-press jeans, braces, Doc Martens and a skinhead haircut. It was an unforgettable sight.

As I got to know Geoff better, I discovered that when he was fifteen he had been approached by Derby County and after a few sessions there he was given the opportunity to sign as a player for their youth set-up but he turned them down flat as it would have interfered with him watching the Villa. These were the days when you could walk out of one job on a Friday and straight into another on the Monday. Geoff and I had a succession of jobs together and with money in our pockets we began to watch every Villa game, home and away. In total we were both sacked from three jobs for taking time off to go to midweek away games. One job we had was working on cars in Little Barr Street, just up from the Blues ground. In the close season, three Blues players, Gary Pendry, Phil Summerhill and Micky Darrell, all took temporary jobs at our place and we would always try to get them to have a kickabout with us at dinnertime. They always refused because they thought, rightly so, that we would kick chunks out of them.

The first recollections that come to my mind when I think about Geoff following the Villa are the following little incidents at away games that still bring a smile to my face:

SWANSEA. It was a very rough place at the time and there had been incidents all day. A smallish group of us had had it on top all the way back to the station. Once we reached the station, we regrouped and went back looking for Swansea and it wasn't long before we found some, who turned and had a go. As Geoff gave one of them a clip, a woman jumped on him and wouldn't let go. 'I've got a hooligan,' she shrieked. 'No you fuckin' haven't,' came Geoff's reply as he threw her off him with some force and ran off.

BARNSLEY. This was another day where it seemed to be non-stop fighting and in the ground Geoff got nicked whilst in the middle of a brawl. The copper was making futile attempts to grab Geoff's hair although this wasn't having much effect due to him still having a shaved head so in the end the copper shoved his fingers in Geoff's eyes, locked his hands and marched Geoff out using his head to open every door and gate on the way. To rub salt into his wounds, Geoff was thrown into a police van which was full of Barnsley fans which wasn't too clever although the police did manage to get Geoff out again once they'd realized their mistake.

MIDDLESBROUGH. Due to lack of funds, Geoff used to hitchhike to many away games, often setting out on the Friday night. In those days, it was not uncommon for you to have your boots taken off you before you entered grounds and this is what happened to Geoff. Our manager at the time, Tommy Docherty, saw Geoff and a couple of other lads outside in their socks and gave them tickets to watch the game from the seats. As an added bonus, Rosco gave him a lift back on the coach he was running.

PRESTON. This was another game Geoff hitchhiked up to on the Friday night and during the night he had problems in a pub, ending with him telling the landlord, 'We'll be back,' to which the landlord replied, 'Yeah, I've heard it all before.' So on the Saturday when we all arrived, he took us all to the pub, which we trashed. I'll never forget the look on Geoff's face as he told the landlord, 'See, I told you we'd be back.'

PORT VALE. There had been a skirmish on the terraces and after everything had died down, a few Port Vale fans were left on the terrace. Geoff told them they'd best fuck off straight away and when after a minute they were still there, he banged one of them. The bloke rocked but didn't fall down and that's when we discovered he had a plaster cast on up to his thigh. We continually ribbed Geoff about that until the time he became ill.

Geoff continued to watch the Villa throughout his life. He was never one to look for trouble but would never shy away and if it did go off, Geoff would be there. Even in his last days, which were spent in a hospice, all he wanted to know about was what was going on at the Villa and when he heard Doug Ellis was selling up he was very happy. Geoff passed away on 18 August 2006. The funeral was attended by several hundred people and six of his closest friends were asked by his family to carry the coffin. He was buried in his new white away shirt which he never got to wear to a game.

GARY M GARY LYTTLE

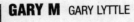

A lot of people would say about Gary that he took over the mantle when Danny left the scene. He was certainly seen by our friends across the city as public enemy number one and I lost count of the number of times they asked for 'Mr Lyttle' in the town. We even had some Nose mugs who we used to have a lot of run-ins with from the Highgate area of Brum who came over to us telling us what they were going to do to Mr Lyttle if they saw him. I politely told them he was standing behind me. Surprise, surprise, they made their excuses.

He was a giant of a man in both stature and personality but he loved the Villa, that's for sure, and he loved the crew that he started to go with, the Villa Youth. Gary would often not bother with the home games, he would always have a crew by the café in Witton Road ready and willing to have a go at any away firm that fancied their chances outside and in the back streets of Aston. One of our lads, going toe to toe alongside him when Leeds were the visitors, copped more than he bargained for when Gary hit some Leeds lad with a plank of wood. The wood split off, hitting Harold in the process and causing him more damage than the Leeds had managed to do. Gary was there that night when Villa gave it Derby on the service station after the England–Holland game and was one of the leading faces in a top England firm who took it to Scotland at Hampden Park in some sort of payback for the silly Jocks rampaging at Wembley in the Seventies. In fact a fair few Villa went to Jockland that day and got a little bit of payback themselves for Glasgow Rangers at our place in 1976, way before my time.

There are numerous stories about Gary but I have picked a few out to try and give some background to how he was revered by friend and foe alike. Scunthorpe in the League Cup in 1985 was a night game and we took a good crew up there. Events started with a lad getting glassed in the pub and it set the tone for a crazy night. The majority of Villa were behind the goal but four of us, me, Rat, Black Roger, who was another good lad, and Gary went on the side.

Gary had the mischievous look in his eye that meant you knew we were in for some fun, and when he said, 'Come on, hop over this wall.' Suddenly we were in their end. We were getting some funny looks and Gary, a larger than life character, couldn't give a fuck. Any nerves he may have had, he steadied. He was the type who filled you with confidence. Next thing we knew, the Rat had disappeared and we heard some commotion. Rat had only hit one of theirs and a big semi-circle opened up around us. The police arrived just as we were enjoying ourselves and escorted us out of the end, with the classic line from a copper: 'Could you politely leave the end, you are upsetting the home supporters.' It was a funny old game, there was an aborted attempt at half-time by the likes of Gary Patt to take their end and afterwards there was a right running battle that seemed to rage for ages. We were told Leeds had come for it but I am not sure about that, it was just another good day out with Gaz.

At another Eighties game, Spurs at home, we were all drinking in the Swanpool Tavern across from Aston Station and were outside the pub when a minibus of Spurs lads came past. They were looking for a row and one of their lads was waving a hammer out the window and went for Gary, just missing his head. Gary had got a broken arm, which was in a plaster cast, but had hidden a blade inside the cast; he was prepared all right. It was a right little ding-dong and must have looked impressive when their bus pulled up screeching on the pavement but for them it turned out to be a big mistake. We literally turned over the van, trashed it and gave the kids the beating of their lives. Gary had fired a flare at the van and when the Old Bill got hold of him to nick him, they asked why he had a flare gun. His reply was that he was going camping that weekend. God's honest truth.

Stu tells a great tale of Gary after we had a great result at Stoke away in 1987. Gary was going round shaking all the lads' hands, proud that they had done the business, he was a mentor to a lot of those lads and nurtured them through some tough trips. Let's just say he didn't do a bad job and above all was a top, top lad. Gary's funeral was a real grand Villa funeral and faces of both Blues and

Albion firms attended and, fair play, sent wreaths in acknowledging a Villa legend of the terraces. Mr Brittle did a sterling rendition of 'When I walked up the steps of the Holte End' and there wasn't a dry eye in the house.

God bless Gary Lyttle and RIP Gary from the Villa Youth.

SILVER FOX STEVE NORTON

Steve was from the Pype Hayes area of Erdington and used to go on the coaches run from a pub called the Norton. The firm operating from the area took the name Norton Flyers and their flag proudly accompanied their many away travels on the back of the coach. Steve was always with his beloved brother Eddie and both were Villa nuts, immortalised in a picture of two young kids in the old uncovered Witton End captured by Villa's resident photographer Terry Weir in his famous book of Villa pictures taken over the years. Steve was a C Crew lad but was known throughout every Villa firm through the generations. If you ask anybody of note from those firms, everyone would say they knew Steve Norton. When you think of Steve you think of him smiling, keeping in the background preferring to let others do the talking, but when it was on top he was never far from the front line. Steve has fought side by side along the best of them and the bloke had good morals.

His funeral was attended by over 500 people and his gravestone is a fitting tribute to one of the quietest and most respected Villa lads of any generation. Where Eddie was the hothead and the joker in the pack, Steve was a year younger and far more reserved but make no mistake, he was nobody's fool and was on the front line on numerous occasions in the heyday of football hooliganism. Steve often frequented the old Aston Hotel in the Seventies and was one of the Witton Warriors who used to greet the away fans as they came off the trains. For the vast majority of his married life he lived in South Birmingham, predominantly a Blues area, yet Steve was never bothered. It was well known that he was a Villa lad but he was held in high respect by the Noses who knew him. I feel privileged to be asked to give my recollections of Steve and just to give an idea of how well he was thought of, a Zulu who became good mates with Steve in later years had a tattoo on his arm in his honour after Steve's untimely death, with the words 'Colours Don't Matter' in the claret and blue and blue and white colours of the two clubs.

My abiding memory is of going to an away match in the Eighties with the Bagot Lads, when I was barely seventeen, and stopping off in Northampton for a drink on the way back. It was a locals' pub but the Bagot lads would never be bothered about that and the lads were having a play-up, as you did. We got talking with the local girls and it seems the men didn't take kindly to us suave Brummies getting all the attention from their women. The next thing we know, we are faced with a seething mob. The trouble was, we were at the back of the pub and there was no way out other than to go forward and they were right in front of us. We literally had our backs to the wall and had to stand and fight. Without going into all of the detail, as there are enough fight stories in this book, we held our own and did well, with the Old Bill coming and us moving through the pub feeling pretty victorious. I was a fair few years younger than the rest but the words from Steve as he patted me on the head have never left me: 'You did well today, you earned your spurs.' From a man as respected as Steve it was something you never forget and I wore my shiner with pride and had a glow inside me for weeks after.

To the brother Eddie would refer to as 'our kid', and to his family, I would like to pay respects on behalf of all those who knew him and knew of his bravery and his modesty, and say he was 'our lad'. RIP Steve.

BLACK ROGER DAVE RAVENHALL

Fearless, totally bloody fearless! You have got more chance of finding rocking-horse shit than you have of finding a Villa lad who would say a bad word about

Dave Ravenhall. Dave was younger than me, and when we were first introduced I remember thinking, look at the bloody size of him, I'm glad he's on my side! I continued to be glad that he was on my side in the years to come, but sadly, as with many great Villa lads, there were not enough of those years.

Dave caught the tail end of the C Crew, and when it disbanded it would be fair to say that he became a main face within the Villa Youth. Dave really was a tough lad and he would always be first in whatever the odds, whatever the opposition. He was genuinely passionate about following the Villa and actually had a very keen footballing brain, although he will mainly be remembered for his ability to kick the fuck out of rival fans! There were not many lads who would fancy their chances against him, and I go back to that day in 1984 when Ipswich's main lad came bouncing up the road towards us and Dave nearly killed him with one punch. I can still hear the poor bastard screaming in agony now, and I bet he was never that cocky again. When they put him in the ambulance we all thought he was dead. He is probably still in hospital now, Dave hit him that hard.

Dave had many friends and was held in high esteem by the Villa boys. He was almost like a god to some of the younger North Birmingham lads, and quite rightly so. When the C Crew fizzled out, Dave suggested starting up a new firm called the VRA, Villa's Republican Army. Much to the amusement of the lads, he even tried to get us all to sing his song: 'VRA, we're Villa's Republican Army, we're barmy, wherever we go.' Thankfully it never caught on and the younger lads from North Brum saved the day with the creation of the Villa Youth. The name quickly spread and eventually all Villa hooligans were being referred to as 'Youth' for many years to come. Dave came from the original heartland of the Youth, North Birmingham, and along with another great Villa lad, Gary Lyttle (RIP), went on to become a major player in their activities.

STU

One Christmas Eve in the mid-Eighties, before the all-day drinking came in, about 50 of the Youth met up in The Cabin pub in town at lunchtime. Our mob that day was mainly made up of Kingstanding and Erdington lads, Jeff Taylor's boys from the Bromford, and myself, the sole representative of the Shard End Lions! As last orders approached, Dave Ravenhall started to rally the lads together with the intention of giving the Zulus an early Christmas present. Full of Christmas spirit and cheap lager, we marched towards the Blues side of town, easily identifiable as it was dimly lit on account of them living in the shadow of Aston Villa.

We arrived at the ramp on New Street, the notorious home of assorted muggers and ambush merchants. There were several Noses hanging about and some got whacked while the rest ran off towards John Bright Street. We all legged it down the old spiral staircase in pursuit, but when we got halfway down the road a large mob of Blues showed up, their numbers swelled by the fact that it was now kicking-out time in the pubs. Dave was first in and he set the standard for the rest of us. It was his shout, he had to lead from the front and he was a natural.

The next ten minutes, which is a bloody long time when you are battling, saw a mad running battle between the two baying mobs. The Old Bill had their work cut out and terrified shoppers tried to get out of the way. Bins, bottles and glasses flew through the air, Merry Christmas Brummie style. That day, with Ravenhall a driving force, we did better than I could ever have imagined. Dave's actions galvanised the rest of us and we eventually got the better of the Blues. Fair play to the Noses, they actually gave us credit for this afterwards.

Contrary to the picture that I have so far painted of Dave, he was not all about violence. He actually had a great sense of humour, and Leicester away in 1984 was an example of this. It was an 11am kick-off and all the lads met up early at New Street Station to get the train. We had big numbers and everybody was looking forward to the day ahead. All of a sudden we noticed that Dave had gone missing and we were all wondering where he was. Just before the train arrived, he turned up swinging a white carrier bag that stunk to high heaven.

Ravenhall had only been to the fish market and bought a bag full of bloody crabs. His plan was to run at the Leicester swinging his crabs at them in order to do a bit of damage. If the Old Bill pulled him, he was going to say that he was only defending himself while walking around town with his dinner in his bag. Our carriage smelt like a fishmonger's wallet on the way to the match. We were all gasping for air, but I don't think anybody had the heart, or the bottle, to try to throw Dave's dodgy bag out of the window, even though everyone wanted to.

We arrived at Leicester and welcomed the chance to breathe some fresh air. It didn't take Dave long to start bouncing around with his crabs. We came out of the station and saw a little mob of ten Leicester standing sheepishly across the road. Dave said, 'C'mon, let's go!' and ran over the road. He carried on running past these Leicester, who decided to have it off on their toes anyway. Ravenhall wasn't bothered with the ten lads because he had seen a larger mob of about forty further on down the road. He was off, a one-man army swinging his bag of seafood. The song 'Bottles and Spanners' doesn't quite fit with '... and crabs', does it? I don't know if it was the sight of Dave and the smell coming from his bag, or the fact that the rest of us were now running up the road behind him, but Leicester ran off. They had either managed to save themselves from a good kicking or a case of food poisoning!

Any mob with Dave Ravenhall in it was capable of pulling off a result. I tell you what, mate, the Villa lads miss you on earth, but along with the likes of Stevie Norton (RIP) and Gary Lyttle (RIP), what a mob we must have up in Heaven. Dave was a great Villa lad, a real main boy, and I can't praise him enough. But much more than that, Dave Ravenhall was one of us.

BQ MICKY RIVERS

I had known Micky Rivers since 1969, having been introduced by Warren McDivitt. In my opinion Micky would have made a formidable boxer, he had a good physique and threw very, very fast punches. A story recounted by Waggy and Micky Rose involved Leeds at Elland Road back in the Seventies. It was a night game and Leeds were laying into every Villa fan. It was so bad that somebody commented that the train home looked like a hospital train, with all the wounded. Micky Rose recalls them all leaving the ground to be chased back towards Leeds Central by warring Leeds fans. Micky Rivers was knocking them back one by one until they reached an island, where even he started to feel the pressure. All of a sudden a big van pulled up and everyone thought, here we go, but luckily it was a big pal of Micky Rivers who got them to safety and dropped a grateful trio at Leeds Central unscathed.

One experience I remember was at Bristol City in 1978. At that time there was a nasty little firm of Bristol City who were very fond of using blades. Warren Mc, Johnny Nixon, Waggy and I were approaching the turnstiles when a commotion broke out in front of us, so we all ran up to investigate, including Waggy who was tripping over his platform shoes. The first thing we saw was 'Rambo' Rivers banging people left, right and centre with the ever-faithful Lorraine, his wife, nearby. Micky's white-collared sheepskin, *à la* John Motson, was sliced to pieces and he had been cut on his arm. This nasty little Bristol firm gathered their wounded and ran off, pursued by all of us. It turned out that a lad called Micky Behan, a non-player, had been attacked by these scumbags, who were on the verge of giving him steel when Micky and Lorraine jumped in. In my book we can all shoot the shit in a nice safe pub with all the lads but it takes real courage when on your jack with the missus to jump in to help a total stranger. Fair play, God bless Micky Rivers, sadly taken from us on 10 October 1988.

RAGGY DOUGIE THOMPSON

I got to know Dougie at school where we both seemed to be absent a lot at the same time, especially when the Villa were playing away in midweek. It was actually Dougie and myself who nicked the flag at Preston that 'Old Pete' mentions in Chapter 1. The home fans were not amused when some older lads grabbed it off us and set fire to it, which was a pity as it would have been a nice souvenir. When we were older, a lot of us had this thing about who turned up earliest at away games. Even if we turned up at somewhere like Crewe or Chester at 12.30 in the afternoon for a 7.30 night game, you would guarantee that Dougie would be sat at the bar when we walked in, probably on his second or third pint. He did it everywhere we went.

Dougie had a great personality, always smiling, he loved the crack and of course the Villa. In the Eighties he married a girl from Oxford and moved down there, becoming a well-known face at the old Manor Ground. He even travelled away with them. When he later moved back to Birmingham, he began to travel away with England for both football and cricket and at some stage you must have seen Dougie's 'AVFC Weoley Castle' flag on the telly at some faraway outpost.

When Dougie died in 1996, we needed a coach and several cars to attend his funeral in Abingdon, Oxfordshire. Dougie was laid to rest with full AVFC honours, as one would expect. A unique guy who is sadly missed. RIP Dougie from all the Steamers.

BRITTLE

A set of lads that anybody would have been proud to have in their firm and a set of lads who just loved their club, Aston Villa.

FINAL WORD

DANNY

Football hooliganism, yes, this was the business we chose! Many will remember the images of football firms running riot in the grounds and chaos on the streets in the Seventies, Eighties and Nineties. Pete the Greek, one of the Godfathers of it all, once told me you can get further with a kind word and a smack in the mouth than you can with just a kind word; in those days it was very true. The order of the day was toe-to-toe combat, the mission was to storm away ends and take them by any means necessary.

When the C Crew did disband, Birmingham City did put a good firm together doing the business nationally. I will give them that. But they never quite reached the level of the C Crew. Internationally, we took football violence to another level. Just like our invading ancestors, the Anglo-Saxons, Celts and African warriors, we exported terror to the shores of other fighting nations. We did it with no shortage of panache, style and, above all, respect. Today's firms could learn a lot from that.

Over the years, I have calmed down a lot and there is no need for my weekly fix of terror any more. Outrageous as it may sound, reflecting on it now and in spite of the consequences, I have to remain true to my beliefs and say I have no regrets nor do I feel any remorse for my involvement and the things I did. I grew up around

North Birmingham in hard, tough neighbourhoods. Fearsome acts and violence were an everyday occurrence, and fear or signs of weakness were not an option for me. The only time it was right to be non-violent was when you were dealing with someone who wasn't violent towards you.

I decided not to come out of retirement for the McDonald's Island mission in 2002; I didn't fancy doing a Frank Sinatra. I have got the stripes, what else have I got to prove? Nothing. Not to say the lads needed me anyway. If the truth was to be told, the firm was a good few players short and we still did over the Bluenoses. I never got the chance to say to the lads well done, you were double naughty that night, you did the business.

They say old age is just a record of one's whole life and perhaps my best years have gone now. Every man should know his own limitations and never try to be something they are not. A fool at 40 is a fool indeed and I am sure there are 100 Black Dannys and Brittles out there ready to take our places, but please lads don't let the grey hair cloud your judgement. Even though I have retired I am not going to stand by and let anyone take advantage of family, friends, or myself, that's for sure.

It was at the Lyndhurst pub on an Erdington council estate in Birmingham on 26 July 1998 that somebody tried to do that. That day is now widely known as Sunday Bloody Sunday, when local protection racketeers decided to make a move on our manor. With respect to my close friend Joe Egan, the events of that day are well documented in the book (*Big Joe Egan, The Toughest White Man on the Planet*). They made *Braveheart* look like a Walt Disney movie, trust me.

I suppose being a retired football hooligan is an occupational hazard. In fairness, most of the West Midlands Police force have been fair with me, even though I have had a few close calls with them, the worst being in 2003 when those horrible lot from Queens Road (the Armed Response Units) decided to land at my place of work, the Roebuck public house, and nick me for a shooting I knew nothing about.

We have all heard it before: 'He was in the wrong place at the wrong time' or 'We told him to put his hands up and he didn't'. Well on this occasion the officer didn't have to ask me twice to put my hands up, they flew up. I shouted at the doorman next to me, who was clueless, 'Unless you want my brains splattered all over your silly face, stand still and put your fucking hands up.' I am not ashamed to say I was afraid that those trigger-happy cops were going to shoot me. They marched over with their guns cocked. 'Hello Mr Brown, you're under arrest.' That's when I noticed who these cops were. They were the same armed officers who took 55 minutes to respond to a 25-minute pitched battle at the Lyndhurst pub.

I was taken into custody and interviewed about an allegation of a shooting outside the Roebuck, which I denied. I was then charged with attempted murder. Whilst in custody, justice did prevail; the so-called witness had a memory loss and was unable to identify me in an identification parade. I was released with all the charges dropped. I was incensed with the injustice of it all and contacted the West Midlands Police Authority asking for a written apology; to date I haven't received one. The one thing that is certain is that the police are the biggest firm in the Midlands and they answer to no one.

In my 34 years as an Aston Villa fan, loyalty and passion have always been needed in big doses. My love for the club can never be in question. Writing this book has brought back so many memories, so many emotions, even a few tears. I don't want to hide my past nor do I want to glorify violence, I will leave that one to Hollywood. It makes me proud and privileged to write this book on behalf of all the Villa lads of my era, oh sorry and the girls. There are lots of people who have helped with this book and without your support it wouldn't have happened. I didn't realise we had so many literary geniuses in our ranks. The other three lads who helped myself and Paul put this together deserve a special mention and my sincere thanks. That was some front line, wasn't it, back in its day?

Finally, to the C Crew lads, it's a cliché but it was true: you were like my second family. We did some crazy things together. The trust and respect I have for you all I will take to my grave, and I hope the feeling is mutual.

My childhood colours, claret and blue, Villa till I die.
Danny Brown AKA Black Danny.

BRITTLE

The end of it all for me started when the rave scene kicked in. I got involved when it started and everybody knows that it brought the football violence to an end. Everybody decided to make money and I went along with that. My attitude was, *forget the violence, let's make money*. The trouble was, I wasn't very good at it and I ended up getting collared. On 24 September 1994, I was sentenced to seven years for drugs and firearms offences. I was released on the 24 February 1999 but received another eight years less than a year later, on 22 January 2000, for a similar offence. I have been away for ten of the past twelve years, and obviously it's game over for me as far as the football violence is concerned.

As Danny has mentioned, there were a few lads missing from McDonald's Island, myself included. I might not have been able to be there in person, as I was being held by Her Majesty in one of her prisons, but I still kept in constant contact with Andy throughout the day. I was delighted when I heard what had happened at the island and a lot of the lads on the wing wanted to know what was going on when they heard me screaming and shouting.

I would like to take this opportunity to thank all the Steamers who brought me up from a very young age, far too many of you to mention but you know who you are. My respect goes out to each and every one of you, not only for what you have done for Aston Villa but also for what you have done for me. Now, to all you C Crew boys. Fuck me, what a firm and what a family. Didn't we have some fun? Not only up and down the country but also our travels abroad. I'd need another few chapters to thank you all. Some of the happiest days of my life were spent with you lads. The Windsor in town was our main pub for many a year and God did we do some drinking, partying and fighting at that pub. I have nothing but happy memories and I wish I could turn the clock back and live it all again, but time moves on, just like we all have.

I'd like to bring my story to an end with a special thank you to my closest friend and my family. Andy Browne has never left my side in many a battle, just as he never left my side during all the years I spent in jail. To my family, I know I've been no angel throughout my life but hey, what the hell? There's never been a dull moment, has there? Love and respect to you all. I will sign off with a message to my two kids, Dillon and Aynsley Vicky Faye Charlotte (AVFC). Do not follow in my footsteps. Love you both, Dad.

Villa until my dying breath,
Paul Brittle.

ACKNOWLEDGEMENTS

Thank you to the following in no particular order for their help and contributions: Sean, Lloyd, Moses, Rosco, Ginger, D.Dub, Raggy, Big H, Deano, Roff, Pete (Old) , Joycey, General, Shana, Heaffy, Eddie N, Mark, Paul Ali, Jimmy Ryan, Fordy, Jimmy Coley, Gary Patt, Mack the Sock, Silver Fox, George, Boris, Foxy, Joe Jordan, Lisa S, Hicky, Stu, Simeon for the photo shoot and those who wish to remain anonymous.